Marlon & Greg

My Life and Filmmaking Adventures with Hollywood's Polar Opposites

By
Joseph Brutsman

Marlon & Greg:
My Life and Filmmaking Adventures with Hollywood's Polar Opposites
By Joseph Brutsman
Copyright © 2021 Joseph Brutsman
No part of this book may be reproduced in any form or by any means, electronic, mechanical, digital, photocopying, or recording, except for inclusion of a review, without permission in writing from the publisher or Author.
No copyright is claimed for the photos within this book. They are used for the purposes of publicity only.

Published in the USA by:
BearManor Media
1317 Edgewater Dr #110
Orlando, FL 32804
www.bearmanormedia.com

Perfect ISBN 978-1-62933-828-6
Case ISBN 978-1-62933-829-3
BearManor Media, Orlando, Florida
Printed in the United States of America
Book design by Robbie Adkins, www.adkinsconsult.com

Dedication

As I will discuss time and time again within these pages, I dedicate this book to two people who made my life worth living, even if they had never introduced me to Mr. Peck and Mr. Brando.

To Greg's wonderful son, Tony Peck. He is my screenwriting partner and nothing short of the brother I needed to have. He's shown me the world, put up with all my problems and he's helped me get through some of my most challenging times, always getting me to smile, laugh and move my life forward.

I also dedicate this book to Marlon's most valued and beloved soul, Avra Douglas, a true Brando daughter who keeps his image alive today as she runs his estate with love and care. Avra became my wife and she has endured so many of my foolish missteps. I hope she knows how much I love her to this day.

I also must add a third dedication: to my angel, Molly Rose, the beautiful daughter I am lucky enough to raise with Avra. Through her own challenges and difficulties, Molly has always been able to give joy and love to her parents and all around her. She's one of those rare magical people who live amongst us.

The baby shower that welcomed her smile to the world was celebrated at Greg's beautiful estate. And she took some of her first steps up at Marlon's Polynesian hideaway, later kissing the dolphins in the bays of his Tahiti. As she still does with everyone, she always made her Godfather smile.

Table of Contents

Introduction viii
A Prologue in Space 1
Single Mined in Many Ways, Before Meeting Those Two Guys 3
FIRST CHAPTER - The Men: Greg & Marlon Essay I 21
Tony (1979) 27
Avra (1987) 31
Meeting Greg and then *really* meeting Greg (1988) 35
Slap and Al (1988) 44
SECOND CHAPTER - Different Hollywoods: Greg & Marlon Essay II 53
The Story Resumes: Writing with Tony - Black Sheep 1 (Fox 1989) .. 58
Century City Fox - Black Sheep 2 (Fox 1989) 62
Carolwood (1989) 65
Ms. Passani (1989) 70
Sunset Blvd. - Lazar (1989) 74
THIRD CHAPTER - Acting vs Stardom: Greg & Marlon Essay III .. 81
The Story Resumes: Doctor DeMott (1990) 86
Meet Marlon (1991) 95
Platinum What? (1991) 100
Water (1991) 105
Private - The Reagan Library (1991) 112
FOURTH CHAPTER - Awards: Greg & Marlon Essay IV 119
The Story Resumes: Spy (1991) 121
Reading DeMott (1991) 130
Thriller (1991) 134
Bob (1992) 143
Goodbye Doctor (1992) 148
FIFTH CHAPTER - 1962: Greg & Marlon Essay V 153
The Story Resumes: Public Men - Avra Meets Greg (1993) 157
The King (1994) 163
Rewriting Bunyan - (1995) 167
Not The Saint (1995) 173
Tony, Meet Marlon (1995) 183

PHOTO GALLERY 197

SIXTH CHAPTER - Navigate: Greg & Marlon Essay VI 205
The Story Resumes: Free Money (1997) 209
Rome (1997) 221
Free Money Rewrite (1997) 224
Greg, the Beg and Free Money (1997) 228
The Devil's Own - During Free Money (1997) 236
SEVENTH CHAPTER - The 70's & 80's: Greg & Marlon Essay VII ... 243
The Story Resumes: Finishing Free Money (1997) 248
CAA, CBS and The Work (After Shooting Free Money 1998) 250
Watch It (Free Money 1998) 280
Molly (2000) 285
Whisper (2001) 288
EIGHTH CHAPTER - Luck: Greg & Marlon Essay VIII 306
The Story Resumes: Tony Kaye - Lying For a Living Part 1 (2001)... 310
Talk (2002) 315
George Englund - Lying For a Living Part 2 (2002) 322
Beatty - Lying For a Living Part 3 (2002) 327
Passing (2003) 339
NINTH CHAPTER - Expectations: Greg & Marlon Essay IX 345
The Story Resumes: Goodbye Carolwood, Goodbye Greg (2003) 350
Greg's Service Revisited (2004) 355
Regret - Goodbye Marlon 1 (2004) 359
Summer in the Valley - Goodbye Marlon 2 (2004) 367
TENTH CHAPTER - Time: Greg & Marlon Essay X 374
Those Roles 381
The Ending 387

INDEX 397

People and things to track throughout the stories: Top, left to right: my talented musician father, Jay Brutsman, my beautiful mother, Marilyn. Tony Peck and me today. Next row: Archie Bunker, from my comic strip of "All in The Family," my drawing of my Juilliard classmates. Next row: me, onstage at Juilliard, with classmate Tia Smith. Low corner right: my wife, Avra, with me and our daughter, Molly Rose. Lower left: my acting years, on CBS TV - "Scarecrow & Mrs. King," with Bruce Boxleitner.

More people and things to track throughout the stories: Top, left to right: Molly as a baby; the great Robert Evans at his cool Paramount office. Next row: me directing Courtney Hansen and Chris Jacobs on the "Overhaulin'" set; me, Marlon and Charlie Sheen on the set of "Free Money." Next row: winning awards for "Living With Ed," with Ed Begley, Jr. and Rachelle Carson. Molly today. Low corner left: Greg during a performance of "A Conversation with Gergory Peck." Right corner: Marlon in 2001.

INTRODUCTION

I was waiting for the phone call.

As an executive producer and a screenwriter, I was about to get a green light. Or so I was hoping. A green light that would put Marlon Brando and Gregory Peck on screen together for the first time in their long, amazing and legendary careers. It was no long shot at that moment.

I was waiting for that call as I was at the film location with Marlon; the movie was about to start shooting. My co-writer was my longtime writing partner and absolute brother, Tony Peck; yes, Gregory's son. We had a great role and script pages for Greg - his scene with Brando, but I was waiting to see if Gregory Peck was going to say "yes" or "no" to the one or two day shoot.

At that time, I had known both Greg and Marlon well for many years, fortunate to have worked on various separate projects with both of them.

I first met each man under incredibly different circumstances, but over time, I grew to know, respect and love them both. They taught me a great deal about both the industry I chose to work in and the life that *should* be led when art, creativity and performance collide with crass and ugly business. In their own individual ways, they had somehow figured out living life as a legend. One was singularly qualified to be a movie star. The other, qualified for anything other than that. Along those lines, as one might imagine, they were also the most opposite individuals one could ever compare, and compare was something I did often. After all, day in and day out, they were both in my life and they were both at such unique and oddly similar levels - both beyond famous, both certifiably iconic, both aging yet vital giants when I was lucky enough to first meet them.

Often, just watching them deal with different "everyday" matters; those moments would provide life-lessons that no conversation could. They were both fully genuine and so unique.

This book is about such real life moments and lessons from those genuine, unique men, as well as those conversations that indeed did happen, frequently and always with consequences.

Oh, I'll get to that phone call later in this volume. But any expert on the world of film knows that, sadly, the screen pairing never did happen, for reasons that were pure Marlon and Greg.

Marlon & Greg

A PROLOGUE IN SPACE

Somehow, I ended up seeing the 1969 Gregory Peck space mission film *"Marooned"* in grade school long before I ever saw *"To Kill a Mockingbird"*. Of course, I was quite young, space travel was epic at that time, and who can fault some young small-town Minnesota teacher for using her 16mm classroom rental selection for, uh, *"Marooned"*? She probably liked the movie in the theater and thought it would be an inspiring watch for kids in this Apollo era.

I was about 9 - (pre-home-video, pre-internet, pre- *"Entertainment Tonight,"* etc.) - and, as I was about to see the movie, I recall wondering: "How in the heck did my school get this film?!"

Even at that age, I was obsessed with the movies. Not just the stars, the music and the art of it all - I also loved the celluloid, the machinery and the whole pack of technological miracles that made cinema. I knew *"Marooned"* had played in theaters not too long ago, and I had no idea as to how my tiny school had 16mm film reels of this recent studio release. My desk was next to the projector cart in the center aisle of my classroom. As I watched our hefty school Principal loop the film onto the 16mm projector that day, I took in all those tiny frames and sprocket holes, the chemical smell of the reels and, ultimately, the magic of projection. To emphasize and reemphasize, I loved film. At that time, my father had an old 8mm projector and I had begun to gather a collection of short Disney cartoons and old Laurel and Hardy silent featurettes. But on those rare times when I got to see my school pull out that big optical sound projector, God! I was in awe!

"Swank Motion Pictures, Inc." - That's what it said on the cases that the *"Marooned"* reels arrived in. The cases lay flat on the lowest shelf of the gray metal projector cart. During the screening of the film, (in the not-quite-dark-enough classroom) I saw a catalog of sorts under those film cases. I slyly lifted those cases and saw

a *"Swank"* catalog. Movie stars and recent film titles were on that cover. My head was exploding. I had never stolen a single thing in my life, but I knew at that moment that I was going to immediately steal that catalog. I had no choice. All the "non-stealing" scenarios I quickly ran in my head; none of them worked. If I asked to "borrow" it? I might be refused, along with some sort of, "The school needs that" or "You're too young" or the sickening, "Why?" or perhaps even the unacceptable, "Well, bring it back tomorrow." No. I was going to *steal* it and I was going to study every page of it forever!

Many years later, I told that story to Marlon Brando, on a lazy afternoon in his den. (As you can see, these stories will not always flow in direct chronological order; please bear with me.) It came up when he asked a "Marlon" question: "We've all stolen things. What have *you* stolen?"

Marlon was often something of a Pope, someone you would confess to. That's because he would sometimes ask you to confess something, and, yes, he was hard to refuse. After he heard the story, he simply thought quietly for a moment. I wondered what he then might say - or ask. I thought he might mutter, "Why did you want a 16mm film rental catalog so badly?" or "What's 'Marooned'?" If I explained that, I knew I was sure to hear some groans about Gregory. In the presence of either man, I would almost always be asked, "So, what's *he* doing today?" This is probably a good time to explain that Greg and Marlon were not exactly friends. They did not in any true sense connect fully with one another. But they did have a keen interest in the other man, whether they would admit it or not, thus me constantly being asked by the two of them, "What's *he* doing today?" Of course, they both knew so many of the same people, the same projects and the same places. Their rare lives crossed over thousands of times throughout their long careers.

Many more details to come on all that. As for that moment in Marlon's Mulholland Drive home: when he finally spoke, it was, of course, Pure Absolutely Unpredictable Marlon. He said, "I think I have one of those catalogs." Huh? "Go look in the library. Knowing you, you're still consumed by such oddities. I think I have one of those. Not sure why, but I think I do." I stood, but then I knew I needed to ask a question I did not want to ask. "Which library?" Wanting to skate past the question quickly, Marlon picked up his TV remote as he muttered, "The big one."

As I headed up the hall, I reminded myself of how delicate certain topics were with Marlon. Technically, the house had two rooms that passed for libraries: a Native American library in a small den, and a much larger collection of books in a big den. But these days, the big den was rarely discussed, and it was seldom visited by Marlon. This was the "Library-Den" where Marlon's son had shot and killed the boyfriend of Marlon's beloved and cherished daughter, a beautiful woman who would then later commit suicide. As a frequent visitor to the house, I rarely went in this room myself. Even with the lights on, the room had a noticeable darkness. I scanned the shelves, somewhat wishing I hadn't told him the story of the catalog. I didn't see it there. As I shut the lights off, I saw a pile of old magazines in the bottom corner of one of the bookcases. I rifled through the old paper - Sure enough, there was the *"Swank"* catalog, of the very same year that I obsessed over back in the late 60's! I was so thrilled! I hurried back to the den with the TV now blaring. And I must've taken longer than I thought, because Marlon was sound asleep.

I quietly sat and paged through the catalog. As Marlon had an occasional snore, along with a jolt from whatever boxing dream he was having, I was near tears looking at the book, seeing so many in the catalog I had worked with. I came upon the ad for *"Marooned"*. There was my pal Greg, looking like the only hero who could possibly get a marooned astronaut back from space.

SINGLE MINDED IN MANY WAYS
BEFORE MEETING THOSE TWO GUYS

While so many of these pages will be about those two men and their journeys through their final years, I of course realize that much of the enclosed context will be lost without at least a cursory view of me and what allowed me to meet and work with

Greg and Marlon. As anyone in "The Industry" knows, there are so many twists, turns and unrecognized moments that shape our career paths. I'm honored to have been cited and quoted in published biographies of both men; I write about that because there are occasions when I still need to remind myself that within my trade, I was indeed fortunate at times. Still, none of the journey was easy or remotely predictable.

As for the journey you'll have regarding this book, please know the stories within will follow a set of curved timelines that, frequently, will fall into their own unique chronological order. That is to say, more often than not, there will be no "concrete" chronological order. For instance, I'll probably tell of adventures I shared with them before I get to the origin stories of actually first meeting them; perhaps it's just the abstract screenwriter in me. Also, allowing for Marlon's timeline, Greg's timeline and my own timelines with both of them, I found the more interesting path to be one of pulling up information when needed. Not to worry; none of that will be as confusing as it sounds; I'll always ground the moments in the places, years and moments that I hope allow for the best telling of these true events. I've also included chapter-break essays about their vast careers. In short: please know what's going on here: I'd like to keep all this incredibly conversational. As for *my* story, please allow me to get some of this part out of the way; I'll just dive right into it, ridiculously obvious beginning and all:

I was born in Cheyenne, Wyoming in 1960.

We were five individuals: my father, my mother, my older sister, Pam, my younger sister, Laura, and me. We moved to Minnesota when I was six. In those days, I don't recall Cheyenne having what one might call a "nurturing" school system or local "community" when it came to the arts. Already at that age, I was deeply into drawing, painting, animation, music, TV and movies. I was no real athlete, what I saw of Wyoming horses and Cheyenne rodeos scared me, and I remember when my first grade teacher heard I was moving to Minnesota. She snarled, "That's good, you're really not much of a 'Cheyenne' kinda boy, are ya now?" Whatever she was saying, I remember being shocked that I had already delivered that much of an impression, even at the age of six.

Today, I don't recall whether I felt oddly proud or oddly ashamed by her observation. All I know is that a bit later in life, I was quite grateful that my parents had made that move. I saw my old dirt-ditch of a Cheyenne neighborhood years after moving, shocked by how little any of it had changed. My father, Jay Brutsman, was a freakishly talented professional musician, playing "One-Man-Band" piano bar and organ seven nights a week. His work took us from Cheyenne to Detroit Lakes, Minnesota, and then two years later to Brainerd, Minnesota, where I grew up until my sister Laura and I got into The Juilliard School's Drama Division in New York City, in 1979.

Going back to toddler-hood, thanks to Walt Disney, Warner Bros. and Hanna Barbera, I understood animation long before I could comprehend film or video cameras; this is vivid to me because I recall looking at *"The Secret Storm,"* a TV soap my mother (Marilyn) was watching; the whole time I wondered, "Who's drawing all *this?!* And so well! Shadows and all?!" Early on, I also discovered that I had a slight degree of my father's musical ability, but honestly, I wasn't near his league. He was one of these rare lounge acts that meant something back when packed lakeside resorts and smoky, well-attended "Supper Clubs" fully depended on nightly live entertainment. He played many instruments, all incredibly well. His "drum" was a taped rhythm track, so I learned drums and started working with him in clubs at a very young age. In that era of chain-smoking fall-down drunks, I was scared-off of both; I've never had a drink or a smoke.

Around that time, thanks to my father's pride (of me), along with his drive and his ingenuity, I also got a job drawing a weekly "Child's View" comic strip in a local small town newspaper - My father stormed the paper's offices with my drawings and before I knew it, I was a published cartoonist in a real newspaper. Between the drumming and the cartooning, I often felt torn between performing in front of people and being hunched over a drawing table by myself. I liked both, but both started to veer off to the side once I eventually discovered high school theater.

That discovery happened thanks to a magical drama teacher named Andre LaMourea. He was that rare small-town instructor who truly stood out, and he was encouraging and key to bringing theater both to me and my sister, Laura. But at the time, my creative world was getting quite crowded. This is not to say that I had mastered any of my skills whatsoever. While my first "jobs" in life were the comic strip and drumming for my father, I also knew at the time that I wanted to make film and TV - in some form or another. Along with all that, in my teens, my sister and I put a band together, getting club jobs, playing younger, louder music our father didn't play. That went on as we were both getting into a great deal of school theater. As if all that wasn't enough, thanks to then modern film cameras and projectors my father got me, I also started creating Super 8 sound films and frame-by-frame animation projects. For better or worse, when you're young and creatively active in a nice small town, you feel that you can do everything.

Looking back, I realize I moved deeper and deeper into stage acting simply as a way to be closer to "film," back when small-town Minnesota had no film classes, no video cameras or any of the access to amateur media-making we see today. Yes, I had my intricate, expensive-to-use Super 8 gear, but my amateur film-making at the time felt less connected to real "Movies" than the school stage productions I was in, all to LaMourea's credit - He shaped his productions into regional events that were beyond high school, treating kids like professionals. And at that time, I was a real student of Hollywood. I started to see that so many of the old plays I was doing were later turned into films that I had already seen. (By the way – side note - unlike today, back then, the opposite was *never* thought possible: making a *play* from an existing *movie?* That was a ridiculous notion!) But it was an absolute Golden Age of cinema (in the early to mid-seventies) - The "G", "M", "R" and "X" rating system popped up in the late 60's, the first group of young, adventurous "film school" filmmakers had arrived, and TV was moving into the bold *"All in the Family"* era of television; mass media that really said something other than the boys of *"My Three Sons"* losing the dog yet again, only to find him before the final commercial break.

All that was happening while I was still in love with then-struggling Disney animation (Made in Hollywood!) and reading that Broadway (in New York City!) was evolving with epic work from the Public Theater, like *"A Chorus Line"*. All along, my Brainerd, Minnesota parents were wonderfully supportive regarding all of my creative endeavors, knowing - perhaps even dreading - that I had sights fully set on both NY and LA. I knew that I needed to find the courage to eventually make a move from the small-town Midwest to a big city metropolis. I think my father understood that more than my mother. As a nightly club entertainer, he was of course quite extroverted and socially brave, while my mother was extremely shy and private. I felt this mix within me all throughout my youth; I still feel it today. I've often thought that my father made me courageous while my mother made me cautious - both in good ways.

Interestingly, to my sister Laura and me, while our father could entertain crowds by himself nightly, four hours at a time, he was never interested in acting - nor could he remotely understand its appeal or craft. At the same time, Laura and I were (and are) far more comfortable when playing acting roles before an audience; hiding within a character and within a script always seemed easy compared to public speaking or other forms of spontaneous stage work.

Our parents were quite proud when we both got into the same small class at The Juilliard School of Theatre, and then graduated four years later. I brought the first video camera into the Lincoln Center school, (as bulky camcorders first arrived on the scene) and I remember it causing a bit of a stir; my teachers reminded me that this was theater, not TV. But I was eager to tape our stage performances and see what we looked and sounded like as young actors. In my summer months between school years, while most of my classmates were doing regional stock theater, I went to L.A. to work in the mail room for Norman Lear, a job I got by trying to get a syndicated comic strip of *"All in the Family"* launched just before my Juilliard years. In short, once I got into school, with Brainerd now fully out of my system, I was constantly torn between NYC theater and LA media. I felt I'd eventually find success in one of those two places.

Shortly after Juilliard, one of my first "successes" in acting came by way of what I first thought was a heartbreaking failure. I played Jim Carrey's boss in a great, short-lived sitcom called *"The Duck Factory"*. That was a MTM show created by the legendary *"Mary Tyler Moore Show"* co-creator and Jay Ward *("Bullwinkle")* writer, Allan Burns. It was a good part, but the heartbreak came as I first read for many weeks as the show lead - the part that eventually went to Jim. That character was "Skip", a young animator from Minnesota! When my NYC agent first heard of this role, she sent me on a bus to L.A. a week after my Juilliard graduation.

Of course, at the time, having just graduated from Juilliard, I thought I had this; "Good God, Skip's an animator from Minnesota!" Well, I tested and tested. Allan was so nice. He often asked questions I wasn't fully shocked to hear after years at Juilliard: "Uh, why are you speaking The Queen's English?" "Why are you projecting to the balcony with the camera right here?"

A brilliant Canadian comic named Jim was far more "A Cartoonist from Minnesota" than I was after four years of classical training at Lincoln Center. It took a bit to learn how to shift from stage to screen acting - something Juilliard foolishly never taught at the time. But the wonderful part of *"The Duck Factory"* for me was how sweet Allan gave me the role of the authoritative TV network boss in the series - and that was a "joke" that then youngish, humorless NBC President Brandon Tartikoff absolutely hated: a young guy (Jim's "Skip") making an animated cartoon for a TV network boss (my character, "Gary Roth") who was the same age as the young animator?! Allan caught network hell for that; Tartikoff limited the appearances of my character, but we did the show Allan's way anyway; as we should've - Burns was a brilliant writer and producer. He's a guy I will always think highly of, in an industry that sometimes seems to have few to admire.

And speaking of admiration - to jump way ahead here in my timeline; as it will clearly be stated throughout this book (and has been stated already), after years in front of the camera, I was able to work on a number of projects with Marlon Brando, a man I met through my one-time girlfriend and later wife, Avra Douglas, the most amazing person I will ever know. Of course, much more on Avra, Marlon's introduction into my life, those projects and those days ahead within these forthcoming pages. But let me just say here: as I'm often asked who I admire in the film industry, a very short list of people come to mind, but few as strongly as Marlon. Much of that was already baked-in as I graduated from an acting Mecca such as Juilliard Drama.

THEATER TRAINING

Marlon Brando and Laurence Olivier were *thee two* religions at Juilliard Drama, but when I was a young film nut, the depth of both those legends actually frightened me whenever I'd see them in a movie; I swear (and only understand now), when I was a kid, the intensity of those two always had me looking away from the screen; I can't explain it any better than that.

I went from Minnesota to NYC theater knowing far more about George Lucas, Walt Disney, Norman Lear and Woody Allen than I did about Brando or Olivier. Of course, once I studied Brando as an actor in school, he was even more intimidating. For me, it took the training of Juilliard, followed by a newfound love of acting, to fully understand the sheer magic of Brando.

So, yes, like most acting students who go through Deep NYC Theater Training, I left Juilliard fully intimidated by the thought of that beyond human deity, Marlon Brando. But meeting the self-proclaimed "lug" years later and really getting to know him changed that.

Marlon was one of the funniest, kindest people — yes, volcanically intense and often filled with epic moods, but a real friend and survivor. He lived a singular life that I'm certain no other artist will ever know. As I teased of in the opening pages of this very book, I executive produced and co-wrote his last starring role of "The Swede" in the comedy feature *"Free Money"*. And that was just one of the many projects, adventures and journeys I was lucky enough to have experienced with him. In his home, I spent over a decade writing, laughing and plotting with him, ultimately spending over a year essentially living there, video editing his final project. By the end, he was working on a series of acting lesson tapes he called "Lying For a Living". And while that title seems to speak to a cynicism many associate with Marlon, people should know that he truly loved acting — he just rightfully hated the ugly "business" of it all.

And that "business" is something that I indeed did get into - in many ways, immediately after graduating from school. Undoubtedly, the best part of my Juilliard experience was meeting a classmate who would become my writing partner and best friend, Anthony Peck. Through Tony, I'd meet his father, Gregory, an actor who - to put it mildly - I admire beyond measure and have much to share about within this book. I won't go deeply into all that now, but I will say that Greg is the reason for me wanting to write all that you are about to read. He could easily be the most fascinating man in all of Hollywood history. I mean that with all sincerity, but I believe you really need to know my views of "The Industry" and its pitfalls to truly understand my thinking. Much more on all that to follow. On certain days, working with Marlon on Mulholland Drive, as well as with Greg in Bel Air, I would often wonder, "How did I get here?" Thinking back (and taking a step back pre-Juilliard) as I outlined previously, I recall always wanting to be in a media center like L.A. after high school, as a writer, actor, director, animator — whatever they'd let me do. Right after high school but before getting into Juilliard, I first saw NYC for a week on an exciting yet tense visit; I had a script to give Woody Allen and cartoons to show MAD Magazine. Well, I couldn't track down Woody and the guys at MAD were polite yet dismissive; they gave me an office tour and sent me on my way. All in all, I quickly thought that NYC was simply too big and too busy. I then drove with a friend to L.A. with a cartoon reel I made to show the Disney animation school, CalArts. These were years when Disney animation was at a precarious threshold, unsure about its future, never dreaming of the renaissance they'd experience in the 90's. Anyway, on that trip, I learned I had missed their next admissions deadline, but CalArts was great and quite supportive; they liked my animation reel and we discussed future semesters.

I then went back to Minnesota and spent months trying to earn for an eventual CalArts enrollment. As my younger sister (one school year below me) was then completing her senior year, I created that aforementioned comic strip of *"All in the Family"*. On a Greyhound bus, I went back to L.A. to show Norman Lear's company. I stormed their offices in the pre- 9/11, pre-security days of the late 1970's and ended up meeting a saint of a Lear executive named Kelly Smith; she was very nice and said thanks to my drive and audacity, I could work in the Lear mail room in the summer if I couldn't get the strip syndicated - and I couldn't; I'd learn that comic syndicators want to own the characters, not be on the less profitable end of promoting someone else's characters. But between that time and "next summer," I went with my sister to Chicago for her Juilliard audition. I also auditioned for the heck of it. Weeks later, we learned that we were both accepted. Surreal, life changing and there I was, on my way to becoming a New York stage actor. Laura and I were the first and to date only set of siblings in the same Juilliard Drama class. It was hard. The training and treatment is famously brutal. Only WE knew it was harder to watch your sibling go through it. As previously stated, I did work for Lear during my Juilliard summer vacations and then moved to Hollywood after graduation as an agented actor, something I hadn't envisioned during my Minnesota youth as an animator, drummer and wannabe writer/director.

As I said, when I was young, in spite of all the music and art I was into, I was shy. So was my sister Laura. But the first time I saw her in a high school play, she wasn't shy at all - in fact, she stole the show from everyone on stage, as a completely different person than the one I knew. I related to wanting to try that, and since I knew her so well and we were so much alike, I think I understood a mental process of just boldly jumping into it. Also, I started to see theater as a path to filmmaking, as opposed to my animation world, where I would spend hours drawing 24 difficult pictures, only to then have one second of a story; yes, an absolute apples-and-oranges comparison, but that's how I thought as a kid. Also, at that time, while I knew I wanted to write and direct films, I was fully aware that I had a lot to learn in many fields of knowledge before I felt comfortable trying either writing or directing beyond my Super 8 attempts.

So once my high school theater teacher, and later Juilliard, said I had acting ability, I grew confident about performing. And that's probably the most important thing anyone in "The Industry" should cultivate: confidence. Not fake "I'll loudly bulldoze through this somehow" B.S. confidence, but *real* confidence, through training, knowledge and a great deal of work. As for directing, producing and writing; as it often happens with performers in Hollywood, I watched, listened and learned from many of the best that I was lucky enough to have worked with; wonderful TV giants like Gene Reynolds, Peter Baldwin, John Erman, Jay Tarses, Ken Olin, Steven Bochco, Asaad Kelada, Gil Cates and so many more. Oh, and yes, - including the great, aforementioned Allan Burns. And by the way, you also learn a lot from the horrible ones as well.

My want to direct, write and produce grew out of life-long desires to make films, especially after I first spent years as a working actor in New York and Hollywood. Any actor will tell you - you want more control, you want more "say" in what you're doing; it's not just ego - It's a very human thing. And I was lucky to find a great writing partner in Tony. We share a sense of humor and off-beat storytelling that we still practice today. Selling screenplays with Tony led to me directing some of our projects, producing others, and ultimately led me to creating and producing TV shows such as *"Living with Ed"* starring Ed Begley, Jr. and his wife, Rachelle Carson.

So today, I still draw and act when I can, I produce, write and direct, and I still enjoy making music. When asked which of these fields I like the best, the answer is easy: I wanna be doing the one I'm not supposed to be working on at the moment. I always find myself wanting to draw when I should focus on writing — or wanting to write when my focus should be video editing a show. Acting, directing - the very same. I don't know why. It's not that I'm such a bad-ass rebel or contrarian, it's simply that I often feel far more creative without the pressure or actual demand of compensation from someone else. Leading to this perhaps sad yet very simple fact: I've always been bad with money. The chance to do something truly creative, no matter how lousy the pay, has always outweighed a smarter financial choice for me. I'm not necessarily proud or ashamed of that; as Marlon often said, "We are what we are." I sometimes felt relieved when I saw Brando also having money issues. I believe those troubles can often be related to those with creativity. Another one of his associated thoughts on all that: "Do what you give a fuck about."

MAKING A LIVING

I have been lucky to always work creatively; even more so, to never be non-working as a creative, often in different fields, but always within professions I love. Acting-wise, there were times when both the experiences and the money were good. I was in the casts of a couple TV series for a number of seasons; *"Scarecrow & Mrs. King"* and *"The 'Slap' Maxwell Story"*. I was thrilled to be making what seemed to be great money at the time, but once I started selling screenplays, I saw what a good payday was really about. Tony and I sold scripts to 20th Century-Fox, Universal Studios and a few others. While the initial payday on an original screenplay is great on a studio project, the odds of the film ever getting made are slim; studios make few original films, preferring the safer-bet worlds of sequels, bestselling books, remakes and reboots.

We often had to become independent producers to finally see our films come to life. In short: you can sometimes earn more as a non-produced studio screenwriter than you can as a produced independent filmmaker, but that's frequently how "The Industry" works. Of course, pay-wise, working unscripted TV today is even worse, *but* - the product gets made and aired. And that's what I love about that mostly basic cable work: at times, it's slightly more than elevated student filmmaking, but you're quickly creating something, it gets done and you're rapidly onto the next episode. Feature filmmaking and even scripted TV - these are slow businesses comparatively.

So while I look back fondly on great adventures and paydays as a studio screenwriter, I remember the frustration of endless script rewrites and project turnaround on those classic motion picture office lots as well. I also recall great days and tough days as a film and TV director. My most difficult day directing was probably on the set of *"Diary of a Sex Addict,"* a Sony film

Tony and I wrote. The production company packed the cast with friends and "favors" — relatively inexperienced performers that sometimes had me wondering if we'd get through a take. I also had "name" performers who were the reason the film was getting financed. These people created other challenges: years ago they were huge stars and now - they were not.

On one take, I really had to focus on the performance of one of these "favors," just as a key "name" performer wanted focus and attention as well. She loudly took me to task in front of my cast and crew. It wasn't fun, and she did more damage to herself in the eyes of the cast and crew, but I learned that directing is often acting — acting focused on everybody at the same time. My best directing day would be any day with Ed Begley, Jr. and his wife, Rachelle. We did three years of comedy on *"Living with Ed"*. It was always fun. Rachelle is one of the great unsung improv artists, and one day with Ed tells you why everybody loves him beyond measure.

So, yes, - there's good and bad in "The Industry". But the one constant truth that I've always worked with is all about the fact that "The Industry" is not mine to control, so I'd better gain control of as many "abilities" and "skills" - for lack of better words - as possible. It's often been a problem — acting agents have dropped me as they thought I was too focused on writing, some production companies think you can't direct if you're also a post video editor, etc. I recall getting comfortable in certain fields, only to have the rug pulled out from me when I least suspected.

I still vividly recall when both *"Scarecrow & Mrs. King"* and *"The 'Slap' Maxwell Story"* ended — both for different reasons, but essentially, both ending by way of issues with the star performers; Kate Jackson felt four years was enough and Dabney Coleman was having creative differences with the show creators by the time ABC was deciding on more seasons. Now, I love both of these incredible performers; I was honored to have worked with them - and given all the circumstances, I blame neither for their shows ending, but as a young actor, I fully recall that frustration over wondering just what I had to do to sustain a working career as an earning actor.

But even after all these years, I try to hang onto memorable moments in my career; moments that had me thinking at the time, "This is what life in this business is all about." I'll go into the following "moments" in a more in-depth fashion later, but in a nutshell, one moment that stands out: Tony and I wrote this giant set piece into *"Free Money"* — Marlon's character worshipped his shiny new truck. The story blows up into a scene where essentially Charlie Sheen's character smashes that truck with a train. Really. The filming day had 10 cameras rolling, Marlon Brando, and I kept thinking, "This was all blank paper until Tony and I put something crazy on it."

Other great memories of course involved knowing and working with the great Gregory Peck. Once Tony and I were established writers, Greg partnered with us. One project was to be a remake of Ingmar Bergman's *"Wild Strawberries"* - with Bergman's blessing! I reread that letter from Bergman to Greg a million times. As that project developed, we worked on it with Martin Scorsese, Sean Penn and many others. I'll get into great detail about this within these pages.

But I must say right now; the real joy of the project was Greg. Take all the warm thoughts you have about this man, multiply them times one million and you still don't arrive at how dignified, gentle and rare he was. I was working with Marlon at the exact same time and the daily comparisons between the two men that swirled in my mind made me dizzy.

That's what this book is all about. They were both so unique, both so different and both with their own firm grasp on handling stardom at the highest level. They also handled fatherhood quite differently, and since my creative partner was Tony, and my wife was Marlon's beloved assistant Avra, both Greg and Marlon became in some ways fathers to me as well. Nobody had a stronger place in Marlon's heart than Avra; she runs his estate to this day.

As this book will explore my love and life with the amazing Avra, I will use this moment to introduce the priority in our lives, our daughter, Molly. People meet me and work with me and I think they see something of a workaholic; I can't really dispute that. But that fierce focus is all about Molly. She has severe autism and much of my shift from freelance scripted work to steady unscripted work today has been about her and her life of therapy. Autism is expensive in this country, and when your child is first diagnosed, you go into a tailspin to change things, to "cure" and to get new life in order. She was diagnosed over ten years ago; it's been a difficult decade. But thank God Molly is a happy, sweet presence - people meet her and fall in love with her.

I believe there's a beautiful purity about Molly that we neurotypical people will never have. I don't really chase a legacy of any sort regarding my work, my films or my creative projects, but I'll always want Molly to know, through all that she either perceives or can't perceive, that I love her beyond words and that I will always do whatever I can to make her life safer, better and happier. My legacy as Molly's father is all that truly matters to me.

My situation with her constant challenges also taught me to always be prepared. And I've certainly lived by that as I watched media and the industry change on a daily basis. I remember when I saw one of the first Avid editing systems; it was next door to my team of editors who were editing my first 35mm feature film on ancient upright Moviolas. I told myself, "I have to get one of those Avid things next door and learn how to use it - *that* is how stories are going to be told." I took the last $65,000 I had as an actor and I bought an Avid system that had a whole 9 gigs of memory! I can do more on my phone today. But that Avid paid for itself many times over.

And that's one more reminder of how quickly and radically things change. As 100 cable networks popped up overnight a few years ago, I recall friends in "The Scripted World" questioning me as I began directing and producing unscripted shows. Today, not a month goes by when one of these guys doesn't reach out and want to propose a few "unscripted" projects.

That's not to say that I'll defend all that passes for "Reality TV," but I always say the same thing to that: just watch in a few years, after more generations of young artists have mastered fast and "non-studio" unscripted storytelling; we're all going to be amazed.

TODAY

These days, my recent projects have been mostly unscripted shows, for different production companies across the country, in places such as Boston, Chicago, New York, Austin, Denver and Miami, currently with a great creative group in Missoula, Montana; talented people who call themselves "Warm Springs Productions". I'm happy to be writing new screenplays with Tony and I'm developing shows for independent producers who are following through on the dream many of us have been cultivating for years: we can make product ourselves, we can distribute it online and we really don't have to wait for networks or production companies to deliver green lights. We're now finding ways to monetize and publicize such projects, in ways that were only in the realm of wishful thinking a few short years ago. Yes, I know many have been having this discussion for awhile, and just as many have already been at this for some time, but I think now is finally the moment for a level playing field when it comes to accessing creative tools and getting a project to an audience. It will probably all change again soon, but I'll say it once more: it's a great time to be creative. Marlon would've *loved* the accessibility of today's technology.

Just as it was when I was younger, my goals are still about creating projects and telling stories; bringing something forth and starting discussions —or sharing a laugh.

I still work with hand drawn art; cartooning and illustration, I'd love to do theater again, but at the moment, I stay creative in my TV producing and make sure bills get paid. I no longer think about white-hot fame or epic success loudly knocking at my door. But I understand how younger artists can certainly chase those types of dreams. And I of course know many enter our business seeking the rewards that come to those who "Make It Big," wanting an estate in Beverly Hills.

There's nothing wrong with that; many feel that that level of recognition lets them be more creative, pick great projects and ultimately support themselves and their families in ways they've always dreamed of. But the real industry is made up of real people you'll find in any industry: blue collar workers, clerical workers, transportation workers; workers! People who work. We're lucky if we get to work in any aspect of an industry that creates a product that entertains, enlightens or flat-out makes us feel better for a moment. Life's hard. As artists, we hopefully get to lessen what's hard about it for many.

I don't know if anything I've written here has merit to anyone thinking about wanting to work in media, but I hope as I share my stories, my history and my experiences, I can share common threads that tie us together. As I spend more years in the industry, no matter what the field, I realize I'm both lucky and often in awe of my fellow creative friends. I wasn't always that way when I was younger and more competitive. I regret those feelings, but I know they were part of the learning process, in a life where the real rewards are what we feel in our heart.

Well, that's a bit about me and even a tease or two about the following pages with Marlon and Gregory, two generous artists who will always have my undying gratitude. I know much has been written about both of them; all I can add to previous volumes is my personal experiences, my observations and my comparisons between the two. Why the comparisons? Because I was so very fortunate to get such a unique perspective. On the day that hit me, I was driving from Mulholland Drive to Bel Air, on a day when I was going to be writing screenplays with both of them; screenplays for them to star in. In a strange way, they had the same "job" - if one could call it that; they were both world famous, Academy Award winning legends in their golden years, both wanting to retain as much dignity, grace and, yes, power, as one could in their rare positions.

They both knew that their names had become as spoken as almost any phrase in the English language. They both knew there was so much more to life than all the superficial things many expect from stars living their giant lives. They both still knew that the people they kept around them mattered, in a business where everybody always wanted something. And, yes, in those days, they knew I was working with that other guy, and they'd both ask, "What's *he* doing today?"

FIRST BIT OF BUSINESS

As teased about earlier, me connecting with Marlon and Greg was the result of two of the most important relationships in my life; relationships that were the result of my opportunity to go to Juilliard - I met my best friend and creative partner at the Lincoln Center school, Tony Peck, and because of my Juilliard training, I was hired as an actor for an ABC TV series, where I met my future wife who then worked in the show's art department, Avra Douglas, an angel of a woman who had long been the equivalent of a cherished daughter to Marlon.

As I'll shout throughout this book, I had no desire or want to meet my friend's famous father nor my then-girlfriend's famous surrogate father, but eventually, both introductions did occur.

Why was I resisting so strongly? I fault my awkward - perhaps cowardly - self when I say that I've never been comfortable around those with that level of extreme fame. As for some of the other famous stars I met before Greg and Marlon - well, I was sure that I had disappointed them as much as they had disappointed me - if indeed, I had made any impression at all.

With Avra and Tony, the situations were even more daunting, thus my want to *not* meet those two legends. I had a wonderful, creative relationship with Tony; if Greg met me and ended up thinking little of me, it might do damage to the joint writing career Tony and I were just starting to pursue. The Peck family was tight, and Greg's opinions mattered. With selective, protective Marlon, he clearly wanted to "okay" or "nix" any relationship connected to those he loved, and there were few in his life he loved or looked out for as much as Avra.

Both introductions came my way for very different reasons, as I'll detail within these pages. But for the moment, in short: after a couple scripts, Tony and I were fortunate and saw success; even though I might have had a handshake or a nod to Greg across a room, after 20th Century-Fox bought one of our major original screenplays, it was clearly time to meet, know and even work with Greg. And years later now, when I recognize the level of Tony's generosity from a more mature viewpoint, I wasn't even aware back then that Tony was indeed allowing me to be a member of the family.

Avra's situation at the time was the opposite of happy success. After ABC's cancellation of the show we both worked on, she left TV and film crew work as she was helping Brando manage the daily fallout of the deadly shooting that took place in Marlon's house. As a longtime friend of the family, after years of being a school classmate of the Brando children, Marlon asked Avra to help him deal with the Christian Brando, Cheyenne Brando and Dag Drollet murder and trial tragedy, sometimes all the way over in France, caring for a troubled, in-therapy Cheyenne.

With Avra becoming so central to so much of this horrible mess (of Christian killing his sister's boyfriend in the Brando home, in front of Cheyenne), Marlon's notions regarding me were clear and even quite understandable: he wanted to know anyone who was seeming to become so permanent in Avra's life. As Avra and I were moving in together in Westwood just as she began working for Marlon full time, I clearly fit into that category. So perhaps fittingly, I met Greg by way of hard work and good fortune, just as I met Marlon by way of unspeakable tragedy.

On the surface, when you think of those two men, that all seemed to make sense at the time.

As I start these chapters, I'll always begin with informational career essays about the men. I don't assume you all know their lives, films and histories. The essays tell of these facts. They won't always be in the chronological "timeline" of *my* time with Greg and Marlon, but these essays will hopefully bring insights into their amazing movies, earlier years and personalities. And these two - Good God - they indeed had personalities. Big Time.

FIRST CHAPTER
THE MEN
(GREG & MARLON ESSAY I)

You might've already noticed that this book is as much an examination of extreme fame as it is a look at my years with Marlon and Greg. When I met these two fascinating guys, I tried to cut through their fame, wanting to understand who they really were, and as importantly, as I worked in the industry, to view how they handled the surreal nature of world famous late-stage careers.

As mentioned earlier, I grew up with a shy mother and a loud father who had his own level of "fame" as a regionally popular 7-night a week nightclub performer. While I felt my father always assumed he would eventually achieve greater fame as an entertainer, I recall my mother's shock when two of her children became "Juilliard actors" - She was actually fearful, while my father saw that event as an almost expected path for his children. Understanding them both, I grasped their respective reactions. It was the possible "fame" aspect that troubled my mother as she learned that Juilliard actors could become "stars". I think I remember her exact words: "What could be worse in the world? You get this one life, and you end up having to live it with millions of strangers thinking they know you? And you don't know any of them? That's terrifying." I told that story to Marlon one day. After a lot of silence, he said, "Your mother is quite brilliant."

That leads me to people who study fame, film history and perhaps even pop culture; I believe they'll follow what I'm about to say here: more often than not, a comparative discussion between Marlon Brando and Gregory Peck will result in the most diverse opinions. Diverse to the point of such discussions really not occurring. Who really compares these two? Not many.

And yet, by way of my travels through Hollywood and The Industry, I've of course heard many talks that compare Marlon with other famous actors - James Dean, Montgomery Clift, or in another sense, Olivier - Who's the greater actor? Brando or Olivier? Just as I've also heard people trying to have equation-theory comparisons with Greg up against everybody from James Stewart to Burt Lancaster, to Cary Grant.

But Brando and Peck? I really don't run across that comparative talk. *But*, when I *do* discuss knowing both men, it's absolutely shocking to hear some of the most surprising things from some of the most surprising people. To generalize, and to put some of it into the most extreme yet paraphrased terms I've heard, it's actually - I kid you not - gone a bit like this:

"You worked with and were friends with both of them? Wow. I would've died if I would've met Gregory Peck; that's kinda like meeting God. He seemed so amazing, so profound, so much integrity. That's a real man among men. Brando? Was he as nutty as people said he was? He seemed like a kook from what I read. Oh, I know some people freak over him, but I just don't get it. If I had to choose, no contest; I'd much rather wanna meet Gregory Peck, - no doubt."

Yes, I've actually heard variations on those themes, as much as I've also heard the following:

"You worked with and were friends with both of them? Christ! I would've died if I would've met Marlon Brando; that's kinda like meeting God. He changed acting. He changed our culture. He changed everything! Gregory Peck? He must've been a nice man, huh? Kinda boring? I dunno, he always seemed a little wooden to me, but, hey, you gotta love 'To Kill a Mockingbird', yeah? If I had to choose, no contest; I'd much rather wanna meet Marlon Brando, - no doubt."

Now, I would not have constructed those above horribly clunky paragraphs if I had not heard many variations on those actual notions time and time again. And yes, I find it to be fascinating every time, not just because I was fortunate enough to actually get to know both of the men in question. No. Instead, my fascination is with the perception of Hollywood images and how they reach and land with audiences - and even workers within The Industry itself.

It would be easy to generalize that wannabe "Art" types "get" Brando more and that "Everyday" folk "love" Gregory more, but it's much more complex than that, and in the end, I believe it's interesting to know that both Greg and Marlon were fully aware of such perceptions, ideas and pigeon-holing. Given that, neither was pleased with the fact that they had both become "products" and "commodities," as well as celebrities. These were all realities they'd often fight against, while at other times, they knew they needed to embrace such images for the sake of career. That's because they both knew that being a legendary international film star was, frankly, a highly unique job; one with no road map, rule book or list of recipes.

All this was also why I often read into both men asking me (about the other man): "What's *he* doing today?" Never once was it asked with good cheer or even some warmth for who they were asking about. Part of that, I believe, was each masking their genuine want to know. While Marlon's delivery of the question was more openly hostile and unfriendly, it was always a bit surprising to feel how mostly pleasant Greg would usually darken when asking. Mind you: I never provoked the question, never brought up "the other guy" - It was just an interesting habit they both got into, usually as I was leaving their respective homes for the day. Avra and I often talked about their "question". Marlon was a curious individual, but he was never curious about movie stars. The same thing can be said about Greg. A simple answer, we guessed, was common "intrigue". *Everybody* we knew would ask us about Greg and Marlon - Why would *they* not ask us about the other? Perhaps, but this was different than mere curiosity. We'd sometimes wonder if it was indeed mere peer interest: being an iconic international star is a rare existence; how does another one do it on a day-to-day basis? Me asking about the daily routine of a star

NFL quarterback is not the same as that question coming from another star NFL quarterback.

For the most part, Marlon *never* hung out with people like Greg. Yet it seemed that Greg socialized with everybody on his own "level" *except* Marlon Brando. Going to the opulent gatherings at the Peck Carolwood Drive estate, I was first amazed that the off-the-chart famous in attendance out-numbered us non-famous; you'd look around, week after week, and you'd see Frank Sinatra, Jack Lemmon, Walter Matthau, Roger Moore, Sidney Poitier, Shirley MacLaine, Billy Wilder, Dyan Cannon, Angie Dickinson, I could go on and on. And as they talked to one another, I realized: they shared a great deal of incredibly rare common experience. I really don't believe that they were being snobs or elite by enjoying this crowd of their peers; they simply liked the camaraderie and relatable short-hand that came with being within this "mutual" group.

A party at Marlon's house (well, more "gathering" than "party") would usually have no famous faces whatsoever. Maybe Harry Dean Stanton would show up from down the road with his worn guitar for a little bit, but that was about it. And there was usually never talk of films, The Industry or "Hollywood" at Marlon's. And yet, Marlon definitely had an interest in Greg. As Avra and I talked about it, I thought of the possible, never-to-be-fully-thought-out "inner-monologues" that might've lived within each man. By writing them out below, please know: neither man *ever* voiced such notions; these are just words I've cobbled together; words that I once thought *could* be possible when it came to both men often asking me that question. So with profound apologies to Greg, my abstract thoughts for him coldly asking the question:

"Yeah, what is Brando doing today? What does he ever do? Such a waste of talent, always angry, always badmouthing the very industry that's made him a millionaire hundreds of times over, and he's even squandered all that away from what I hear. I remember when he first rolled into town and the press made him "God," with some kind of "technique" that was supposed to make all the rest of us immediately and permanently redundant. Both Sinatra and Bette Davis called him "Mumbles"- They got

that right. Well, maybe Joe Brutsman and much of the rest of the world bought into you, "Mumbles," but not Ms. Davis, not Frank - and definitely not me."

Okay, perhaps that seemed harsh and out of line for sweet Greg, but I heard him say far worse about Ronald Reagan and Richard Nixon. And it was just a fantasy speculation anyway, based on things that many others have spoken and written about Marlon for decades. Moving on, my fantasy speculation for Marlon's thoughts on Greg might seem even more harsh - Marlon *could* be more harsh than Greg, *but,* I do believe there's something to these thoughts that I'm about to hoist onto Marlon. In fact, they are thoughts that made me want to write this book. Because if you put all of it together, all of the decades, fame and uniqueness of both these men, I will make the case that Gregory Peck alone gave other giant, possibly envious male stars of his era some of these same thoughts and frustrations, simply by being Greg. And mind you, Greg would often be spared negative thoughts from others because he WAS Greg; you might envy him, but he was just too magically gracious and genuinely loved to truly criticize.

Also, Marlon *did* have some of these following ideas about fellow actors, even though I never heard them fully spoken in regard to Greg. And with that, here goes: with sincere apologies to Marlon, my abstract inner-thoughts of him, as he coldly asked: "What's *he* doing today?"

"Yeah, what is Peck doing today? This guy, somehow having the love of the world and why? Over a few movies? He's probably out buying more tuxedos today; there's not a weekend where he and his wife don't end up in the paper at some flashy shindig, all dolled up at the latest "charity" of the day. And how the hell does he look that good?! And thin?! Jesus Christ, all of us old gypsies know: there's no dignity in painting your face at our age and getting out there to pretend, yet somehow, this guy, he's the only one in The Old Guy's Club who's still doing it with complete dignity! How the fuck is he doing that?! And harder yet, how is he both fully liked and totally sincere - in this shit-hole business?!"

Many have the mistaken idea that deep-thinking Brando never thought of "trivial" things such as male dignity, his own likability, his own appearance or public perception, but he did. He often liked to display otherwise, but those feelings were there, especially later in life, when he knew time was getting shorter, opportunities were disappearing and money was often in short supply. He'd grow angry constantly needing to "brush off" the media's barrage of "Fat Jokes".

Having anger, envy and insecure thoughts; all of that is human. And Marlon was the most human human I ever met - hands down. Getting the "human" truth out of him was a totally random exercise. Some days he would say nothing that was remotely true, deep or from his heart. Yet on other days, he was an absolute fountain of truth; sometimes dark, sometimes joyful, sometimes so brutally harsh that you wanted to find the valve that would allow you to shut it off. Truth-wise, Avra and I often liked talking to him when he was falling asleep as he sat in his den in front of his television. Falling asleep was a joyful intoxication for Marlon; he'd sometimes mutter like a drunk, even though he hadn't had a drink for months. During those sleepy times, he'd occasionally talk "Hollywood," in ways that he would avoid when fully awake.

One such time, he brought up the term "Movie Star," and he slowly, quietly muttered, "Being a movie star is the greatest job in the world. Being an actor that nobody knows, being an actor looking for a break with your picture in your paw, that's worse than having skin disease."

Both young Marlon and young Greg first broke onto the film scene in ways that nobody had ever witnessed before. They both showed up as perfect looking, powerful performers who could make women literally swoon by merely walking into the room. They both dove directly into a string of hit films and Academy Award nominations; track records few actors ever experience. By the time I met them in the 80's & 90's, they were the first ones to admit that their respective, personal entry chapters into stardom contained far more luck and more excitement than most. But now, as I grew to know them past those intense, amazing glory years, I believe they were both on the same hunt - For a substantial film project to "End" with.

Throughout this book, I'll talk about the years I was lucky to have spent with Greg and Marlon: their final years - Years when, whether they personally would ever admit it or not, were both looking for a fitting "Third Act" success. I use the "Three Act" structure not just out of simplicity; looking at many artists in any medium - especially in American pop culture - one sees a familiar pattern. When artists become the "Household Names" that Greg and Marlon became, there's Act One - again, that amazing "Burst Onto The Scene" that is near blinding, an entrance that makes everybody feel that *this* is someone who is here to stay.

But given that we're talking about Hollywood and the U.S. film industry, only one thing is clear: there's no real set pattern for success or career sustainability. Both Marlon and Greg certainly checked that box when it came to their entrances in their 20's, both making everybody sit up and notice these new amazing actors. Their blinding entrances carried them all the way through the 60's; by then, they both had "Best Actor" Oscars. Then there was their "Second Act" of box office and hit-making, a marker that can be identified by Greg's *"The Omen"* and Marlon's *"The Godfather"*. And as I'll be saying in different ways in different places within this volume, I feel I met them as they were both trying to figure out and execute their "Third Act."

They were looking to shape some form of a worthy final chapter.

Mortality, like skin disease, has a way of getting your attention. Even if you're a movie star.

TONY (1979)

Being a writing and producing partner with Tony Peck was something neither Tony nor I could've remotely guessed about back when we both arrived at The Juilliard School in 1979. My sister Laura and I came to Lincoln Center pretty-much directly from high school in Brainerd, Minnesota. Tony already had a degree from Amherst, having seen most of the world a few times over.

My sister and I had yet to ever ride an airplane at that time. Tony had crossed every ocean, met world leaders and partied with major stars, models, celebrities and rockers, still doing all that as he was attending what many say is the most challenging acting conservatory in the world.

In short: Tony and I were from different planets, but with a class as small as ours - 27 upon entering, 14 of those from the original 27 at graduation (yeah, about as close to half as it gets) - it was impossible to avoid one another over the four year period. In fact, we grew to understand and respect one another, even as we might not have, at first, seen one another as the best of friends beyond the walls of our school or outside our trade. We were just too different, that's all.

But even with those cultural distances at school, I saw that Tony was such a fun and sweet presence, incredibly likable and approachable, eager to laugh or make you laugh. But one thing was obvious as school began for Laura and me: certain students were not gonna stop chasing Gregory Peck's son, for whatever reasons they had; self-serving or otherwise. As accusatory and crass (on my part) as that sounds, it was clear as day, especially when everyone would watch the pursuit of Tony by classmates such as Kevin Fowler, later to use his Scottish middle name and go by the moniker of Kevin Spacey. A student two classes above ours, a one-time high school classmate of Kevin's, Val Kilmer, also made sure he got Tony's attention as often as possible.

It's perhaps no accident that these two actors found their way to great fame; yes, they were incredibly talented, but they were also persistent, not afraid of chasing limelight, and most of all, had no fear of going after what they wanted. Today, many in the industry will claim that these two talented actors would later pay career-ending prices for volumes of questionable behavior, even after achieving their fame. Back at Juilliard, their "chasing" of Tony was awkward for many to watch, but once one grew to know Val or Kevin, it was easy to see that their "chases" were in tune with their personalities. As for Tony, he was always trusting, good-natured and very polite in these matters - Never naive, but always aware and knowingly tolerant of those who had interest in him for matters of industry advancement, social climbing or even simple Hollywood fawning.

For the very reasons listed above, I guess it's fair to say that I perhaps did somewhat avoid Tony to some extent during our early school years, only because those of us in the class with self awareness did not want to be seen as Another Young Actor Chasing The Movie Star's Son. On top of that, I was ridiculously filled with issues of class, fame and money that first came from my parents and TV. Example: as a little kid, watching *"Gilligan's Island,"* I actually felt incredibly sorry for Ginger and the Howells, feeling their situations in life made them sadly and horribly unaware. I laugh and cringe thinking of such notions now, because I realize how unfair so much of my mindset was regarding Tony, a man who would not only become my best friend; he's a guy who anyone would be lucky to know. Hopefully within this book, I'll make his value, charm and creative brilliance clear. He's an amazing man, closer to me than any brother could ever be.

He's taught me so much about so many things; things I never experienced as he did; more on all that later. Back to those school years: Tony and I graduated in the summer of 1983 as friends, finding humor by way of our opposite worlds, our different sides of the tracks, our "Country Mouse and City Mouse" views, and our amazement over the fact that two actors from such diverse places could share the theatrical stage so many times, get each other to laugh so often, and yes, somehow both get through the four cut-throat years of The Juilliard School of Theatre. Right after graduation, we were the only two from our class to go directly to Los Angeles, even though Tony was not in California long, quickly getting a part in Roman Polanski's *"Pirates,"* an epic film shoot that took him out of the country for months. When he returned, we began an exercise regiment together, running the epic bleacher steps of UCLA. We often talked about writing together, talking about it so much that we finally decided to do it, starting in 1987.

Prior to that, I had never written with a writing partner. In fact, in my mind, I felt I was still teaching myself how to write. When I think back as to how I believed I could teach myself writing as a young teenager, I recall a certain play by a certain author. Allow me to explain:

In 1974, *"The Good Doctor"* was a Neil Simon play that I had read a number of times in the Brainerd Library. It was a collection of comedy sketches based on the stories of Anton Chekhov.

I've never seen a production of it, but as a young person, I found it to be a fun read, and I knew this author was responsible for one of my favorite TV shows, *"The Odd Couple,"* even though he had never written a single episode. But I read his original *"Odd Couple"* play, and like *"The Good Doctor,"* it was fun to read. That was the magic of Neil Simon back in his golden era; when he was "on" you loved it even when it was just on paper. I checked *"The Good Doctor"* out of the library for one purpose and one purpose only. I was 14, I knew I wanted to be a writer, and I knew that I had no idea of how to become a writer. Well, that's not entirely true; now that I had just found a used typewriter, I *did* have an idea of how to at least *start* to become a writer - My juvenile, perhaps absurd idea: word-for-word, I would retype *"The Good Doctor,"* so I could see what it looked like from my typewriter.

After that, I'd re-type what I had just typed, changing a word here and there with messy, chalky "Wite-Out". After that, more "Wite-Out", more re-typing; changing even more words, names and locations. My hope was that the simple steps of typing, formatting and viewing pages would start to get my mind thinking like a writer. To be honest, to this day, I'm not sure if it worked, but I do know that I am now a self-taught writer who has worked for many years as a professional - never doing any of it with any abstract near-plagiarism. So, hey, maybe there was something to what I call, *"'The Good Doctor' Method"*. I later did the same thing with episodes of *"M*A*S*H"* and *"The Dick Van Dyke Show,"* transcribing, changing-up words, taking the scenes to new conclusions; basically using an art method: essentially tracing until I could draw, so to speak. Years and pages later, I felt I had enough confidence to begin writing with Tony.

At that time, I was finally starting to date, coming off a troubled 10-year relationship that went from Brainerd to NYC to L.A. I had my own apartment in Westwood, meeting one "wrong" girl after another - until I met Avra. Tony and I wrote a comedy about it called *"Tie You Up,"* and as uneven as it was - being our "first" joint screenplay - it did get made, and it was the start of a fellowship that brought Tony and me great joy. We'd laugh like hell while working and we became the daily "life" sounding board for the other guy. We were still working and auditioning as actors at the time, but that too was part of the excitement of those days - We were young and it felt as though anything was possible.

When Tony and I would write, there were days when the best part of the session was going to lunch. We'd sometimes go over to the Peck home on Carolwood Drive to lunch with Tony's parents, Greg and Veronique, or we'd have a healthy lunch with Tony's fiancée and later wife, Cheryl Tiegs. But often, we'd go into Hollywood, Beverly Hills or even the Valley, to talk over the day's writing and more often than not, eat bad food. Tony has always been a much healthier eater than me, but occasionally, he'd have his waves of burgers, fries, pizza and junk. Still, being something of a natural athlete, it never seemed to show on him. During one of those lunches, after writing *"Tie You Up,"* we talked about a second script. We were both close to our sisters; I knew Cecilia Peck well and my sister Laura was a Juilliard classmate of Tony's. I talked about how Laura always hated me being the perceived, well-behaved "favorite" of my parents. Tony discussed being annoyed over how clearly Cecilia was seen as the "white sheep" of his family.

And with this, we knew we had a second screenplay to write. Yes, more on all that coming up.

Avra (1987)

Playing Dabney Coleman's son in ABC's *"The 'Slap' Maxwell Story"* changed my life. I really did think that this was a show that was going to both succeed and stay on the air. Along with Hugh Wilson's *"Frank's Place," "Slap"* was the best reviewed show of the 1987 fall TV season. It was a series that brought Jay Tarses and Dabney Coleman back together, after their critically acclaimed yet ratings challenged NBC series, *"Buffalo Bill,"* a dark comedy about the kind of character Dabney played well: a self-absorbed egotist who also happened to be a highly questionable father. In *"Bill"* he had a daughter (played by Pippa Pearthree), in *"Slap,"* a son.

I had just finished two years as "Agent Efrem Beaman" on *"Scarecrow & Mrs. King"* for CBS and I was so hoping that *"Slap"* could be the steady, quality series I had dreamed of being a part of since I was a kid. My first *"Slap"* episode was the fourth of the new series, a "recurring" character - perhaps - *if* I did well. But that was my situation on *"Scarecrow"* years before, and I had confidence after being able to turn the guest role of "Efrem" into ongoing employment. With *"Slap"* I of course saw the obvious ongoing possibilities of playing the son of the series lead.

Getting the part reminded me of the fragile, often horrible nature of casting. I first heard of the part by way of two Juilliard classmates, friends who came from New York to Los Angeles for "Pilot Season". We all had the same agent. As we hung out, having a happy reunion, I heard they were both reading for some great part for some great show: a broad, complex comedic character: half fool, half brilliant; he makes his tough sportswriting father, played by the singular Dabney Coleman, crazy. Both my friends talked about the difficulty of this odd role; a writer's abstract creation that's fun to read but nearly impossible to act alongside grounded characters - especially within this "new" form of TV: the "Dramedy" - part comedy, part drama, laughs but no audience or laugh-track, all shot in single camera format like a feature film. This was all quite new in the mid-to-late eighties. (side note: it took years to train U.S. TV audiences to laugh on their own.)

Anyway, I asked my agents if I could read for this interesting part. They said I was not right for the role. When both of my friends - two good actors - failed to get a call back, I asked my agents again. They told me to stop bugging them. I then heard that the *"Slap Maxwell"* casting people were going to New York to search for an actor. I put it out of my head and went on with my life. Weeks later, I got a call to go in and read, basically told that I was essentially the very last actor my age on both coasts to read for "Eliot Maxwell". I went in and read for writer/producer Jay Tarses, someone I met briefly back on the MTM set of *"The Duck Factory"* sitcom years earlier; that previously mentioned comedy about a small, rundown animation studio.

In *"Duck Factory"* Jay played the Morey Amsterdam/"Buddy Sorrell"-like writer of the *"Dippy Duck"* cartoon, I played the head of the network that aired the cartoon. Auditioning for Jay after small talk about *"Duck"* and the work we did back then with Allan Burns and Jim Carrey, I read "Eliot". And I quickly had Jay laughing. I got the part, was made a recurring character after my first "trial" episode and talk began about making me a regular in season two.

While shooting the show, I met and fell in love with a young beauty in the art department named Avra Douglas. I was crazy about her from the moment I saw her. Much more about Avra, her family and our lives together as these pages unfold. When we came together, Avra was also working on Jay's other dramedy of the moment, NBC's *"The Days and Nights of Molly Dodd"*. These shows were shot in strange warehouses-ala-soundstages in the San Fernando Valley, far from the fun and community of Hollywood studio lots. Avra and her fellow art department crew members did a lot of driving and searching when it came to putting the shows together. There was no simple running over to the studio costume shop or prop house when needed; we were really out in the middle of nowhere, even needing to cease shooting when the frequent noise from the next-door tile-cutting shop would kill a take. Dabney would throw fits over this.

He'd throw a lot of fits about a lot of things, and however it happened, an angry stalemate soon formed between Jay Tarses and Dabney. When they both talked to me privately about the seemingly certain season two, they had very different plans: the show was essentially about a small newspaper where Slap worked, called *"The Ledger"*. Jay said, "Next season, that's the show title, without Coleman." Dabney told me, "Next season, the show will be a live studio audience comedy, but with no Tarses." Yeah, I did wonder how all this was going to shake down.

Avra and I started dating as the series was reaching the end of its first season. We were both shattered to learn that the show would not have a second season in the Los Angeles Times. The head of ABC, Brandon Stoddard, blamed the cancellation on the feud between Coleman and Tarses, claiming that while the season's best reviewed show *could* survive not-so-great ratings, it could not live in an atmosphere where the star and head creative can't be in the same room with one another.

Avra and I immediately looked for new work, as we were making plans to move in with one another. I continued to audition for other acting roles as I also kept writing screenplays with Tony. Avra did a couple art directing jobs, soon finding her skills as a pastry chef to be both more rewarding and more lucrative, especially when it came to work more steady than anything in the worlds of film and television. Without the grind of two TV shows such as *"Slap"* and *"Molly"* (Tarses took that NBC cancelled show to NYC for Lifetime) it seemed she had more time to see her friends. Avra lived in the town she grew up in, and many easily picked Avra as their "best friend" - She's a sweetheart who was and still is always in demand. Back when the always funny Jay Tarses learned I had interest in Avra on the set of the show, he said to me, "Oh, she's amazing - nobody can get enough of that girl; she's like heroin!"

One of her "best friends" was Rebecca Brando, a daughter of Marlon's that Avra went to school with years back. During those years, Avra also got to know all of the Brando children, along with the rotating cast of ex-wives, ex-girlfriends and assorted characters in Marlon's orbit.

Avra also got to know Marlon quite well. Avra and Rebecca would spend time with Marlon occasionally, and even in these months before Avra was hired to work for Marlon, I declined all invitations to meet with him. Like anybody, I found stories about his everyday life somewhat interesting, but I did not want the unnecessary, nerve-racking experience of meeting "Brando".

After the horrible May 16th, 1990 incident at the Brando house involving Christian Brando, his sister, Cheyenne and her boyfriend Dag Drollet, Marlon needed new people in his universe on all fronts: legally, medically and emotionally, and they all needed to be people he could trust. While that trust level wasn't always possible in some areas, like say, needing to hire lawyers with the, uh, "integrity" of soon-to-be O.J. Simpson attorneys, Marlon did want a beloved friend such as Avra around, to help with shattered Cheyenne and other related matters.

As Christian's trial took place, Marlon wanted to spare the incident's fragile sole witness from a courtroom, from maybe having to testify against her own brother regarding the murder of her boyfriend. It's easy to understand Marlon's tragically unique concerns - Cheyenne was the only other person in the room when intoxicated Christian goofed around with his loaded gun in front of Tahitian guest Dag Drollet. A week after Avra and I moved into a new apartment together in Westwood, Marlon sent Avra and Cheyenne to France, so his daughter could seek therapeutic help. Avra was gone for so long I flew to Paris to have an American Thanksgiving with her. When she finally did return with Cheyenne, Marlon asked Avra to stay on as his assistant. So here we were, Avra and I, living together in Westwood, California; I was a struggling actor and screenwriter, spending most of my days looking for or trying to create work.

And here was Avra, with her new full time boss. If you were to ask Marlon at that time in his life, he'd say that he too was a struggling actor and screenwriter (at the age of 67), spending most of his days looking for or trying to create work.

Oddly, as Avra and I would witness, there were days when he wouldn't be far off about all that.

Meeting Greg
And then *REALLY* meeting Greg (1988)

In the small town I grew up in, Brainerd Minnesota, there was an automotive race track that had a well known, oddly oversized profile within the world of international raceways, "BIR" - Brainerd International Raceway. At least, I think that's what it was called back then; before that, it was called "Donnybrooke Speedway". If I knew more about the divisions of professional car racing, I could tell you exactly what type of racing took place there. Whatever it was, the heady national fame of the track eclipsed the town of Brainerd at that time. To give a little perspective: a top headline in the local paper in those days would actually be something like "Local Cat Stuck in Tree," with a photo of an arriving fire truck. No joke; it was a small town. Much of the movie, *"Fargo"* took place in Brainerd, even though it was filmed elsewhere. The Cohen Brothers who made the film came from a Minneapolis suburb, knowing the tiny, provincial nature of Brainerd.

But I always tell people without jesting, "The movie *'Fargo'* made the place look far more sophisticated than it is; when I was there, they never would've had a female sheriff, let alone a pregnant one." Still, I experienced a great and beautiful place to grow up. Returning to the race track: I barely knew much about BIR as I was deep into heavy film study, film worship and film obsession, all on my own. So one summer night, as a young teenager, I was walking down the street, having just gotten out of a movie; there wasn't a film that came to Brainerd that I did not see. Who is in a car on a quiet street waiting at a red light? In Brainerd, Minnesota? Race car driver Paul Newman in a small convertible. *What the fuck?!* I think I had a heart attack right there and then. Seriously. From a few feet away, I started screaming, yelling, probably crying. I shouted, *"I've seen every movie you've ever made!"* He smiled, laughed and then gave a little Newman-esque tip-of-his-fingers-to-his-forehead salute as the traffic light (mercifully for him) turned green - And to cobble together two of my favorite characters - Cool Hand Butch drove away. The whole thing happened within the span of a few surreal seconds.

Up to that point in my life, hands down, that was the most famous person I had ever seen in person, and you might say, sorta-kinda "communicated" with. Leading to this: there are many ridiculous aspects to being a self-involved teenager; a key one for me was self-reflection to the point of self-destruction. For months, I, perhaps oddly, hated myself for the foolish display I staged in front of Paul Newman. The whole matter had taken me by surprise, but I was already picturing myself as some sort of future Hollywood Player - and *this* is how I was going to act in the presence of the famous? Pathetic. I made star-struck Lucy Ricardo look sophisticated by comparison. By the time I was a student at The Juilliard School of Theatre, you'd think I would have been a bit more at ease when it came to meeting famous people, but you would be wrong.

Nobody from the "Outside World" gets to see young Juilliard actors until those performers finally enter their third year of training; at least that's the way it was back when Tony, my sister Laura and I were Juilliard students. In a drama student's first two years, only Juilliard teachers and fellow students get to witness your efforts. In the third year, you do plays in acting studios made into theaters, with folding chairs and limited sets, but they are plays that are open to the general public. In the fourth year, you move onto the Main Stage at The Juilliard School. For the first two years, the somewhat pretentious young students of our class occasionally had a quiet conversation that they tried to pretend they were not having, a conversation that involved everybody except our fellow classmate, Tony Peck. But I'm certain Tony was familiar with this kind of conversation - the type of whispered chatter he's known since childhood.

The "conversation" amongst those in our class: "Won't it be strange when Gregory Peck is out there watching us?!" When things like this were whispered, I found it to be oddly annoying, and yet I really didn't know exactly why. I'm sure it crossed my mind as well, but I think I found the spoken question among our classmates to be ridiculously pointless and uncomfortably distancing regarding our friend and fellow cast member, Tony Peck. *And* - incredible but true: maybe I was having cringeworthy flashbacks as to how I had embarrassed even myself as a young teenager when race car driver Paul Newman stopped at a red traffic light in Brainerd. Whatever the case, I didn't meet Greg at Juilliard, even though I heard he was in the building to watch his son in our plays. I'd meet Greg later when I moved to L.A. after graduation, at first just saying "Hi" as his son's friend, as Tony also moved to Los Angeles when school was finished; his move west was a homecoming. Mine was a search for a career in Hollywood.

Looking back, I feel I now know some of the reasoning for never wanting to meet Greg or Marlon as a young, yet-to-succeed actor and filmmaker, or even perhaps Tony, when we were first year students at school. Yes, Shrink-Alert: it all came from my parents - No, I'm not blaming them, but as you mature through the years, you grasp elements of your mother's and father's nuance, along with aspects of their behavior; you try to understand more. Hopefully, you also appreciate some of it along the way as well. I've discussed how opposite they were from one another, but of course, they both strongly influenced me in their own ways. My shy mother had a firm rule that she so clearly lived by - "Never bother people. *Never!* That's the worst thing you could possibly do, especially people who get bothered a lot - why would you add to that?"

My father - the self-taught solo nightclub entertainer in the Midwest; he couldn't read music, he taught himself eight different musical instruments, along with teaching himself carpentry, auto repair, plumbing, electrical work - he was totally intuitive about everything. In fact, he thought that certain forms of education were actually the same as "cheating". When I was a young cartoonist learning my "craft" by watching and drawing Mickey Mouse, Bugs Bunny and Fred Flintstone off the television, my dad would proudly show me off to others, telling people that I draw "without looking at anything!" Of course, once I had those TV lines memorized, yeah, I guess you could say that. But I'll never forget when I had my first "real" art classes in junior high school. On Day One, my teacher started us off with a simple still life vase and flowers. I looked away and started doing some Hanna Barbara-like cartoon version of a flower in a vase.

My art teacher had already heard of this Great Boy Cartoonist of Brainerd - my wall murals and artwork displays were all over town, but he wondered what the hell I was up to with that, uh, "original" flower vase. Keeping me after class, he asked about my process - I explained that it was "cheating" to look at something and draw it. He laughed, "Are you crazy? Do you know how many great artists and illustrators trace, use projectors and flat-out cut and paste their 'art'? Who put all that nonsense in your head?"

The same thing happened when I joined the school band as a percussionist; my band director knew I was already drumming professionally in clubs with my father on weekends, but he had a hell of a time getting me to learn sheet music.

That odd aspect of my father's "independent" thinking stayed with me for quite some time - whether I realized it or not. The strict notion behind it: you don't need other people or their assistance or their "cheats" to accomplish something. Anything. Period.

Of course, in line with all that, I also recall his constant irritation/envy with the many musicians, actors and artists he'd see on TV. He'd always have some gripe about "who they knew to get ahead," how big pop singers *really* had great unknown, unnamed musicians behind them - *those* were the real talents - not some pretty girl or pretty guy in front holding a microphone. Okay, sometimes true, but to what point? He always had dreams of going to Las Vegas, hitting it big and only *then* - on his own terms - meeting Wayne Newton, Frank Sinatra, Johnny Cash, etc. My father had such great talent but he also had such great pride. Perhaps too much pride.

Growing up quite poor, he also had a "Class Structure" chip on his shoulder the size of a cinder block. Heritage-wise, he was part working-class German and part reservation Native-American, always feeling that he was pretty much all on his own. And given his temperament, he was. So while I believe I didn't *fully* cling to my mother's "Never bother anybody" notion or my father's "Never need anybody" edict, I know elements of all that shaped me when it came to meeting two people as big as Gregory Peck and Marlon Brando. No doubt about it. But as I explained earlier, those meetings happened once Tony and I were doing well as writers and Marlon insisted on knowing who his favorite assistant was living with. Actually, the real firm, lasting and transformative meeting of Greg was on an incredible night at the Peck estate on Carolwood Drive. First, a few words about that elegant piece of property in Bel Air, California.

Warren Beatty's *"Shampoo"* was a 1975 film that was as "Los Angeles" as a movie could possibly be. To this day, Southern California film buffs know all the locations, streets and houses seen in the Columbia Pictures film, with the most famous location probably being the opulent "Party House," the packed mansion seen the night of the presidential election. It's a sprawling Bel Air estate with acres of wooded areas, its own flowing creek and a picturesque log cabin down by a spectacular tennis court. A couple years after *"Shampoo"* was made, the place would be sold.

That very house on Carolwood Drive would go on to become the residence of Greg and Veronique Peck, an estate that Tony taught me to simply call "Carolwood". (As I would later call Marlon's Mulholland Drive home "Mulholland". After Marlon's death, some in the press claimed he called the home "Frangipani" - I never heard Marlon call it that once.) Rented out for a while as a film location (mostly by Universal Studios) before the Pecks bought it, "Carolwood" pops up today in old movies and TV episodes; you'll see it in *"Columbo"* reruns, which is perfect; just the kind of prestigious mansion unwashed mutt Detective Columbo shows up at (and looks out of place in) as he's outsmarting the always tall, white, handsome, estate-owning, guest star murderer. And speaking of "unwashed mutts," yes, that's exactly how I felt when I first arrived at Carolwood. An unwashed mutt looking wildly out of place.

Back to that night when I feel I finally, really *met* Greg; before that night, I had a lunch, a wave or a "Hi" from Greg a few times, perhaps shook his hand once in a while, seeing him now and then from a distance as I would have the occasional visit to Carolwood. I was probably seen as perhaps another friend of "the kids," maybe referenced as one of the Juilliard classmates, but nothing more. In the mid-eighties, Tony and I created that aforementioned first screenplay together, *"Tie You Up,"* the youthful sex romp that we got to make into an unreleased feature in the 90's. In the late 80's, with our writing then clicking, our second screenplay was sold to 20th Century-Fox. *"Black Sheep"* (not the Chris Farley film) was a mafia comedy of diametrically opposed siblings; a script that was agented by Irving "Swifty" Lazar, thanks to the prodding enthusiasm of Tony's mother, Veronique.

Greg pretty much stayed out of these matters, but when the screenplay sold, Greg was proud and supportive. The Fox deal was announced on the same day that Greg and Veronique were already planning a huge dinner party at Carolwood. They often had many grand dinners and parties at the house throughout the year, but this one was epic, sprawling through the house and out into the yards, celebrating some birthday, anniversary or arriving guest of honor that I was never fully informed about. Whatever it was, it was clear: celebrations at Greg's house were pretty damn big. Tony invited me to this gigantic party, and of course, by coincidence, part of the celebration turned into this sub-event regarding our script. Like I said, while all of the dinner gatherings at Carolwood were star-studded, and often large, this one was insanely off the hook. Tony and Cheryl sat with many family members as they seated me at a great table with three women who happened to arrive that night without husbands, boyfriends or escorts: Dyan Cannon, Angie Dickinson and Shirley MacLaine. Tony introduced me to them as his Juilliard classmate, his creative partner and, as of today, a sold, agented WGA screenwriter thanks to Swifty Lazar and 20th Century-Fox. All of that apparently was enough to get the conversations started at our table.

To say I was a bit nervous would be a fully ridiculous understatement. But they were all charming, shockingly beautiful and wonderfully interested in the newly sold screenplay, the acting work I had recently done and my years at Juilliard. While MacLaine was the most quiet, not talking a whole lot, often visiting those at nearby tables, Dickinson and Cannon were funny and chatty, wanting to know the entire story of *"Black Sheep,"* the way I worked with Tony and what Peck and I were going to write next.

Only years later can I fully understand what I perhaps represented to them at that table on that evening - either subliminally or fully realized: I was full potential and promise, without the slightest bit of real accomplishment to my name as of yet. Still, in spite of that, I was a young, unknown screenwriter in an hour of certified success for that night, then without baggage trails behind me; "Industry" trails of public failure, show business cynicism or Hollywood male ego.

Both then and now, my respect for those three women was and is immeasurable. Think about it: I was sitting there with true industry stars who had been through so much, who knew all the highs and lows of a very brutal business. Thinking back, they were amazing; all three so smart, supportive and giving. Talented, beautiful and female - in their youth, that combination was probably great to a point. But I can only imagine what they had to deal with years back, and how incredible their survival skills were as I was meeting them on this evening in the late 80's.

Later that night, after the desserts, drinks and chatter, Veronique pulled me aside to talk of her excitement over the script sale. I couldn't thank her enough for her support and endorsement; after first reading *"Black Sheep"* weeks ago, she was the one who approached her friends Mary and Irving Lazar, and while I had faith in the script, I knew that Irving was positively key to all this - He could sell just about anything to just about anybody. Greg soon joined our conversation as Veronique trailed off to talk to others. So here I was, in a sense, in my mind, really, fully meeting Greg - for me - for the very first time since I knew him. You'd think that all those other passing waves and handshakes would've at least gotten me over the "Jesus Christ, you're Gregory Peck!" phase, but no, that wasn't the case. But at least I didn't pull a "Paul Newman in Brainerd".

Greg laughed, "I think I saw your name in 'Variety' today, landing that 'six-figure deal at 20th.'"

I also laughed because I felt I knew where this was going. Greg continued with, "Anthony told me of the one hundred thousand dollar payday. You see, that's good agenting; I guarantee you, when the press wanted the actual number, Irving simply said, 'six-figure deal' and left it at that."

I congratulated him on throwing such a great party for, uh, whatever it was that the party was for, with me politely faking my way through the illusion that I knew what it was for. I thanked him for inviting me, along with more small talk about the recently sold screenplay.

Feeling the evening was getting late, I was making my exit, reminding myself (and telling Greg) that my upcoming weekend would be consumed with preparing for an acting job on Monday morning, an episode of *"Slap Maxwell"*. I recall this moment because I then got to hear Greg bask in some of the elegant language he often liked to use - language he sounded so good using.

"For now, you and Anthony should keep all your irons in the fire. But one day, one of you, or perhaps both of you - you might need to decide between being a thespian on the boards or an ink-stained scribe. But you both have plenty of time to figure that out."

I smiled and shrugged, "Or maybe, one day, it just gets figured out for you."

He smiled with a nod, asking, "Do you like 'Joe' or 'Joseph'?"

"Uh, really, whichever you like best."

"'Joe' it is. I'm 'Greg'." We laughed, shook hands and parted ways as others approached Greg for a valued moment of his precious time. I then said "good-bye" to the three beautiful women at my table, having, of course, fallen madly in love with each one of them; anything short of that would've been impossible. I then slyly made my way out of this ocean of Hollywood elegance, finding a shadow in the corner of the yard, one that led to a groundskeeper's gate I knew of. That brought me out to the dark residential street, where I could then start my walk to my junk car - the automobile that I did not hand over to the valet at Greg's gate, a heap presently parked about half a mile away up Sunset. After that night, Greg and I saw each other quite differently. I was starting to understand what Greg's world was. It was a world where he always knew that so many eyes were constantly on him; eyes belonging to so many that he would never, ever know, even though so many of those staring strangers thought they really did know the wonderful Gregory Peck. I wasn't one of those people any longer to Greg. To him, I was a thespian on the boards, as well as an ink-stained scribe named "Joe," who wrote movies with his beloved son.

And now, to me, he was "Greg".

We still didn't know each other well at that moment. But all that was about to change.

That aforementioned Monday morning, when I went to work on a final *"Slap"* episode, I had scenes with all of my favorite cast members: Dabney, of course, as well as the beautiful Susan Anspach, who played my mother, and a latecomer to the series, Shirley Jones, who was playing Slap's new girlfriend, "Kitty". Shirley was as sweet and warm as you'd assume she'd be. I was still a bit giddy from the sale of my script, the night at Carolwood and, of course, my talk with Greg. As many in and out of The Industry know, there's a lot of waiting around and chit-chat on a film or television set - Especially by the actors, waiting for the lighting and camera set up.

Some actors like to relax on the set, some hide away in their dressing room or trailer. With both Susan and Shirley working today, Dabney made it a point to "hang out" more in the soundstage than usual; it was as though important guests were in "His House" today. I sat with them as we all discussed our weekends. After blurting some variation of my news, talk of my screenplay was quickly eclipsed by talk of Greg. I remember Shirley and Susan swooning over Peck, as Dabney told of his want to study in 1958 under Sanford Meisner at New York's Neighborhood Playhouse, specifically because it was where Peck, one of Dabney's favorite actors, had trained.

As only Dabney could say it, he ended his story with: "Gregory Peck. Goddamn. That is a man."

Coleman was a uniquely passionate man, often masking huge emotions behind that singularly cold facade. He was actually tearing up over his "Gregory Peck" proclamation. Seeing that he was being noticed, he rebounded with, "And Shirley, you two together in *"How the West Was Won"*- Shirley quickly interrupted with, "That was Debbie Reynolds," and Dabney smoothly went straight into, "And Joe, doggone it, for you to confuse Shirley here with Debbie Reynolds, well, I'd say you owe this great lady an apology."

God. *That* was Dabney Coleman - As original as it gets.

Slap and Al (1988)

As I was working on *"Slap Maxwell"* in the late 80's, Rupert Murdoch, to many, was already becoming a Known Force of Evil in the Universe, mostly thanks to his *"New York Post"* and his *"Star"* tabloid. While not everyone saw him as an arch villain, he was certainly hated by many in the Democratic Party and among liberal organizations. He'd later go on to build Fox News and without a doubt, use it to reshape the country's political landscape. He was also buying-up major organizations left and right when I first arrived in Los Angeles. Just as I was about to be profiled in *"TV Guide,"* by way of my acting work on ABC's *"The 'Slap' Maxwell Story"* and CBS's *"Scarecrow and Mrs. King,"* I got a call from the TV Guide writer, a wonderful woman named Susan Littwin. She was telling me that the story was now much shorter, if it would run at all.

Murdoch had just bought the magazine, and the new directive for the *"new"* TV Guide was to be more bubble-gum *"People"* magazine-like; no longer the place for a story about a Juilliard trained actor coming off of a failed "quality" series like *"Slap"*. The article did run, and I while I've never blamed Murdoch for the editorial change, I knew then that I was getting a very vivid picture of who this guy was; incredibly powerful and a real player in Hollywood. But buying TV Guide was clearly small potatoes compared to his other financial adventures within that same time frame. Murdoch was also busy with his newly fully acquired toy, 20th Century-Fox.

With that, he was about to change the face of TV. As disliked as Murdoch has always been by mostly liberal Hollywood, he was a bit of a darling to the working actors and creatives within the industry in the 80's, when he took it upon himself to expand the town's workflow, by creating that longtime elusive dream of a Fourth Network. Back in a world of three networks, a handful of primetime shows and an always limited set of opportunities, *any* expansion and new promise was welcome. So with the help of then media master Barry Diller, Murdoch gave Hollywood's performers, writers, directors and producers a few hours of new primetime possibilities.

Of course, if you were there, you know that early on, "few" is the operative word here. While the network did arrive, it was limited by its small number of nights, hours, shows and even local affiliates. Still, simply by letting creative people *be* creative, without excessive network notes or interference, Diller and the new Fox network built hits. After a rickety start, they let Keenen Ivory Wayans shape *"In Living Color,"* they allowed James L. Brooks to morph the cartoon shorts from *"The Tracy Ullman Show"* into *"The Simpsons,"* and very early on - their first real hit - the bawdy *"Married... with Children"* shocked audiences after they had just been lulled back to sitcoms by way of the safe, warm embrace of NBC's *"The Cosby Show"*.

I was working a great deal as a TV actor back when the Fox network arrived, and like many in town, I too welcomed the notion of more shows and more opportunities. So given that, along with my love of television, I watched all of the first Fox shows, rooting for this young, small enterprise to flourish and grow, returning me to the aforementioned *"Married... with Children"*.

Today, it might be easy to forget that the very first episodes of *"Married... with Children"* were daring, provocative and really quite good. The show creators had worked on some of the Lear shows, and while *"Married"* never wanted to reach for the social messages or the sweet golden "final act lesson" moments that came with some of Norman's shows, it actually did something a bit more risky: it started dark, it seemed to stay dark, and when it wasn't staying dark, it was finding ways to just get darker. Of course, this is why it only took a few episodes to slide the whole enterprise into a very greasy form of pro wrestling. As an actor, I was focused on the brilliance and ease of series star Ed O'Neill, a guy who was making a very tough job look very easy. No matter the story or material of the week, he was funny, lovable and even with a very good supporting cast around him, he truly was the horse that the entire show was riding in on. Not since Carroll O'Connor had there been such a central tentpole to a hit situation comedy.

Working on one of the final episodes of "Slap," near the time of the *"Married... with Children"* debut, I arrived at a baseball stadium location one day to see from the new call sheets that only 3 actors were called for the entire shoot: Dabney, Ed O'Neill and me. What the hell? I knew the story, my lines and the script - sportswriter Slap and his son meet with a washed up baseball player - but I didn't know who was cast as the ball player. I went to the make-up trailer, hopped into a chair next to Dabney as I exclaimed, "Ed O'Neill?! Holy cow!" In perfect Dabney cold tone and dry sarcasm, he softly muttered, "Yeah. Gee. Oh my. Golly. Who the fuck is that?"

Coleman knew by then that he could make me laugh uncontrollably by being as "Dabney" as he could around me. But I had to force my laugh a bit short at that moment as I realized that call-time-wise, Ed could walk in at any moment; I should quickly give Dabney an education on Ed.

"He has his own show on the Fox network."

"What's that?"

"Fox network. It's a new network. He's the star of *'Married... with Children'* - he's really good."

"How long has he been doing that?"

"Uh, since about April of last year, I think. I mean, that's when it first came on."

"He's got a big part in the thing?"

"He's the star. Like, if it was *'All in the Family,'* he's Archie."

We both felt the vibration of the make-up trailer; someone was coming up the stairs outside, about to enter. As the door opened, Dabney jumped out of his chair, grumbling, "Nobody tells me shit around here; 'glad you know all this" - And at that moment, in walked Ed, with Dabney smiling, thrusting out a handshake, giggling, "Ed! There he is. Welcome! Damn, I, I like that darn show a' yours, I really do." The wonderful audacity of Dabney Colemen knew no limits. Did he say all that to make Ed feel good? To ingratiate himself with O'Neill? Or to entertain all of us in the trailer who knew he just learned about Ed seconds ago? Very easy answer: all three.

Ed was sweet and even blushing; he quickly brushed *"Married"* off as some sort of "goofy fun" as he quickly went on to praise our show, reminding us that it WAS indeed the best reviewed show of the season, seen as quality by anyone who cared to grade it. Of course, the joke was on us: at that moment, *"Slap"* was weeks away from being a cancelled one season show, while the "goofy fun" of *"Married... with Children"* would go on for 11 hit seasons.

The series of scenes we'd shoot that day would go deep into the cold night. While *"Slap"* was a sportswriter who was reaching a stage of possibly being "washed up," Ed's character was "Dewey Freeman", a 39-year-old ballplayer who was now learning (at spring training) that he too was on the verge of being "washed up". As Dewey and Slap traded barbs and insults about faded masculinity and a lack of future potential, my usually sweet, wide-eyed character breaks loose with a long and angry defense of my father, telling Freeman off and then some. In the eyes of Eliot Maxwell (my character), Slap was and *is* "The Greatest Sportswriter who ever lived!" The long series of scenes were shot all across the empty ballpark - from the dugout, in the outfield, on the diamond, at the mound, etc., etc., etc. As the chilly night dragged on, Dabney invited Ed and me into his deluxe "Star" trailer, and the three of us talked and laughed the night away.

As the two veteran actors were exchanging the requisite Hollywood who-they-knew and where-they-had-been, it was clear that Ed knew a great deal about Coleman, talking about *"Buffalo Bill," "Nine to Five"* and *"On Golden Pond"*. Dabney was wonderfully generous that night, talking of his love for Jane Fonda (even though they were worlds apart politically) and his first acting jobs and training areas. He brought me into the conversation as he "Dabney"- mocked the "hoity-toity" training of Juilliard, actually doing it like a proud father, showing Ed the level of people he had here on his team at the show.

As it can often happen with skilled actors of certain generations who love their craft, talk moved to Marlon Brando. I saw this kind of thing all through school in New York, and on other TV and film sets as well. It can sometimes be something of a pissing match, where male actors will soon be working hard to "Out-Brando" one another, going on and on about Marlon's films, performances and life. Ed and Dabney knew a great deal about Marlon Brando's movies, both wanting to praise the more obscure titles especially, volleying shouts like, "But *'The Appaloosa'!* Good God! Incredible!" Mind you, all of it was enthusiastic, heartfelt and I loved every bit of it.

I was already a fan of Ed O'Neill. I always thought Dabney was one of the greats and it was thrilling to hear what they found so inspiring and motivating as working actors. It was especially enjoyable to watch Dabney like this; he rarely brought real warmth or fun to the set, and he was having a blast, talking to this Ed O'Neill guy about everything and all things "Brando".

And then it hit me! Big Time. I had never met Marlon Brando at that time, but I knew that he had seen Dabney and me on *"'Slap' Maxwell"* - My new girlfriend, Avra Douglas in the art department of the show; she had just told me days ago: she's friends with Marlon's daughter, Rebecca - Avra and Rebecca were up at Marlon's house - Avra wanted Marlon to see her work on the show. Avra told me that Brando found the show to be funny. She had pointed out the guy she had started to date (me, on the show) and Marlon made mention of how funny Dabney was.

Wow - To have *that* information at *this* moment! Hell - Time to spill it! Just as Ed and Dabney were reaching a crescendo of Brando Love, I blurted out, *"He likes Dabney."*

Silence. Dabney stared that icy Coleman death stare. He then muttered, "What the fuck was that?"

I explained the whole situation with Avra from the art department (whom Dabney knew and loved a great deal) and the Brando family. Both Dabney and Ed were stunned. They didn't even know what to say. There was some disbelief. Ed asked, "Who knows Marlon Brando?" Dabney snapped, "No, Ed, this Avra; she's a pearl!" After the convincing was over, Dabney was giddy as we all shared more talk about Brando. Again, it was oddly thrilling to hear how inspiring one single actor could be to so many other actors - especially actors at the level of Dabney Coleman and Ed O'Neill. When the night shoot was finally over, it was such a great feeling to have those amazing conversations with Dabney and Ed. We were also all thrilled with the work; all three of us had a great deal of dialogue, a lot of intricate blocking and movement, a variation of takes Dabney insisted on and a wonderful connection as characters. Some days and some nights on a film or TV show really remind you as to why acting can be - every now and then - the greatest, most rewarding job on Earth. As he was leaving, Ed again praised our show and said how happy he was to be a part of "'Slap' Maxwell". Before he disappeared, I asked if he could arrange for me to go to a taping of his show. He said he'd like that and that we should have dinner or a drink after the taping. He was good enough to line that up for me a few weeks later.

At the show taping, it was obvious that the still-then-young series was already getting a colorful following, with loud young fans clearly liking the rapidly escalating crude humor and increasingly zany plot lines. Due to schedules, happenstance and just plain life, I had not seen the show on TV for quite a while; many of my perceptions were still with the very first episodes; the stories, plots and performances that I found unique, dark, non-Cosby and wonderfully funny. I had heard from one of my agents that the show had become far looser and more crazy with each passing week. I didn't know what that meant, but I certainly found out that night of the taping.

In my viewing absence, "Married... with Children" had gone full circus. While I can't fully recall the plot, I remember it had something to do with Ed's character, Al Bundy, having to deal with an incoming visit from a pack of hideous in-laws. There was a freak-retro trio of mature female singers, a giant wrestler who put his head through a door, an overly effeminate guy who was used for a slew of offensive jokes, and capping it all, much talk about Al's mother-in-law, an unseen woman so obese she could not be displayed within the confines of the living room set.

As always, Ed was funny, inventive and in charge of doing absolutely all of the heavy lifting when it came to getting legitimate laughs. After the taping, I met with Ed on the Bundy living room set, as he had an almost sheepish laugh over how insane this episode was. He said he was tired at this post-show moment, requesting a rain-check on the dinner and/or drink we had once discussed. I certainly understood, but I also felt that it would probably be the last time I would see Ed O'Neill - unless we were to work together again someday. The magic of our fun night on "Slap" was - of course - not there on the "Married... with Children" soundstage that evening.

Years later, I'd marvel over Ed's great work on *"Modern Family,"* one of the best shows television will ever see. When it first aired, I thought it was incredibly brave for the show creators to go with "Al Bundy" on a show that was clearly so high in quality and so different.

To Ed's credit, I was wondering if a television audience could ever get past a character as famous and memorable as "Al". But then I remembered "Dewey," his washed up ball player on "Slap", a performance that was nothing at all like either Al Bundy of *"Married... with Children"* or Jay Pritchett of *"Modern Family"*. Incredible. (Odd footnote: Ed received no billing on our episode. I suspect our casting director knew Ed's work, knew of his love of *"Slap Maxwell"* and wrote up some sort of "Unbilled Guest Star" contract.) Anyway, back to Ed's career: try being central to *one* hit show as a lead performer. But *two?* Statistically impossible. And no, I'm not talking about, say, a *"Cheers"* to *"Frasier"* spin-off. And again, no, one can't compare nostalgic coupling like Andy Griffith in *"Matlock"* or Dick Van Dyke in *"Diagnosis: Murder"*. To me, that's simple TV history on replay mode. With O'Neill in both *"Married"* and *"Modern"* nearly back-to-back, that's sheer talent. For me, the only bottom line is the obvious one: Ed O'Neill is a great actor.

Guess what: Marlon liked him too. Years after working with Ed, back when *"Married"* was still on in both primetime and reruns, I was watching television with Marlon in his TV den one night, looking at the screen as he madly channel surfed away. Marlon and I had been good friends for years at this point. On TV: there was Al Bundy, trying to put a too-small high heel on some heavy female customer in the shoe shop he toiled away in. I couldn't help it - I blurted out, *"Hey! That guy loves you!"*

"Huh?"

"That actor, Ed O'Neill; I worked with him years ago. He thinks you're the cat's ass!" Marlon laughed - he had taught me that term, back when we were once discussing Sophia Loren; feeling she displayed vanity during the making of *"A Countess from Hong Kong,"* he told me, "She thinks she's the cat's ass." Tonight, Marlon watched as Ed (as Al) droned out a dry line that got a huge laugh. Marlon muttered something about how he had seen this show before. I asked, "Do you watch this show?" He shrugged, "No. But I've seen this guy. What's his name again?" And again, Ed got another big laugh, one that made Marlon cough out a chuckle as well.

I said, "Ed O'Neill." Marlon nodded, "The man knows his stuff. Funny".

As Marlon continued to channel surf, I thought back to those last days of *"Slap"* - Those days unfolded as I was shifting from acting to writing. I missed those production days a great deal.

Moving from a performer on ABC to a writer at 20th Century-Fox - Life was changing fast.

SECOND CHAPTER
DIFFERENT HOLLYWOODS
(GREG & MARLON ESSAY II)

Great actors like Dabney Coleman and Ed O'Neill found inspiration in actors at the level of Brando and Peck; I did as well as a young actor. That inspiration had me constantly studying their histories.

Their April calendar birthdays are a mere two days apart, but eight consequential and historic years separate the births of Gregory Peck and Marlon Brando. And while they both broke into the world of stardom in their late 20's, both jumping into acclaimed, lead roles, both racking up multiple Oscar nominations at record paces, they were doing so in radically different times - different for the world, America and especially for the artistic community of Hollywood.

Greg's *"The Keys of the Kingdom"* was released in 1944, with a world at war, Hollywood's classic "Golden Years" fading away and all of creativity on the verge of great and irreversible change. *"A Streetcar Named Desire"* hit the screens in 1951, and new leading man Marlon Brando arrived as the crowned king of a new creative era. Seismic shifts in music, literature and perhaps most visible, film, were taking place. Amazing to think: the talking picture was only 22 years old at that time, but both filmmaking and acting techniques had matured rapidly, and both "Brando" and *"Streetcar"* were markers of naturalistic acting and adult storytelling, elements audiences longed for as television was about to start making radical changes in American film-going habits. When TV did come along, Hollywood was still creating projects around aging "Golden Age" legends such as Gable, Bogart, Cagney, Tracy and others, but not one of those idols was immune nor unaware regarding the tremors Brando created; film acting was changing, and whether Marlon liked it or not, he was the certified ambassador of that exciting change.

As dynamic as Marlon's arrival was, one must also examine Greg's quiet entrance into the spotlight and his quick rise to stardom in the mid-forties (as one of the first stars who refused to sign a long-term studio contract, making Louis B. Mayer literally cry). *That* entrance was perhaps far more astonishing - *and* Industry Changing. Greg often told me, "Every generation wants their own heroes, their own stars," and he saw that up close and personally as he arrived in Hollywood at a time when the four "Golden Age" actors I named a few sentences ago ruled the screen, along with women like Hepburn, Bergman and Garson. Then, all those "Golden Age" performers had been around for quite a while, with a star like Clark Gable going back to the early 1930's.

So if it can be said that "Gable" was a marker for the "Golden" years and "Brando" was a marker the "New" era, it falls to "Peck" to represent that unique and incredibly hard to describe period between the "Golden" and the "New". Beyond just being "The War Years," this time frame was transitional and influential, and it included new arrivals such as Burt Lancaster, Charlton Heston, Kirk Douglas and other unique leading men. On the surface, more handsome, and in some cases, more classically trained. Still, as a young NYC acting student, Marlon had great admiration for the "Bogart" generation; more than he had for Peck, Lancaster and that group - simply because that's what ambitious young NYC theater students do - I know, I was one of those at Juilliard - you romanticize those actors you grew up watching, just as you envy and resent those just ahead of you - those you'd like to "replace". Marlon agreed with me on that.

As crude and seemingly simplistic as those generational gauges might be, I often found them to be useful shorthand when I was dealing with certain creative aspects of Greg and Marlon. While they both did their best to stay current in later years, both eternally insatiable when it came to knowledge and awareness of modern day ideas, they were also products of their youth, products of their stardom eras and products of those golden moments that marked their years as Kings of The World; and they each experienced exactly that: Kings, at certain times in both world cinema and pop culture.

A direct example; one that is more than merely an abstract story: screenwriting with and for Gregory was at times challenging for a number of reasons. I was a self-taught screenwriter, but as a working actor, I kept and studied every new script that came my way. I'd model my writing off those current scripts and I'd always make note of when styles in dialogue, stage directions and camera indications evolved - or devolved. As William Goldman wrote about in his brilliant 1983 book, *"Adventures in the Screen Trade,"* professional screenwriting styles were changing all the time. Screenwriting was like any other aspect of Hollywood filmmaking: susceptible to style trends, shaped by new generations and often great fodder for debate.

Greg saw "new" scripts all the time as well, but as a producer and co-writer, he was quite traditional when it came to telling actors, directors and fellow filmmakers what to do - and what not to do - by way of a script. He showed me a script Alfred Hitchcock had scribbled in, telling me not to give a dialogue line an exclamation point ("See, Hitch would never dare to tell an actor that he needs to shout here.") In turn, I noticed where "Hitch", along with screenwriter Ben Hecht, occasionally included excessive camera angles and shots, incredibly by modern standards, often being listed all throughout the acting script. Conversation on this often had me frustrated: it was as though I was asked to sometimes indicate more to the DP than I was to the star. Greg would say, "Ignore that tutelage! It's not written for you!" I asked, "How can I ignore it? This, uh, 'tutelage' is cluttering up the read!" That was a rare moment when I took stock in the notion of *when* Greg's most influential eras were and what was the time period that shaped so much of his filmmaking process. But beyond that, a greater reality hit me: it wasn't that Greg was stubborn, locked in a time period or refusing to keep up with the times, so to speak - The reality was both more complicated and far more unique. See, Tony and I were freelance screenwriters in the '80's; at that time, we sold a great deal on spec: readers or producers would read our "unattached" work. Please remember all that as this equation unfolds. As we wrote, I always told Tony, "While I don't want us to over-write things, I want us to remember that we only get one chance to tell this story to some bored studio reader - a reader who has a stack of scripts before him or her today - maybe on their weekend. Let's make every word and bit of punctuation count." I was pretty nuts about all that back then. When Tony and I would finish a script, we'd read them out loud together, as actors, over and over, always finding something we'd want to change, cut, or in some cases, reinvent entirely.

But - on the other hand, Greg's experience and situation with scripts was a totally different thing. Essentially, from his very first film, this man was a star. By the time Gregory Peck was getting a script, ANY script - it was already bought, green-lit, set with an accomplished director, etc., etc., etc. In other words: my screenwriting life was from blank pages, then having to jump over hundreds of hurdles to exchange those pages for a check from the studio. Any script sent to Greg was an absolute offer. He was the last stop on a very long train of script development. If he read an offered script and said, "No," well, the studio would then, perhaps, send that "perfect" (maybe heavily rewritten) script over to the home of Kirk Douglas over on North Rexford Drive.

Defending my exclamation points as I delicately explained these differences to Greg, he laughed and said, "When the new script we're writing goes to the finance people, I know it will get a careful read. Why? Because it will be coming from me." He was right about that - A script from Greg going to finance guys was being sent because Gregory Peck wanted to make that script into a movie - It wouldn't be read as though it was coming from a pair of spec writers.

Greg being confident about that - it wasn't arrogance - that was pure knowledge, fact and absolute self-awareness. Greg never did boast, but he was also completely secure and steady when it came to his stardom and how others viewed him. So when he wanted no exclamation points and yet - at times - seemingly excessive retro-camera angles in a script, I listened.

As for writing with and for Marlon - *that* was a whole other ball of wax; many balls of wax.

More on all that later. Let's just say, Marlon never referenced his previous screenwriters when we were writing, often saying, "I always wrote all my own stuff," sometimes tossing a few film titles into that claim, one time even dropping *"Julius Caesar"* onto the list. So as you can see, as I needed to do for years, these pages will continue to whipsaw from the 40's and 50's - to the 80's and 90's - and everything else before and in between. My mind often spanned all those decades because I was working with men who had solid sensibilities and viewpoints from certain eras, long before I met them.

Or - to put all this another way: I actually think I was a good match for these guys in many ways. Example: as a kid, I knew a lot (too much) about Hollywood films of the 1950's. In small-town Brainerd, Minnesota, in the 1970's, I recall boring a high school date to tears, discussing the screenplay of a great film she had never heard of, *"All About Eve"*. I recall her ending the night with, "You're just plain weird!" She was probably right. But that's the great thing about certain pieces of knowledge: you never really know when you might need that exact kind of "weird".

Interestingly, thinking of that amazing *"All About Eve"* screenplay by Joseph Mankiewicz, I'm about to reach a point in my written journey here where I will be crossing into a time in my life where I was becoming more of a screenwriter and less of a working actor. It really wasn't by design; it's just the way things unfolded for me. Looking back, screenwriting was key when it came to me really getting to know both Greg and Marlon. Along with Tony, I wrote for both legends. In the scheme of things, I might've meant very little to them as just one more actor who admired talented icons. But as a working, selling, optioned, produced, solid screenwriter, I was somebody who could work alongside them. Because here's a bit of news that perhaps is not much of a secret: Greg wrote magnificent letters, Marlon could create incredible improvisations that, when transcribed, shaped fascinating dialogue. But neither could write a screenplay.

They didn't need to have that skill, but yes, they did want that skill. They of course saw that possibility as one more way to have more control over their films, more ownership. But it was something they never fully mastered. I believe they both knew that was the case. Many stars kid themselves into thinking that if they just sat down and did it, they could write a screenplay. Easy.

Frankly, Greg was grounded in a more realistic place when it came to those notions - Of course he was! What area of life *was there* where Greg was *not* more grounded than Marlon? But still, even with all his bluster, talk and desire to be a screenwriter, I think Marlon knew his limits.

With Tony, script by script, I feel we learned what can work in a screenplay. And thanks to Tony, our work was judged by many to be unique, different and interesting. I brought structure, pace and order to his fantasies, his color and his unexpected inventions. And since we loved working together, we solved what is often the hardest part when it comes to any writing:

Getting it done. And with that, onto my professional writing career with Mr. Anthony Peck.

THE STORY RESUMES: THE FOX (1989)

Back when Tony and I were rewriting our *"Black Sheep"* script at 20th Century-Fox, we were also writing new and original work we were hoping to sell to Fox or others. Like most studios, Fox would buy, redo and beat to death a number of projects at the screenplay stage. No one really knew what might make money, so, obviously, better to work lesser paid writers, until somehow, some Fox executive would then - maybe - start releasing the script to "A-list" talent, to see if someone with real power (a star or star director) would bite. The original sold version of *"Black Sheep"* was a complicated script with a number of moving parts. The studio did their best to make it into a commercial moneymaker on paper - in other words, a script that would feel like something you had seen or read before. The studios' constant dilemma was (and still is) obvious: please make it original while being completely and totally derivative at the exact same time.

Of course, as every film decade experiences, the box office dictated much of what was made in the 80's, especially "in-house," as executives tried to forecast the zeitgeist; difficult when your green light may be two years before the premiere. But a certain type of script (or at least a certain sub-group of genre) had obvious requirements: comedies like *"Black Sheep"* needed known stars of the moment, and the humor and story (for a studio film) could not be too bleak, too dark or too adult. Even though a few "R" rated comedies had been successful, there was a constant want in the 80's for "mature" humor that would also somehow play to a family audience as well. Really.

With our comedy of a mafia hit man, a prostitute and two badly estranged families, we were constantly asked to add characters and subplots you'd recognize from TV sitcoms. Example: a family of snoopy neighbors (who were brief sight gags and had 4 lines in the original script) - these snoopy neighbors are rich: let's give them a prize-winning poodle to show how wealthy they are; a nice looking house with a luxury car in the driveway - that's not enough. In fact, by studio demand, let's move some of the actual plot to a posh dog show itself - It will be a scream: a filthy mob hit man and a sexy hooker at a high class dog show (even though the traffic of the characters made no sense for that possibility). You get the idea. Suddenly, "nothing" characters like the "rich" neighbors were driving the plot of the rewrite for pages and pages. This is the nature of the big studio rewrite; every nightmare regarding an assault to your creativity is true.

As we did rewrites, Tony and I met with pros he knew by way of his life in Hollywood. We'd often hang out with veteran producer Elliot Kastner (*"The Missouri Breaks"* and many more films) who I knew a great deal about by way of his long career in the industry. Greg liked Elliot and would invite him to the Carolwood parties; Marlon hated him and had worked with him a number of times - both typical for Greg and Marlon. Elliot was a fun and likable guy; often more of a stand-up comic than producer. He treated Tony and me as professionals; we'd hear his ideas and give him ours, hoping we could find a vehicle for all of us to put together someday - maybe. I liked Kastner. Elliot was always enthusiastic, full of energy and filled with industry knowledge.

    I assumed whenever he met with anybody in the business, he was "on". I suspected his colorful image of a fun Hollywood guy was the exact opposite of the man underneath. You could see he was a razor sharp professional, intelligent, canny and tough as old leather. He was a successful money-raiser when it came to film. His business was "Elliot Kastner". We'd talk at length with Elliot and his then assistant, Bruce Charet, and I always found Kastner to be quite interesting. I have no idea what he made of me. Nothing ever came of all those long conversations, but I'm glad I got to spend time with someone with his volume of experience. We also hung out with *"Godfather"* producer Albert S. Ruddy, a great guy we'd eventually write a war comedy for. So I was gradually getting the hang of Hollywood as a writer, how it worked and how stuff got made. The problem was that the non-creative aspects of the business offered nothing of any interest for me. In short: I disliked "The Business." I needed money, of course, like anyone. The romance of poverty can only be enjoyed by those who've never been threatened by it. I knew many young actors in New York who despised money, choosing to forget they were still funded by their parents. But money ceased to interest me when I was busy being creative. Tony once half-joked: I was never allowed to negotiate anything for us or even for myself; I'd offer to do anything for free, and once that gets known, you become that guy who can be had with any promise of "creative" expression. Tony told one producer, "Making a 'deal' with Joe; that's child abuse."

    In Hollywood, money can create an appearance. The typical newcomer to the film studio system rents a nice house in Brentwood and leases a new Mercedes. "Front" is everything. I was horrified when I got myself a one room apartment in Westwood and a new Hyundai, knowing I'd now have Westwood rent and monthly payments to make on the car. Worse yet, even when the car was new looking, it would still be fully out of place parked on the Fox lot in Century City.

Still, in spite of those "classist" things that irritated me, I was fascinated by the Hollywood studio system of filmmaking and learning from it each day. It was more and more horrifying and wonderful as I peeled back each layer of its history and uncovered its complexity. I realized that each time I hit on a "fact" about the studios, the opposite was also true. It was not wall-to-wall "McDonalds," as tiresome New York snobs assumed. I longed to be a part of the studio system that had given me the movies and TV of my youth. But as time went on, I felt I was failing. *"Black Sheep"* was not getting a green light, no matter how many rewrites took place.

I tried not to feel bitter about that as I struggled. I was learning that Hollywood has more madness, psychopathy, Machiavellianism, narcissism and people dissociated from their true feelings than most places. This is because enormous rewards of riches and power are dangled daily and the fight for them is ruthless. The town offers sun, sex, celebrity and wealth. Winners take all. But the casualties are many. Look closely at most faces, look behind the tan, deep into the eyes; you will see fear. Just beware of those whose fear you can't see. These are the socially functioning psychopaths and they're dangerous. All of "Show Business" now seems to trend this way. But the individual isn't the problem. It's the system which offers fertile opportunities for the worst to thrive. But my sticking point back then was my disinterest in embracing their definition of success, as well as their frequent disinterest in what I really wanted to make: My Films.

Despite this, I learned many professional lessons at Fox. Some very bright and talented people are drawn to studio opportunities, especially writers. I worked with and admired some of the best, brilliant technicians lost to rewrites, their original screenplays taken from them and given to others to "improve"; Tony and I were on both ends of that exchange. Back then, Fox had many films in what it called "Active Development" - *"Black Sheep"* was one of them, written by two then un-produced writers. See, it's comparatively cheap to "punt" at that end of the process.

One day, after a weary year of rewrites, I read the first draft Tony and I sold - and then the last draft. This last draft was like a Swiss watch, perfect in its structure; I had learned a lot as a studio writer. Oh, yeah, this final draft: it was also lifeless, dead on arrival. The first draft was a structural puzzle, with action occasionally ending with some line or odd bit that only Tony and I found funny - *but* - it was alive, bursting with energy and the characters popped off the page.

This is why it first sold. This formed a question for me. I never forgot it.

Early on, if I knew the tricks of "Professional" Hollywood - would this have made our early projects more "successful"? A good question with no good answer. Some questions can be that way.

Most helpful of all from my Fox days, I shaped a phrase I still live by today creatively. It calms me. *"I cannot hit the molecule in the universe that is your as of yet unformed idea."* As Marlon would tell me years later: "The key to 'knowing' is understanding what *is* and what *ain't*."

Moving forward here, before leaving *"Black Sheep"* altogether, please allow me to tell a bit more about the process, the key characters, and the sheer "Hollywood" elements that work to create a dead-end script in L.A. - The writing is one thing - *Who* you write for is another story entirely.

More on the Century City Fox (1989)

The studio had two opening fanfares for their films back in the 80's: a long one and a short one. The opening of a 20th Century-Fox film would start with those drums, trumpets and lights shining up at that giant number and those glowing letters. But at one time or another, the studio would revamp that opening, and by the time Tony and I were studio writers, one thing seemed clear: most 20th Century-Fox films had a nice, short logo opening, while the studio's more "important" prestige films had a longer, more traditional opening; more bars of music, more weight and more of an indication that something substantial was about to be presented.

That longer opening was the one I wanted for the first studio script Tony and I sold, *"Black Sheep"*. We knew our script title was good, having it before the Chris Farley and David Spade film. But our story was totally different. Again, this was a film about a blue-blood Connecticut family that learns (on Thanksgiving Day) that they have married into the mafia, along with the additional shock that one of the key members of the blue-blood family moonlights as a hooker. But allow me to back up a bit as I again go into this fun and sexy romp of a screenplay. When Irving Lazar sold the script to Fox, that was at the moment when the studio was being transferred from Marvin Davis to Rupert Murdoch. *That* event had every Fox executive very worried and nervous. After all, if you don't even understand your high-paying job in the first place (as none of the Fox executives of that day did), how sure are you of keeping it when new bosses enter the scene? - New bosses who *also* have no idea of what they are doing. God, one "Boss" of ours was a veterinarian-newly-made-producer, thanks to some grateful dog-owning studio Big Shot.

What I left out of the previous chapter was this: after having us do a number of "in-studio" rewrites on *"Black Sheep,"* Fox turned us and the project over to Sandollar, an entertainment-producing entity created by Dolly Parton and Sandy Gallin. Gallin was a successful manager and producer who had been part of overseeing the careers of Parton, Cher, Michael Jackson and many others. Sandollar now had a deal with Fox, and Tony and I were being handed over to them. While we didn't see much of Dolly or Sandy at their offices, we did work with a man named Howard Rosenman. In my opinion, Howard was one of those very "Hollywood" guys who seemed to have one sole purpose in life: meeting and being around famous people. It's not that uncommon out there in L.A., but it was not all that helpful as I was just learning how these movie-making companies worked, and we were tasked with trying to rewrite *"Black Sheep"* for Howard.

Most of our "story" meetings involved Howard fawning over Tony's family history, wanting to pick Tony's brain on the "Famous Carolwood Parties," wanting to discuss Greg, wanting to discuss how he could meet Greg, wanting to discuss how he could get invited to the Carolwood parties and making sure he never made a moment of contact with me; as a non-famous, not-related-to-fame individual, I was literally invisible to Rosenman. In his presence, my voice was on mute - even in a small-room, three-man meeting. I learned a lot about that kind of industry type by way of Howard, and I'd go on to meet so many others exactly like him.

I can actually laugh about it all now, but at the time, I was frustrated with the situation because I felt it wasn't helping the project. My goal was to get a movie made; while I knew that a good relationship between Tony and Rosenman was a positive thing, I really wanted Howard to have a passion for our script, not merely a passion to network within a situation that he thought would bring him access to a family line he saw as Hollywood royalty. Frankly, I was naive. Yes, of course, Howard knew I was Tony's partner, but Tony - he was an actual Peck. Looking back, I realize all this is a real and common syndrome in the business; one that is probably quite human, I suppose. People come to this world famous Los Angeles industry fueled by both ambition and those legendary images that motivated them; stars that made them want to get into this difficult business to begin with. They create a tunnel-vision that is driven by a determination to succeed, as well as some inner-demand that they be included into those exclusive ranks. All *other* non-famous, non-"opportunity" human beings represent mere noise, boredom, service, failure or just some series of invisible vapors that get filtered out.

But once you have any sort of fame and/or success, or you are directly connected to people with some sort of fame and/or success, well, there is a shift.

I truly noticed this shift when I'd meet a Rosenman type in the presence of Greg or Marlon. I'd be non-existent until Greg or Marlon would speak to me, ask me a question or give me a pat on the back. After that, *whoa!* Everything would change for these people locked into "Star-vision"; they'd then ask for my phone number, perhaps a dinner invitation would be tossed out there. I know - this whole analysis might all sound like some sort of unique bitterness or envy on my part; it's none of that - Actually, I get it, and if you work in the industry, you "Get it" as well. It's Hollywood. And for some, it brings great success, opportunity and financial reward.

Anyway, as I mentioned in the previous "Fox" story, after *"Black Sheep"* was rewritten into an unappealing mess thanks to both Fox and Sandollar, the studio gave the project a pass. And that was the end of our first studio project. My disappointment was great.

But - I also had a newfound knowledge of how Hollywood - and some of those in it - "worked".

CAROLWOOD (1989)

As my story of Howard illustrates, it's clear that the industry is filled with "fans". Of course, film and TV stars can also be huge "fans" of other stars as well; sometimes more so than civilian fans not within the industry. And it makes sense - many performers go to Hollywood *because* they're so enthralled with stars, desperately wanting to join that club. I always found it quite interesting when major stars would try to "Out-Marlon" one another when it came to their early and ongoing worship of "Brando". Nicholson, Pacino, Sean Penn - It was almost as though they felt their own stock would rise every time they'd mention their respect for Marlon's work, craft and accomplishments. And why not? They were backing the horse that came in first, in the race that was all about changing and expanding the art of cinematic acting. Yes, it's easy to find major Hollywood names still gushing over Marlon; his existing body of work does speak for itself.

Given all that, it's hard to overstate the ways in which Greg's fellow stars seemed to look up to him. I don't mean those who did not have his stature, I'm referring to those who you would think would be "equal" or, if possible, "higher". Yes, I know these types of determinations sound crass, somewhat tacky and even impossible to fully gauge, but when you work in Hollywood long enough, you clearly know it when you see it, and you fully sense it when you feel it. I had no greater proof of that than the way Marlon reacted when Greg was ever mentioned. Of course, Marlon's attitude might have been due to the fact that Avra and I knew the

Peck family well, and therefore, Marlon was not the only "star" in our orbit. That was an unusual situation for him.

That sounds like Marlon had thoughts that were a bit petty, but after all, he was human - and yes - he was quite used to being The Giant Sun in anybody's orbit. He also saw that I had great respect, love and admiration for Greg, knowing that I was not often impressed with all that many film stars. Most of all - and it's the one thing I've been saying here time and time again - Marlon was a star like no other, seemingly without a single rule or a guardrail. *That* - as Greg meticulously followed Hollywood's near-impossible rules and yet, still, almost singlehandedly, came to his natural end with pure dignity, pure stature and pure respect. While Greg bristled at Brando's world famous rule-breaking, Marlon *never* understood *anyone* wanting to follow "order".

That leads me back to the way Greg's peers seemed to view him. Basically, nothing says it better than Frank Sinatra himself looking up to Greg - and Sinatra clearly did. When Sinatra needed someone to vouch for him in a 1981 court as he was trying to get a Las Vegas gaming license, Frank called Greg. And while voices such as Johnny Carson gave Greg a bit of a rib over a saint vouching for America's crooning gangster ("I just got word Gregory Peck was nominated for an Oscar - for his performance at the Frank Sinatra hearing"), the public chalked it up to the personal loyalty of a mensch like Greg, helping out a rascally scamp like Sinatra.

Once when I was talking to Marlon about the Pecks, I was shocked when he seemed aware about something I had never brought up; he sarcastically asked, "And they hang out with Frank Sinatra? Wow. He's a real fun guy." Quite openly, Marlon didn't like Sinatra. The two men didn't get along when they made *"Guys and Dolls,"* and it was one of the few work relationships that he was not shy to discuss with friends; that and his dislike of tyrannical director Charlie Chaplin after working on *"A Countess from Hong Kong"*. Still, I was wondering how he knew of that Peck/Sinatra friendship. As public as it was, it was not the kind of news that Marlon would either bother to know or bother remembering. It was also a Peck-related thing that I didn't want to pry Marlon over. When I asked Avra about that, she shrugged and said, "Probably Carol."

Carol Grace was a wit of a character who was once married, in her younger years, to author William Saroyan. She was a busy socialite, a colorful storyteller and a popular personality in the New York intelligentsia of the 1950's. The fictional "Holly Golightly" in Truman Capote's *"Breakfast at Tiffany's"* is said to be based on Carol. In 1959, she married actor Walter Matthau, and through the 1960's, up until her death in 2003, she was known all throughout Hollywood as Carol Matthau. I was never sure where or how she met Marlon, but they knew each other well, and into the 80's and 90's, they would talk on the phone at great lengths on any given night, discussing 1950's New York, today's Hollywood, or perhaps, Walter's pals like Frank and Greg.

If you went to a Carolwood Peck party, you were sure to see Walter and Carol. He was the funniest and sometimes the most seemingly intoxicated person in the room; she was an intense, totally-powder-white-faced chatterbox who held court with Veronique and the other wives. Running into Carol often at Carolwood, I never had the nerve to ask her about her friendship with Marlon. I always assumed she might bring that conversation up to Marlon, and then there it would be - Something Marlon would hate - Me out there in the world talking about him to other people. I also didn't see a way to have a coherent conversation with Carol; when at the Peck house, it seemed she was there to only talk to stars or their glamorous spouses.

Walter, on the other hand, was a fun and fully approachable joy; my absolute favorite person at the Carolwood parties. We hit it off right away and he quickly learned that I knew all about old Hollywood - And not just "Old" Hollywood - But *ancient* Hollywood, able to talk about the very first stars of the silent era; a topic Walter loved to discuss. In that Matthau "W.C. Fields" voice, he'd ask, "How the fuck does a pisher like you know who Emil Jannings is?!" He also had a billion horse racing stories and dirty jokes at the ready, and if you took a breath or paused for a second while talking to Walter, he'd have a comedic bit or a quick line that would make you cry with laughter. One joke he'd often repeat was about an old guy who proudly urinated every morning at 6am sharp; the problem: he never got out of bed until 7am. Maybe Walter just saw an easy audience in me, but he seemed to like talking to me at the parties, and I could not get enough of Matthau; he was as brilliant about history, science and politics as he was funny.

Returning to Sinatra; I always felt there was a strange and recurring routine to the intimate Carolwood parties regarding Frank; while his wife Barbara always seemed friendly, wonderfully interested and legitimately inviting to non-stars such as myself (perhaps it was political; she was smart, knowing today's Hollywood unknown is tomorrow's Hollywood big-shot), Frank would arrive there in Greg's living room with a pained look and an uncomfortable stance. At times, you'd wonder if he was showing up with half-a-bag on already - or under some sort of medication. Of course, to me, he *was* Sinatra, so how could you not give him some slack.

I didn't expect Frank to be as chatty as Walter Matthau. But as Tony would tell me of the many Peck family stays at the Sinatra Palm Springs compound, it seemed that a simple, fully understandable equation was at work: if Frank was "home," in charge as The Boss, he was a lot of fun, even the life of the party. But if he was a guest in someone else's home - discomfort-ville, baby. Marlon wasn't that different, but after a few moments of unease at someone else's home, Marlon would soon be psychoanalyzing a stranger in the corner - probably one of the housekeepers, where it seemed like Frank away from his comfortable home would just slither away.

At the elegant Carolwood parties, it felt like the "Sinatra" formula was the following: the guests all seem to be here; now, just a touch later, the Sinatras arrive, almost on cue after the others. Barbara looks beautiful; actually, perfect. She makes the rounds and greets everyone, making a special effort for those she doesn't yet know, all as Frank kinda fades into a more comfortable shadow. Nobody even seems sure as to whether or not "new" people should be or could be introduced to Frank. Even old friends like Jack Lemmon simply give Frank a nod from across the room, almost saying, "Hi. I see ya. Don't worry; I'm not coming over to talk to you."

At one of my first Carolwood parties, Tony breaks the rules and introduces me to Frank; Tony explains that we were Juilliard classmates and we write screenplays together - Without any exchange of words, Sinatra and I shake hands, smile and we both then blend back into the party. It was fine. I got to meet Tony's idol, Frank. More than I was expecting to do, actually. Many parties later when I again saw Frank, I simply tried that across-the-room Jack Lemmon nod to Sinatra, as Frank then just looked at me, blankly, confused, while finding his dark corner.

But getting back to what seemed to be "The Routine" for Frank at those Peck parties - Yes, Barbara makes the rounds as Frank seems to want to disappear. Seeing Frank's discomfort, Veronique goes to get Greg, who has yet to fully join the party himself. Moments later, everyone turns, looks and smiles as Greg enters the room; he's warm, charming and frankly, flat-out stunning; to say the least, he's a presence. Everyone feels uplifted by his glow. He scans the room and then rescues Frank from that dark corner he's crawled into. Greg then takes Sinatra over to a little two stool bar that is in the corner of the Carolwood living room. Frank is finally smiling, now only having to deal with Greg, who will, more often than not, sit with Frank for the rest of the night. Of course, everyone else at this intimate party chats, jokes, and has a good time. But nobody, not even the wives, nodding Jack Lemmon, nor other giant stars seem to approach Greg and Frank. Warm and protective Greg will make sure that Ol' Blue Eyes is comfortable.

And of course, every now and then, you can't help but to look over there across the opulent room, over at that cozy little two-man bar, and yes, you will be saying to yourself, "Holy shit: that's Gregory Peck and Frank Sinatra. What the fuck am I doing here?"

Occasionally, when I was trying to *not* be overwhelmed by the famous faces in the room, I'd look out a window and marvel over what was perhaps the strangest aspect of the gatherings: the literally insane and not remotely logical property values in this neighborhood. Sure, it was a very nice area, with every large estate perfectly kept, but - *hey* - it was essentially a residential community in Los Angeles. Drive your BMW a few miles away and get on the 405 - There you now were, on The Great Equalizing Non-Moving California Freeway; no further ahead of the guy in the VW in front of you. Clearly, you lived on Carolwood because of those who lived there and those who lived there before you: a collection of names that include, past and then-present, Elvis, Streisand, Sonny & Cher, Tony Curtis, Clark Gable, Sinatra, Rod Stewart, I could go on and on. Today, homes on Carolwood go for as much as 150 million dollars. I guess it's like Steve Martin once said, "You're nobody in L.A. unless you live in a house with a really big door."

I believe it was often that level of "surreal" that had me never fully at ease at Carolwood. But as awkward as I was at those parties, there was one person there who was the full definition of *not* awkward. She handled it all quite beautifully. Incredibly, she wasn't necessarily a "star" herself. But through the years, man, she learned how to outshine everybody else in the room.

More on this dynamo below.

MS. PASSANI (1989)

Being a mother is perhaps the most difficult job on Earth. And I've been told, in many cases, it doesn't get any easier simply because your children become adults. In fact, the difficulty can increase for some. Becoming a parent yourself of course allows one to more fully appreciate the challenges of navigating the lives of children, and as the years go by, I am more and more amazed by the accomplishments of *my* parents *as* parents.

Given all the circumstances, I feel they did a good job. They were quite young when they had children, but that was a norm in their generation. Again, my father was that pro supper club entertainer on a nightly basis, as my mother was a shy, German-heritage homemaker, raising her children, keeping an immaculate house and knowing that my father was not like any of the other husbands in our small, Minnesota town; he didn't work at the paper mill, he didn't work during the day - He was a handsome, charismatic talent who was not ordinary - in a very ordinary town.

Analyzing the small-town level of my life and the lives of my family members, I've often thought of what Veronique Passani was up against when she took over the grand scale operation of Gregory Peck's enormous life; a life that was already epic when she met Greg. His was an existence that was always under the Hollywood microscope, filled with the history of an ex-wife and three sons that came before Veronique.

In the mid 1950's, many in Paris knew that Veronique Passani was a force to be reckoned with. She was that beautiful, dynamic journalist at France-Soir who won the heart of the then already legendary and world famous Gregory Peck. When they married, she then had to win over Greg's young sons from his previous marriage, as well as raise the "new" family that would eventually include Tony and his sister, Cecilia. As I would meet Veronique years after all that family raising, she was also welcoming a world famous daughter-in-law into the Peck family, Cheryl Tiegs, Tony's first wife. Like Veronique, Cheryl was also a strong woman, and it seemed that much of Tony's understandable anxiety in those years was about making sure that strong Veronique and strong Cheryl were agreeable with one another and not crossing signals regarding matters such as interior decorating, style, fashion and many other non-aesthetic matters as well.

Back before Tony and I began writing scripts together, I could see that he had a big life, one that included time always (rightfully) put aside for both Cheryl and his family, his expected attendance at many weekly large parties, frequent plane rides between L.A. and New York, a number of extended holidays throughout the year, and from what I could see, limited hours within any given day to write screenplays. With all that in mind, I pressed hard for his time once we became writing partners, arriving daily and at his doorstep early, accommodating his hours when he had them, and teaching myself how to work with a partner when I, at the time, was barely any kind of writer myself. As I've sketched out previously, we were both still working as actors as we began to write, so I too often needed to call out for needed time, to go learn lines, go out on auditions, and when lucky, go to the TV or film set to work as an actor.

As I was understanding the schedules, dynamics and logistics of Tony's life, I could see that Veronique was, of course, quite key to it all. She was a gatekeeper, a security guard, a Hollywood agent and most of all, a devoted, protective wife and mother. To put it bluntly - Juilliard or not - when she and I first met, she had no idea of what to make of this Midwestern guy who was writing screenplays with her son. Given my age at that time, I'm sure I wrongly saw her skepticism, frequent lack of invitation and even coldness as some sort of elite classism.

After all, I *did* see her light up and even glow as she would greet some of Tony's other friends to Carolwood: the grown children of Frank Sinatra, Roger Moore's kids, and many others of that ilk. But of course, I now see how common sense explains so much of that; Tony and those people grew up together, all within the same world of Hollywood, and yes, privilege.

Frankly, how could Veronique *not* test and analyze new people - strangers - who were coming onto the property of the family, entering their world and going into a 50-50 creative business with her children? I'd later see how Marlon's "loose" world could've used a Veronique.

For me, it would ultimately become a true badge of honor to fully, finally win over Veronique.

That came about thanks to Tony's constant endorsements of me, the success we would share as co-writers, the years of respect I would always give her, and mostly, trust; she could see Tony had become a true brother to me. Now, "Winning Over" Veronique didn't mean you suddenly had a gal-pal who was warm, open, or at times, even happy to see you. But you knew when her main guards were finally down and she saw you as a friend. When I could make her laugh in our one-on-one conversations, or she would share a family confidence with me; that meant a lot.

At times, I think she struggled to be as loving to her children as she was to Greg; Greg's life and career were epic and all-encompassing. Where Marlon often let his children see the world as their playground, Veronique made her children know that they were Official Representatives of a Worldwide Icon; one that represented integrity, intelligence and, yes, even justice for all.

These were the elements she promoted, even as her kids were growing up in the Hollywood and New York worlds of 70's and 80's sex, drugs and rock and roll. As Tony and his sister became adults, you could sense her mix of pride and frustration; she could no longer tell them what to do, and if they had missteps, they would not be the unseen, common, youthful missteps she herself knew growing up overseas; they would be missteps that could often be widely published, fully criticized, and most important to Veronique, viewed as matters that would publicly reflect on Gregory Peck. That *was* a lot to put on her kids, but in her mind, she had raised her children well; to her, being born into fame was no excuse for bad behavior. Still, in their defense, I often thought of how little she might've understood their unique lives from the day they were born.

I have two warm moments I recall with Veronique. The first one: when Tony and Cheryl divorced, understandably, Tony was in a sad, depressed place. Veronique, in a rare state of tears talked to me, wanting my take on Tony's state of mind; she was scared and we discussed ways to help Tony. The other moment: after Greg had passed away, Veronique moved to a manageable estate on Mapleton Drive. She threw a small party for one of Tony's birthdays at the new home. I had not seen her for quite some time on that evening. With Avra busy that night, I had to bring our toddler daughter Molly, who was fully, deeply into her loud autistic behavior. I struggled with Molly at the dinner table. I took her outside as her tantrum raged. I got her to calm as I sang to her, letting her put her feet in the swimming pool. I turned to see Veronique watching in tears nearby. Spotted, Veronique ducked back inside fast; she didn't like people seeing her softer side.

After she passed away in 2012, many in Hollywood had plenty to say about Veronique Peck; she was often outspoken, seemingly cold to some, and at times - to those who didn't really know her - she simply gave the cliched appearance of being the attractive requisite second wife to a movie star - a wife who was skilled when it came to presentation, appearances and protection of her husband, a bit like, say, Nancy Reagan, a name liberal Greg would hate being cited here. But it oddly makes sense. In fact, in their final years, Nancy and Veronique would often cross smiling paths within the society circuits of Bel Air, both widows who knew the very rare worlds beside a pair of very rare men. But in that twilight, while Nancy had the support, fame and facade of White House history, along with Secret Service protection and all that comes with being a former First Lady, Veronique was where she had been for years: still the most determined, devoted and fiercest protector of all things Greg. But now, she was doing it all without Gregory next to her.

For decades, she ran the singular "business" that *was* Gregory Peck, a mysterious job she both learned and created. A job that became more difficult in Greg's later years. And because of the love that the couple shared, it seemed to me, she was oddly - yet incredibly - good at it.

SUNSET BLVD. (1989)

I never tire when it comes to watching Billy Wilder's *"Sunset Boulevard"*. For those who might not know, it's the story of a desperate young screenwriter, caught in the (oddly) romantic and (barely) professional web of a faded, desperate silent film actress, a diva who lost her huge stardom when talkies arrived, now trying to reclaim her fame in the 1950's. I would view it on TV late show movie presentations before I even lived in Los Angeles or worked in The Industry. Of course, with every year that goes by, I "get" more and more out of the film: the old "Industry" Dream Factories, the old City of Los Angeles, and the changes in film, pop culture, technology and styles of every kind. As Greg often said to me, "New generations want their own heroes" - Norma Desmond couldn't understand that. And the other themes that get deeper to me as time goes by: desperate screenplay writers, aging stars, accepting questionable opportunities in Hollywood, faded fame, on and on and on. It all sounds cliched, obvious and over discussed, but somehow *"Sunset Boulevard"* continues to resonate with me more with every single viewing.

When I was 15, thanks to the generosity of my father (who selflessly traded his pickup truck for a film collection on my behalf), I had a giant 8mm and Super 8 collection of sound and silent films, long before home video ever arrived on the scene. As little as I truly understood about *"Sunset Boulevard"* as a young teen, I *did* understand that very few of those silent stars I had on those soundless reels were able to cross over into the era of talkies. I knew that I loved Stan Laurel and Oliver Hardy in both silent and sound films because they were rare - Two of the few performers to crossover, maybe the most successful, along with Greta Garbo. Almost all others - Chaplin included - are debatable at best when it comes to their success in sound filmmaking.

I'd think of those old films in the 80's and 90's, when I was then watching Peck and Brando in person, seeing them as relevant, sought-after and still fully in the game. And indeed they were. Unlike some of their peers and contemporaries, they seemed both uniquely insulated *and* elevated by their own distinct brands of legend, seclusion and iconic presence. At times, their occasional absences and disappearance from mainstream view for a bit even enhanced their mystique. While that might seem obvious and even common knowledge regarding Marlon, the same could be said for Greg, who knew that he wanted to be selective about when he should and should not be seen. I recall a time when he was on his office phone discussing yet one more film role offer he was politely declining. After charming his way off the call, his tone changed; he hung up, grumbling, "I swear, if one more director is looking for another goddamn 'foxy old judge'!" Obviously, many older performers don't often have the luxury of getting to be standoffish about any aspect of the industry, and of course, that was also the case for many aging stars in the 80's and 90's. Shelley Winters once half-joked about Marlon's seclusion, suggesting that people would forget about her if she tried "that routine." And then, of course, there will always be actors and performers who truly seem to *love* show business, "The Industry" and basically everything connected to it. They love getting out into the public, or diving into almost any given project, at a moment's notice. I occasionally understood those performers on different levels - Why not love it? It should be easy to see and appreciate the good luck of it all. And especially those connected to comedy — Whether they liked it or not, those comics almost *needed* to keep popping up with a smile, an appearance and a joke, simply by the nature of their personas and their product.

Marlon often chuckled at the kind of old celebrity who would "show up at the opening of a door" as he put it, mentioning people like Bob Hope in that discussion. I saw his point. But at the same time, Tony and I would constantly laugh with, marvel at and fully love those loud talents who seemed positively shameless regarding their love of "Show Business"; grateful, exuberant balls of fire like Mickey Rooney or Jerry Lewis; while it was easy for younger generations from the Too-Cool-School to mock jesters like Lewis and Rooney as they unapologetically aged in their later years, you also had to examine the totality of their careers and what they did. They were insanely talented, skilled and prolific. Were they as "Happy" as they seemed? Doubtful.

Of course, advanced age and strong opinions are nearly impossible to separate. Greg disliked films and books that would leave viewers and readers with extreme moral ambiguities or fully negative elements that, for him, overwhelmed an ultimate positive and/or lasting impression. He felt the remake of *"Cape Fear"* was a soulless bloodbath; a gory reworking of his original film. He thought the new version left audiences momentarily thrilled, drained by the end - and perhaps nothing more once leaving the theater. While he understood that Martin Scorsese was a singular craftsman, he also had issues with Marty's embrace of darkness and highly conflicted characters.

This brings me to Scorsese's *"Goodfellas";* when it opened in 1990, Tony and I would go to see the film in theaters time and time again. I readily admit that I was perhaps overwhelmed the first time I saw the picture, not even sure what it was in certain places; where was it going? So many threads, pop songs, narrated segments that turned the story into B-roll theater? I knew I did not hate it, but I certainly didn't see it originally as a work of art that would eventually consume me; admittedly, I am positively addicted to that movie. It's one brilliant moment after another.

Perhaps Tony and I oversold it to Greg, but after a few weeks of the film being in release, we finally got Greg to see it. Or perhaps it was finally screening over at Irving "Swifty" Lazar's house; Irving and Mary Lazar often had first-run screenings in his home for guests like Greg and Veronique. The day after Greg saw it, he was quite firm about how little he liked it; from the way he was talking, I'm not even sure that he got all the way through the movie before it was over. He saw it as an endless parade of irredeemable characters committing one irredeemable criminal act after the other. His reception reminded me of how film styles and even "movements" in cinema can be just as strong as pop music, fashion or any art form that flows from era to era. That's not a revolutionary notion, but it's often possible to forget when, say, the same actor is in two different versions of *"Cape Fear"* as Greg was - One where he's the star, one where he's a supporting player. But even with the same basic story, they were not comparable to somebody like Greg. Some might say that it's all a matter of "age" - and *that* brings me to old Irving Lazar.

First, a little about that unique Hollywood character with the shiny head and the giant glasses.

In his later years, Irving built a connection between his own image and the Oscars. Those awards were a religion to me as I grew up. I had a book of all the winners through 1978, and yes, I had that book fully memorized by the time I arrived at Juilliard. As the awards evolved through the years, the hype, glitz and festivities around the Oscars grew as well. Even the Flower Power "Aloof Hippies Shrugging it Off" years that showed a young apathetic Dustin Hoffman or a political Jane Fonda did nothing to slow down the public's - *and* The Industry's - love of Oscar. Even with all of the other awards that have evolved throughout the world, throughout the years, and in so many other mediums, it's still The Academy Awards that symbolize The Holy Grail.

Greg spent time as head of the Motion Picture Academy, even producing the worldwide telecast. All as Marlon, of course, was famously walking away from his second Oscar. That's a perfect split-screen view of those two men: one is protecting, nurturing and proudly presenting this pinnacle of their craft, while the other is essentially saying, "Fuck You" to the whole enterprise.

Somehow, even before vast internet, modern social media and smart-phone communication, The World would grow to know about Irving "Swifty" Lazar's annual "Oscar Party" at the legendary "Spago" restaurant in Hollywood - Well, technically, West Hollywood. When Irving was my agent, he often had me thinking about the evolutional aspect of film; it was a constant consideration as I conversed and worked with Greg, Marlon and those of their generation. Swifty was a guy who had made deals for everybody from Ernest Hemingway to Humphrey Bogart to Richard Nixon. Many in Hollywood in the 80's and 90's still wanted to think of him as current, happening and still in the swim. Much of that was because of his Oscar party. He rejected our third screenplay, *"Free Money,"* saying, "Nobody cares about Midwestern characters!" That made me ponder Irving's ideas regarding what was "current" and "marketable" in the era of unique storytelling such as *"Goodfellas"*. Nothing hit that home for me like a 1989 screening over at Irving's house. Tony's sister Cecilia had justifiably fallen in love with the sweet, sensitive film adaptation of the Christy Brown autobiography, *"My Left Foot"*. She was thrilled when it was going to screen in the Lazar private home theater. As Tony and I would go on to do with *"Goodfellas"* a year later, Cecilia perhaps "overtalked" the film up to the skies, having seen it already in theaters, eager for her parents and others to view it. On the night when I was invited to Irving's to see it, I had previously viewed it as well, marveling over the incredible, challenging performance of Daniel Day Lewis. He was playing the lead in a true story, the journey of a paralyzed, spastic quadriplegic; a physically trapped individual who would eventually become a famous painter, poet and author, thanks to his sole working body part - hence the title.

For those who have not seen it, the film is often difficult emotionally but ultimately uplifting - even very funny at times. If you have strong empathy, you'll be profoundly moved. But given all that, none of the positive aspects of the picture seemed to reach 82-year-old Swifty Lazar as he viewed it. After watching just a bit of the lead character struggle, writhe, groan broken language and twitch uncontrollably, Irving wanted the projector shut off. Perhaps because of Cecilia, Mary had a hushed talk with Irving and the film kept running. But not for Swifty. He left the screening room as the rest of us watched the remainder of the film - uncomfortably in Irving's house.

As the end credits rolled, Cecilia was heartbroken, wondering how a man with Irving's legendary intellect, perceived literary sophistication and lifetime of worldliness; how could he storm away from something she saw as a masterpiece? When the lights came up on this small group, I said "goodnight" and got out of there; I was rarely in Lazar's opulent house and I can't say I ever found the atmosphere to be pleasant or inviting. Before leaving, I looked around a bit, wanting to - I guess - "thank" Irving for the evening, finding myself relieved when it seemed he was nowhere in sight. I sure as hell wasn't gonna knock on his bedroom door for a "Bye-Bye".

The next morning, Tony and I were writing in the Flicker Way screening room. I had to ask how the rest of the previous evening went - *if* there was any more evening after I left. I asked if Greg and Veronique liked the film. He shrugged, suggesting that, given the circumstances, they probably made a good effort over it for Cecilia. I asked Tony if he himself liked it. He said he wanted to see it again, correctly suggesting that Irving had pretty much thrown the whole night off track. After discussing how upset Cecilia was, he then went into a series of ideas that were pure Tony: incredible humor, wonderful insight and his own beautiful brand of common sense.

"Look, Joey, Irving's over 80. He's a little rich guy who's been around the world and back a few thousand times; there's nothing he hasn't seen or done. Now he wants things *nice!* Now! *Nice!* At the end of the day, he wants a nice dinner with his nice wife and nice friends. *Nice.* He wants to watch a *nice* movie with maybe a few laughs, a few adventures that keep him interested for an hour or two. Then he wants everyone to get the fuck out of his house! He then goes up to the bathroom; he prays *that* goes well! He then crawls into bed and he hopes to God that he wakes up the next day. I'll tell you what he *doesn't* want after a long day: he doesn't wanna go into a dark room to stare at some actor moan and stutter and crawl on the floor and get put into a wheelbarrow and hurt and drool and alla that shit - no matter what the story! He doesn't need that. That might rock my sister's world, it might rock our "Juilliard Theatre" world, but that's nothing but a nightmare to Lazar; a fucking nightmare he doesn't need!"

Tony finished with, "Irving is at a place and an age where he deserves *niiiizzze!*"

His hilarious ring of extreme passion and sincere understanding on that incident still resonates with me to this day. While Tony knew he was being funny, for my entertainment, he also knew that he was speaking something that was quite true.

I said, "I guess I see what you're saying, but I find it interesting that a guy so in love with 'Oscar' no longer recognizes Oscar-worthy filmmaking."

Again, with his response, Tony nailed it - "Pallie, these days, for Swifty, 'Oscar' is only a party."

As we started to write again that morning, I thought I would close the topic by muttering, "Well, let's get this next script finished; maybe Irving can sell it." As one last beat of the morning to make me spit up with laughter, Tony sighed, "We gotta jump ship from Lazar." I laughed, but I saw he was serious. As I squinted a "What?," he added, "Irving's not the agent for us anymore."

Tony closed with, "The old guy doesn't even get *'My Left Foot'.*"

Weeks later, we did have a new agent. And frankly, I think Irving was relieved to be done with us. He first took us on as a favor to Greg and Veronique, and day-to-day agenting with "new" clients was ceasing to be a part of his everyday routine. On top of that, our next paid assignment as writers was going to be a tangle of personal relationships and challenging material, with a producer who demanded excellence. It was a situation where I would've had a hard time seeing the involvement of the shrewd, calculated and elevated Irving "Swifty" Lazar.

Oh, this next, demanding producer:

A very special breed of "tyrant" named Gregory Peck.

THIRD CHAPTER
ACTING vs STARDOM
(GREG & MARLON ESSAY III)

"You have to be a little bit crazy to be an actor"
- Gregory Peck
"You have to be willing to take a shit on stage to be an actor"
- Marlon Brando

Marlon did say those words to me - and variations of those exact words - a number of times. And that quote from Greg was as "disrespectful" as Greg ever got about those within his profession; if what he said can even be considered remotely disrespectful. It certainly wasn't to Greg - He enjoyed that whimsical part within himself - the part that was "a little bit crazy." He loved to laugh and he knew he could make others laugh with just the right vocabulary word, just the right phrase, or best of all, a skewed delivery of what he knew was a "Gregory Peck"-like line. He knew that epic voice and that tone of his could make you laugh when used in just the right way. A version of this self-awareness and a beautifully extreme example of it was the much-viewed straw hat song and dance he did in 1969, towering over and soft-shoe shuffling with Jack Benny and George Burns on Benny's TV special. It blew my mind as a nine-year-old movie nut and I still love watching it on YouTube today.

It's Greg goofing on "Gregory Peck," and it's a wonderful bit of magic.

Even in personal areas, Greg knew the Gregory Peck mystique. He famously left a letter at Lauren Bacall's home after Humphrey Bogart died. Bacall talked about the letter for years, saying how supportive, kind and empathetic the letter was, how it helped her during that difficult time. Greg was a human embrace, and something of a famous letter writer, knowing both the importance of each word and the lasting impact of any effort to mail his thoughts. Sometimes his letters were elaborate and certifiably romantic (thanking Audrey Hepburn for speaking at a Peck tribute), and sometimes they were just hilariously to the point; turning down the role of a senior citizen in a nursing home, he ended his short refusal with: "Don't want to do it. Too vain."

So what shaped young Greg? I met his mother a number of times but never really got any clues; Bernice Ayres (who her friends and family referred to as "Bunny") had divorced Greg's father (Gregory Pearl Peck, who died in 1962) when Greg was only five. Young Greg went to military school and lived with his father when he was 14. Decades later, I'd listen as Greg talked about how much he loved his father, while Marlon would tell me repeatedly how much he hated his own father, Marlon Brando, Sr., a man who had a rocky marriage with Marlon's alcoholic mother. I'm sure any psychologist could do a lot with all those facts. It's quite possible that those realities also had an impact on how they viewed and approached parenting, but as I'd witness time and time again, the biggest impact on their parenting was constantly the giant, crazy lives and careers both men had - and how those careers affected the women and children in their lives.

Throughout these pages, I hope the following is coming across: in their insanely different ways, Marlon and Greg were both genuine and authentic, in an industry that is often more illusion off screen than on. Some would say that you might get that "privilege" to be that "real" when your stardom is at that rare level. But I know through my years in the industry that that is not the case. As talented as they were, they both knew that it was indeed the industry itself that had given them both such big lives, big audiences, big money, and of course, big problems - problems that are only clear to people in their tiny circle - problems dealing with privacy, expectations, family and many things that are not remotely thought about by any struggling actor who would read this and easily be thinking, "Oh, I would *love* to have such problems!"

Again and again as I've mentioned, I've tried to figure out the fascinating and distinct interest - and disdain - I felt these two had for one another. I was so fortunate to be present for so many honest talks, so many open conversations and so many free exchanges of ideas with them. When I boil it down to the simple "Respect for The Industry" vs. "No Respect for The Industry," I think I'm close to understanding the essence of both men, but I know it goes deeper than that.

As I brought up pages ago, at a very young age, I was lucky to work as both a professional cartoonist and a professional drummer. Given that, I always felt I was a visual artist first (hiding behind my easel), then a musician (hiding behind my drum set), moving on to wanting to be a writer (to hide behind my typewriter), wanting to be a filmmaker (to hide behind my camera), arriving at "acting" after all that, where I first felt I could "hide" within the role - until Juilliard, where I learned I needed to "become" the role, if done well, with no hiding involved whatsoever.

Greg and Marlon both saw themselves as character actors, even though the two of them knew - full well - that they were a combination of "Leading Man" and "Star," two terms they both disliked. You don't take roles like Peck's Josef Mengele in *"The Boys from Brazil"* or his Captain Ahab in *"Moby Dick"* if you think you are only a "Leading Man," no matter your age. Today, a white actor like Brando would probably never be cast in the ethnic roles he took on with *"Viva Zapata"* or *"Teahouse of the August Moon,"* but for him, back in those days, it was pure "character" work, in the tradition of his idol, leading man, character actor and star Paul Muni.

Through all their films and roles, Greg and Marlon constantly tried to balance their craft with their private lives, and I thought about that as I watched an old classmate of mine on YouTube a while back. I've mentioned Kevin Spacey in this book a few times, perhaps in less than flattering ways. I've never been an admirer of naked ambition, but I've always admired talent, and I knew the moment I got to Juilliard, Kevin had extreme talent. The YouTube video I cited above featured Kevin giving a teleconference talk during the 2020 quarantine days of the coronavirus pandemic. I watched it because I had read that he caught hell for making that video, for comparing his "Me Too" banishment from the acting world with all of us who were finding ourselves in sudden quarantine. As a reminder of his situation: In 2017, Kevin's huge world of stardom turned to ashes after a young actor went public with a recollection of Spacey making inappropriate sexual advances on the actor back when Spacey was 26 and the actor was 14.

As far as people being angry with Kevin's 2020 video, saying they hated that he found comparisons with the world in quarantine and his own isolation-by-way-of-pariahdom, tone-wise, I didn't hear his words in that way. I was instead hearing Kevin - perhaps for the first time - talk about trying to find the person he was without "acting." As I've often written about: in my small Juilliard class, there were those training to be "Actors," those clearly training to be "Stars" and those training to just be as creative as humanly possible; on many days, I felt I was the only one who fell into that last amorphous category. Faculty members often told me as much.

Kevin was clearly in Juilliard with my sister and me to become a star, and I was not shocked at all when he became one. And he achieved that in many respects by being an exceptional actor. But as I've stated previously, I felt that nobody ever really knew the guy - not during our school years and not in his professional life - Because acting - and then stardom - fully consumed him.

On the day when Spacey did the 2020 teleconference video, he gave, what I believe to be, a heartfelt confession of being totally lost about who he was. No, I'm not here to defend Spacey for all or any of the stuff that erased him from film, TV or theater during the "Me Too" movement, but I did hear him - as I was writing about Greg and Marlon - when Kevin spoke about not remotely recognizing himself with "acting," "stardom" and "performance" out of his life.

I met Marlon and Greg in their later years, somehow both becoming more revered just as they were also becoming less relevant to modern day filmmaking and storytelling. Of course their ages had a great deal to do with that. But it was also about how box-office, acceptance of ageism and young audiences were changing. To some extent, they were both fine with that, both private individuals who were often offered any number of "elderly" roles on any given week. But as their "lasting" images and their status as icons grew, they also struggled to make sure the world knew that they were human beings first, with thoughts, opinions and ideas that made them more than screen images. Greg toured his live audience Q&A evening, *"A Conversation with Gregory Peck"* in different cities - he did 70 evenings with the event - and when Marlon couldn't stay silent on certain matters, he'd pick up the phone and then find himself on *"Larry King Live"* that night, not always to positive effect, but still, he had things he wanted to say. Marlon also felt that his reality show-like *"Lying For a Living"* would be the lasting set of statements from his winter years, and to the shock of many, for 13 days, that reclusive, by then allergic-to-work genius actually got up off the couch and went to a Hollywood studio to tape it. Much more on that epic project within these forthcoming pages.

In short, I believe both men late in life wanted the world to know more about them apart from their roles. Yes, by way of various interviews and appearances, they had done variations on that theme all throughout their lives. But as life was winding down, I believe they knew what I saw Spacey only now discovering on that teleconference: as an actor, finding the character in a role is one thing. Finding a way to make stardom work - and *keep* working - that takes a rare series of tricks and maneuvers.

And finding *yourself* - when your passions are "characters" and "stardom"; that's the most important - and difficult - task of all.

When I was young and viewed famous people from the distance of print, film and TV, I recall show business lovers like Mickey Rooney telling talk show hosts about a perk regarding being a star. To paraphrase those Industry journeymen like Rooney, "Stars" never really die; their work allows them to be with us forever. Then I read a quote from Dustin Hoffman, who said, basically, being a big star takes your mind off of ever dying. The reason: "You're already dead. You're embalmed," is how Hoffman put it. It took me years to understand how correct that probably is.

Marlon and Greg struggled with that imbalance: being "okay with" and even appreciating the immortality a "star" receives, all while being realistic about how much is taken from you when billions can "love" you as a "star" but not know *you* whatsoever. Often, for the most simple of perspectives, I find myself going back to the joy we get from the movies themselves. One of my favorite, most surprising moments with Marlon came one day as we were watching TV, channel-surfing until we came upon a Laurel & Hardy short. Marlon had to stop and watch; he loved those guys. Between huge laughs, he said, *"This* is why everybody loves the movies!"

To him, Stan and Ollie weren't "stars". They were a couple guys who brought him great joy. And it's that very "Joy" that seduced a very young Marlon to chase that tangle known as "Stardom".

THE STORY RESUMES: DOCTOR DeMOTT (1990)

It's safe to say: all the films of Ingmar Bergman were personal, sensitive and beautiful, each in their own way. As I grew up in small town Minnesota, I first knew of him only as a name that my parents mixed up with actress Ingrid Bergman. In my teens, trying to be a huge film wonk, always looking through my aforementioned stolen Swank Film Rental Catalog, I'd see that this Bergman guy was viewed as respected, revered, loved, honored and clearly one of the certified geniuses of cinema. (Quick side note on the "Swank" catalog: along with the then new MPAA "G", "M", "R" and "X" ratings, each film had a Catholic Church rating: a "C" = "Condemned" - and I swear, nearly *every* film in the book - new or old - The biggest films: 1929 - 1969 - *all* had a "C"! As a young Catholic boy, this thrilled me to no end!) Again, remember, in my youth, there was no way for me to see Big City "Art" films, thus my love of the Swank catalog, a book I'd cross-reference with film study books in my school library. But alas, Bergman films did not play in small town Minnesota theaters, on TV, and there was no video rental, no internet; you get the idea. As a teen, much of my Bergman education was by way of Woody Allen and his love and tribute of Bergman, within Allen films such as *"Love and Death,"* *"Interiors"* and others.

When I got to Juilliard in New York, I'd go the art house cinema as often as possible, finally seeing the films of Truffaut, Fassbinder, Herzog and of course, Bergman. I must've sat through *"Fanny and Alexander"* half a dozen times, at first, not sure if I was "getting it" as a Midwestern 19- year-old. But with multiple (three-hour) viewings, I came to finally understand more and more about the Swedish class structure of 1907, the influence of August Strindberg (a playwright we were studying at Juilliard) and most importantly to me, the filmmaking of Ingmar Bergman.

By the way, some people today like to laugh and smirk over the hoity-toity education young people submerge themselves in once they leave their small towns for cultural centers like New York City (and yes, the still-maturing personalities of some college students can be insufferable). But you know what? I loudly say, "Fuck You" to all those critics; it shouldn't need to be said, but in this current era of often elevating stupidity, thank God for higher education, and especially art films, for that matter. No, I don't kneel down and bow to every work of abstraction, literature and foreign cinema that comes along, but to this day, I am so incredibly grateful that New York City, intelligent professors and The Juilliard School of Theatre taught me to appreciate and understand our want for culture, art history and most of all, the desire to understand the unique voices of elevated ideas. Am I a snob? I have an easy answer for that: I'm the biggest snob in Brainerd and I'm the biggest hick in The Big City. Kinda - and painfully - balances itself out. Okay, sorry for the rant. Having said all that, I now need to whipsaw back to my Midwest Love-of-TV culture.

Once I got to Los Angeles in the mid 80's as an actor, writer and director, I didn't have agents who were at all interested in my love of foreign art films or God forbid, working on such stuff. And that's fine, because I also had (and still have) a deep love and knowledge of all things U.S. commercial network TV, box office cinema, top 40 radio music and youthful pop culture (See, I told ya, still the biggest hick in The Big City.). Still, when home video finally arrived, I no longer needed to wait for a Los Angeles art house cinema to screen a 35mm print of the classics of artists such as Ingmar Bergman. So why all this about Bergman? Hang on. We're getting there.

Please allow me to first tell you a bit about a man named Victor Sjostrom. He was a Swedish actor and director with a giant resume. He worked from the earliest days of silent cinema, right up until his death in 1960, with his most famous piece of work blooming two years earlier in 1958, when Ingmar Bergman cast Sjostrom essentially as Bergman's own father (a retired college professor as a film character, while Bergman's real life father was a Lutheran minister) in the lyrical, strongly biographical masterpiece, *"Wild Strawberries"*. Acting at the age of 78, with a tall frame, prominent eyebrows, healthy head of white hair and a warm smile, Sjostrom in the 1958 film had a strong resemblance to the Gregory Peck of the early 1990's.

"It happens a lot," Greg said as he first mentioned *"Wild Strawberries"* to me. I asked, "What happens?" He laughed, "I'm in some country, in an international airport, someone says, 'You look like that old man in *'Wild Strawberries'*!'" My only thought at that moment: "Good God, Greg lives in such a rare, sophisticated, geographically cosmopolitan world! What world airports do you find yourself in where it sounds like they know *'Wild Strawberries'* better than *'To Kill a Mockingbird'*?! - Hell, where they know friggin' *'Wild Strawberries'* at all?!"

Greg brought it up because he had been harboring an idea for quite some time; the idea of doing a remake of *"Wild Strawberries,"* with Greg as the retired professor, a character Tony would go on to name *"Doctor DeMott"* - and that became the title for this possible remake. And since Tony and I were now working as WGA 20th Century-Fox writers at that time, Greg wanted to hire us to do the American adaptation. Okay, this is where things begin to truly intertwine.

Before I go into Greg's project, know that this is when I was about to meet Marlon and start spending days with him on his screenplays - As always, a very different experience than writing with and for Greg. (My meeting of Marlon is a big chapter coming up next; allow me to tease a bit of that material right now.)

See, Marlon's scripts were both new and old - old ones (original screenplays) he had written years ago with others, and new scripts based on "new" stories that were banging around in his head. At that time, I was also still writing new original scripts with Tony, *and* still going on auditions as an actor, occasionally getting a role and doing that work as well. It was a lot to juggle and it was an exciting, albeit often exhausting time. Some of Marlon's "old" scripts were films that almost got made back when Marlon had great clout. *"Fan-Tan"* was a South Seas adventure inspired by his Tahiti love, a script that he kept dabbling on throughout the years. *"Jericho"* was a spy thriller that actually had a green light at one time, complete with a waiting cast, crew and production facility. Some reports claim it was all set to go and Marlon just never showed up. I had read such stories, I asked him about it, and he just dismissed it all with a shrug and a sour face, saying, "Joe, you are not looking at a Let-Down-Artist. That is tittle-tattle."

Whatever the case, *"Jericho"* was just one of six scripts he and I "worked" on throughout the years - in various degrees of seriousness, and in some cases, collaboration with others. *"Bull Boy"* was a poetic tale of animal appreciation that PETA would love, *"Skuzz"* was a new anger fable that the paparazzi would hate, *"Tim and His Friends"* was a comedy starring Marlon's dog, Tim, and *"Platinum Toenail"* was a spy adventure that he felt would be good for Tom Cruise, Robert De Niro and Marlon Brando. More on that project coming up.

The "new" scripts with Brando required me recording conversations with Marlon, making transcripts and then shaping his ideas into some form of page-count. The "old" scripts always had Marlon saying, "Let's shine this up," letting me know that he felt any of the old drafts were stale, dated and not worthy of current production - even when that wasn't the case. Older drafts of *"Fan-Tan"* showed the interesting work of Donald Cammell, an acting, writing chameleon of a collaborator who probably knew well the joys and frustrations of working with Marlon.

Where Marlon was undisciplined and freewheeling in his approach to screenwriting, of course, Greg was cautious, careful and precise. I worked without pay for Marlon on most projects.

Greg made sure he set up a Producers Guild/Writers Guild contract with me and his own son, assuring we would be paid through an agent as we began work on the Bergman project.

By the way, as much as I wanted to get Tony involved with my Brando writing, that was not to be for some time. Marlon allowed very few people up to his house and he had a clear dislike regarding what he called, "Hollywood Kids". *And* as I've brought forth many times within these pages, Marlon clearly had some sort of dislike of Greg. Tony and Marlon coming together would occur much later; I promise I'll get to *that* down the road here as well. Okay, back to Greg's *"Wild Strawberries"* script - As the rights from Bergman were obtained, personally by Greg, we got ourselves an amazing Executive Producer, in the most amazing way. I'll try to keep it succinct, but it was quite a path. Around the time that we were beginning the *"Doctor DeMott"* project, Greg was learning something that got him quite angry. I've read different versions of how all this went down; what follows is the version of events I saw at the Peck estate - Events that gave *"DeMott"* a boost and eventually gave Greg a great payday.

I'll back up a bit here and then ramp up into it all. Actually, I'll need to back up quite a ways to get started.

Early on in the film world, two actors, a director and an actor/director gauged their stardom and then did what they could to retain some control and profits. United Artists was founded in 1919 by Charlie Chaplin, Mary Pickford, Douglas Fairbanks and D.W. Griffith. All four of them understood their immense power, knowing that they themselves were essentially the actual reasons for much of the success of this new industry. Many years later, long after color and sound faded in, after the old studio heads had faded away, First Artists would be founded, led by Barbra Streisand, Paul Newman and Sidney Poitier, soon to be joined by Steve McQueen and Dustin Hoffman. Ahead of them in that line of evolution, Greg and Marlon were also in an era where film ownership and profit participation was possible for stars at the rare level of Peck and Brando. It's fair to speculate that Greg lived a life of financial security in large part thanks to owning pieces of both *"To Kill a Mockingbird"* and *"The Omen,"* as well as a few other films.

Marlon's constant chase for money was, in part, due to producing only relatively unsuccessful films through his production company, while taking flat fees for some of his more successful films. He'd also get into lengthy legal battles over profit participation, perhaps most notably, his battle over what he felt he was owed in points from the vast haul of 1978's *"Superman"*. In short, it was often the same picture with these two guys: Greg would quietly pay all his bills on time, knowing he had a steady flow of well-managed income, while Marlon would constantly half-joke to Avra and me that he was incredibly tired of living his entire life, "A day late and a dollar short."

In the early 60's, both Greg and Marlon worked with Universal, both as part-owners of the films they were in. *"To Kill a Mockingbird"* was the perfect, non-recurring miracle combination that every studio still dreams of: shot on the studio backlot and within its sound stages, it was not a budget-buster, delivering incredible reward and prestige, along with a golden self-life that will probably last as long as time will be measured. Within roughly that same era, a few sound stages away (when not on costly locations for MGM's *"Mutiny on the Bounty"*), Marlon was shaping his own set of Questions for Humanity with *"The Ugly American,"* a political essay on U.S. diplomacy and foreign civil war; subjects that fascinated Marlon, even if Cold War audiences of the day were not all that interested. (Note: On this book cover: Marlon in costume for that film shoot.)

This is the very same era when Greg also made and became part owner of the film, story and screenplay of the previously mentioned *"Cape Fear,"* that 1962 hit thriller starring Greg. Again, as many of us know, it was also a highly successful remake years later, directed by Martin Scorsese. About that: okay, the way some say Martin Scorsese has told it, he's reportedly stated that he was fortunate throughout his young career when actor Robert De Niro agreed when asked to take part in a fair number of the early, pivotal Scorsese films. That's a modest assessment on Scorsese's part, given that many might say that a young De Niro was just as lucky to have then young Marty; together, the two of them really are a rare case of great actor and great filmmaker creating their mutual careers in tandem with one another. But as both men became bigger, both becoming their own film factories with their own production companies, it seems that one of the first "asks" of De Niro to Scorsese was the request that Marty direct the remake of "Cape Fear".

So, that's one version of the partial "Origin Story" I heard; of how the 1991 *"Cape Fear"* began to come together. Within that version, Scorsese reportedly didn't want to do a remake of an old film - any old film - but De Niro convinced him, with Scorsese later having demands that involved using actors from the original film, as well as the classic 1962 Bernard Herrmann score.

Other stories tell of King of the Universal lot, Steven Spielberg, first going to town on *"Cape Fear"* under his Amblin Entertainment banner. In this version, Scorsese was about to direct *"Schindler's List"* and Spielberg was trying to find his own want to direct *"Cape Fear,"* but neither project satisfied its then-attached director, thus a "trade" took place, where Spielberg would tell the holocaust story and Scorsese would do the remake. Frankly, all of these elements together might hold certain degrees of truth, as the finished 1991 *"CapeFear"* would go on to be produced by Amblin Entertainment, De Niro's Tribeca Productions and Scorsese's Cappa Films.

That's a pretty amazing slate of companies; if a team like that wants *your* old property, *your* old rights to *"Cape Fear"*- Man, you'd think that would be a big payday. But here's the deal: as Universal squabbled with Greg over the selling of his rights to the film, he was never told that the folks behind the "want" were a trio of ordinary guys named Spielberg, De Niro and Scorsese.

This, of course, was all unknown to those men just listed above. When you're that big, the studio does that messy "rights buying" stuff for you. So whatever happened with the coming together of the project early on, *"Schindler's List"* and all, again, all I can tell is the portion of the story I witnessed over at Greg's house. When the studio made the first *"Cape Fear"* offers to Greg, I heard they were ridiculously low. While the 1962 version was no gigantic hit, it was a great thriller; Greg didn't care to see it turned into some TV movie. The probability of this "remake" being a TV movie; that notion, of course, came from the reported nickel-and-dime offer. But Greg had been in the business long enough to sense that Universal really wanted this deal - like, super bad. As offers and counter offers went back and forth for some time, the studio was soon playing both hardball and lowball with Greg's representatives, barely raising their numbers as they insisted how good Universal had been to Greg, citing *"To Kill a Mockingbird"* and other titles that were part of the long history between the studio and the performer.

By the time it all devolved into a "Take it or leave it" stage, Veronique convinced Greg that the "Final Offer" was a good amount of money for a property that was just sitting there. Greg sensed something amiss in all this, but as the studio clock was ticking, he reluctantly agreed to the deal and signed the papers. A day later in The Hollywood Reporter, Greg would read about his old film being remade, by, what's this? Three guys with kinda famous names. He was furious, angry that he got worn down in an offer that clearly was all about concealing the "buyers."

As we were just starting the *"Doctor DeMott"* project when much of that was going on, Greg and the family received an invitation to join Scorsese for an honor Martin was receiving in New York. Thinking back now, I believe Scorsese was already in motion regarding his want to feature original 1962 *"Cape Fear"* cast members in the remake; perhaps this invitation was part of that plan. Knowing that Martin was far outside of Universal's deal-making, Greg thought it would be a good evening for the family to attend. That's exactly the way Greg was - He did not want to misplace his anger against an artist like Scorsese. Just before the Pecks headed east for the event, I asked Tony, "Do you think Greg will say anything to Scorsese about the film rights deal?"

Tony smiled, "I don't think so. But I'm going to."

Sure enough, after the gala for Scorsese in New York, Tony found some private time with Martin and explained what he saw go down between Universal and Greg. Scorsese said he felt terrible, having no idea about the deal. That's when Martin talked about how badly "Bob" wanted him to direct it, how much he never wanted to do a remake of anything, and how he'd like to make it up to Greg with an amazing salary for a two-day cameo in the new version. Tony said, "That's great." Tony then did something incredibly brilliant, knowing he was talking to The Mega-Film-Nerd of all time. Tony pitched into a deep-dive explanation of Greg's new project, a remake of *"Wild Strawberries,"* with permission given by Ingmar Bergman himself. Given all the elements: the Universal *"Cape Fear"* deal, "Ingmar Bergman," *"Wild Strawberries"* . . . it all must've hit Scorsese in just the right way, because within that very micro-meeting, Martin Scorsese offered to Executive Produce *"Doctor DeMott"*. Again, the brilliance of Tony Peck.

I think I actually did fall off my chair when Tony told me the news upon his return to L.A. As we started to write *"DeMott,"* we'd have phone conferences with "Marty," as he liked to be called. A few weeks after that New York event, a Los Angeles function was also throwing an evening honoring Scorsese at the Beverly Hilton. Tony and I went and I was introduced in person; it was thrilling for me, even though we had already had a number of phone calls over the script. That night, Scorsese gave a speech that mentioned a real hero of his, Michael Powell, the British filmmaker who had recently died. During his career, Powell made unique masterpieces such as *"Black Narcissus," "Peeping Tom"* and *"The Red Shoes"*. For the next week, if I wasn't watching my VHS copy of *"Wild Strawberries,"* I was watching one of those films by Powell.

For the next few months, we'd write and send scripts to Scorsese. When his distinct voice and rushed cadence would come rat-a-tating over the phone speaker, you had to smile.

"Page 8 - So guys, why are these characters speaking The King's English? Didn't we go over this before?" He'd ask questions like that to me and Tony as he'd go over a draft of *"Doctor DeMott"*. That note would come up more than it should've. There were a few reasons for those words that Scorsese was asking about. We all shared a bit of the blame; Tony, Greg and me. Greg often hated script dialogue that told actors when to use conjunctions, and even certain forms of slang, while Tony and I were perhaps keeping too much of the icy tone and pace first established by Bergman's story. But whether it was dialogue or story structure, it was no surprise to learn that Scorsese was a script wizard, able to see what's wrong with a page, what works in a scene, and everything else, all as he remains wonderfully polite and filled with contagious enthusiasm.

Eventually, after a great deal of writing with Marty, we were close to having a workable draft. Before long, he said he was talking to Sean Penn about possibly directing the film. That was exciting news that motivated Tony, Greg and me into then completing what felt like a draft we were happy to circulate, or, at least, a draft that Scorsese was happy to circulate and give to Penn and others.

And with that draft, - well, if you know anything about Hollywood filmmaking, you know the following is true: the writing is often the easy part. Sometimes even the joyous part.

After writing - now comes the hard part. Sometimes - even the fully miserable part.

MEET MARLON (1991)

Okay, you're probably thinking, "This many pages in and you now *finally officially meet him?!*" Trust me, it's The Brando Way. Always. He's worth waiting for, and once he arrives, he totally takes over. So, yes, please allow me to jump back within this collage, when I actually *did* "officially" meet Marlon. It was simple *and* profound at the same time. One night after she had worked a long day up on Mulholland, Avra came home. She was more tired, irritated and frazzled than usual. After plopping down onto the couch, she sighed, "He wants to know why you're ducking him." Earlier that day, I was getting much of that same stuff from Tony when we were writing. As he had said a lot, he said again, stating, "Pallie, enough. You gotta meet this guy. You gotta."

By now, I had spent years avoiding invitations from Marlon. I often hoped that his want to meet would eventually fade away. But I knew much of his family through Avra, having spent time with Rebecca, Miko and even Christian (before the incident). I also knew Marlon's home and property far better than I knew him. When Avra was not off on locations as part of the staff of Brando movies - on films such as *"The Freshman,"* she was taking care of things up at the Mulholland house. I'd see the home with Avra when he wasn't there, realizing that I had spent decades reading about this place, this property and this region. That's how famous Marlon was: his hideaway home had been a true (and written about) Hollywood curiosity for quite awhile.

And remember, I knew he had seen me on TV. As I mentioned in my Ed O'Neill story, Avra was a frequent guest to the home before working there, back when she was working in the art departments of *"Molly Dodd"* and *"Slap Maxwell"*. She'd watch these shows with Marlon and his daughter, Rebecca, up at Mulholland, proudly showing the Brandos the set work she was doing for Jay Tarses. She pointed me out one night while watching *"Slap,"* all the more reason that Marlon wanted to meet me. Brando harbored a strong, perhaps rightful distrust of "actors".

So, yes, one day, I was told it was finally time. After one of her work days, Avra came back home and then brought me up to the house, to "officially" meet Marlon. By then, I somehow felt that I was less nervous over the meeting than Avra. I had resigned myself to the whole thing, and after a few years of acting on TV and now knowing Greg quite well, I had become much more at ease with the known and the famous - Still, yes, this was Marlon Brando.

Going into the house, I got the same chilled vibe I received back when I had first gone in a few times before, as mentioned, back when Marlon was out of town on a film shoot and Avra was taking care of the place. This was still the era of the Drollet murder; I swear you could feel it in the atmosphere. Along with that, I knew that Marlon was still dealing with so many residual aspects of it - *huge* matters, such as the incarceration of his son and the mental health of his daughter. And that's where Marlon's need and love regarding Avra was so extreme at that time. After the death of her boyfriend at the hands of her brother - at close range, right in front of her, in her father's house - Cheyenne became mentally unstable, famously so. This was after a previous car accident that had already brought mental challenges to Cheyenne. She loved Avra and seemed able to communicate with her, in a way that she could not with her siblings or with Marlon. At the time, there were so many therapies and doctors that Cheyenne was dealing with, and all of the details, transportation and father-to-daughter communication fell to Avra.

As for the house itself, when Marlon first designed his Mulholland estate - and yes, he did design it, by expanding a small set of rooms into a sprawling multitude of unique spaces, he went out of his way to make it unlike almost any other home you might see. The house was on a series of hills - You'd drive up the hill of Mulholland to get there, you'd then drive up the hill of the driveway he shared with Jack Nicholson to get closer still. Left to Marlon's, right to Jack's.

You'd then go through Marlon's gates and then drive up yet another hill to the parking lot, where an old sign said something about staying in your car and honking your horn for assistance; Obey that sign or dogs will attack and eat you. And then, once you ignored that sign, because you'd soon learn that nobody was going to assist, attack or eat you, you'd get out of your car and walk up a hill of old railroad ties: the steps up to Marlon's house. You'd pass the giant windows of that library of a den (the murder den) as you walked a deck around to a kitchen entrance. A funky half-log of a dining table near a not-so-clean aquarium was lined by one of the largest pieces of window glass you've ever seen.

Marlon liked to brag that the dining area glass pane (lacking "official" support beams and safety guided size and weight limits) was completely illegal; it broke every building-code rule known to man, and if L.A. City Planning-type authorities ever learned of it, he'd go to Architecture Prison for the rest of his life. Seriously. He was *"The Wild One"* even about his kitchen window. And at night, all those aforementioned hills paid off. He had one of those few, very cool lots where one side of the property looked down onto the lights of Hollywood - The other side of the house gave you the lights of the San Fernando Valley - Both regions in equal measure, both looking far more beautiful, sexy and glamorous by night-twinkle than they could ever look down at street level.

Once in the house on the day that I met Marlon, Avra and I were trying to get comfortable in the living room during a bit of a wait. After a fair number of minutes went by, in came Marlon in his underwear and a robe. We shook hands as he muttered with a smile, "There he is. Finally."

We all sat. Still smiling, he stared for a bit, studying me. Leaning back, he asked, "So, why did this take so long?" Somehow hearing a prompt from my mother, I said, "Well, I didn't wanna bother you." He squinted. Suddenly becoming the shrink that I knew he was, Marlon intoned in his low, quiet voice, "That is a very odd thing to say. Interesting." That made all three of us laugh. He broke more of the undeniable tension with, "We had to meet. This had to happen. Nobody is more dear to me than Avra, and here you are, lucky enough to live with her." Avra giggled, "That's not always so 'lucky' for him. Oh, Marlon, do you remember Joe on the TV? *'Slap Maxwell'?"* After she reminded Marlon, he laughed and asked the name of "that funny guy with the mustache" who played my father.

I said, "Dabney Coleman."

"Oh, yeah, that's it. Yeah, he's funny, that guy. Avra says you went to Juilliard? And she says you sold a script to a studio?'

"With my writing partner - Tony."

Avra added, "Tony and Joe went to Juilliard together. I told you, Tony's father is Gregory Peck."

Pause. Marlon thought for a beat. He then smiled oddly, sarcastically muttering *"Gregory Peck."*

Within this weird moment, I could only think to say, "He's a very nice guy."

Another odd beat. Suddenly quite serious, Marlon asked, "What's he doing these days?"

By then, on that date, thanks to the validation via the script at Fox, I told Marlon that Greg had already hired Tony and me for a project that Greg would produce and star in. I mentioned bits of the *"Doctor DeMott"* script as Marlon then interrupted, blurting out, "I write scripts too." I nodded, with the quick, clumsy response, "Oh, yeah, I can imagine."

Since that came out a tad wrong, I sorta tried to recover with, "I'd love to read your scripts."

Without the slightest pause, Marlon said, "Avra, get a few of them together - Have Joe here give 'em a gander." I blinked. That seemed somewhat strange. Matter of fact. Perhaps not the first time that someone passing through this house was suddenly handed a stack of old scripts? After an odd pause, he added, "Well, actually, I've written all the parts I've done."

Knowing his films well, I didn't want to throw Tennessee Williams or William Shakespeare in his face at that moment, but I certainly knew of his improvisations all throughout *"Last Tango in Paris"* - I brought that up, with Marlon greeting my praise with both a happy nod and a flinch at the same moment - the flinch hitting me with a very sharp inner-rap to the head: "Here I am, just meeting Brando and we're already talking about his films?! It wasn't supposed to go like this!"

I changed the subject, recalling that he spent many years of his youth in Minnesota. We talked about the Midwest for a bit. After a while, Marlon soon felt I was far more farm boy than Hollywood shark - a perception that was the absolute truth. Yes, I knew a lot about films and television, but he could see that I was still the wide-eyed hick who was trying to figure out the industry. I think he liked the fact that I had extreme knowledge of his work *while* still clearly being skeptical about the business - perhaps even illustrated by my obvious want to *not* meet him.

About four hours later, we said "Good-bye" with a laugh and even a hug. He said we should write together and that "Now" I was "a member of the gang up here." It was all quite sweet, but I also knew that much of this was about how much he loved and needed Avra; he was taking up so much of her time - She lived with a guy he had not yet met, cleared or vetted - until tonight. I guess I passed the test. For now. On the drive home, Avra and I discussed both how well this went and how we needed to be cautious moving forward. Marlon can take your life over.

Steering my Hyundai up Wilshire, I said, "He's pretty charming when he wants to be. But now when he wants all of your time, you won't be able to pin your need to exit on some faceless boyfriend he's never met." She sighed, "Yeah, I know. But he really did like you." As I was driving, I looked at the stack of scripts in her lap; a pile of non-produced stories she grabbed from the office on our way out, all those odd screenplays I mentioned here a few pages back. Avra added, "Be careful with this writing stuff - He'll wanna do it all day. But you can say 'no'." I asked, "Really? How?" Silence. Avra pondered, "I don't know." I thought as I drove on - The evening was good but undeniably different. I spent years avoiding him. Now I knew Marlon - the actor that other actors love to talk about. I was about to get proof of that yet again.

Days later, I was doing a week as a guest lead on NBC's *"L.A. Law"*. Robert Duncan McNeill and I played brothers in a courtroom donnybrook, where I was represented by Blair Underwood. It was a busy set with many actors and extras, and yes, as it was that night with Dabney Coleman and Ed O'Neill years back, two actors on set loudly discussed "Brando".

I kept my mouth shut, thinking, "Wow, can actors *ever* gather without mentioning his name?"

Platinum What? (1991)

It took quite a few weeks to learn how to write with Marlon. Once we agreed that we were going to make scripts together, after I looked through his stack of "work" - scripts he said he had written - not co-*written* - but written - I started to calculate how I was going to do this. In this pre-internet era, I set out to do some Writers Guild research on these scripts and Marlon's way of "writing". Avra had some information, but I found many more answers at the WGA library, even running across magazine articles and book passages about Marlon I had read before.

Of course, now these articles and book chapters had new meaning to me. Trade publications and biographies that wrote of his screenplay-related tantrums and difficult behavior; it was abstract to me until now. *Now* - it was something I was going to deal with, in a close and personal arena.

In the WGA library, I kept thinking of a phone call he gave me right after I met him - He said, "Let's write scripts together." Of course, as I've been saying here: I knew one thing and one thing only at that time: I had no idea of how this was supposed to work, this "writing scripts" with Marlon Brando thing. But having already sold scripts with Tony, I did know how certain aspects of the business worked, even though I was still learning how "The Business" worked when it came to working alongside Brando. Honestly, even though I knew that some within The Industry saw Marlon as a troublemaker, I thought there would be no shortage of people who would drop everything and run to work with him, especially as the world might be recognizing that, time-wise, he probably only had a few projects left to do. I saw that syndrome from a distance with Olivier years before; even Greg said he only took *"The Boys from Brazil"* to work alongside Olivier. At this time, I thought this is where the film world was with Marlon Brando.

But of course, coming from Juilliard Theatre and frequently working as an actor, I soon realized what a warped view I had of this, especially when it came to ultra-revered artists like Olivier and Brando. While Oliver (in his final years) seemed to be doing whatever role came attached to a million dollar check (witness *"The Betsy"* and *"Inchon"*), financial people working the money end of filmmaking in the 80's and 90's were beginning to see Brando as a costly gamble, a situation that first haunted Marlon through the 1960's up until *"The Godfather"* in the early 70's. But still, as I began to work with Marlon in the early 1990's, I thought every actor was still seeing something else. I assumed all performers, even big name stars, saw a legend they wanted to work with. But that doesn't always get a film made. And it's easy to forget that actors - and yes, even stars - are often the *last* to be hired for a film, long after writers, directors, and, of course, The Money People have perhaps spent years putting a costly motion picture together.

Actually, almost everyone who worked in film at any level and in any job at that time; they all *wanted* to work with Brando. But if there was no clear sign that Marlon (or his name on a poster) would be directly responsible for putting paying asses in movie theater seats, well, Marlon was then only a possible-tantrum-throwing-and-delay-inducing problem; a liability The Money People did not care to get involved with.

But when he and I started writing our first original script together, *"Platinum Toenail,"* I was excited for two reasons. Reason One: he wanted to write this (from a story he had come up with) as a spy vehicle for himself, Robert De Niro and Tom Cruise. "Wow," I thought. He had yet to work with De Niro at that point, and in my mind, how could Tom Cruise *not* want to work with Marlon? Reason Two: I had yet to work with Marlon at this point, so I had no indicator as to how the "writing" would work, or what the reception would be once we had a script. In short: I was excited because I was still completely naive regarding absolutely everything involved.

In true Marlon fashion (combined with pure Brando fantasy), the title of *"Platinum Toenail"* referred to a secret set of plans, maps, blueprints and formula charts, all needed for the spy story's ultimate solution, all put on a tiny platinum micro-micro-microchip that would be hidden - you might've guessed by now - under somebody's toenail. Story-wise, Marlon didn't have a lot more than that microchip and that amazing potential cast. As we began, I learned how he liked to work: as I spoke of a few pages back, the two of us would have long, marathon conversations about the story, it would all be recorded on tape, professionally transcribed later, and I would then take the transcripts and try to shape the ideas and improvised lines into a screenplay. Not fully the worst way to work, but it all seemed to come with an unworkable catch: he never liked any of the scripts that came out of this process.

Mind you, I wasn't foolish about how to work this way; I felt I really did know the difference between his good ideas and his lousy ones. I knew when an improvisation from a transcript was solid or throwaway. I knew how to shape a scene, arrange the ideas and give him back all the best "Marlon" stuff from our conversations. In short: when writing various projects with Marlon through the years, I never reached "The End" without feeling that it was a workable screenplay. Of course, it's easy to lose sight of all this when you work with someone like Marlon.

Hell, maybe I was merely thrilled when I knew we finally had enough pages together that looked like a script. Kinda like the old "Dancing Bear" notion; you don't marvel over how *well* the bear danced; you marvel over the fact that he danced at all.

Going back a beat or two here - Yeah, it was always hard to "finish" with Marlon; he liked to keep "working" on a script, never satisfied. In what ways was he dissatisfied with our co-written screenplays? For starters, he always wanted to start over from page one on any given day. He'd wake up with new ideas; sometimes those new ideas came to him by staring at the wall for a few hours, sometimes they'd come from something he saw on TV last night. Often, most infuriating, he'd look at dialogue *he* had written (spoken in a taped improv), only to gripe, "Nobody talks like this! Nobody!" Whatever the case, the frustrations or the set of problems, we did get screenplays completed, and even without his full approval, I would occasionally go out into the industry with some of those screenplays to test the waters, to see if people might have interest in making a film with Marlon. I did just that with the best draft we had of *"Platinum Toenail"*.

Talking with producers who knew both De Niro and Cruise, I'll never forget the education I received regarding "New Hollywood" - a Hollywood that was now more calculated, disciplined and perhaps more realistic than previous generations. Take the messy "Star Tantrum" era of Marlon's *"Mutiny on the Bounty,"* fast-forward up through the "Spoiled Director" years ending with *"Heaven's Gate"* - What followed and unfolded out of that was a business that really *was* a business: actors and directors knew they were replaceable, studios needed major outside partners to finance projects, and actors like De Niro and Cruise knew that they themselves had become a combination of producer, megacompany and perhaps in distant third place, performing product.

This was all a long way to say that *"Platinum Toenail"* was only going to be offered to those two superstars if it was an "In Place" project (at a studio) with a good director, a solid producer and a deal on paper. Based on fact or not, I was often told that Cruise and De Niro were well-past being excited about "Brando" and signing onto any unattached script. As one producer told me, "Tom and Bob don't wanna see their names in the trades, (film industry newspapers) looking like starry-eyed kids who hopped onto Brando's latest pipe dream. They're way too big for that."

When I tried the whole thing from the other angle, talking to an agent who was an ace at packaging studio projects, his thoughts were just as cryptic, telling me, "Yeah, I see Marlon's name on the script, but come back to me when you really do have De Niro and Cruise on board."

The agent then said something I already knew, "Hey, you wanna make this fast and cheap; that can happen - If Marlon takes a pay cut and will do this with guys like (Ralph) Macchio and (Steven) Seagal instead of Tommy and Bobby; fuck, I'll talk to (Yoram) Globus or (Ovidio) Assonitis at Cannon and *that* will be a signed deal by noon." Quick education for you who might not know, this was 80's and 90's shorthand for making a fast, inexpensive film; one of, say, a highly questionable caliber. That kind of thinking always scared me when I was out trying to line up projects with and for Marlon: I never wanted him to think I was out there lowering his stature. Not that he would go through with such a film, but with enough talk in those circles, career damage can be done, especially when dealing with a character as unpredictable as Marlon.

Of course, reading this, you probably have a simple question: "Why not have Marlon call Cruise and De Niro?" Good idea. One key problem: Marlon would never sign off on the script; he always wanted to keep writing. Oddly, it's not as though I was finding out that industry people didn't like *"Platinum Toenail"* - I suspect few even bothered to read it. No, it was the "deal" I thought I could "easily" move forward for Marlon - "easily" because, hell, he was Brando!

I pictured a fantasy day where I could tell him that I "stumbled" onto interest for the project, an advance check for him; the whole bag of great news! He knew I actually *did* work within the industry and really did know some of the right people. Years later, all of this actually did happen with a project I wrote with Tony; a project that really did get made and really did star Marlon.

But with *"Platinum Toenail"* I learned quite a few lessons - lessons about how projects can be hatched as too big from the start. I learned about hypothetical deals that require far more resources at inception - even if you really do have a legendary "draw" firmly in your corner. I also learned things about an industry that no longer played star-driven games with studio money. And most of all, I learned many lessons about how to write screenplays with and for Marlon Brando.

At around this time, as Tony and I were still doing drafts of *"Doctor DeMott,"* Greg was busy with a couple other projects: playing the stoic, noble copper-cable manufacturer in Norman Jewison's version of the hit play, *"Other People's Money,"* and before that, playing the attorney to Robert De Niro's evil Max Cady in the remake of *"Cape Fear".* It was perhaps a bit too cute as Greg played the lawyer for the character who was his nemesis in the original version, just as the original Max Cady, Robert Mitchum, was now playing the lawyer for Greg's 1962 character, Sam Bowden, being played in this new version by Nick Nolte. And as if a cherry on the cake was needed, the Police Chief from the original, Martin Balsam, presided as courtroom judge in 1991.

When I told Marlon of the *"Cape Fear"* cast and remake, he shook his head, along with, "God! Re-heating old shit! With the same actors? How about something original for a change?"

He answered his own rant of a question with, "I'll tell you what's original: *'Platinum Toenail'!"*

And with that, he sat back into the sofa, adding, "The title alone is gonna knock their socks off."

Water (1991)

One day, after years of knowing Marlon, I saw him hanging up the phone as I was entering his den. When it felt right at a moment like this, I'd have no problem asking, "Who was that?" When I sensed it was family or business, I'd never ask, but at times - as it was with this call - I'd feel compelled. Even though I heard next-to-none of the call, I could tell that this was not a fully "casual" call for Marlon; he had just put on the charm and the smile with that call, as well as a louder, clearer voice. I wondered to myself, "Who the hell was he just talking to?" Ever the mind-reader, he looked at me, asking, "You wanna know who that was, don't ya?" I shook my head, "No." Some silence. Marlon then muttered, "'Nice guy." More silence. I could only laugh, "Who was it?" As he turned up the television, he muttered, "Paul Newman." This was one of those odd "Marlon" conversations where he wanted you to ask more. By now, I knew what to say to get more information, knowing that Marlon would often respond better to statements rather than questions. I said, "Nice of him to call." Silence, then, "No, I called him." More silence. Then, Marlon sighed, "Time to sell stuff; get out of pictures. It's time to stop working."

Throughout the years, Marlon was constantly convinced that he had to finally go through with one or all of the plans that he had been formulating; plans that would make him rich and he could then stop working job-to-job in motion pictures.

Back to that talk in the den: it was all clear to me after Marlon's mention of "stop working," because this was not the first time he had conversations with Newman about Star Marketing. Avra would tell me later that there had been other such phone calls. And I knew what those calls were really about. Marlon always wanted to make a successful business outside of anything to do with filmmaking. He had many ideas for gadgets, musical instruments, educational videos and more, all attempts to market his name and fame into profitable products. Occasionally, he'd talk to those who - he assumed - had accomplished what he was setting out to do. Seeing many products with Paul Newman's face on them, Marlon always figured that Paul was raking it in, even as Marlon was constantly told, especially by Paul Newman himself, that the attraction of the Newman product line was the very thing that Marlon wasn't interested in: "Newman's Own" was and still is today, an entirely non-profit organization; all of the money goes to charity.

While some might wonder why Marlon couldn't think more like charitable Paul Newman, Marlon had his own reasons for wanting to profit off of his world famous name. It's no secret that Marlon was an incredibly generous man; if he had money to give away to those who needed it, he'd give it away. Very much in line with that, he was not at all good with the sheer "numbers" of money, always thinking he had more than he did. He loved the actual exercise of "acting" but he hated the machinery of "the business" - Not an uncommon set of attitudes in Hollywood. As he supported nearly a dozen family members from L.A. to Tahiti, Marlon was always finding out too late that it was time to make another film, to fund the many costly aspects of Brando-World.

One example of this want to "merchandise" came in 1991, after I had only known Marlon for a relatively short time. One day, Avra came home from work with a new assignment from Marlon; a new "product" based money-making possibility. After having heard about a few of the less plausible notions ("Brando's Paint-Ball Emporium" or perhaps my favorite: getting everyone in China to simply give him a nickel), Avra told me about something that actually made an interesting bit of sense. Marlon's new idea: "Tahiti Rain," a bottled water that Marlon titled, at a time when the American "bottled water" market was growing every day. He also had a slogan to go along with the name: "If This Isn't The Best Water On Earth, We're On The Wrong Planet."

I recall telling Avra that she'd need to explain more to me as we went over to Cheryl's and Tony's — They were going on a vacation and Cheryl had asked me to house-sit in their absence, at her house on Flicker Way, the Hollywood Hills home where I spent most days writing with Tony. When we got over to the house, Avra showed me some Polaroid photos of Marlon wearing a straw beach hat. These were photos she had taken earlier in the day in Marlon's den. I laughed at Marlon with a big grin on his face. She said, "He was super mad when that one was shot."

When I asked why, she just shrugged, muttering, "Marlon."

I asked, "What are these photos for?" She sighed, "He wants me to make labels for the water bottles, with his face on them." Avra was very artistic, but this was the kind of thing I was born to do; I love putting together marketing art, logos and mock-ups that look like real products. Before computer art, I had become quite good with rub-on letter transfers, Zip A Tone shading graphic screens, colored cut paper, sheets of double-stick adhesive, Xerox paste-ups, and ultimately, running layers of colored cut paper through a full color Xerox process, spending a great deal of time (and money) at the Westwood art stores and copy centers.

If you're at a younger age where all those arcane art methods make no sense to you, don't worry - Just know this: the result: people would look at my final color Xerox work and ask, "How did you do this?" Not wanting to be presumptuous, I asked Avra if I could kidnap this project from her and turn it around overnight. She tiredly agreed as I set up an art shop in Cheryl's giant basement screening room. My goal for Avra: tomorrow, she would walk into Marlon's home with six actual bottles of water that had six different professional-looking real color labels on them - Labels with Marlon grinning, presenting "Tahiti Rain".

Oh, as my mind is now taking me into a very familiar house, please allow me a quick side note regarding the owner of the place. She's someone who was always incredibly good to me, and man, did she know how to successfully merchandise and put her name on quite a few products.

I'm first going back in time here for a spell, to the 1970's. Long before the mess of 90's reality television, pop culture was trying to find its way when it came to bridging the gap between the many different types of "Famous". When I was young, a few known fashion models were starting to become film actresses, pro football players were becoming movie stars and the cross between newscasters, politicians and pundits was already starting to get confusing. A key media moment for me was when I saw a relatively young show called *"Good Morning America"* - ABC's knock-off of NBC's *"Today Show"* - do something that I thought was daring, interesting and even odd: they brought on a stunning woman known only to much of the general public by way of a bikini poster, and they let her talk. Not as in they "interviewed" her. No. They let her talk as though she was some sort of broadcaster.

She was beautiful and she was verbally good on camera - beyond "good" - she lit the screen up when she laughed and smiled.

Many years later, a good friend of Tony's, model Janice Dickinson, would tell me that she herself was "The World's First Supermodel". As acclaimed and as beautiful as Janice was when she told me that, I smiled as I was (somewhat) laughing inside, knowing that what she just said wasn't remotely true, at least to me anyway. I felt that because I recall being there as a young man, watching ABC's *"Good Morning America"* that previously mentioned morning, seeing that stunning Cheryl Tiegs wasn't JUST the world's first supermodel, she was also the world's first "spokesmodel," essentially inventing that role herself. You could actually feel pop culture change in that moment. In fact, years later, in 1983, when the Ed McMahon *"Star Search"* series debuted and became instantly popular, I recall early episodes where McMahon would introduce the "spokesmodel" category with a somewhat clumsy, "Spokesmodel, like Cheryl Tiegs" - Yeah, *now* you knew what the category was; Cheryl was the absolute originator of all that.

It goes without saying that when Tony and Cheryl got married one weekend at Frank Sinatra's Palm Springs compound (after a long and quite famous courtship), she was a beautiful addition to the Peck family. Cheryl and the Pecks knew so many of the same people, the same places and the same rules when it came to the etiquette, the nature and the flat-out difficulties of fame. Of course, it was also another set of pressures that Tony was required to deal with; not only was he the son of an iconic legend; he was now the husband of someone who (you could make the case) was at the time as famous as Greg in *her* very different field of fashion-mixed-with-marketing-mixed-with-celebrity. The added challenge for Tony: he himself was something of a famous "rascal" at that time; handsome, party-loving and fun, just as both his wife and his father were seen around the world as figures of discipline and order: Dad was "Atticus Finch," his wife was Ms. "Sears & Roebuck". At times, Tony would joke that his life might be easier if he was married to then party-girl Bianca Jagger and his father was Rat Pack Boss Frank Sinatra.

Built by actress Jane Seymour and her then husband, David Flynn, Cheryl's beautiful house on Flicker Way is where Tony and I did much of our best writing work. When Tony and Cheryl would be out of town for any sustained period of time, she'd ask Avra and me to look after the place and to use the house as needed. That evening creating Marlon's water bottle labels was memorable because I always turned any art project into a sprawling mess. With this endeavor, there was so much drawing and cutting and pasting - Before computer art, your art mess was really only as contained as it related to the number of flat surfaces you had available. In short: A small art project on a small table: maybe workable. A small art project on a big table: much better. A big art project on a - well, you get the idea. In her screening room basement, Cheryl had an absolutely epic horseshoe-shaped bar. It was perfect for this giant, multi-layered project.

By morning, after being up all night, I was double-sticking the color Xerox labels on real water bottles. And there they were, a variety of pictures and colors revolving around different label samples featuring Marlon as the smiling logo-face in a beach hat. They looked store-worthy, and I was eager to have Avra get them to Marlon.

When Avra came back to the Tiegs estate that evening, after a day of showing Marlon the labeled water bottles, I pounced on her for a response, assured that they must have been a hit. With a tired shrug and a plop onto Cheryl's sofa, Avra tiredly sighed, "Oh, he really didn't have much to say." I was confused, asking, "Really?" She muttered, "He was excited about the idea yesterday; he was thinking about other stuff today." This was around the time when I was just starting to write screenplays with Marlon.

Yes, I knew of his wandering attention span, his ever-shifting interests and perhaps most challenging, the always possible chance that he could receive a three million dollar acting offer at any given time during any given week, thus taking his brain somewhere else entirely. But still, after a full night of exhaustive arts and crafts, I was really put off by this reception. And while I knew that he wasn't offering Avra any sort of "partnership" with the possibilities of this "bottled water" dream, I was at this moment concerned that I myself was putting too much time in lately with Marlon's scripts, ideas and yes, projects like these labels. By then, I had read books and magazine articles about Marlon spinning the wheels of others, of being a "time waster," and as one writer put it, a "Professional Let-Down Artist". Look, it's not as though I was searching for a grand payday from Marlon in any way. But as a young freelancer in Hollywood, during perhaps my most valuable earning years in a youth-obsessed business, I didn't want to simply be an unpaid senior caregiver with a very interesting client. And even though she was on Marlon's payroll, I didn't want that for someone as creative and vibrant as Avra either. You dream of getting to be creative with those who inspired you to be creative before you ever got to Hollywood. I loved that Marlon also thought of selling bottled water, conga drums, acting tapes and any number of projects that I'd help him with or watch him pursue, but if absolutely everything was a dead end - either by way of his own self-sabotage or rapid lack of interest, well, I wasn't sure just how much "Marlon" I could put in for.

A week later, when I guess he came to life on the water project for a moment, Avra told me that the bottles were shown to some representative from Poland Spring - an offer was made, Marlon found the offer to be lousy, and that was the end of that. I wasn't shocked, least of all by the fact that a major company would respond when they got a random call from Marlon Brando.

As I made clear, I really did like the way the labeled water bottles turned out - and it's not as though I always fall in love with all or any of my art projects. And I believe their pro "look" was helpful regarding the Poland Spring offer. With an extra bottle and an extra label I had leftover that morning after I made the sample bottles for Avra, I put together one for myself as well; it was my souvenir of the adventure. When Tony and Cheryl returned from vacation, I recall showing them that water bottle of "Marlon Brando's 'Tahiti Rain'". Marketing Diva Extraordinaire Cheryl lit up with her beautiful smile, exclaiming, "Oh my God! Wow! Is Marlon selling water now? What a great idea!" I told her, "He got an offer from Poland Spring, but he passed on it."

Cheryl gasped, "He could make a fortune! Is he *crazy?!*" Hearing her own question ring in the air, just as she instantly recalled previous wacky Marlon stories I had told her, Cheryl could only answer herself, with that distinctive Tiegs laugh. "Oh, yeah. 'Crazy'. Right."

And please allow me this footnote: for years, Cheryl was a kind, generous and beautiful presence in my life; she continued to be even after she and Tony ended their marriage. As I'm writing here of Tony and "marriage," I'd be remiss if I didn't mention that Tony went on to remarry, finding a true saint and goddess of a woman, Paula Rice. Tony Peck - Man, this guy sure can pick 'em.

PRIVATE - THE REAGAN LIBRARY (1991)

It might seem odd to say, but it was often clear that Greg was much more of a private man than Marlon in later years. Not necessarily more reclusive, but certainly more private. I'd gauge this often only because I found it to be somewhat surprising. When this thought first hit me, I knew I had a skewed view of the situation, simply because Marlon was a single loner who often would call me and say, "Come up to the house today - We'll shoot the shit." This was not the behavior of Greg; not with many or any, and certainly not with me. But over the years, it was clear that even with his family, Greg spent a great deal of time alone, but always with a purpose.

He was a reader, a thinker and an avid news watcher; politics were on his mind most of his life, and his later years were no exception. He kept himself in amazing shape, even beyond "for a man of his age". He often worked with a fitness trainer and frequently just got down on the floor when in casual conversation, to either work his back out or do a few sit-ups. He also had a great greenhouse on the Carolwood property, where he'd garden, ponder and find peace with his own thoughts. Yes, it's not hard to think of a satisfied Greg in that holistic, natural atmosphere.

While it might seem humorous to mention "fitness" regarding the later years of Marlon, perhaps sadly, it was something that was always on his mind. Frankly, his thought process was that of many of us: "I'll get to it tomorrow, and once I commit to it, I'll get back to that look and weight that will amaze everybody." He had a lifetime of fluctuating weight, and when he was younger, it seemed he was always able to get himself back to the movie star look he was famous for. And even after he had long-crossed the physical threshold of "slim boy" to "sturdy man" (if you know his films, think *"The Men"* (1950) to 1968's *"Night of the Following Day"*), for decades, he still found ways to come off as the handsome star that he was. But that was all a few years ago. Now, at this stage of life, perhaps there was no turning back, no matter how many costume tricks, lighting set-ups or camera angles a film shoot might be able to come up with.

Up at his Mulholland house, he'd invent different diets and weight loss methods, often wanting to believe that just the right mindset could address his weight issue. But he also thought about physical exercise as well. He invented a set of weights that he would take into his swimming pool, convinced at one time that weightlifting while swimming could be key to getting his appearance back to where he wanted it to be. I first discovered the weights as I jumped into the pool, hit one of them and asked, "What the hell? What is this?" With a very serious voice, he answered, "That, my boy, is the future." That meant that he saw those weights as yet another one of his "Get Rich" schemes; a product that could be marketed to the masses.

So while one-on-one days with Marlon were more common than those with Greg, I did have fascinating one-on-one experiences with Gregory as well. As the years went on, Tony was generous enough to convince all of the Pecks that I was indeed something of an extended family member. This was on display on a chilly L.A. morning in November of 1991, when Greg, Tony and I met down in the casual Carolwood "basement" living room, to go over one of the latest drafts of *"Doctor DeMott,"* a draft that we were about to send off to Scorsese. This living space at Carolwood seemed rarely used, but like all of the estate, it was originally retro in the coolest of ways, and of course, immaculately kept.

Greg was in his comfortable work-out clothes; his shorts, sweatshirt and some golf-cap style hat he got from the admiral of an aircraft carrier. Tony didn't have a lot of time that morning; his son, Zackary had been born a month earlier; it was time for the baby's 30-day check up. As soon as we went through the script, Tony was leaving to join Cheryl, to take Zack for his check-up.

Thinking I was leaving with Tony, I started up the stairs, just as Greg said, "Oh! Joe! You will *not* want to miss this travesty!" Running late, confused and a touch frazzled as he checked his watch, new-father Tony said to me, "Uh, I don't know what he's talking about, but I gotta go." Tony disappeared. After hearing that excitement from Greg, I didn't think I could just vanish as well. I looked down the stairs, around to the main room, seeing that Greg had turned on the television. It seemed that all three of the major television networks were now live-airing the ceremony commemorating the opening of The Ronald Reagan Presidential Library.

Greg and I often talked politics, and he knew that he and I shared many of the same interests, biases and flat-out infuriation over the same politicians, issues and ideas. He clapped his hands together, laughing in that distinctive voice, "Have a seat! *Oh!* This is gonna be good!"

Marlon also loved talking politics, but it never took long for Brando to go down into a dark, international place when it came to the topic. A conversation about local California problems would quickly move into the areas of world hunger, mass exterminations and man's overall inhumanity to man. At times, I felt that Marlon avoided the then current politics of the 90's, often seeing news reports as anger-inciting game shows; programs to make a buck that were disguised as news. He knew his own rage level, and on some days, he'd do what he could to avoid anger.

He also had a lifetime of getting emotionally involved with politics, to the point of personal pain. Of course, as this book contains in another chapter, there were times when a news report could still get him into trouble; he'd see something, get mad, call Larry King, end up on CNN a couple hours later, and as it sometimes was back in his younger days, the end result of the public tirade was not always good for Marlon.

Unlike Marlon, Greg knew how to keep his political rage dignified and productive in public, just as that same rage was almost hilariously out of hand in private. I say "hilarious" because Greg was incredibly self-aware and he loved to laugh. He also knew that a raging, swearing, out-of-hand "Gregory Peck" voice mocking every word of Ronald Reagan's was enough to literally make me cry tears of laughter. That morning of the Reagan Library opening, I sat there as Greg got down on the floor and did a few leg-lifts, along with some back exercises and half-sit-ups, all the while, swearing a blue streak about Reagan, George Bush and most of all, Richard Nixon, all up on the TV podium after Charlton Heston's opening of the "show".

To get all that commented on from Greg was a blast. Every now and then, he'd get up off the floor and pick up the phone, calling upstairs to Veronique, who usually watched TV in a stylish, floral-lined den the family jokingly yet lovingly called "The Casbah." He did this a few times throughout the broadcast, and it was those calls that often reminded me of something that hit me as totally profound as I sat there: "Good God, not only does he know all these epic people, in many instances, one could easily make the case - he's actually *'bigger'* than they are!"

He'd ask Veronique, "How do you think she looks? I think she looks good. Poor Lady Bird, having to sit through this garbage." Yes, it hit me: Greg and Veronique were good friends with Lyndon Johnson. Years after Johnson, Greg literally changed the shape of the Supreme Court with his anti-Robert Bork campaign. Greg was a giant film star when Reagan was a D-grade actor. On and on, so much history, as I looked at the TV; it was hitting me in every way, just how much Greg had been a part of the American fabric; his politics, his marches for civil rights, along with Martin Luther King; marches he did with Marlon *and* now-conservative Charlton Heston.

In fact, getting lost in all those politics made me think of the only correspondence I knew of between Greg and Marlon; it was in one of the files of Marlon's storage spaces: telegrams between the two, asking one another to bring who they could to the next Civil Rights march in the 60's. They both knew how much influence the other had over certain actors, and white famous faces helped back when the marches were first being televised. The telegrams (between Greg and Marlon) suggested that Marlon contact Paul Newman, that Greg contact Tony Quinn - on and on. Yes, in their younger days, Greg and Marlon had so much in common.

Watching this on TV with Greg, I was also thinking of how Reagan would *never* have gone into politics if he had achieved the stardom of a Gregory Peck. Back when Greg and then Reagan wife Jane Wyman were starring together in giant films such as *"The Yearling,"* Reagan was an unexceptional actor with none of the depth or talent of either Peck or Reagan's Oscar-winning wife. (By the way, his *second* wife could *also* act rings around him; check out Nancy's great performances next to Ronald's usual Squinting Canned Ham in either 1957's *"Hellcats of the Navy"* or better yet, a 1961 edition of *"Dick Powell's Zane Grey Theater,"* an episode that stars them both.) In short, it's not hard to see how a guy like Reagan saw that his limited abilities were better suited for sales or politics - two areas he first explored by way of being a product spokesman and Screen Actors Guild president. Yes, I obviously shared Greg's dislike and full skepticism of Ronald Reagan, a man I always thought of as ill-suited for the job of Leader of the Free World. But my view was from a distance; Greg's was lived.

As the televised ceremony went on, many things I had read years ago were coming back to me, perhaps explaining much of Greg's attitude regarding Reagan. Greg saw up close as Reagan shifted from a Democrat to a Republican. He watched as MCA, General Electric and agent-turned Universal Studios titan Lew Wasserman "created" the new "dignified spokesman" Reagan with a sweetheart deal via G.E. In return, as SAG President, Reagan allowed an agency like MCA to get into the studio-running game, something that was seen as illegal at the time. By the time that sort of thing was going to be investigated by then Attorney General Robert Kennedy (thus ending Reagan's cushy high-paying gig as a shill for General Electric), like Nixon, Reagan found his "true" conservative roots, primarily by way of petty Kennedy resentment and envy.

Being accused of having sold out SAG with the MCA deal (a deal that gave studios greater bargaining power over actors), Reagan became bitterly "Anti-Union," a stance that Big Business loved, as did the failed operatives who ran Barry Goldwater for president. Before long, those operatives drafted Reagan into Republican politics by way of the California governorship. Yeah, Greg saw all that from the front row, knowing all the shifting facades of Ronald Reagan. Back then, many tried to draft Greg into running for office; any office. He resisted, understanding the differences between politics, leadership and images. He also knew then what it took a few generations to figure out: Reagan, Schwarzenegger, Trump - it's the conservatives who are fully, shamelessly star struck, all while they bash the "Hollywood Liberals" and the "Coastal Elites".

Still crying with laughter as I listened to Greg comment on every aspect of the televised Presidential Library ceremony on that day, I was almost relieved when it was over; my stomach was actually hurting. Greg smiled as he saw me wipe the tears from my face. What started as "I can't let Greg see that I'm laughing *this hard* over what he's saying" turned into Greg trying to torture me with every uttered phrase. An example: when Gerald Ford nobly intoned, "To paraphrase General Douglas MacArthur: Old Presidents don't fade away" - it was quickly followed by Gregory Peck shouting, "Well, *you've* disproved *that*, Gerry!" With the long ceremony finally ending and the TV eventually off, Greg's smile went away. He was quickly lost in thought. He shook his head. "That clown Reagan; he's bad enough, but how in the world does anyone still invite a crook like Nixon to these things? Politicians. Absolutely Amazing." As a young boy, I recall reading about the pride Gregory Peck said he felt when he learned he had made Nixon's extended "Enemies List". I was also thinking of those back and forth telegrams between Greg and Marlon about the civil rights marches. They really did put a great deal on the line back when they were young, famous and filled with the want to make things better. Fan-base-wise, movie-studio-wise, it would've been far easier to just stay out of it all and let others speak and march. Yes, back then, Greg and Marlon were rich, handsome, fortunate white men, but I believe they were also quite aware of injustice, and they did what they could to help.

Greg walked me out to my car after the Reagan laugh-fest. That viewing was the only time I ever heard Greg use that level of profanity. He was now calming down in the driveway, but he was clearly growing pensive about what we had just watched. He said, "Mrs. Johnson, Rosalynn and President Carter - they looked horribly out of place there." It was only then that I realized: Carter was standing there at that ceremony with *four* Republican Presidents and their wives. I told him, "Wow. You're right. I was too busy laughing at you to even realize that." As I got into my car, Greg sighed, "Well, it's no laughing matter; our party is *due*."

One year later - actually, to the very day, Bill Clinton was elected President of the United States. As I watched TV on that day, seeing the young Clinton and Gore couples greet a crowd to the sounds of "Fleetwood Mac," I really did think back on that day the year before, crying tears of laughter as Greg did sit-ups on the floor, answering Ronald Reagan with, "You fucking liar!"

Today, I have a photo of the entire Peck family in the White House from 2012, all standing with President Barack Obama. Of course, Greg's not there; he passed away before Obama was elected. The family was there to celebrate the 50th anniversary of the film, *"To Kill a Mockingbird"*.

Greg would've loved Obama.

And he would've loved that photo, seeing his family standing there with *that* President - the embodiment of something even Atticus Finch probably could not have dared to dream.

FOURTH CHAPTER
AWARDS
(GREG & MARLON ESSAY IV)

Awards of any kind are a funny thing; given any amount of context, what do they mean?

How are matters judged? On and on, the questions are there, in any arena, competition and field. Even in something seemingly as ruled-structured as sports, someone will find a way to question the judges, the referees and even the very rules themselves. Of course, all that is nothing next to awards in purely artistic arenas. And when commerce, marketing and sentimentality are brought in - forget about it - It's easy to say that any award in "The Arts" can essentially be meaningless.

As we know, in Hollywood, artists, actors, crafts-people and musicians dream of the Oscar, and it goes without saying, both Greg and Marlon had complicated relationships with the award.

As I stated previously, in the first five years of his stardom, Greg was nominated four times for Best Actor. Losing the fourth time in 1950, he probably had to think that his day may never come, especially when he'd often see that award go to the star of that year's Best Picture - he watched that happen three times, but when HE was the star of a Best Picture, *"Gentleman's Agreement,"* he still couldn't land the statue. He wouldn't be nominated again for over a decade, until his *"To Kill a Mockingbird"* win in 1963, an Oscar that was supposed to be a lock to go to Peter O'Toole for that year's Best Picture, *"Lawrence of Arabia"*.

Marlon's first four nominations ended with a 1955 win for *"On the Waterfront,"* and he was actually thrilled to get it, showing up to accept it and giving press interviews about the win afterwards. A couple times, I heard him grumble about his earlier loss for *"A

Streetcar Named Desire," when he watched all his co-stars get Oscars along with Humphrey Bogart getting Best Actor - "When he should've gotten it for 'Casablanca'," Marlon told me. As much as Marlon liked the work of Bogart, he thought the "African Queen" award was a "Now or Never" prize; an award given to a legend who might not see many more nominations into the future. Marlon *did* want that "Streetcar" Oscar. He was a young actor who knew he was one of the key reasons - maybe *the* key reason - for the success of both the play and its film adaptation.

There's no doubt that Hollywood rates the "stock" of performers by way of Oscars, award nominations and, of course, the rate of how often and sustained those honors are, especially when it comes to big studio, mainstream filmmaking. Young Marlon and young Greg knew those statistics fully. In fact, as I've referred to that "Gap" between the "Golden Classics" of Bogart, Cagney and Tracy and the "Method Players": Brando, Clift and Dean - with Greg and his contemporaries falling in that "Gap," I sometimes think Greg felt baffled by the "arrival" of Brando, an arrival that happened to coincide with the end of Greg's early Oscar nominations.

Ironically, some probably saw Greg's 1963 "Mockingbird" nomination the same way some saw Bogart's "African Queen" nomination, wondering if he'd ever be back up to bat again. I say "ironically" because Greg's "Atticus Finch" win is now seen as perhaps the most perfect and deserved Oscar victory in Academy history, certifying the film as the classic it has become.

As time moved on, Marlon clearly became less enchanted with Oscar, as Greg grew closer, becoming President of the Academy, producing one of the telecasts and becoming one of the Grand Old Men of The Motion Picture Academy. Greg would get a second Oscar in 1968 - The Jean Hersholt Humanitarian Award. Acting-wise, Greg and the Pecks felt there was another "Best Actor" due to Greg, especially as history presented multiple winners such as Spencer Tracy, Katharine Hepburn, Jack Nicholson, Tom Hanks, Marlon Brando and others. Greg's roles in *"The Boys From Brazil,"* "MacArthur" and "Old Gringo" all had an "Oscar" aura to them, but the nominations didn't materialize. There was even a

"Supporting Actor" buzz for his role in *"Other People's Money"* - mostly due to the status of Greg - but again, that didn't happen.

This is not to say that Greg sat around and pined-away for that second acting Oscar. But as I was always reminded, both Marlon and Greg lived in that rare world. It was a world where the highest entertainment award on Earth was actually a real and constant rotating presence in their lives. Those are very special lives.

Perhaps hilariously and appropriately, while Greg's two Oscars (his "Atticus" award and the honorary award) are today in the safe hands of his children (Cecilia has the acting trophy, Tony has the honorary), Marlon's two awards continue to swirl in the worlds of rumor and mystery; even Leonardo DiCaprio got dragged into the mix in 2018, as the "Waterfront" Oscar was auctioned-off and then given to DiCaprio. I believe Leo had to hand it over to The Academy, where there's talk of displaying it in their new museum.

I laughed when I read about it all. Greg knew his Oscars would rightfully mean a great deal to his family and children. To Marlon: hunks of metal that can swirl in mystery - for all he cares.

As for what Marlon *really* cared about: well, for one thing: Tahiti. These next pages contain a South Seas tale that's both absolutely true and seemingly impossible at the exact same time.

Just like Marlon.

THE STORY RESUMES: SPY (1991)

Avra was almost always drained as she came home after a workday with Marlon up at his Mulholland home. As you'll recall, when she started as a full time assistant to Marlon, the Brando family was still dealing with the many tragedies that began with Christian Brando firing his gun in his father's house. Cheyenne's many therapies, Christian's trial, Marlon's financial troubles due to the whole nightmare - All day long, Avra was confronted with a string of related horribleness that stretched from Los Angeles to Tahiti. Shifting gears here, I've never been much of a dog person, but I bought Avra a happy little Boston Terrier to try and cheer her up; Avra named her "Billie" and the two of them became inseparable.

Avra would take little Billie up to Mulholland, always making sure to keep her apart from the two gigantic mastiffs, Frannie and Tim. I later bought Avra a companion for Billie, a small half-Boston, half-French bull Avra would name "Charlie". Marlon also loved our dogs when they were puppies, always insisting that his big dogs would never attack them; that's something we never allowed to be tested.

During this time, Marlon was not only depressed about all the trouble with his family, he was also quite frustrated by the fact that the complexity of the incident (the killing of Dag Drollet, whose father was a prominent Tahitian judge) was pretty-much keeping Marlon out of Tahiti. But, of course, Marlon's well-known love of Tahiti was also part of what challenged his financial situation; if he was on one of his islands, he wasn't doing the only thing he could do to make money: acting in films. And as many knew for years, Marlon loved being on those islands; they were places of beauty, of peace and of solitude. Marlon famously fell in love with the place when shooting *"Mutiny on the Bounty,"* later brokering a deal that gave him decades-long leases on a small string of tiny, picturesque islands. One day, Avra came home from work and said, "I made reservations for the pups at the Kennel Club (a luxury kennel) - We're going to Tahiti." I was confused yet intrigued. I asked, "We're going with Marlon? I thought he can't go there?" She explained, "He's not going; we are. He heard a guy is giving tours for profit of his islands without permission; he wants us to videotape it as tourists, so he can take the trespasser to court."

Silent Pause. I could feel it already - This was not going to be some sort of pleasurable vacation.

The next day in his TV den, Marlon showed me some video recently shot by two women he had already sent for this very same "spy mission" - video that he considered unusable, poorly thought out and a waste of his money. The women were friends of Marlon who had shot what I was watching; they made this video just a few weeks ago. I could see and hear that they were scared, unfamiliar with video cameras and worst of all, unwittingly set up to fail - by Marlon.

He had given them a "script" to follow; they were playing "tourists" - with fake names and all - trying to simultaneously video and essentially "frame" the Tahitian native who was indeed giving tours of a few of Marlon's uninhabited islands. The tall, muscular native "Tour Guide" seemed to speak no real English, the women *only* spoke English and they ineptly kept the camera (mostly) pointed in unfocused close-up on the sand, all as they tried to get this very intimidating-looking guy to confess that he was doing these profit-making excursions without Brando's permission. He "confessed" to nothing, occasionally seen grinning at these two scared, pretty Americans in bikinis, once the camera was finally aimed at his face. He then shrugged over their collective lack of translation and lit a cigarette, heading off camera to tend to his tour boat, along with the other "guests" he had brought to the island.

And the TV screen went black. The women had nervously shut off the camera.

"They blew it," sighed Marlon. He then went on to tell me why *my* excursion into this confession of a "trap" would work, in ways that would succeed where the two women had failed.

Marlon began with, "Sex, money and Carl Dodge from Quebec. You will be Carl Dodge."

"From Quebec?" I asked. Marlon nodded. He then went on to explain, "Like those girls, Avra will wear a revealing swimsuit; this will get him discombobulated to an extent. You'll keep the camera rolling as you introduce yourself as a tourism businessman from Canada, Carl Dodge. You're there to make a deal with him, along the lines of, 'Listen, I have dough to make a *real* tour business out of this - Look at you; you work alone, all by yourself. You only have the one boat. I can get you a fleet and a crew; we'll really take dumb old Brando for a ride. Whadda ya say? Fifty-fifty. Do we have a deal?' - And when he says 'yes,' you got him."

I smiled, hoping this was perhaps a joke.

Of course, it wasn't.

He went on, "Joe, you're an actor; this won't *just* be a piece of cake; it'll also be fun." I asked, "Does he speak English?" Marlon shrugged, "I think he understands well enough; he was playing dumb for those girls - I think he was on to them."

I continued to stare. My mind was spinning. I knew that the very costly plane tickets and hotel accommodations were already in order - Yes, I was immediately at that place: how do I get out of this? I'm supposed to "frame" an imposing muscular stranger who looked like a Tahitian knife fighter? On a desolate island? While simultaneously videotaping him *and* performing an insane "Tourism Businessman Carl Dodge" script written by Marlon Brando? And Marlon would know if I followed his script or not - It would all be on video.

Really? Really?! Really?!!!

By now, I knew how much Marlon adored cons, scams, games and even lies. He lived for "adventures" like this but was now at a place in life where he was too famous, old and heavy to get in on the action himself. So there he was, now writing, producing and directing it all from a distance. And he didn't accept people failing at this type of bizarre "mission" gracefully. He had been so lucky, charming and even somewhat devious all his life; his own "craftiness" had always been rewarded in different ways. He couldn't seem to understand how others could *not* pull off the same shenanigans that he recalled a younger Marlon effortlessly getting away with.

And of course, perhaps most "Marlon" of all, he was just putting all this ridiculousness together on his own. It's not as though one of his lawyers had said, "Marlon, you get me a tape of that guy saying he'll screw you, and we'll haul his ass into court." No. This was just Marlon cooking-up and envisioning his whole dream version of this from start to finish: from the frame-job, to the fantasy court case, to the imaginary punishment this "Tour Guide" would suffer once my brilliantly shot and perfectly performed tape would play to a packed and astonished courtroom. I could hear it now: "Ladies and Gentlemen of the jury, let the record show that Businessman Carl Dodge of Quebec is actually actor and videographer Joseph Brutsman." *("Gasp!")*

No, to be honest, I really wasn't thinking about any of that at all - I was only wondering how the hell I was gonna do anything close to what he wanted once I got to Tahiti.

Avra and I were already getting tense during the long plane ride over the Pacific.

Once there, I was angry that I wasn't allowed to just enjoy the most beautiful place on Earth. I was almost shocked to see that Tahiti really is as off-the-chart amazing as you think it will be. Marlon gave us instructions on where to find the guy who was boating tourists out to the Brando islands. I felt like Martin Sheen in *"Apocalypse Now,"* going up the river to get Kurtz. But in this version, Kurtz was the guy I was supposed to report back to after this impossible mission.

I could already hear Marlon after watching my failed video work: "The horror. The horror."

As we got on the boat for a multi-leg set of tours, I thought it was best to just keep the camcorder running all the time - I was already editing the "evidence" tape in my mind; if I couldn't get that clincher moment between the Tour Guide and Quebec businessman Carl Dodge, I could at least get B-roll to tell the story: Avra paying cash to the man for our boat ride, shots of the other tourists he was bringing out to the islands, shots of trash and garbage people had left on Marlon's islands, etc. But I knew these bits of logic would be lost on Marlon; he wanted that one moment on tape - the magic footage and performance that would show the devious deal being made between the Criminal Tour Guide and a fake corrupt Canadian tourism businessman.

Marlon had a number of small islands; our first stop was a tiny one called "Bird Island". As Avra and I shot video of trashed soda cups and thrown candy wrappers in the grasses, she made mention of wanting to look up friends while she was here: Marlon's ex-wife and her children. Realizing that I had forgotten all about them, I shut off the camera, angrily asking, "What the hell?! That's right! He has a whole family here! Why can't they do this for him?!"

"Because the tour guide knows who they are," she said.

I asked, "And this tour guide just *knows* that the Brando family is watching this every day, he knows that they don't like it? He knows that they're telling Marlon about it?"

"The Tour Guide, the Brandos here - they're all super laid-back, they all live here with each other; it's a tiny community, even the law here doesn't wanna to get involved since Marlon's not actually here. Look, Marlon sent us here - Let's just do this."

She was right. It was a Marlon Plan - it was a mistake to think there was real and legal logic attached to it.

Ugh, I was getting so uneasy about this, trying to figure out how to video the Tour Guide while I was talking with him. Avra and I talked about her shooting the video as I would then talk with the guide about financing tours behind Brando's back. After too much talk, we decided it would be better if I just held the camera and "left it on" as I talked with the guy. If I got any kind of picture, great, but the main thing for Marlon was to "hear" the Tour Guide agreeing to the continuation (and expansion) of doing tours on Brando's private property.

As the day went on, I never found a good time or place to talk with (and video) the Tour Guide. By nightfall, Avra and I were with a group of tourists on a small, beautiful mound of sand and trees called "Turtle Island," the place where we would all be spending the night; the video had to happen soon. I thought I should stay "in character" as I mingled with the small group of tourists on the island. As I introduced myself as "Carl Dodge from Quebec," I was shocked, stunned and horrified to meet a man and his wife - yes - born, raised and still living in Quebec.

We were all elbow-to-elbow around a campfire as this was going on, with the Tour Guide listening to all of this. As the Quebec couple asked about my whereabouts in Quebec, I copied their accent as I immediately realized how little I knew about Quebec. Trying to think as quickly as I could, I discussed my many "Tourism" offices around the world - New York, Madrid, Fiji, London, Paris, and yes, Quebec. As they asked more about me and Quebec, I launched into more "Big Shot" talk about branching-out my empire to include Tahiti. It was around this time that the Tour Guide stood and went over to his tied-up boat for a cigarette.

I looked at Avra, knowing this was now or never. Since we knew this video was going to be for our Audience of One, we knew we should stick to Marlon's script, complete with Avra walking up to the Tour Guide in a bikini.

I cradled the large, switched-on camcorder on my right arm, holding up the huge lens in the direction of the Tour Guide. Yes, I could feel the bright red "on" light glowing, I saw the erratic auto-focus lens flip and spin as it tried to find a clear picture - It was all getting me SO unnerved. Standing before the strapping, muscular Tour Guide, he looked more like a prize knife fighter than ever. As I sussed-out his English, I learned that this language issue was far worse than I thought - or in my paranoia, "Was this guy onto me?! I'm staying on a desolate island with this guy tonight?! Jesus Christ!" I told myself, "Think 'Juilliard'! Calm down! You *are* Carl, a confident, big shot tourism tycoon! You have this beautiful wife here in her bikini! You can do this *Carl!*"

After some smiling babble from both the Tour Guide and me, I made a conversational leap to the "money" aspect of all this, along with the mention of how people like to visit these small islands, often by way of their curiosity over Marlon Brando. The mention of that name brought a noticeable shift in the Tour Guide Knife Fighter; he was clearly uncomfortable with this talk of Brando, this mention that was from Marlon's script. Damn, by now, I just had to go for it, telling him how much I wanted to expand his tour operations here in Tahiti - "I can fund such a thing; more boats, more business, more cash coming in from all over the world, and dumb ol' Brando won't be the wiser." The man gave me a confused nod as I shot out a big grin, getting him to grin back. I then gave him a cartoon-sized handshake, as though he was fully agreeing to "The Deal".

He finished his cigarette and went back to the group. Avra and I went to the other side of the island; it was just a few yards away; this place really was the size of the kind of deserted island you'd see in a philosophical New Yorker cartoon featuring some bearded guy, a note in a bottle and a talking bird. I shrugged, "Well, we did what we could." Avra figured, "Let's just put the camera away; try and enjoy what's left of this trip." After a nervous night sleeping on the sand, followed by an uneasy boat ride back to the mainland (where a short swim along the way seemed to give Avra an instant case of lasting tinnitus), Avra and I met briefly with some of Marlon's Tahitian family. We then caught our flight out of Faa'a International in Papeete. Returning home, we picked up our spoiled pups from their luxury kennel and I quickly started to "edit" the video. This was before I had any sort of editing system. Instead, I used two VHS machines, a narration track from a cassette player and some handmade titles made from tag board and magic markers. I labored over the presentation for a couple of days, knowing I didn't quite "get the goods" on "the target". After there was nothing left to do but surrender, I arranged a time on a late Friday night, where I could "drop off" the VHS tape without talking to Marlon - at least until he watched it.

After the weekend, he called and wanted me to come up to the house later in the day. As I went into the TV den, I could see that Marlon had watched the tape - The plastic VHS bookcase box container I delivered the tape in; that container was open and empty on top of Marlon's tape machine. I quickly did *all* the math; through the clear window on top of the VHS machine loading door, I could see that the whole tape had been played and had yet to be rewound - Yes, I was *that* nervous about this whole thing - and yes, I knew all aspects of VHS video that well.

He asked what I thought of my first trip to Tahiti - I expressed my awe and wonder over the place. I so didn't want to discuss the tape. I shifted into talk of Marlon shooting *"Mutiny on the Bounty"* there. He laughed about the filming of that picture, saying how it was both wonderful and horrible at the exact same time. He then talked about being wrongly blamed for the failure of that film. For the next few hours, we talked about everything under the sun - except for the tape.

It was getting late. He got a call from his friend, Carol Matthau - They started to talk as I made a motion to use the bathroom. I slipped out the den door, hearing that Marlon was getting tired. From experience, I also knew that Marlon and Carol could talk for quite a while. Note: after you've spent a great deal of time with Marlon in his house, you learn there are times when you can and cannot sneak out the door after a marathon conversation. Please know, this was never out of rudeness, it was just the laws of time and human endurance at work. When topics of the night were urgent, center stage and important - even in a long conversation, you would put in the hard time until Marlon was ready to call it a night. But when he was just shuffling around, even avoiding a topic - as I felt he was doing that night - I found myself slipping out the kitchen door, getting into my car and making my way down Mulholland Drive - as quietly as possible.

Days later, after Avra had had a couple days back working with Marlon, I asked if he had mentioned the tape. She said, "He gave it to his lawyer."

I asked, "That's it? That's the end of it?"

"I guess."

"How are you so calm about all this? After all we went through?!"

"He must've liked it well enough. Stop worrying about it."

A bit shocked, I asked, "And the two of you didn't talk about it?!"

"He didn't want to and I didn't want to. Do you wanna talk to him about it? Of course not."

As always, that was the calm beauty and common sense of Avra Douglas, the best Marlon Whisperer in all of Brandoland. Ultimately, nothing ever did become of the tape and whatever it was supposed to do; I think the Tour Guide continued doing tours for quite some time, and sadly, due to so many miserable complications, Marlon never did get back to his beloved Tahiti.

The day after Avra told me that the tape was given to Marlon's lawyer, Tony was going to have a breakfast at Carolwood with his folks; he asked me to come along. This was the first time I had seen Tony since my return from Tahiti.

Over breakfast, Tony and Veronique wanted to know all about my trip, the mission Marlon sent Avra and me on and all of the insanity that was pure Brando. I got quite caught up in it as I told the complete tale, chapter by chapter, move by move. Tony laughed wildly and gave his usual generous assist and prompt when needed. Veronique was also laughing and shaking her head, finding the whole thing to be both ridiculous and thoroughly entertaining.

Across from me was Greg, who rarely smiled during the whole, long adventure. After I completed the story and Tony, Veronique and I were done laughing, an odd pause followed.

It was a pause eventually broken by Greg, with a quietly asked, totally serious "Greg" question.

"Does he ever do anything correctly?"

READING DeMOTT (1991)

As we all know by now, the black-tie parties at the Peck Carolwood estate always had a star-studded list of guests and world famous faces. Meanwhile: at Marlon's, you'd see maybe one famous face, every once in a while; perhaps more "familiar" than "famous". As I said earlier, that was the craggy mug of Harry Dean Stanton. Harry Dean was known and loved in almost every circle I traveled in or worked in. When I worked with Sean Penn, we'd talk about and often hang out with Harry Dean; Sean and Harry were close. Greg also loved Harry Dean, having worked with him on *"Pork Chop Hill"*. My good friend, Ed Begley, Jr. talked to Harry Dean everyday on the phone: they did the crossword puzzle in the Los Angeles Times together six days a week.

Unlike Tony, I never hung out with Jack Nicholson across Marlon's driveway, but Jack was incredibly tight with Harry Dean. Harry Dean also became close to a dear friend of Avra's and mine, Los Angeles author and journalist, Patt Morrison. Yes, it seemed Harry Dean Stanton was everywhere at all times, often carrying his worn guitar — and always stashing a few packs of cigarettes. He was also the only "celebrity" who was within the recurring cast of Marlon's orbit. And while Marlon did have ongoing talks and calls with people like Johnny Depp and Michael Jackson, it was Harry Dean who you might see on any given day or night up at Mulholland.

Maybe that's why I wasn't all that shocked when I saw him now turn up in the home of Cheryl Tiegs. Good God! This guy is everywhere! He was there that day for *"The Read"*. It was quite a cast of star performers who joined him: it was Harry Dean, along with

Reese Witherspoon, Gregory Peck, David Morse, Jason London, Robin Wright, Jeremy London, Ed Begley, Jr. and Eileen Ryan, all in that basement screening room (with the giant horseshoe bar) belonging to Cheryl, with Martin Scorsese on an open New York phone line for hours.

That was the day there was a "table" reading of *"Doctor DeMott"* in the Tiegs West Hollywood home, an exercise brought together by (and directed by) Sean Penn, who constantly paced, prodded and choreographed with wonderful energy and motivation throughout the read. As the writers, Tony and I sat with the cast and spoke the stage directions aloud.

The read went incredibly well - you could see and hear the movie - but this film was always going to be a hard sell; one of the producers working with Scorsese correctly called the project a "Mass Art Film" - meaning: it had to be one of those rare Oscar-worthy films that would be critically acclaimed yet box office enough to be attractive (before getting made) to investors - to the tune of millions and millions of dollars. Essentially, the type of film I call an "Un-recurring Phenomenon". The cast I listed showed up free that day thanks to the collective power of Martin Scorsese, Sean Penn and Gregory Peck. Paying their asking prices for a lengthy film shoot would be a whole other matter altogether. Still, we were optimistic that day. Even by way of a cold sight-reading exercise, I believe that cast grasped the power of Bergman's story, and I'm certain they felt what Greg would bring to the central figure - Most likely, his final starring role.

But even after that great day, the project stalled. Before long, it felt as though Sean had to tend to other commitments and we were losing his interest. Regretfully, we needed to move on to other directors and other contributors, but at the root of the problem was the film financing world itself - a limited pool of cautious investors who were having resistance issues with an adaptation of an old Bergman film starring a legend who had not been "Box Office" for quite some time.

Still, through all of our continuing and numerous meetings, rewrites, initiating of newcomers and journeys through the challenges, Greg was the constant driving force. Everyone who came onboard was immediately under his spell; you'd listen to Greg tell the story of the film and you were hooked, sure that this project had to be made.

By now, I was starting to know a few money guys and investors in the industry as well. As a creative person in the film world, it's oddly easy to vilify these guys. You somehow think that these rich swells are the horrible cads who are keeping us creative geniuses from doing our thing. Of course, that's a ridiculous notion. So many film investments rarely pay off. And the investors who really love film; they so want to be part of something that succeeds - of course. They could only get burned so many times before they wanted out of the crap-shoot of filmmaking.

Often, large film funds in those days were financed by foreign investors with pools of disposable income. It had to be that way, because the investment of a film was so risky. Some of these investors took part simply for the excitement and thrill of being part of Hollywood, knowing that a movie investment would be a long-shot. There were times that I had to admire the kind of gambler who would roll the dice like that. It was probably much easier to create another mini-mall, business or apartment building. Private investors aside, we were also trying to work a deal with the then relatively new StudioCanal, a division of Canal+, a French television channel that was launched in 1984. StudioCanal came along in 1988, making features at the time of our *"DeMott"* project. When working with blockbuster producers like Mario Kassar and Andrew Vajna (and their Carolco production company), StudioCanal was able to hitch their wagon to big Hollywood titles such as *"Terminator 2: Judgment Day," "Total Recall"* and *"Basic Instinct"*. But StudioCanal also had a smaller "art" side to it, financing then popular auteur David Lynch and his projects; his unique art films such as *"The Straight Story," "Mulholland Dr."* and *"Inland Empire"*. Without perhaps the often signature hazy ambiguity of Lynch, these were examples of the kind of unique thought-piece we wanted with *"DeMott"*. But as it often is in Hollywood (even by way of Paris), you sometimes need to wait in the foreign "money" line for your turn. *Agh!* I hated these money-chases in my life at that time. Thank God I had Avra to keep me sane.

During these days of *"DeMott,"* Avra was often doing what she could to comfort a fragile, emotionally unstable Cheyenne Brando. One afternoon, after a day of work with Tony and Greg, Avra told me that we had tickets to see *"Phantom of the Opera"* at the Ahmanson Theater. We were going with Cheyenne and Marlon's neighbor (who took care of Jack Nicholson's place), Helena Kallianiotes. Avra and Helena wanted to keep Cheyenne active; Cheyenne said she'd like to see that show. But when we arrived up at Marlon's to pick her up, in a rage, she had just then shattered a giant glass door with her bare hand; we actually drove up as the pieces were crashing! Incredibly, she didn't have a scratch on her, but Marlon was fully shaken. Amazingly, Cheyenne hopped in the car, wanting to see the show. As the lights went down at the Ahmanson, Cheyenne had a loud breakdown. Avra, Helena and I got her out of there and we got her back to Marlon's.

Cheyenne was a beautiful girl. Avra often thought that a new man in Cheyenne's life could be a solution, especially since Cheyenne did talk about such things occasionally. One night after a Carolwood party, Avra suggested that we introduce Cheyenne to the handsome son of Roger Moore, Geoffrey. As I struck the idea down, Avra said, "Too late; I already talked to Tony about it." Nights later, Cheryl and Tony were gracious enough to host a great meal and a movie with Cheyenne, Geoffrey, Avra and me. The possible couple was not hitting it off, and things got worse as we all went to the screening room for *"Blazing Saddles"*. The film and the night ended early. I felt bad for Cheyenne, but I also felt horrible for Avra, who so wanted to help her friend.

The next morning, Tony, Greg and I had a quick *"DeMott"* meeting, as Greg then went off to start a long weekend. Around this time, when Greg wasn't working on the development and progress of *"DeMott,"* he would sometimes spend time - even a weekend - with a very eccentric friend. Veronique was friends with this eccentric as well. So was Marlon. The eccentric probably made sure that Greg and Marlon were not houseguests on the same weekend, even though the eccentric had the epic property of a whole resort on which to entertain guests. Still, anyone who knew

Marlon knew that he didn't care to share his weekends with other movie stars - no matter how much space everyone got.

The eccentric - he was no movie star.

He was much bigger than that.

More about him below.

Thriller (1991)

New York City radio was a fascinating thing to me when I moved to Manhattan. I loved local radio back in small town Minnesota, and being a media-nut, I loved learning that New York had flagship stations in affiliation with the Big Three TV networks: WNBC, WABC and WCBS. How cool was that?! Howard Stern arrived in New York around the time I got there, and I had to pinch myself as I listened; I couldn't believe that a so-called mainstream "network" radio network was that hip, that cool and that outrageous. The last time I pinched myself like that was when I was 11, having then watched the first episode of *"All in the Family"*.

And yes, I really did literally pinch myself, thanks to both Norman Lear and Howard Stern. The non-talk music stations of NYC in 1979 also seemed very cool to me. Yes, I heard current pop music growing up in Brainerd as well, but there was something quite real about living in New York City and hearing the top 40 music of the day, knowing that The Brill Building, Rockefeller Center and Madison Square Garden were just a few blocks from where I was going to school, and even my school itself of course had its own musical pedigree, being The Juilliard School at Lincoln Center. Let's face it: everything's heightened quite a few notches in NYC.

Listening to New York music radio of the late 70's and early 80's, drawing cartoons after a long day at school, I'd turn the dial back then and the music and the soundtrack of that era was starting to be owned by Michael Jackson. Years later, when I moved out to L.A. after graduation, he was even bigger. It was something of an amazing feat - For many years as I was growing up, it did seem like he might just be a former child sensation, one that would eventually fade away, or perhaps, at best, be part of an "Oldies" act. Few could've seen how gigantic he would become.

Those who make it into the high levels of show business, of course, want to stay there. But there's no real map or true plan for that, any more than there's a plan on how to arrive at the top to begin with. Sometimes, retaining fame seemed to be a game of "contacts". As I watched Greg and Marlon through the years, I saw that neither man wanted to necessarily reach out and keep those "valuable" contacts merely for the sake of career. Both men also assumed that they had reached a place where any kind of "networking" was both unnecessary and, perhaps, demeaning. But they were both powerful and influential in their own ways. A casual phone call or "Hello" from either of them went a long way, letting studio heads, fellow stars or top agents know that they were still there, they were still in the game and most importantly, they were still open to new projects. I rarely witnessed either man actively "networking" for the sake of their careers, but I did see them keep ties with major players, often, for any number of good reasons.

One big name they both had in common was Michael Jackson. Once Jackson arrived in the stratosphere of show business, graduating from a one-time child star to a major superstar, it seemed he wanted to make something clear to the world: his "contemporaries" were not Donny Osmond, or God forbid his brothers (whom he kissed goodbye-have-a-nice-life with the profitable "Victory Tour") — No, *his* contemporaries were Katharine Hepburn, Frank Sinatra, Elizabeth Taylor - the major stars of the world. Of course, many could argue that Jackson did indeed earn that kind of privilege. He must have, because at the peak of his career, if Michael wanted you within his pack of famous friends, few resisted. And while Marlon was a tough "Get" even for Jackson, Michael solved that by hiring Brando's son, Miko, as a bodyguard, even though bodyguarding was not a real skill that Miko possessed. More on all that shortly.

Often, when I'd learn of a famous "younger generation" friend of the Pecks, I'd sometimes suspect that it was the doing of Veronique; she was always smart and practical, knowing Greg needed to keep certain ties, appearances and connections when it came to his career, something I've discussed throughout these pages. And while Greg did have true bonds and friendships with peers such as Sinatra, Lemmon, Matthau and Roger Moore, I was at first a bit surprised when Tony told me of the family friendship with Jackson. I say "a bit" because I had heard for years that Jackson, like more than a few of the mega-powerful, was a true "Head Hunter," a Hollywood term for someone determined to meet, court, wine, dine and associate with big stars. Surprisingly, as Jackson demonstrated - you can be a big star yourself and still be as star-struck as anybody.

In turn, it obviously served older stars as they brushed-up against someone (at the time) as hip, young and locked into the mega-fame zone as Michael Jackson. As many of us remember, there were years when Michael was as big as something could humanly get. For a time, it seemed as though there were only two types of people Jackson wanted to hang out with: major superstars or young boys; mostly unknown kids who were his friends for sleepovers or playdates at his sprawling Neverland Ranch. Once in a while, we'd see a young actor next to Michael for a moment who had some fame attached - an Emmanuel Lewis, Macaulay Culkin - names of that sort. But years later, we'd all learn that those young boys closest to Jackson were not stars - and perhaps for very good reason: Stars - even young celebrities - have degrees of independence and power. Unknown kids with starstruck, naive or accommodating parents; not so much.

While I wasn't always privy to what Michael and the Pecks were up to when together, I do know that Greg and Veronique took part in a number of invitations extended by Jackson: concerts, Neverland visits, music video shoots and more. At the time, it was hard not to have respect for the success of Michael Jackson. His talent was unquestionable, his music crossed generations and his self-promoted eccentricity was both intriguing and back then seen as (odd to think now) oh so endearing; he was a unique phenomenon, as though he fell to Earth from the heavens to save us all - especially the children, landing in a world that didn't deserve such a precious, fragile gift. Much of that was simple cultural popularity - in 1979, critics swooned over the age-challenged courtship between Woody Allen and Mariel Hemingway in *"Manhattan;"* ask those same critics today; still so charming? So - going back a bit in the timeline: as Michael the "Head Hunter" did indeed begin to rack-up names between his *"Off The Wall"* through *"Bad"* period - names such as Greg, Liz Taylor and others, of course, the prize of Brando was a more difficult capture, even for a singer who was becoming the most famous person on the planet.

Once Marlon's son was a member of Michael's staff, Jackson had a clear and open channel to the elusive, reclusive Marlon. And like all interesting individuals, Michael did indeed fascinate Brando. Marlon would do his therapist routine on MJ, something the great actor would do with almost everyone he'd meet with in his house, whether you be the new gardener, the new plumber or The King of Pop. You'd sit there, and there was Marlon - a cross between Freud and The Pope, and before you knew it, you were confessing everything, to someone you thought could keep your secrets. Why? Because Marlon was, by legend, secretive. And why were you doing this sudden confession? Because open, self-confessing, sharing, caring Marlon Brando was asking you to do so. I know, it sounds crazy, but those who knew Marlon knew how it worked.

To cut to a certain obvious upcoming spoiler: long before certain tabloid stories and world famous trials, Marlon did say to me: "Michael - he likes little boys. It's not good." Marlon said that to me not all that long after I first met him. (Oddly, it was within this same conversation that Marlon abruptly, seemingly out of nowhere, strongly denied legendary rumors of his own bisexuality.) Hearing Marlon Brando tell me that about Michael Jackson; well, I just kinda stared and shook my head, not knowing what I was supposed to do with that high level of gossip.

Back to Miko - As I've written about here, Greg and Marlon were two very different types of fathers. Greg valued education and made sure his children received the very best possible. Marlon took the education of his children on a case-by-case basis because, in Marlon's eyes, he did not want to pressure his kids into anything they didn't want to do. On top of that, Marlon had such complicated relationships with all of the mothers involved with these children; at times, certain kids were out of the fold, and then, back in as matters changed or evolved. While Marlon might be funding the college education of a child who was the daughter of one of Marlon's girlfriends, at that very same time, a biological child might be skipping higher education altogether - not always because Marlon was nixing it, but because that kid would rather be a welder than an Ivy League honor student. And yes, a star at the level of Marlon could more than likely get his kids into just about any school possible - *If* Marlon knew that child wanted that.

From Christian to Cheyenne, to Rebecca and Miko, Marlon's kids all had vastly different experiences when it came to education, higher learning and careers. By the time Marlon met the biggest star in the world, Michael Jackson learned that Miko Brando was open to work that would pay well and not tax his limited experiences with education and previous employment. Posing as a "bodyguard" to Jackson fit the mold of Miko's large size, and to a degree, massive presence. Jackson liked to gush that it was "Marlon Brando's son" who "saved" his life during a Pepsi video shoot; a session that included a famous accident where Jackson's head caught on fire due to some hair gel and hot lights. Michael claims it was Miko who bravely dowsed the flames.

However it worked out, Miko eventually became a permanent member of Jackson's staff, moving from bodyguard to general gofer; running errands, manning a Westwood office and handing out invitations to Neverland - a standing offer that was always available to Marlon.

In the early 90's, I recall discussing Jackson with Greg after Michael was famously interviewed by Oprah Winfrey. The conversation was vintage Gregory: careful, diplomatic and positive when it came to Jackson's talent, wealth and accomplishments.

Jackson often told Veronique how much he adored Greg; not a difficult thing to believe knowing Peck's charm and Michael's love of legendary stars - especially "handsome" men such as Greg. Through plastic surgery, Jackson longed for the facial features of actors such as Greg, Cary Grant and others from that classic era; Jackson kept framed photos of both young Greg and young Cary in his Neverland home. As I talked about the Oprah special with Greg, expressing a giggling disbelief over how "adult" Jackson displayed his eccentric "Ferris wheel" lifestyle to Winfrey on the TV special, amusement park rides and all, Greg cautiously talked of how he believed that nobody really "knew" a mystery like Michael. As it was with Marlon, I believe Greg saw Jackson as a rare enigma: an extremely talented singer and dancer who was both a recovering victim of some kind *and* a mysterious, calculated operator. About Michael, Greg once said to me, "You can't accomplish all he's done on pure wide-eyed innocence alone."

In the heyday of Neverland Ranch, the place really was something to see; incredibly manicured and well kept; a mutant form of Disneyland up in Santa Barbara County. Again, at various times, Greg and Veronique were guests, climbing on rides such as "The Zipper" to Michael's delight. And of course, there was always a deluxe cottage ready on the premises for Marlon.

Jackson's adult life as a living legend can easily be broken into two very separate halves: before molestation accusations and after. As it was with Frank Sinatra, Greg was a loyal friend to those others sometimes questioned. I believe he saw unique characters like Jackson and Frank as colorful eccentrics, in a club occupied by those Greg would sometimes tell stories about - John Huston, Alfred Hitchcock, Anthony Quinn and others - Greg seemed to see the oddity of Michael as part of Jackson's genius: MJ was a complete original in Greg's eyes.

As for Marlon getting a direct and dark confession from Michael years before certain accusations, Marlon admitted that he had no proof of Jackson ever "acting" on his desires. I also think that Marlon thought it was quite brave of Michael to admit his "wants," while (maybe, hopefully) not following through on any of it. Marlon saw Jackson as a fellow reclusive rebel and eccentric, secretly in touch with his own dark thoughts but perhaps too big as a public figure to actually cross forbidden lines. He also thought that Michael had a religious moral compass by way of his life as a Jehovah Witness; perhaps in Marlon's mind, Jackson had the occasional "illicit" thought - *but* - he was too "good" and "famous" a person to actually molest a child.

Lastly, Marlon had a somewhat understandable inner lock that always seemed to trust celebrities over what might turn out to be negative public speculation or accusation. This of course came from decades of his own press battles, along with the adjacent legal problems that might follow a mess within the life of a celebrity. I made a film about the O.J. Simpson trial, *"October Three,"* where I played three brothers discussing the verdict on the phone. Marlon liked my film, but he'd argue with me over the case, insisting that the police more than likely really *did* frame the guy who I say indeed *did* kill Ron Goldman and Nicole Brown: O.J. Simpson.

As for me, when Marlon first told me of Michael's "confession" of desires, I was really not shocked in the least. And even though this was long before the public accusations of Jackson, I'll say it loud and clear: you didn't need to be some sort of detective to figure that out. Maybe two things were in my corner when it came to my self-proclaimed clear vision on this: One: I was no real fan of the music; something rare at that moment. I *loved* the old "Jackson 5" music. Maybe I was too old for new pop music by the 90's, but his over-produced *"Thriller"* and *"Bad"* stuff left me quite cold; don't get me wrong - it was wonderfully done pop-dance music, but it wasn't for me. And two: Michael and I were about the same age, and that somehow had my gears turning.

While I in no way consider myself to be (or ever to have been) a career contemporary of Michael Jackson, I do recall my mindset back when I was a working, and at times, "known" TV actor within the industry. My only goals at that time before meeting Avra: getting girls, meeting women, extreme dating! When I would read that a guy my age, one who could get essentially any woman he wanted, this guy was, - what? Having sleepovers with young boys? What sane person didn't think, "What the hell?" Well, the media at that time seemed to think otherwise. They really bought into the whole thing, acting as though only The Beautifully Pure Michael Jackson could be trusted with young boys in his bed. It made no sense to me back then, and to borrow a later phrase from Donald Trump, "When you're a star, they let you do it." Oh, I know, I'm no psychologist, and I do understand his fully bizarre childhood, the possible damage done by his oppressive father, and all the Michael Jackson history that has circulated through the years; yes, I've read it all and I grasp it all. Perhaps all the more reason as to why I feel that my mind was made up regarding Jackson and the behavior in his private life early on.

Long story short: for years, I declined any invitation to Neverland that came my way from Marlon. He loved the place. For him, it was a grand hotel with 24-hour food and room service. Avra would take Molly there often, as our young daughter loved the gentle rides, the free first-run movies, the many animals and the park-like atmosphere. For whatever reasons, both Greg and Marlon were fully impressed with the size and the layout of Neverland, both telling me of how it really should be seen if the opportunity ever exists. I sometimes thought that was because they both knew big money and they both knew the scale and value of owning such a property.

In turn, I knew nothing about owning a massive property of any kind, I cared little about such things and I really didn't want to visit a place that I suspected to be an elaborate "Boy Trap" from the moment it was on a blueprint, designed in the same way that the Playboy mansion took shape, with a real agenda as part of its construction. Face it: Hugh Hefner knew his grotto would come in handy. I could be wrong, but I suspect Jackson saw the bedrooms in his candy-filled movie theater in a similar fashion.

So, as it might be clear from my previous words, I *did* finally get out to have a look at "Neverland". "You're coming with us," Marlon said one day, as there was a planned trip with Avra, Molly and Marlon. It was years before the infamous Martin Bashir interview but after Jackson was first accused of child sexual abuse; back when the police never pressed charges for accusations made by a family in the early 90's. He'd be accused again and go to trial in 2005, ending up with an acquittal on all counts. Years before that, I got out to this estate that both Marlon and Greg were so impressed with. Scale-wise, detail-wise and by any measure of "unique," yes, it was quite interesting. But by then, I was fully convinced, right or wrong, that it was that day's equivalent to what years later could be labeled "Jeffrey Epstein's Island," a private retreat in the U.S. Virgin Islands designed as a haven for sex with underage victims.

When Avra, Molly and I left, Marlon stayed for a few days more; thanks to Michael, Miko and many other means and methods, Marlon would be able to get back to Los Angeles whenever he wanted. Driving through Santa Barbara Country, thinking of that garish estate, I chose to put certain thoughts aside as I marveled over how incredibly talented Jackson was - a freakish talent that only comes along once every few decades. Of course, it was also an overwhelming talent - One that collided with just the right moment in pop culture history; the perfect atom-smash of ability and timing, creating a fame that impressed even those who knew fame quite well.

About five months before he passed away, Greg wrote a letter of support for Michael; this was around the time that the Bashir documentary, *"Living with Michael Jackson"* finally alarmed audiences as Michael calmly discussed his sleepovers and young friends. By the end of that year, Jackson would be booked on molestation charges and Greg would be gone, passing away in that summer of 2003. Marlon didn't live long enough to see Michael go to trial over accusations of child molestation. I suspect he might've gone on TV in a heated rant, in support of Michael, saying many of the same things he said to the press when his own son was accused of murder, or when he was arguing with me about O.J. Simpson. I sense even the powerful testimony of Wade Robson and James Safechuck in 2019's *"Leaving Neverland"* wouldn't have fully swayed Marlon. In the documentary, the now adult men give graphic, vivid accounts of sexual abuse by Michael.

So, why write so much here about Greg, Marlon and Michael? That's a good question.

I believe the answer is wedged somewhere within the following: when I was in the lives of these two elderly men, I often saw their accomplishments and their fame as elements too vast to understand. But being overly-analytical and prone to over-thinking everything, "understanding" was something I was always striving for.

Then at around the same time, I saw *both* of these very different men fascinated with an artist from my generation. And they seemed to be as fascinated with him as *he* was with them. "World Famous and Legendary" - it's a small club; these three were in it. Of course, the acting world is different than the music world, but on that rare level of being Famous World Citizens, all three of them, I found myself observing "fame" from a very unique set of perspectives.

I knew that Michael understood Greg and Marlon in a way that I will never understand them.

But I'm also certain that I understood Michael Jackson in ways that - I think - Marlon and Greg totally missed.

BOB (1992)

The Paramount Studios of the late 60's and early 70's put together a number of artistic victories. I've always felt that the studio was kinda bright about how they did it. All the young, cool directors were breaking out back then, and by pairing these directors with best-selling books - favorites such as *"Love Story," "Rosemary's Baby,"* the list goes on - the studio had a formula. It was a formula that allowed the studio to appear both smart and hip at the very same time.

Meanwhile, across town, it seemed that Columbia was occasionally letting the hipsters do what they wanted to do, scripts or not. Bob Rafelson and his pals were sometimes allowed to shoot first and figure it out later, with funky pieces such as *"Easy Rider,"* The Monkees' *"Head,"* and other youth-based fare. Around this time, Universal was making kinda plastic films, but they were also deep into kinda plastic television production, and many of their kinda plastic films were looking like kinda plastic TV shows in the process - and vice versa.

Within this same period, Disney was trying to figure out how to survive as a studio in a new "G", "M", "R" and "X" rated world (what Disney nerds now call "The Dark Era"), and Warner Brothers seemed to be making films that still looked and sounded old cinematically, while they were basically young in theme - Exhibit "A" in that mode: *"Bonnie and Clyde,"* a film that only gets "hip" looking once it becomes a slow motion bloodbath. Up until then, it's two pretty fashion models in designer clothes, filmed studio-style, pretending to be naughty people.

Meanwhile, United Artists seemed to be dialed-in in every way; in look, feel, vibe, storytelling, on and on. There's no other way to explain an unexpected masterpiece such as *"Midnight Cowboy"*. But whatever the case, all over Hollywood, things were moving and they were moving fast. How schizophrenic was it all at that time? A studio like 20th Century-Fox could offer-up a cheap cool-fest like *"M*A*S*H"* right next to an expensive cousin of a dinosaur called *"Hello Dolly"*.

All that is a big fat lead-up to my two friends: before Brando's *"The Godfather"* and Peck's *"The Omen,"* Marlon and Greg were making "new-ish" movies in the 70's without a great deal of success. Of course, those two films named above changed it all for them, both artistically and financially, strongly launching them both into the final chapters of their careers.

Returning to the top-of-the-page topic of the Paramount Studios of the 70's, it's not possible to view that place or that era without having a look at The Kid That Stayed in the Picture, Robert Evans. While it was strange enough for a certified failed young actor to be running a major motion picture studio, it was perhaps even stranger to witness the wild success that Evans shared with Paramount. Marlon never forgave Evans for the hoops he had to jump through to get the role of Vito Corleone in *"The Godfather"* - The stories of Marlon's home screen-tests, his pay-cut to get the role, all as a young Francis Ford Coppola needed to beg Evans for Brando - these tales are both undisputed and legend.

Not far from that timeline, Greg was both thrilled and relieved when Evans agreed to have Paramount distribute the sailboat saga, *"The Dove,"* a homeless passion project that Greg put together as an off-screen producer. The film taught Greg a great deal about independent producing, in some ways forcing Greg to return to a more cautious place; a place he was *trying* to step out of as he wanted to devote more time to the world of producing from a blank page, as opposed to getting your "Movie Star" production company a producing credit on a film you are acting in as an International Screen Icon.

Jumping from the 70's to the 90's - Watching Greg essentially producing *"Doctor DeMott,"* just as I watched Marlon claim to be "producing" every script I would work on with him, I grew to learn the differences between Superstar actor-producers and flat-out "Producers" - Producers Tony would introduce me to; men such as Elliot Kastner, Mike Medavoy, Albert S. Ruddy and yes, Robert Evans. In their different ways, Marlon and Greg were equally as passionate when it came to wanting to produce pictures - as passionate as the producers I listed above.

But Greg and Marlon were also equally passionate when it came to great acting, the great performances of other actors, the perfection of the shooting script, etc. In my mind, these were all lesser thoughts to men like Kastner, Medavoy, Ruddy and Evans, at least in the early stages of the deal. In fact, to guys like Elliot, Mike, Al and Bob, the "deal" was everything as a film was coming together; more often than not, the picture would get figured out as time went on; hopefully by "The Artists". This is not to speak ill of the "Producing" methods of any of these men; it's just a simple fact that great actors and great deal makers are very different animals.

And then, of course, there is a level of producer like the guys Tony and I got to work with in the foreign and indie worlds. This is where you can find the crooks, the cheats and the flat-out criminals. Of course, many would say that *that* is the world Evans entered after he left Paramount and became an independent producer, especially as he became mixed up with a pack of unsavory characters while trying to finance, complete and distribute his 1984 film, *"The Cotton Club"*. That's a whole other story that has its own set of books, and by the time I met Bob, he was just getting past those difficulties, claiming to proudly have all that drug, murder and illegal stuff behind him. By the early 90's, he was living a "new" strange life as a dapper "Gentleman" producer, working out of both his signature home in Beverly Hills and his boutique-ish "Office for Life" he somehow had on the Paramount lot. It was an odd, fully bizarre set-designed, strange fake office-of-an-office-of-a-set that he'd occasionally use for meetings.

As much as it sounds like I might be goofing on the history, lifestyle and pure essence of Bob, please know this: I personally found Evans to be amazing; a character like nobody I had ever met. He loved Tony, became his good friend and we'd often go to see Bob when taking a break from writing. Whether it was going to his cool retro house or to that cool retro "office" at Paramount, getting to go see Bob was something of a thrill. Oh, and by the way - two people who really, truly didn't like Bob Evans in any way, shape or form: Greg and Marlon.

Marlon I understood; not only did Marlon dislike and mistrust almost *all* studio guys, he also had that *"Godfather"* baggage I mentioned a few lines back. Greg's dislike seemed more complex. While I never knew the full story of how or whether *"The Dove"* proved profitable (or not) for either Greg or Paramount, I did see Greg bristle every time Bob's name would come up. Always ahead of the curve, Tony saw the "hip" appeal of Evans long before it was the popular stuff of books, Hollywood legend and caricature. Tony and I loved riffing "as" Evans, doing his famous strange voice and laughing over Bob's daring and even reckless exploits. And *that* I think is where Greg was with his "Evans" anger; somewhere in that area, anyway.

Yes, Tony was a grown man who could take care of himself, but on the simple, emotional level as a father, Greg had no want for his free-spirited son to be associated with someone who had so openly been steeped in drugs, vice and legal hassles. Love or hate Robert Evans, all that stuff was open and seemingly ongoing knowledge. Marlon occasionally had almost the exact same thoughts regarding his grown children and Mulholland neighbor Jack Nicholson, wondering if Christian Brando was crossing the driveway to get into "drug trouble" with Jack. And as all the world seemed to know in those days, Jack's very best friend - was Robert Evans.

I remember having a dinner with Greg and Tony at Spago. We had finished, were leaving, as Bob walked in with a very Evans-esque young and sexy circus of an entourage. With Bob was some shady-looking stubble-guy, along with three very noticeable women who could easily have passed for adult film actresses. Tony politely went over to say "Hi" to his friend Bob. As smiling Evans started to make his way over to Greg, many in the restaurant watched Greg forcefully walk out the main entrance door; those famous eyebrows angrily arched. Of course, Tony and Evans saw all that too. Maybe the most "Un-Greg" thing I ever saw him do, only because Greg was usually so incredibly polite - especially in public.

Wanting to ease the moment up, Tony chatted and shared a quick laugh with Bob. Seeing that Tony had matters covered on this end, I really saw no other choice but to join Greg at the valet stand as we waited for the car. The vehicle arrived. I'll never forget Greg's words: "Get in. If he wants to talk to Robert Evans, he can walk home." Just then, Tony came running out and got into the car. Nothing else was said about Evans that night, but the next day, Tony said, "Uh, around Greg, let's not talk about Evans, or do his voice anymore. Okay?" I nodded in agreement.

Weeks later, I had a birthday. Tony got me VHS copies of two of my favorite films, *"The Godfather"* and *"The Godfather Part II"*. He said, "You gotta get Marlon to sign those; they'll be worth something." I laughed, "I could never get Marlon to sign these." More to the point, I would never think of asking him. Tony kinda chuckled, "Yeah, what was I thinking? Hey, get in the car." Tony drove me over to Bob's house. Once there, after Bob and Tony first shared some hushed chat about some woman, and then another short chat about "Jack", Tony announced that it was my birthday as he handed Bob the VHS tapes and a silver sharpie marker.

What a great idea; Bob ran Paramount when these films were made. As I always found him to be, Evans was uniquely warm and cordial; he smiled as he was about to sign the movies. I watched him as he thought about what to write on the tape box. He and I: we were in no way great friends nor best buddies, but I could see that he wanted to write something that meant something.

He sat on an odd circular sofa as he thought. Within this quiet moment, I recall studying his well-constructed hair, his painfully dark brown tan, his blinding-near-glowing white shirt and the intense blue lapis lazuli stone in the medallion of his bolo tie. I also thought, "What does he even know about me? Of course he's stumped." But as he started writing, I remembered that he does indeed know two things about me: Evans knows I'm a working screenwriter and I'm good friends with Marlon. Sure enough, to those points, he wrote (on the original *"Godfather"* box), "Joe, the writer is king! Without Puzo, there would be no Brando today! Keep writing! Your Friend, Robert Evans". On the *"Godfather II"* box he wrote, "Happy Birthday Kid!"

With the mention of *"Godfather"* writer, Mario Puzo, (and even with the jab he gave Marlon) I was moved. Evans didn't need to do that for me, but he did.

Later, I showed the signed *"Godfather"* video box to Avra. Her only words, "'Better not let Marlon see that."

GOODBYE DOCTOR (1992)

After quite a few rewrites, directors, producers and frustrations, Greg finally decided that he was done trying to see if he could get his *"Wild Strawberries"* remake, *"Doctor DeMott"* to the screen. Back when the project began, the Paul Kohner Agency wrote-up a time-limited option and contract for their client, Ingmar Bergman; Greg had a choice: he could let the project go or he could retain the option for a pretty high price. But after such little success while getting so much time from Martin Scorsese, Sean Penn, Martha Coolidge, Noel Pearson, Arthur Penn, Jim Sheridan and even Jerry Weintraub (who owned the rights to the original film {not the screenplay} and agreed to not question technical "script" legalities only because, hey, this was Gregory Peck), Greg felt it was the hour to put the entire project to rest.

I believe that his past experience was guiding him. Many years back, he had chased a remake of *"Dodsworth"* (the 1936 Walter Huston film, based on the Sinclair Lewis novel) until it didn't happen. In 1972, he did get a film version of the Vietnam-era play, *"The Trial of the Catonsville Nine"* to the screen, and it cost him a great deal of his own unreturned money. And then there was his long and difficult road producing the sailboat romance *"The Dove"* in 1974. Thoughts of all those projects probably reminded him of when his practical mind was telling him that enough was simply enough.

Also, at the time, he was busy working on a project with (and for) his daughter, Cecilia. The Tina Howe play, *"Painting Churches"* was about to get a made-for-TV adaptation for Ted Turner's TNT network; it would be retitled *"The Portrait,"* starring Greg, Lauren Bacall and Cecilia, directed by one-time potential *"Doctor DeMott"* helmer, Arthur Penn.

It was very much like Greg to do the work (and the *quality* of work) he did with both Tony and Cecilia at this time. By then, he knew that the number of his remaining projects was probably limited, he loved his children beyond measure, and as always, he went about these "family" projects in such a professional and structured way. If he was going to act in a film with Cecilia, it would be with an established director like Penn, with a name co-star like Bacall, within a successful story from a hit play. And even if it was going to be a made-for-TV endeavor, it would have all of the production values of a feature film.

"The Portrait" - I'll label "Cecilia's project" - that was all just as professional and on-the-level as *"DeMott"*: "Tony's project," as I'll call it here for the moment. As I wrote previously, *"Doctor DeMott"* went through Writer's Guild contacts, through the agency that represented Tony and me at the time, with Greg working as a Guild Signatory Producer, attaining the assistance of professional industry giants like Marty, Sean and all those big names I previously listed - Kind of amazing, when you think about it.

But he was Greg. Of course he did it all one hundred percent right, proper and By-The-Book. Every "i" dotted, every "t" crossed, even on a project that never made it to a film set.

On the sad day when I learned that *"Doctor DeMott"* was finally over, I left Carolwood and I went up to Marlon's, as he had been asking me to do for a while, to begin a free rewrite on one of his old scripts, his espionage thriller, *"Jericho"*.

I must say, it was a depressing moment. I had read this old script many times, I didn't know what Marlon liked or didn't like about it, and worst of all, at this very moment, I had just finished working with and for "Above-Board Greg" for such a long time. None of that work was a free-for-all, and none of it was a drain on my bank account, a time-killer nor random in any fashion.

I also recalled that I had read many stories about this *"Jericho"* script in the press years ago; I had so many questions that I know Marlon didn't want to hear - Hell, he might not even know the answers to what I wanted to ask. Questions like, "Do you still own this script?" Or "Are there other writers with legal attachments to this script?" I once read that it was beyond-close to a real production a number of times. So, uh, how could it still be a "free & clear" property to Marlon?

These were the kind of legitimate industry "Call the Lawyer," "Have the Agent Draw-up a Deal" questions that would totally consume Greg, just as they would totally bore Marlon.

Feeling that this forthcoming "work" on *"Jericho"* might eventually leave me a bit broke financially, just as I was then still feeling frustrated and agitated over *"DeMott,"* I found the nerve to ask Marlon, "Why don't we get a deal to develop this correctly? We could be getting paid at this very moment by a studio or a production company just to rewrite this."

Silence. Marlon looked at his phone. He started to reach for it. He stopped reaching. He then shrugged.

"Naw, 'better just to brown-bag it for now."

And with that, I opened the old shopworn screenplay to a very weathered Page One.

I looked over to see that Marlon was now lazily playing with one of his old dime store magic tricks Avra had given him, one of the many little items he kept on an end table near his sofa. With nothing better to say, I asked, "Did you wanna be a magician when you grew up?"

With a straight face, he muttered, "I still wanna be a magician when I grow up."

Later that week, my *"DeMott"* depression and *"Jericho"* frustration had both subsided. After a few days of trying to write, Marlon kinda grew bored with both musty *"Jericho"* and our slow rewriting process. Knowing I had spent years as a percussionist, he wanted to again show me his collection of conga drums, particularly a conga that he had patented with the U.S. government, by way of a unique design and mechanism he had invented. Inside the drum, he had a series of spokes that would tighten or loosen the drum head - thus changing the pitch with the turn of a knob that was mounted on the side of the drum. It was clever, but for the fact that the large spoke-mechanism itself (nearly up against the head) was clearly not helping the sound of the drum. This was evident by just one tap on the head. Congas are long, fully empty and tuned with a drum key on top of the instrument, and those three elements create a distinctive sound.

When I *very* gently suggested something I'm sure nobody had dared to tell him - your brilliant invention is making the drum sound lousy (not said in those words) - he got out an un-sharp stub of a pencil and a too-small pad of paper - He then drew a new design that he thought could improve the sound. I smiled as I saw how he sketched plans, blueprints and schematics exactly like my father: childlike, determined and most of all, without the slightest notion of failure. I was actually quite touched: I kept thinking, "Look at this rare giant, this incredible soul. He's still such a dreamer. Such a free spirit. I love how he just follows the flow of his turning gears."

Days later, I was waiting for Tony as he was on a call with Cheryl. We were at Carolwood. As the call went on for some time, I wandered the property a bit, shuffling over to Greg's greenhouse. I could see him in there, alone; I did what I could not to be seen, inching my way closer. He was tending to a large white orchid, and I could swear every now and then, he might be saying a word or two to it as well? I felt as though the anxieties and pressures of the *"DeMott"* chase had clearly faded from his demeanor. I knew he loved those growing bits of nature in that greenhouse, and of course - no - while I could see Marlon studying a wild plant on a Tahitian beach, I couldn't picture him nurturing that beautiful greenhouse orchid for a single moment.

Just as I could never picture Greg excitedly drawing out a new design for a tunable conga drum. Or telling me that he still wanted to be a magician when he grew up.

FIFTH CHAPTER
"1962"
(GREG & MARLON ESSAY V)

Both my father and his father were quite frugal men. When these guys worked as carpenters at different times of their lives, they'd tear old houses down without ruining a single board, a single piece of sheetrock or a single - and this is true - nail. They'd keep it all for the next project. While driving anywhere, they'd always be ready to throw the brakes on if they saw anything of value being thrown away or sitting on a curb, ready for a trash collector: old furniture, plumbing, boards, auto parts - you name it; they were scavengers - and I suppose, in more contemporary terms - technically - hoarders. But in their defense, I will say this: they were hoarders who almost always did put their overstocked finds (eventually) to good use; building with "recycled" materials to save money. So, yes, whatever the labels, they were indeed frugal.

With all that as fact, it's also somewhat surprising to me as I look back and recall what "Early Adopters" they both were when it came to certain forms of pricey merchandise. If they saw a gadget, invention or new product that truly lit their imaginations, they'd find a way to buy it. I distinctly remember this at a very young age in the early 1960's, when my grandfather got one of the first color televisions in Cheyenne, Wyoming. I was already TV crazed before I could walk, so seeing Grandpa's color television blew my child-sized mind beyond description. We'd go to his house on Sunday evenings to see whatever Walt Disney was showing, followed by the Ponderosa guys on *"Bonanza,"* two of the few color shows on television at that time.

Being somewhat competitive with both his father and his younger brothers in Cheyenne, it didn't take long for my father to get a color TV of his own - well, I mean, a color TV for his family to enjoy. That led to a beautiful situation that I should've been more grateful for at the time, as a preschool television addict: the old family black and white TV was then put into a bedroom I shared with my sisters. My parents knew my TV love - I could recite every TV schedule prior to knowing how to read or tell time. But, "Damn," I thought (a word my father used often): "This old TV in *my* room; it's black and white. Shit!" (another one of Dad's favorite words.)

This was still a time of "Rabbit Ears" on television sets; at least it was in our house. Knowing that, I woke up one morning at 5AM with a great idea: I would put the "color" rabbit ears from the color living room set on my lousy black and white bedroom TV. I tried to be as quiet as I could be, especially after I learned that I was not living in a "wireless" era; it took a lot of pulling, tugging and ruining to get the "color" ears off the new TV. But once they were off, I ran to my bedroom and put them on the old black and white set. With the sound turned down on this early morning, I turned on my new "color" TV, only to see that the picture was still black and white. I got my eye real close to those dots on the screen, swearing I could see some purple starting to form. But no, it was a failed experiment. I then turned to see my father standing there. Looking back, the best part of the attempt was my father's response. In general, he was often a loud and instantly angry man who wildly overreacted when his kids damaged things or did something "stupid". But with this, he only laughed, clearly appreciating my childish thought process, and more importantly, knowing my hunger for film and TV. He saw me as a media mogul before I was in kindergarten. His expert handyman skills had his color TV back up and working in seconds, even though I was certain I had ruined his new television beyond repair.

So at the very moment, when I was busy trying to reinvent the electronics of color TV, Greg and Marlon were in "color" and "black and white" worlds of their own, bringing me to a year that perhaps defines them and their lasting images more than any other moments in their respective timelines; the year: 1962, when Greg made *"To Kill a Mockingbird"* while Marlon was making

"Mutiny on the Bounty" - and "color" and "black and white" were not just supporting elements in these stories, as you'll see along the way here - for obvious reasons.

By the early '60's, Greg and Marlon were clearly in transforming phases of their careers; both superstars that many thought of as "classic" in their earlier "black and white" years, both with a library of films from years ago that locked their images within the minds of many filmgoers - to mention a few: of course, *"Gentleman's Agreement"* and *"Roman Holiday"* with Greg, *"A Streetcar Named Desire"* and *"On the Waterfront"* with Marlon. And while there were other hits and memorable films through those years for both actors, it's hard to imagine that Marlon was about to make a film (in Tahiti in 1962) that would define almost every aspect of "Brando," his private life, and his future family difficulties, while at the very same time, Greg was about to make the film that some would say totally defines every aspect of him to this very day.

Harper Lee's book was a bestseller when Alan J. Pakula and Robert Mulligan decided to bring *"To Kill a Mockingbird"* to the screen, or as it's often referred to in literary circles and within the Peck family, "TKAM," a needed abbreviation for the Pecks as it continues to be central to their estate today, used in contracts dealing with everything from Broadway show rights to "Atticus" style eyeglasses. To save space here, I'll use "TKAM" when needed as well.

Even though there are stories of Pakula, Mulligan and Universal first approaching Rock Hudson and others for the role of Atticus Finch, it of course now seems impossible to imagine anyone else in the part. In fact, Greg was not even a full-fledged "partner" in the project as filming began, but to the credit of Pakula and Mulligan, it only took a few of the first filmed scenes on the Universal lot for the producer and the director to settle on a rare but simple thought: this actor in this project IS the project. Mulligan, Pakula and Greg then entered into a legal three-way TKAM partnership that lasts to this day, through the respective estates of that trio of principals.

While all that was going on, Marlon was busy turning down most films offered to him, and almost every great male lead at that time -

except for Atticus Finch - *was* offered to Marlon. I once asked him about one from that very moment that he famously passed on; in the 90's, I brought up *"Lawrence of Arabia"*. He laughed, "Hmmm. Meet beautiful women in Tahiti or sit for months on a camel's ass - Pick one!" Of course, he was referring to the time when David Lean had to go off to England to discover Peter O'Toole, because Marlon was not going to be Lean's T. E. Lawrence, instead, accepting MGM's offer to remake *"Mutiny on the Bounty,"* the film that led to Marlon's future family, his future second home and in that more immediate time frame, his airtight reputation as "The Greatest Troublemaker Hollywood Had Ever Known."

To be fair to Marlon and more accurate about this "early 60's" timeline I'm bouncing around on, MGM's remake had started production long before the smooth and near perfect shoot of TKAM, with huge *"Bounty"* production delays and problems that first had very little to do with Marlon. The first director on the project was the legendary Carol Reed, who left the film with very little footage in the can. His replacement, veteran Lewis Milestone, was almost starting from the top of the shoot, even though the film had been in production in Tahiti for months.

Sadly for Marlon, his perceived behavior in those days was often lumped together with the seemingly star/brat shenanigans reported via 20th Century-Fox and their bloated *"Cleopatra"* folly, with Elizabeth Taylor and Brando together cited as "Exhibit A" in how it might be time for Hollywood to reign-in anyone with "power" in front of the camera. Frankly, I believe TV saved stars like Brando and Taylor at that time; actors on those TVs in your home couldn't behave this way! Publicists kinda made the case: these exotic movie star creatures must be worth it when it comes to leaving your home and going out to the movies. Interestingly, the earlier Clark Gable version of *"Mutiny on the Bounty"* seemed to have a theme that was totally foreign to Marlon: "Without order and discipline, human beings destroy each other." Later in life, Marlon might have seen the wisdom in that, but in the early 60's, he saw that thinking as both laughable and dangerous. While at the same time, Greg was making a small, black and white film (within a smoothly-running, disciplined production) about the good and evil human beings are capable of. Given all that, it's easy to see that both films were indeed about race, class and social behavior. Three things that obsessed Greg and Marlon. Disciplined production or not, they had that in common.

THE STORY RESUMES: PUBLIC MEN (1993)

While dinner out with Marlon would have the two of us at burger joints such as Carney's, Fatburger's or even McDonald's, dinner out with the Peck family often ended up at places like Le Dome, Chasen's or an oddly fascinating place that first opened in 1963, a favorite Sinatra haunt known as "Matteo's" over on Westwood boulevard. As it was with the Carolwood parties, Greg seemed to dominate the moment he walked in, no matter who else was in the room - or in the main dining area of Matteo's. On an evening that coincided with one of Tony's birthdays, I joined the family on a Saturday at the famed bistro, a place that was crawling with famous people everywhere you looked. You could gauge Greg's status by a simple fact: Gregory sat at his table as all of the famous in the place came by the table to say, "Hi". There was only one time, later that night, when Greg was possibly out-ranked, and even then, that individual came to Greg's table just like everybody else. More on that in just a little bit.

Some of the best moments of the evening came when legendary comics would come to the table, basically to "perform" for Greg, who always laughed loudly and warmly for these guys; for good reason: they were incredibly funny in person and in your face. Whatever you might think of club comics you shrugged off while watching Johnny Carson or Ed Sullivan, trust me: when they're right at your table doing schtick - Don Rickles, Buddy Hackett, Red Buttons, Jack Carter; these guys knew how to make you literally wet your pants. Hackett was funny even when in simple conversation, knowing that every shrug, giggle and crossed eye was side-splitting.

Oh, and that aforementioned "possible" out-ranking of Greg that evening. Late into our meal, we noticed a number of men in distinct suits with stealth ear-piece-rigged communication radios enter Matteo's - Well, I didn't notice this, Tony did, with his ever-perceptive awareness, knowledge and love of such gear. He tapped me as he muttered, "Secret Service?" Sure enough, as it appeared that these likely "agents" were clearing aisle-ways and looking all around the restaurant. Their behavior began to force many others near our table to squint with the same question I heard Buddy Hackett squawk from a distance, "Who dis 'bout?"

Buddy soon got his answer as former President Jimmy Carter entered the restaurant. I had never been in a situation like this, but of course, it wasn't new to Greg. He started a standing ovation that quickly had everybody politely but strongly applauding; it would last until Carter was at his table. As the former President passed the tables of the aforementioned comics, he waved and smiled, showing a very famous set of teeth. When he got to Greg's table, he stopped and shook Greg's hand; Carter then shook the hand of everyone at our table. Shaking the former President's hand was a surreal moment for me, but if I had given it a thought, it was just as surreal to be at the same table where Jimmy Carter was shaking hands with Gregory Peck.

Very much related to that, as I move on to a story about Brando, I must say, after knowing Greg and Marlon for some time, I'd often pay little attention to the oddities involved with going out into the regular world with them - But to think back on it all now, odd it was. Casually going out there with Marlon (outside of his Mulholland home) was always a challenge. Even when he was overly "mature," large, a bit heavy, squat and buried behind jackets, sunglasses and giant hats, I was always shocked how quickly he was recognized, and equally as shocked by how fast news of his presence within any certain area, store or restaurant was reported and responded to.

I of course understood that his fame went beyond legend, but the seemingly uncontrolled behavior of people wanting to see him and be near him; that actually was pretty scary. I wasn't any sort of bodyguard, security expert or assistant - none of that. But there I was, often the only one with him when he wanted to step out for our mutual "fun" activities: eating bad junk food, going to electronics stores or heading to other places that included our shared interests. It wasn't often that he left the house, but every now and then, seemingly out of nowhere (with, of course, Marlon-Unpredictability) he'd appear fully dressed in his Mulholland house hallway (not in his usual robes and underwear), and he'd say, "Let's go. We'll take your car." Miles later, when making me park in illegal red zones, he'd laugh, "Don't worry; you're with 'Mister Lucky'."

As many of us have seen, in more than a few films and TV shows, Hollywood has had some fun with the egos of stars, showing them secretly (and not-so-secretly) wanting that occasional jolt of public fan worship. A great example can be seen in 1991's *"Soapdish,"* as Sally Field's daytime-drama star character gets an emotional boost by being swarmed by fans at a mall. Sally Field is a brilliant actress, but it's hard to watch that scene without thinking of her famous Oscar speech where she was thrilled to realize that people "Like" her.

Actually, I loved that speech from her, because as many know, she had the strangest, child-star life, and she deserved (after all the TV, tabloids and the rest of it) to know she had the full respect and artistic rewards from an industry she had worked in since her youth. That's all a long way to get to perhaps a more unique reality: Marlon Brando never went out to be noticed or remotely "liked". He would step out occasionally because he sometimes felt trapped in his house.

Of course, he had been private and reclusive for most of his career. And to many, that was a huge part of his mystery, his singular legend and his unique appeal. When it came to the love affair between a performer and an audience, Marlon perhaps rightfully figured that his performances on the film set completed his end of the bargain. Of course, he sometimes would even sabotage those performances and films with a number of odd publicity methods, but those are subjects for other chapters within this book.

Returning to our field trips out into the worlds of the San Fernando Valley, Sherman Oaks, Montreal (where he shot two films) and other regions, Marlon's appearance always caused quite a stir. In the same way that Richard Nixon had a fetish for audio recorders, Marlon loved home video cameras, always thinking that the then newly-evolving devices could perhaps do some "spying" for him (as witnessed in my Tahiti mission), replace film cameras in movie-making and maybe even document his personal thoughts beyond a mere microphone. In short - as he often was - Marlon was pretty much ahead of his time. Yet oddly, he'd purchase a number of camcorders but rarely ever used one himself.

Nonetheless, when we would often check out new electronic devices at "Fry's" in the valley, an overly interested mob would tightly form around him as he looked through the viewfinders of the powered-up floor models. When we couldn't even move forward or backward through the aisles, he would lower his sunglasses and give me a "Do Something" look. I could only stare back at him, almost angry that he got me into this shit yet again - *He* had known this scene for decades - and no matter how many times he'd put me through it, I did not. Fortunately, these were not screaming music fans or even autograph or handshake seekers; nobody seemed to expect The Pope-and-President-like Brando to sign anything or even shake their mortal hands.

No, they just wanted to tell others later that they had seen him, had stood near him, touched him, or, hell, I really couldn't say. I finally learned a certain truth in these situations: those who worked in these places were as slack-jawed by "His Arrival" as anybody in the building. Not wanting to cause a scene, or act like some sort of traffic cop myself, I'd look into the crowd, and sure enough, I'd spot a store worker, waiter, or someone who was paid by this place. This person was also immobilized and star-struck, like the customers. I'd look at this individual with my best Marlon "Do Something" look. That's when that worker would then - hopefully - wake up and take charge; I'd then see them act like a big shot by clearing the area and occasionally getting a "thank you" from The Star. I'd thank that worker myself and then rush to pay our bill, make our purchase, whatever the escape fee was, to then get the hell out of the place as soon as possible.

This is something Avra dealt with far more than I did, and she was much better at it then I was.

Now, if an amazed, confused open mouth was what you saw when someone spotted Marlon, the look when people out in the world spotted Greg was from an entirely different place. Even though the immediate body posture of "There's The Presidential Pope" was exactly the same, the expressions that followed were polar opposites. It's hard to categorize all the levels of sheer joy people quickly displayed when spotting Greg; it's as though they had laid eyes on a Beautiful Lord God of Our Universe, their long-passed-away grandfather, The Actual Breathing Abraham Lincoln - Take your pick; the smiles were big enough to look painful. And, of course, Greg was always gracious, warm - fully "Greg". Somehow, to the public, it seemed to me that Gregory was both wonderfully embraceable and yet profoundly intimidating at the exact same time.

That rare combination allowed him a certain, dignified distance, even if he was in his summer shorts, sweatshirts and golf caps. It's almost as though an immediate love of Gregory Peck forced people to keep a respectable distance, even as they clearly wanted to touch him, shake his hand or get him to sign something. I rarely witnessed Gregory needing to return strangers more than a smile, but that was more than enough for those who were lucky enough to spot him out in the world. It was a smile in person that people never forgot. And his instinctual brilliance was simple: he made sure he had that smile for everyone. (No, Marlon did not.)

Perhaps my favorite public moment with Greg also happened to be the moment Greg first met Avra in 1990. I had known the Pecks for quite some time by then, but for a number of reasons, in the first eras of our then-courtship, Avra had met all of the family but Greg - *that* aspect of the Peck family was not unusual; Tony, his wife Cheryl, sister Cecilia and mother Veronique were far more public, accessible and mobile than Greg. While Peck wasn't the same brand of recluse that Brando was, Greg was indeed something of a rare sighting in his later years.

By the end of the 1980's, Greg and I had discussed Avra many times; he said he wanted to meet her. That moment arrived when a premiere of one of Cecilia's films was taking place at a theater on Wilshire Boulevard. Cecilia occasionally performed in movies, and of course, her family and friends were always supportive and in attendance when one would launch. While the premiere of this foreign indie in L.A. (a Middle Eastern "Romeo & Juliet" titled *"Torn Apart"*) was not the product of a big-budget studio, it did have something that caused a traffic jam, forced-up blue police barriers and brought out a herd of paparazzi: an early evening attendance by Gregory Peck.

As I often did with my problematic junk cars and severe lack of funds, I parked blocks from the event, not wanting to deal with the pricey valets or embarrassing comparisons of my old economy heap next to the new luxury cars of the rich. It's a real "Los Angeles" thing as many within the industry might tell you. Being the saint that she was, Avra never complained as we would then need to run for blocks in thick Southern California heat to get to the theater on time. As we finally arrived, we could barely get across the street and could not get near the theater; the traffic congestion I mentioned a few lines ago was in full jam. I could see that most the focus and attention of this mob scene was on a very tall elderly man in front of the theater. Guards, police and others were not allowing Avra and me through; we could not get to the theater entrance. Behind a blue police barrier, I shouted with my loudest, Juilliard-trained set of lungs, "Greg!"

His head snapped, turning toward me, and I then saw one of the most magical moments of my life. Seriously. First of all, a background note: Tony and I had been working with Greg at his house a great deal at that time, seeing him day after day in his comfortable sweatshirt, shorts and golf cap ensemble. When he turned to me fully dressed up, fully combed and fully in mega-star mode, well, Jesus Christ, what do you say? That's Gregory Friggin' Peck! Not at a Carolwood house party but out on the street. Better yet, he then started walking toward Avra and me, causing all traffic, police, paparazzi and smoggy Hollywood atmosphere to part, as though he was a more dignified, more handsome version of Charlton Heston's Moses in *"The Ten Commandments"*.

I'd swear later that he actually picked us up and gently placed us on the VIP side of the police barriers, in front of the theater, but the reality was, that's exactly what it *felt* like. What I do remember more precisely and realistically was how he greeted and embraced Avra, taking her by the shoulders and telling her how happy he was to finally meet her. Seeing him look down at her as he held her shoulders, I immediately thought of how much brown-eyed Avra looked like one of Greg's beautiful leading ladies, Jennifer Jones.

As we were all asked by the film producers to get into the theater, Greg, with his typical mix of levity and truth, turned to us and said, "Avra, Joe, it's a mess out here. I'd say you two were lucky that I arrived just in time, able to pluck you from The Great Unwashed." That was his way of mocking the paparazzi, his own fame and all the bizarre noise-making that goes with the opening of a film in Hollywood.

Avra was working full days, five days a week for Marlon up at his house at that time. She grew up in the business, having met hundreds of stars, ranging from Clint Eastwood to Michael Jackson - She was no stranger to fame and she doesn't have a star-struck bone in her body.

Still, as we took our seats for the film in the cool theater, she seemed quiet, even breathless.

As the lights went down, I asked, "Are you okay?" In the dark, she sighed, "Oh My God. He's so beautiful."

The King (1994)

For a number of months in the early 90's, Marlon refused to turn on the television. He *did* watch a lot of TV before that, and he felt it was something he should do a lot less of. So one day, he started his own self-imposed TV ban that, surprisingly, did last for a while; he *did* have willpower. *But* this also happened to be around the time he first discovered (and was first learning) "The Computer". The internet was waking up in stops and starts during that era; so was texting in group chat rooms by way of early forms of anonymous communication. This amazed Marlon.

He'd go into those early "AOL" chat rooms, pretending to be all sorts of people, thrilled that he could just exchange views with those who had no idea of who he was. Eventually, Marlon did turn the television back on, and like many people of his "mature" generation, he was usually quite interested in any given evening's presentation of CNN's *"Larry King Live"*. Back at the height of the show's popularity, King was indeed a talented and smart broadcaster, able to get top guests by allowing them to talk, knowing audiences were tuning in for the guest, not the host.

King seemed to be from that generation that had a hyper-gasping, near-fainting reverence of Marlon Brando. And since Marlon rarely did TV appearances, King clearly saw Brando as the ultimate "Get," as many other broadcasters also did at that time. Luckily for King, Marlon got himself into a certain situation - a unique situation. Brando figured the easiest way out of it: endure a session answering the fawning, soft-ball questions of CNN's top talker of the day.

Ah, the "situation".

Many months before Larry was able to growl-shout his dream-show opening with, "Tonight: on *Larry King Live*: Marlon Brando," Marlon's "situation" began. Always looking for an income stream that did not include film acting, Marlon reluctantly agreed to go along with a lucrative, long-asked-for project - He would finally make a deal with a publisher that would give the world, in book form, his autobiography. It was to come out in 1994, and working with writer Robert Lindsey, it took awhile to put together. Lindsey had performed a similar role four years earlier when Ronald Reagan decided to "write" his own story, but as Lindsey would figure out, Brando and Reagan were two very different men.

Reading both books, it would seem that Lindsey needed to *add* to the blank slate that many found Reagan to be as a person. In turn, I know for a fact that Robert had to *subtract* from the color, sheer life and controversies that Marlon refused to post in his autobiography.

As a hilarious side note, one that made Greg laugh like hell - When Reagan's "Official Biography" (not the Lindsey book) was put together with the blessing of Ronald and Nancy Reagan, they chose Pulitzer Prize winning Theodore Roosevelt biographer

Edmund Morris. Unlike the fluffy celebrity autobiographies that Lindsey would ghostwrite for Reagan (and later, Marlon), the "Official Presidential Biography" is a big thing, especially when the author is handpicked by the former President and First Lady. Morris named the book after one of Reagan's nicknames, "Dutch," and the finished, published book horrified Reagan worshippers, most of the GOP and perhaps most of all, nearly every member of the entire Reagan family.

In it, Morris created an observing, fictional character who went through life with Reagan, a character based on Morris himself. This after Morris was given full access to White House logs, Reagan's private diaries and even Reagan in the flesh. It was clear: a brilliant writer like Morris found Reagan to be too dull a person to write about - Reagan could only be observed and then commented on by someone with an analytical mind. Greg said *that* was the Ronald Reagan he knew as well. Greg laughed like a banshee when Morris was interviewed about it all on *"60 Minutes"*. On the Monday morning after the broadcast, Greg was still howling, quoting Morris to me with, "Nobody around him (Reagan) understood him. Every person I interviewed, almost without exception, eventually would say, 'You know, I could never really figure him out.'"

Anyway, back to Marlon, Larry King and the "Brando autobiography" - As many who follow celebrities know, stars now usually have contracts that demand they promote their films, books or products. No book publisher was going to *not* have this contract with reclusive, unpredictable Marlon. He was given a few choices to promote the book (a network morning show, a late night talk show, etc.), and his agent got him a clause that said he only had to do *one* major promotional appearance - Yes, the chase we've already cut to: he picked Softball Larry.

The night of the big interview, King came to Marlon, and not the other way around. CNN set up a broadcast stage in Marlon's living room and a control center in the kitchen. Avra and I were up at the house that night and we sat at the kitchen table along with the CNN crew, their glowing monitors and Marlon's giant mastiff, Tim. Avra was supposed to release Tim on Marlon's live on-air secret cue, so the giant dog could then run into the interview and assist Marlon in his live TV mission; his mission being to create anarchy and talk about anything other than the book.

Earlier in the day, Avra had helped Marlon gather samples of Salicornia, a genus of succulent, halophyte flowering plants in the family Amaranthaceae that grow in salt marshes, on beaches, and among mangroves. Marlon had invested in a Salicornia farm, and he saw it as the plant of the future, usable to solve world hunger, possible for energy conversion - you name it, according to Marlon, the solution to all problems: Salicornia. Marlon had a table set up with Salicornia there for Larry; it would be the key topic of the evening as far as Marlon was concerned. That and maybe a few minutes killed by big Tim's entrance; Marlon always loved to watch visitors as they first laid eyes on an approaching dog who was the size of a cow.

By the time the interview was over, the book was barely mentioned, Larry was cradled in Marlon's palm, the men kissed, and the whole scene was already being written up to be a skit for a forthcoming edition of *"Saturday Night Live,"* with Kevin Nealon as a fawning King and John Travolta as a controlling, out of control Brando. The skit wasn't far off, as John's Marlon made Nealon's Larry don a bonnet, accept magic marker on his face, force-eat strange food, drop his pants and then serve as a ride, as "Larry" got on all fours and "Marlon" hopped on him like a child on his daddy's back - all as "King" shouted, *"Anything* for The Great Marlon Brando!"

As Avra and I drove home that night from the CNN interview, we had one of our frequent, odd Marlon discussions. We weren't sure of what we just saw, we didn't know how we felt about being part of it, and we didn't know if the whole thing was a bizarre failure or a bizarre success.

Both Marlon and King were thrilled with the broadcast, and why wouldn't they be? Larry King finally bagged an interview with Brando, and Marlon was now officially done with his entire book tour. As we discussed all that, Avra shrugged, "Well, that was strange, but it could've been worse."

Two years later, it would be. Marlon's next "Larry King" appearance was after he saw a Los Angeles freeway incident caught on a TV chopper news-cam, where a truck of undocumented Mexican workers had a violent run-in with law enforcement after a high-speed chase.

The event enraged Marlon; he snapped his fingers, got King to set up a show in an instant and Marlon hit the airwaves before he had a chance to cool down and gather his thoughts. As the live broadcast went on, Marlon went from attacking the California Highway Patrol to taking on Jewish film executives who he saw as running Hollywood while promoting ethnic and racial stereotypes. This led to instant protests from Jewish groups, Avra hiding Marlon in a car trunk to escape an angry mob and Marlon eventually making a tearful televised apology at a synagogue.

I stayed away from all of that one. When Avra returned home from the synagogue, she sighed.

"Well, that was strange, but it could've been worse."

Rewriting Bunyan (1995)

In the early-to-mid-nineties, I often asked myself volumes of questions about how both movie content and film process was changing. After directing an unreleased feature film that was edited by a team of elderly editors on ancient 35mm Moviola cutting machines (editors who had used the same exact machines when they worked on *"Five Easy Pieces," "Easy Rider"* and *"The Monkees"*), I discovered and then bought one of the early Avid editing systems. With that, I taught myself this then-new form of media creation, clearly seeing that *this* is how films and TV will now be put together. In fact, my first jobs in basic cable TV taught me the very thing that I knew Avid was key for: reality TV; no scripts; shoot it first and "write it" later, something that was next to impossible to do quickly with "old" film cameras and classic editing systems.

It was also around this time that giant special-effects-based movies and "epic" films were becoming more and more popular, even more so than the years that immediately followed the original *"Star Wars"*. While Tony and I were writing and selling quirky, dialogue-based scripts such as *"Black Sheep"* and *"Free Money"* (more on that coming up), we knew that studios were producing fewer in-house films that did not feature heavy action, giant fantasy creatures and, yes, "epic" themes. It was around that time that I reminded Tony of my Minnesota roots, wondering why nobody at the time had produced an epic, special effects-driven rendition of *"Paul Bunyan,"* a mythic giant of a character I obviously grew up with in the Midwestern Land of 10,000 Lakes.

After I explained this wild tall tale in detail, Tony agreed. Before we dove into the creation of such a script, I recall a lunch where we first ran the idea past Veronique and Greg. Greg just kind of laughed and shook his head, wondering if this might be some sort of children's film. When we said, "No," he laughed again, poorly masking his dislike of a theme that was running rampant in Hollywood: "Mass Audience" films based on juvenile ideas. It was nothing new, but it was now becoming more than just the norm; it was becoming *the* green light for studio filmmaking. Greg had easily passed on perhaps hundreds of offers to stalk around movie space ships, in capes and outer galactic headwear, always feeling that this was the road to ruin when it came to great American Cinema. In truth, Greg really wasn't a snob about such things, he simply felt that as both a viewer and an artist, it wasn't for him. When Greg saw fantasy well done, he was actually a huge fan, having once pushed for an animated film to be the first nominated for Best Picture, loving the craft, skill, art and sheer spirit of the 1967 Disney feature *"The Jungle Book"* decades before Disney's *"Beauty and the Beast"* earned that distinction.

As brilliant and well-read as she was, Veronique, with her fully European upbringing, knew very little about Paul Bunyan and his blue ox, Babe. As we explained the strange American tall tale of the gigantic lumberjack to her, she shook her head and laughed, asking, "Are you sure this is a character people outside of Minnesota know?" Such a smart question; she knew just how important that was. I assured her it was well known all across America. A nod on that from Greg confirmed it for her. She suggested we try it, fully aware of this new film studio obsession with fantasy, blockbusters and perhaps most of all, projects based on known names, characters and ideas. Tony and I wrote the script after we figured out a way to update the fable, make the story relevant, and (just as "Eco" ideas were becoming mainstream) create an ending that had our lumberjack learning the value of *not* chopping down trees. We went down to a progressive L.A. bookstore called "The Bodhi Tree," bought two copies of Al Gore's *"Earth In The Balance,"* read the books and then started to think of "green" themes that could work in the script.

Looking back, it's almost humorous to think that when we needed a model for a "Villain" who was both a land developer and the kind of man with an ego who thought he could go up against a 100-foot tall walking miracle - and *win* - Well, even way back then, there was only one person we could reference. The evil "Dick Brick" of our script was, of course, a then (some would say) self-publicizing, then achievement-fabricating D-grade "celebrity" of sorts; a worthless, egomaniacal gadfly who would later go on to somehow become the nation's 45th - and very worst - President (again, some would say). Tony was such a master at knowing what would be funny and Hollywood-accurate regarding a character with this many narcissistic insecurities, intellectual deficiencies and demands to brag - What private plane would he insist he fly on? What names would he drop in a contemporary story, stupidly thinking he was impressing those around him, all while allowing others to see his reckless, dangerous incompetence? It was a screenplay that took longer than almost any other script that we wrote; the result was a big, epic, funny, overstuffed thrill ride of a fantasy film.

And yet, we could not find a buyer. While we knew that a script of this nature presented challenges on many levels; at first, we weren't sure as to why it was not resonating with others once we took it to market. Our agents simply saw an epic non-sequel from writers new to this genre, a script that demanded a huge budget. In short, our reps saw this script as unmarketable. Back when Tony and I first started writing, he'd often give Veronique a final draft to read. I'll admit, early on, I was uneasy with this practice; she had great intuition, she spoke her mind but I wasn't sure as to whether or not I wanted to hear criticism from my creative partner's mom.

Of course, for me, all that changed back when she read *"Black Sheep"* and insisted that someone no less than Irving "Swifty" Lazar represent our work. So years later, here we were with a dead script. Tony asked Veronique to give it a read. She found *"Paul Bunyan"* to be dense, unmoving, and perhaps most damaging, hard to get through in a scene-by-scene read.

In my gut, I feared she was right. After spending weeks not looking at it, I thought of her words as I set out to read it once more. I wanted it to be good and I wanted to see where she was wrong, perhaps missing the value of the script. I had to figure this out. I really needed to sell something; I was a freelance writer and actor and I saw no other potential paydays on the horizon.

But given the epic, special-effects-driven wanna-be "Blockbuster" that we thought we were designing, I saw exactly what Veronique understood when I reread *"Paul Bunyan"* — It was a rare moment where I felt I was looking at my own screenwriting, perhaps for the first time, with full objectivity. I blamed myself; Tony was often generous enough to allow me to impose what I felt to be structure, form and order within our scripts. His brilliance as a writer often surfaces with unique dialogue, fully original characters and wild situations one could never predict. All of his contributions were there; I felt I needed to make this into the clear and fun-to-read narrative I felt it could be - or more precisely, simply *had* to be if it was ever going to sell.

With Tony set to leave on a vacation, I asked him if he would be okay with me trying a restructuring of the script. We loved working together, but this story on this canvas was larger and more sprawling than our previous work; I felt I needed to clear my head and remap a new version. Tony agreed to let me give it a try. Of course, I also needed to ask myself, "Would I find the time, motivation and space to actually accomplish this in a realistic amount of time?" As anyone who writes understands, it doesn't take much to get blocked, stalled and dizzy with indecision. As I was having these thoughts, Avra came to me and said, "Pack a bag; Marlon's doing a film in Ireland. We're gonna house-sit Mulholland and take care of the dogs for a while."

The thought of being away from the loud streets in front of my Hollywood apartment, to be way up there on the quiet, secluded hill, in that giant, sprawling Tahitian style house — *without* Marlon — This was something that greatly appealed to me to this exact moment in time.

Given Avra's role as Marlon's assistant, she and I had been up to the house countless times when Marlon wasn't there, but this was different; it was going to be many weeks and it was going to be great. During this time, Marlon had another assistant working with him on *"Divine Rapture,"* a movie filming in Ireland that ultimately fell apart financially and never got finished.

Yes, as I love saying, much more on that coming up. Now remember, Marlon loved computers and he always had the latest and largest monitors, printers and Mac towers, all when this stuff was still quite new and evolving. His main computer set up was in his TV den, on a giant table that looked out onto his property. Back then, you'd often move data with small, insertable flat drives that looked like square drink coasters. I brought *"Paul Bunyan"* into his den on just such a disk, opened it up on his screenwriting program and spent the next few weeks rarely leaving that den. Since the story was American folklore, I thought I'd first chapter-divide the dense script, breaking it up every few pages with oversized-text quotations from Davy Crockett, Ben Franklin, Mark Twain, Will Rogers, Teddy Roosevelt and others - Quotes that always framed-up our story.

Within the script, you'd later learn that Paul (new to this modern world after decades frozen in ice) kept a book of folksy quotations as he was making his way through this contemporary America he found himself in — These quotations were in that book of his. Would this type of "page-turning" device even make it into a final cut of a big, epic fantasy film? No way to know at this stage. By this time in my writing career, I had learned something people like to dispute:

It's not a real "newsflash," but hear me out: I understood that a "read" is not remotely a "film". Almost everybody likes sitting down to watch a movie. Almost everybody hates sitting down to read someone's script. Of course, the argument you'll get from much of Hollywood is that the read has to be as good as the movie - perhaps better. True enough. Perhaps. But as an original screenwriter, I'd often shape scripts on paper in ways that forced a page turn, divided text for the sake of the page design, the ease on the reader's eyes, and I tried to make sure that people could - maybe - enjoy reading it. This is something that I had not done on *"Paul Bunyan"* until now.

Once it was done, Tony and I both felt that it was ready to be shown again. Our timing was right as our then agent was about to become a film executive; Jon Sheinberg was the son of then Universal Studios titan Sid Sheinberg, and Sid was about to leave Universal to start his own family film business; a business he would run with his two sons. This new company run by the Sheinberg family would specialize in making "family" films. Oh, but just before all that, Jon was an agent at William Morris, and as stated, he happened to be our agent. Jon liked this new *"Paul Bunyan"* so much, he gave it to Sid. Sid liked it so much, he had Steven Spielberg read it, and before we knew it, Tony and I had a contract at Universal, along with a deal to develop another fantasy idea of ours: the flying, arrow-shooting baby *"Cupid"*. Both projects went with the Sheinbergs as they went on to start their new company, "The Bubble Factory".

It was a life-changing payday and a series of extensive rewrites that eventually, years later, amounted to - I dare say - nothing. Ultimately, neither *"Bunyan"* nor *"Cupid"* got made.

But still, as all these types of adventures prove to be, it was also a collection of educations that gave me further understanding - and even clarity - when it came to knowing more about the sheer joys, as well as the sheer impossibilities of Hollywood filmmaking - *and* - rewriting.

NOT "THE SAINT" (1995)

I guess it's common knowledge that Australia is a ways away from America. When Avra went there with Marlon to film a remake of *"The Island of Dr. Moreau,"* it took me a while to understand just how far away she was. Frankly, she was far away to a point that was beyond my comprehension. I never did get the time zones right for our phone calls. While I had previously gone in that general direction 4,125 miles to Marlon's islands in Tahiti for his assigned spy mission, the over 7,500 miles to North Queensland, Australia seemed somewhat mind blowing to me. Not to be such a small-town Minnesota boy about it, but I remember how fascinated I was when I was discussing the distance and flight with Marlon as he was getting ready for his trip.

By that time in his life, quite understandably, he positively hated crowded airports, commercial flying and extreme travel. As we discussed Australia, he talked about other trips he'd taken there. I asked, "So you've been there before?" Without the slightest bit of bravado, sarcasm or attitude, he very simply explained, "There aren't too many places I haven't been to."

I recall the moment because it was one of those odd moments when you're brought back to the realization that this isn't just funny old Marlon you're hanging out with; this is Brando, and yes, of course, there really *aren't* that many places that he hasn't been to, this boy from Omaha.

I was talking to him before his trip because Avra said he had questions about one his co-stars in the upcoming film shoot; Avra told Marlon that I had gone to Juilliard with Val Kilmer.

As I've written about within this book, in my Juilliard years, the pursuit of Tony Peck by obvious fame-chasers such as Kevin Spacey and Val Kilmer was the topic of much conversation in the small, tightly-knit Juilliard theater community. I don't know if Val ever met Greg when Val landed the privilege of dating Tony's sister, Cecilia (who also lived in NYC when her brother was at Juilliard), but when that relationship ended, nobody was shocked, simply because different members of his class (two years ahead of the class I was in with my sister, Tony and Kevin) all constantly said the same thing about Val - the verdict was always clear and never-changing: "Val's a horrible guy" - Yes, it was spoken time and time again.

I really didn't know him all that well at school; he was one of those upperclassmen who *never* talked to those in classes below him, unless that person was either a very pretty girl or someone like Tony. But still, to me, it seemed clear that Val was indeed set for stardom. He had a great look, the school facility gave him leads in his all-important much-seen fourth year plays, and as demonstrated, he had no problem when it came to actively pursuing what he wanted.

Jumping back to the years ahead - to the mid 90's, when Marlon needed money and agreed to do a remake of *"The Island of Dr. Moreau"* for New Line Cinema, Avra was set to assist Marlon in Australia for the shoot. As Hollywood history shows, that production, even before filming, was a mess of casting, recasting, shifting directors, etc., etc., etc. When Bruce Willis dropped out of the film, he was replaced by Val Kilmer. Knowing all about my school years, Avra asked me about Val; like most people who had worked in Hollywood, Avra had heard many bad things about Kilmer. I told her a story that I would later tell Marlon, when he asked me about Val before heading off to Australia.

As Marlon was grumbling about having to pack up and travel, he sat down in his TV den with the question, "Avra says you know this Val Kilmer guy?" I shrugged that I never really knew him all that well by way of school, but I feel that I got to really know him one odd afternoon at Universal Studios in the early 80's; know him in a way that seemed to explain all the things I'd heard about him at school.

Preface and reminder: in my summer years during Juilliard, I was invited to work for Norman Lear in L.A., thanks to my first bringing my ideas and samples of an *"All in The Family"* comic strip to Lear just before entering school in New York. Some of those summers were filled with industry strikes that shut down Hollywood and kept me either in New York or in Minnesota visiting my parents. During the summer between my third and fourth year of school, I arrived at Lear's just when the bulk of his company was moving most of its production to the giant lots of Universal Studios. It was a great summer as I ran mail to different bungalows, wrote spec scripts for *"Archie Bunker's Place"* and pitched episode ideas to shows such as *"The Jeffersons"* and the new *"All in The Family"* spin-off, *"Gloria,"* starring Sally Struthers.

When possible, I'd go to as many tapings of the Lear shows as I could and I'd constantly sneak into the Universal screening rooms where there would be nightly, ongoing "exclusive" lot screenings of that summer's biggest film, Universal's *"E.T. The Extraterrestrial"*. Lear was producing a few features at that time as well, so his casting executives such as Eve Brandstein and Marc Hirschfeld occasionally held readings for those projects.

I was often torn between asking to read for roles and being a "team" on-lot "non-performing" worker, clearly seeing the difference between those in front of the camera and those behind it. It really is a set of two different worlds, especially in TV, where the actors can sometimes be both revered and hated at the same time, an odd equation that sadly makes sense when you live in that unique TV universe long enough.

TV shows can occasionally run a long time. An actor can go from one lucky audition to a major, powerful star in what seems like no time at all. Egos develop, power struggles ensue, on and on through the journey of television, a medium that is totally unlike the short-run of a feature shoot or the "live" rigors of theater. In TV, almost everyone behind the camera sees the actors as the odd, exotic creatures that they are; often pretty - or at least different looking, insanely abstract and either one of two things: desperate or successful. I remember when one of the Lear executives who saw me as The World's Greatest Mail Boy learned I was a Juilliard Drama student who was about to enter my graduating year. He said, "Oh? Aw, that's too bad. Wow. I didn't see that in you. Well, you're gonna blow that off and stay here, aren't you?"

At that moment, I thought it was the most ridiculous thing I had ever heard, especially from a guy who knew actors, understood creative craft and worked in the arts. Years later, I totally understood his thinking. From his POV: after three months that summer, I had many friends at Lear's, many friends at Universal and through all that, many friends in the industry. And I was leaving all that to finish my time at a New York theater school? Where, of course, only neuroses, desperation and narcissism can reign? All that, when my DNA was clearly designed - or so it seemed to the Lear people - for factory-like L.A. TV?! Good God, maybe he was right.

Anyway - my Val story - One morning at the Lear casting office, I was running a package of tapes for Eve Brandstein when I ran smack into Boyd Gaines, a Juilliard graduate who had become a regular on the Lear show, "*One Day at a Time*". Being both a Lear-Head and a Juilliard-Know-It-All, I knew that Gaines had graduated just before my sister and I entered Lincoln Center; he was "Group 8", Laura and I were "Group 12". I felt I had to say "Hi" and introduce myself. At first, he just politely listened to my odd introduction and then asked, "Uh, why are you here?" knowing full well that a good Juilliard Theatre Student was supposed to spend their summers doing regional theater, stock musicals or Shakespeare in some park-of-a-festival off in the wilderness. When I explained my odd comic strip history with the Lear company further, he asked, "But geez, you *are* going back to finish, right?"

That was asked like a pure Juilliard Drama student - he knew of the horrible "Student Cutting" slaughter that used to take place after the second year of Juilliard Drama (your small class is cut in half; half the class is told they are no longer Juilliard students), and he couldn't believe that my sister and I were in the same class - *and* that we had both survived the cut.

Given all that, Gaines wanted to make sure that I wasn't tossing all that aside to suddenly become a mail boy in Hollywood.

When I assured him that I was going to finish school, we laughed, had a brief chat and discussed Juilliard - its eccentric faculty and all that goes with that strange, tiny world. In short, Boyd could not have been nicer. We talked about having more chats, seeing each other around the lot and sharing more stories in the future. Given our schedules, not much of that ever transpired, but he always left the door open. When I'd occasionally see him on his way to the "*One Day at a Time*" set, he'd shout, "Group 12," I'd shout, "Group 8" and we'd have an inside laugh.

Again, so completely nice, positive and encouraging. A super talent and a super great guy.

The day I met Boyd was a real "Juilliard" day, as later that afternoon, I ran past one of the Lear casting lounges only to see Val Kilmer looking at some pages of a feature film script; as most in the industry know, those pages in Hollywood are called the "sides" - the few pages you will audition with. I was running because I was behind on my company errands for the day, and there were three things Lear's people really liked about me: I was always fast, I always smiled and I was always on time, with whatever they were asking me to do. In fact, all pre-planned: I actually gave myself an acting role that entire summer; I told myself that I would play the most efficient, dependable, happy mailroom guy in the entire world. I can honestly say that I succeeded.

Anyway, back to seeing Val there - Val and I both blinked as we recognized one another; I went over and said, "Hi!" explaining my presence there as I had done earlier with Boyd. The difference: Val stopped me mid-explanation with, "Okay. Stop. I really don't care." Was that snarky? Funny? I really wasn't sure. I just chalked it up his "Val" act. I learned he was there to read for a film role, a part he felt he was wrong for, but his agent had told him he should go in anyway and meet the casting people; always a smart thing for any actor to do. There was a long line of actors waiting to get in; as it can happen in casting, performers pile up as the scheduler books too many auditions within a certain too-short time frame. Val really didn't like this wait; he was loudly telling those running the audition that he had no time to wait and that if they wanted to see him, they'd better do it soon. Mind you, he was no star at this moment whatsoever. I recall feeling stupid as I felt that the big smile on my face was only being met with an angry, beady-eyed scowl. Shifting gears, I said I had to run across the lot to get a package to some *"Silver Spoons"* producers (that was a new Lear show) and I wished him well.

As I ran the errand, I recall that I had just read about Val in a magazine; only a couple years out of school and he was dating Cher, of all high profile individuals. As I mentioned, Val was not even a star yet, but as it was with Cecilia Peck, I just figured,

"Yeah, I guess it makes sense: he's a great looking guy who truly knows how to operate. Good for him."

After the errand, I was passing that casting area again and Val was just coming out of it, not thrilled to have wasted his time; he did get in to meet with the casting team, but felt he left with all in agreement that Val and this role did not arrive at a good match. I was almost shocked as he approached me, asking about my access to the production company here. I explained my odd set of roles here at Lear's as he then asked for a favor: he told me that the "sides" he just read from also went to a friend of his; an actor who was set to read here tomorrow. Val asked me to go get him a copy of the whole script. Val explained that he (Val) was wrong for the role, but this friend of his - this was more of a role for him. I was both busy and filled with the knowledge that I probably wasn't supposed to be doing that - In those days, there were often reasons as to why producers did not want full scripts circulating around town, thus only the few-page sides for each role. As I told Val that this task would be difficult, he continued to press for it.

Feeling like the slack-jawed Juilliard freshman I once was to Val's then senior class star, I soon found myself tiptoeing around the Lear casting office as I eventually found what seemed to be the sole copy of the complete script. He met me at a hallway Xerox machine as we tried to appear official, hand-feeding the script into the ever-jamming machine, one page at a time, getting further and further off my errand schedule for the day - along with feeling nervous as hell about having the script in my possession - and copying it! When it was finally done, I got a large envelope for Val (for the script copy) and said it was sure nice of him to do this for his friend.

With a totally straight face, Val now made it absolutely clear: this guy who was getting the script; he was no "friend": he was a fellow actor who was about to break out, and this gesture would mean one thing and one thing only to Val - According to Kilmer, this actor would now owe him a favor, no matter what might happen regarding the casting of this film. I instantly put myself in the place of that actor, and I knew that Val was correct about that plan; an auditioning actor suddenly getting a full script he wasn't supposed to have? That's gold. You can then understand the whole character, from start to finish.

I could only nod, thinking that this was probably a very smart "business" move on Kilmer's part. But something else also hit me at that moment: now that he had the script, I was (only now) learning that this other actor was no real friend of Val's. Should that have made a difference as I was sneaking around and essentially stealing the script from Lear's office to copy? You bet it did.

At that time, I was a very young, trusting, positive individual; painfully so. Val saying he wanted to do this for a "friend" when he first asked - That had me wanting to do Val the favor. Learning it was just future leverage for Kilmer; I was getting flashbacks of how people talked about him in school. But all that was about to be eclipsed: as Val was leaving the Lear building - that's when the full "Kilmer" hit. Here we were, both Juilliard students, both in L.A. - Maybe I could learn more about "The Business" from Val. I said, "Hey, I have a message service number (pre-cell-phone days) - Lemme give it to you; maybe we could get together, maybe have a bite." As he was walking away, Val said, "I could lie to you and tell you that'll happen, but it won't."

Wow. After I did him the "favor". For his "friend". He really said that. And with that, he was gone.

Years later, I told a shorter version of that story to Marlon before he went off to Australia to do the film with Val. Marlon nodded as he muttered, "Sounds like a real piece of work." I said, "Who knows? Maybe he's a good guy and that was a bad day for him; I don't know." Many weeks later, when Avra returned from the movie shoot, she had horror stories about Val; so did the entire film crew, stories they'd later share in a documentary about their filming experience in Australia. Marlon never wanted to discuss Val, and I rarely bring up Kilmer when Tony and I reminisce about Juilliard classmates; it seems Val might still be a sore subject when it comes to the Peck family. After *"Moreau,"* Val had a few more shots as a lead, one of the last being a feature film of TV's *"The Saint".* It didn't really work. So - whatever the case back in the 80's, I'll just put it this way: back then: Val Kilmer; he was no

Boyd Gaines. Today, I suspect he's tamed many of his demons; he's been through a lot, and Val has always been one thing for sure: smart.

On the day I told Marlon that "Val Kilmer" story, he wanted to hear more about Lear and his company. I shared further regarding that summer of 1982, particularly a set of thoughts I'll share here. I had a great time working on the Universal lot for Lear. But as it is with any workplace, especially one containing "known" products such as popular TV shows - there's always room for disillusion and disappointment. And don't forget, I was a *huge* fan of the Lear shows. Perhaps it's like working at a restaurant where you once loved the food as a customer; of course, if you toiled in the kitchen of that place long enough, you might change your mind about the cuisine. That leads me to more of what I shared with Marlon, recollections about "race" and the Lear company of the 70's and 80's, a set of stories that first requires me to recall how influenced I was as an 11 year old first watching "All in the Family". If I can begin here: I wish my father was more open-minded when it came to race. As I grew up in small town Minnesota, I also wished that town as a whole was more open-minded when it came to race. At age eleven, when you think you might be surrounded by racism and your best friend (to me at the time, network TV) tells you that you're not wrong to be troubled by this, well, as I've stated in different ways previously: *"All in the Family"* told me as a very young person that racism was wrong, and those around me spouting racism; they were no better than that icon of "wrong," Archie Bunker.

From 11-years-old to 22, I kept up with all the media and news about Norman's company and shows; the big contract negotiations with the stars, the show cancellations, etc. And as Hollywood was becoming more gossip-driven thanks to People magazine, the emerging tabloids, Rona Barrett and even TV Guide, I of course also followed the off-camera behavior of the stars. One would often read about the challenging trials and tribulations of Lear performers such as Mackenzie Phillips of *"One Day at a Time,"* Demond Wilson of *"Sanford and Son"* and many others. There was always news of "walk outs" in television all the time;

Carroll O'Connor, Redd Foxx - and, of course, not just on Lear shows. When a struggling performer suddenly becomes a major "Star," and they begin to feel that *they* are the reason for the triumph of a hit show, a show that makes millions of dollars for networks, studios, sponsors and production companies - well, it's not hard to understand the friction, contract dealings and heated negotiations that come with a huge financial success. Great TV ratings are incredibly powerful, mind-altering drugs.

I got to know a number of high level TV executives at Lear's that summer, and as I was in friendly conversation with one in their office, I'll never forget as this executive was handed a memo from an assistant.

The executive looked at the memo, took a silent beat and then muttered the following:

"Jesus. If you're not racist, work for Norman long enough; you will be."

Such a strange phrase. Such strange wording. And overall, to me at the time, incredibly shocking. Nothing that I expected from this person - at *this* company. I guess my awkward silence did the job of asking, "What do you mean?" The groaning, sighing executive went on with, "To Norman, every black actor is always right, no matter what they say or want. And all the white people who pay 'em; we're all horrible bastards."

As the executive continued to stare angrily at the memo, I found an uncomfortable way to detach from this odd conversation and head away.

But I never forgot the moment or his words.

Unfortunately, that tone felt replicated to me as I was later pitching storylines to the white producers of *"The Jeffersons"*. These two showrunners, a pair of guys who would go on to win Emmys and produce giant shows at other studios and networks, they could not stop chattering during my pitch session; chattering about the obsessive "eye rolling" of their cast, the constant "over-acting" of the cast members and their frustrations with the difficulty of lead actress Isabel Sanford, who they referred to as "The Queen". Were these "racist" remarks and observations? All I can say, in the room at that moment, they most definitely felt that way, as they would jokingly bite their tongues as they exchanged awkward giggles and shifty glances with every comment. Combining their behavior with those comments from the executive, I often had to remind myself how innovative the Lear shows were, not just *"All in the Family"* but also *"Good Times," "The Jeffersons," "Diff'rent Strokes"* and *"Sanford and Son"*. While it was hard to maintain the quality of so many different shows throughout the years, it was easy to forget that these shows were breaking new ground in a new era. And they gave real power to star black performers. By way of a few (very few) old shows such as *"Amos 'n' Andy," "Julia," "I Spy," "The Flip Wilson Show"* and, of course, *"Roots,"* 1980's white America had convinced itself that network TV was pretty much an open, "non-racist" arena, free from the old shackles of prejudice and bigotry.

Of course, nothing could be further from the truth. At the time, I knew Lear himself was always mindful of the then "newness" regarding an all black cast or individual black cast members becoming fully aware of their talent, their value, and perhaps most crucial in the high stakes world of network TV, their newfound bargaining power thanks to the success of a show - hence that executive's gripe. No, to me Norman was always such a pure soul. He and I had a great set of talks years later after a movie pitch. He walked the walk. But for some of the white writers, executives and creatives working for him in those transitional years of TV - and transitional years for American society - clearly, not every Lear employee got the unwritten office memo. To me, that would be a seemingly unneeded memo stating that the company that changed TV with Archie Bunker simply *had* to be a place where racism wasn't allowed. That summer was great, but between those race issues and Val, my thoughts later on those months: "Wow, human beings, just *try* to be nice to each other, for God's sake!" Years later, telling those recollections to Marlon was interesting; he loved discussions like this. After I finished talking, he muttered, "Mankind somehow mistrusts differences. If you could magically have world peace between all races, creeds and colors, achieving that with the snap of your fingers - you'd snap those fingers, and there it would be, no more racial or religious intolerance." He then concluded his fable with, "And after that snap, it would take all of one second for some guy to whisper to his son, 'Now remember: we can't trust all those left handed people'." He then sighed, "Okay, enough about this. I gotta go pack my toothbrush. I'm off to make a picture with this 'Val'."

As Marlon stood, he noticed that I saw him glance at a photo on his end table; a photo of his daughter, Cheyenne, who had committed suicide weeks before this talk. He patted me on the shoulder as he left the den, telling me, "Thanks for all your gab; 'took my noggin elsewhere."

Tony, Meet Marlon (1995)

As you've read, Tony introduced me to so many great and important people, friends of his such as Frank Sinatra, Robert Evans and others. Those were people beyond his family inner circle, a circle where he was generous enough to invite me in and indeed be family with Greg, Veronique, Cheryl and the rest of the Pecks. Tony's heart and open arms always amazed me; to this day, his friendship is one of the brightest aspects of my life. Given all this, it pained me when I was not able to - at first - introduce him to Marlon. Why was this an issue in my mind? Because there are few people in Hollywood who would pass up an opportunity to meet Marlon Brando, and like I said, Tony never hesitated when it came to allowing me a handshake, an introduction or (especially) a laugh with so many powerful, and often, interesting famous individuals.

Of course, even someone as big as Michael Jackson had to learn (as he ended up hiring Brando's son), that Marlon was a rare "get" in the fame orbit, mostly because Marlon stayed far away from any of those circles. Perhaps that's why Greg's silences and occasional dissatisfied grunts about Marlon fascinated me. The more I stumbled upon old Hollywood history, stories and lore, the more I saw that Greg and Marlon probably knew each other well, often crossing paths, sharing political interests and many common industry friendships and working relationships. Oddly, and I simply can't say it often enough, neither man ever really wanted to discuss the other guy - and you really couldn't push that issue with either of them, either. As I now underline currently established ideas here, please know this is essential, as these worlds are set to collide. As I've elaborated on throughout: Greg's and Marlon's polar opposite personalities just instantly rejected "Him" - especially as both men saw how much respect I had for both of them. Don't get me wrong, it's not that either icon cared what I thought, but it's clear that I represented a trigger regarding their mindsets: Marlon had zero respect for "The Industry," while Greg did the impossible: he supported The Industry as he remained his own man - Not like a John Wayne or Charlton Heston, but instead, on an incredibly singular high wire that impossibly balanced "Hollywood" with Integrity. Of course, that's the stuff that puzzled Marlon; he'd easily laugh at a crass, obvious "Industry" cheerleader like John Wayne. But there was no laughing or mocking Gregory Peck. At the same time, it seemed Greg could not fully fathom the industry's acceptance and at times rewarding admiration of Brando's rebellion and shenanigans; all that baffled Greg - Leading me back to long days of writing with Marlon, and the upcoming entrance of Tony Peck.

Oh, slight necessary preface: I never initiated a single photo with Marlon. Ever. And I knew it was never my place to just bring someone up to Mulholland. I knew Marlon even appreciated that I declined many of his frequent invitations, and even knew that I tried hard not to initially meet him back when he was first pushing Avra for it. Again, I just didn't want the stress and burden that would come from meeting my then girlfriend's boss - a man who happened to be Marlon Brando. Once I eventually found myself to be a full-blown member of Marlon's small Mulholland circle, mostly by working as Marlon's "writing partner," I'd be talking to Marlon about Tony far more than I would ever mention Greg. This was for obvious reasons.

I was often trying to discuss how I worked with my "real" writing partner; a guy who laughed with me as we took blank paper and actually turned those pages into scripts; work that had sold for good money to 20th Century-Fox, Universal Studios and Sony Pictures.

Maybe the system Tony and I had wasn't perfect - no creative partnership ever is - but it worked. Writing with Marlon, there was no system, and some days, as I was cancelling appointments or *not* writing with Tony because of my time with Marlon, I'd find myself getting frustrated, peeved and often, depressed. Having gone through the same exhausting "writing" system with Marlon, Sean Penn once said to me, "Joe, I love Marlon, but I can't do that anymore with him. He calls it writing; he talks into a tape recorder - I get the transcript later, I try to make it into a script or I write it all myself - he never likes anything. I don't do it anymore - You wanna keep doing it; knock yourself out." And I did, thanks to the circle I shared with both Avra and Marlon.

Now occasionally, Marlon would ask how Tony and I formed a script together, as every partnership is different, challenging, and at times, in need of evolution. I would often turn the tables and ask how *he* had done it with other writers. I'd find myself fighting to keep a straight face as he'd always say something like, "Those other guys; they never wrote anything. I always ended up having to write it all myself." He'd say this as we were often "rewriting" "old scripts". The fact that those scripts existed at all told me one thing for certain: *someone else* wrote; I knew that for sure.

Marlon seemed to have a certain aversion to finishing something, completing something or even making a firm statement. Part of that - of course - was because he would be immediately graded in ways that most people wouldn't be judged; he was The Great Brando; committing to a finished script or even a line of dialogue, this was something he was often uncomfortable with.

On top of that, in a creative writing process with Marlon, he was the last stop on the train before getting money and other filmmakers involved; in short, if a script *was* ever finally to his liking, all around him would now expect the project to become reality, and in the years when he had true clout (1950's - 1970's) that *did* happen with projects, whether they really were "ready" or not.

Lastly, as an artist and an ever-seeking intellectual, he enjoyed the process of exploring ideas far more than he valued completion or conclusion. *And,* (let's not leave this one out) - it goes without saying, he had *time* on his hands when I met him in the 1990's. On those days up at Mulholland, when I was wondering how my rent might get paid for that month, he was often taking time away from ant watching to dabble in screenwriting with a friend.

Of course, today (and I state this because I do mean it), I cherish every memory of every moment with him. But at the time, I must admit, Marlon could often be a source of incredible frustration.

Ah, yes, I digress - Tony. On one frustrating day in the living room with Marlon, I suggested bringing Tony up to the house, so the two of them could meet and, perhaps, Tony could assist in the writing of the day. As had happened before, the topic of "Tony" would be something of a triple whammy for Marlon: 1) at this stage, Marlon considered Marlon to be my writing partner, 2) this Tony; his father, (groan) and 3) in Marlon's mind, Tony was a "Hollywood Kid," an odd "creature" Marlon had severe across-the-board issues with. Whatever the case, the conversation was interrupted as Avra called on the speaker phone and asked if Marlon was going to be ready for tonight's dinner at Yachio's. What? A lot here - Let's back up a bit. First: The History:

Yachio Tsubaki was a one-time girlfriend of Marlon's. Like many in the Brando Universe, she never really escaped his orbit. But Yachio was different than any of the "former girlfriends" or ex-wives I met. Yachio was a beautiful, wonderfully cultured Japanese woman who Marlon often described as his greatest mistake, within the special category of "The One That Got Away." She and her adult siblings lived in a stunning house in a gated community within the Mulholland region, clearly coming from a certain degree of wealth and privilege. The heightened aspects of her upbringing, appearance, education, independent wealth and certain degree of detachment from Marlon; all these set her apart from most of the women I met from Marlon's past.

Marlon and Yachio had been a longtime couple, but that ended in 1989 when Marlon's then housekeeper gave birth to Marlon's daughter. Horribly hurt but probably not all that shocked when it came to Marlon-being-Marlon, Yachio and Brando parted ways for quite a while.

But after a few years of talks and sustained friendship, Marlon and Yachio became something of an occasional, seemingly platonic couple; they had years of shared history and they both seemed almost humored by their mismatched pairing; he loved describing himself as the rambling, uncultured Midwestern "lug" who was somehow tolerated by this wealthy, educated, beautiful Japanese "princess". Seeing them together did indeed paint that oddly sweet picture.

Back to Avra's call during our "writing" session: she reminded me that she and I were *also* going to this dinner at Yachio's, something I had forgotten altogether. An immediate headache hit. After a long day of "writing" with Marlon, I was hoping for an evening of TV with Avra, or maybe we could go down to our favorite nearby revival house, "The New Beverly Cinema," - something, anything other than a fancy dinner at Yachio's. And they were fancy; when Yachio would have Marlon over, the food, the service and the evening was all quite special. *Ah!* That's when it hit me: Marlon must be up to something! Unlike the Pecks, Marlon had *no* skill when it came to presenting a grand meal, a sophisticated evening or an impressive gathering. But he *did* know when such a thing needed to be thrown. I was starting to understand that this evening was just such an occasion. So I asked Marlon, "I have to shave and put on a suit tonight? And you do too? What's going on?" He groaned as we finished our call with Avra, as *he* was now painfully reminded of a "ruined" evening as well. This is the moment, I thought, that maybe there was a way out of this tonight - Nine times out of ten, at this exact moment - this would be when Marlon would pick up the phone and cancel; just the thought of getting dressed up, combing his hair, getting into the car, etc., etc., etc. All that stuff made Marlon furious. But no. I could see he was resigned to the schedule and the evening. Huh? What gives? So since it was *my* ruined evening as well, I asked, "What's the dinner for?" He then picked up a nearby calculator.

Marlon kept a number of small, battery-powered pocket calculators throughout the den and living room; it seemed, on almost every flat surface. Avra and I often laughed about all those calculators, because they were all only there for one very specific reason: fantasies regarding his finances. Throughout any given week, day or hour, Marlon would seem to have any number of "Get Rich" schemes - As I've discussed: no fantasy was too wild and no possibility was too impossible. Somewhat ironic for a man who could've been at that time one of the richest men in the world; he certainly had enough epic paydays to set up such a reality.

But, no, the money was never well organized nor well invested, and here he was, constantly dreaming, scheming and clicking to see if the fantasy numbers checked out on those calculators. Example: he'd think of a product his name could go on. He'd ballpark the costs to make said product. He'd then think about the millions of customers for said product - click, clack, click into the calculator - In his mind, he was now rich. If such a thought would hit at 3 am, he'd call Avra and tell her to start the research on such a project. Why call at 3am? How could he not? The calculator was telling him that this was a sure thing, a sure fortune. Let's get on it right now!

So - Yes, no screenwriting was getting done that day; both Marlon and I needed to get ready for a dinner at Yachio's. He had picked up the calculator - I had to ask again: "Why this dinner tonight?" He smiled as he looked at a number that had just come up on his calculator, asking me, "Do you know that the United States has one of the highest tax rates in the world?" I knew where this was going. He had often thought that citizenship in another country would spare him when it came to paying U.S. taxes. But as I had this conversation with him before - a number of times - I could see that he was just pretty much making a lot of it up as he went along; he really hadn't done the actual research, but at times such as this, hey, actual research wasn't key to his plan: as he liked to say, "It's not *what* you know, it's *who* you know."

Tonight's guest of honor at Yachio's was to be then Ireland's Minister for Arts (and later President of Ireland) Michael D. Higgins. Higgins recently became friends with Marlon during the brief and quickly aborted filming of *"Divine Rapture,"* in the coastal town of Ballycotton. Marlon said he was thinking of changing his citizenship to Ireland, for the sake of taxes. Gently, I mentioned something I recalled hearing from some newscast - or someplace anyway. My unwanted mention: "I think I heard that Ireland has a higher tax rate than America." He smiled as he kept working the calculator, "Maybe that's true for some people. But I got Higgins."

As the discussion went on, we talked about the tax rates of other countries; I didn't know a lot, but I recalled a recent conversation I was having with Tony about taxes in France, shocked to learn that France had a lower tax rate than America. I recall Tony and I talking about all this because a very close friend of Greg's and Veronique's was the then President of France, Jacques Chirac. I mentioned this and Marlon stopped clacking and clicking on the calculator. He thought in silence for a moment, then asking, "Where'd you hear this about Ireland's taxes?" I shrugged, unsure of his newfound interest with France and Chirac. He then asked, "What do you mean 'friends' with Peck? Chirac's thrilled to meet a big movie star?" I said, "No. They're tight. Close. That's what Tony tells me." Marlon *loved* this kind of discussion - it made his gears turn; as I mentioned previously, he so enjoyed planning, scheming and fantasizing. Having "inside" info!

That night at Yachio's, I met Michael Higgins and an associate of his who traveled with him, another gentleman who also worked in Irish government and had, like Higgins, met Marlon during the film shoot. Upon entering, Marlon quickly pulled Higgins aside and began a hushed conversation in a room corner. With just the six of us here, Avra immediately joined her good friend Yachio in the kitchen and I was left to make conversation with this other Irish politician. He was a sweet old leprechaun of a man who still could not believe that he got to meet Brando.

As we made small talk, I kept on eye on the hushed conversation in the corner between Marlon and Higgins. Whatever Marlon was hearing from Higgins, he did not seem happy.

Before long, Marlon left a somewhat puzzled-looking Higgins in the corner as he loudly asked, "Yachio! Where's the grub?!" The nice man I was talking to had a giggle hearing "grub," but I think everybody else - including Higgins - knew that Marlon's question wasn't playful. Avra, Yachio and I knew that that was pretty much

Marlon-Code for, "How soon can I get the hell out of here and get back home?" Yes, I believe Higgins had already straightened out Marlon on Ireland's tax codes, and right then and there, I figured that the rest of the evening could be long and uneasy.

And indeed it was. The food was exceptional, Yachio was her typical near-silent self and Marlon had very little to say, talking most of the evening to Avra. This left me to awkwardly, politely talk to Higgins and his associate. Whether it was the politician in Higgins or just that he did not know Marlon well, the Minister began to enjoy the evening immensely, especially as I politely peppered him with constant questions and did my best to be both his interviewer and his audience. I occasionally caught Marlon literally laughing at my attempts, only because he knew that he had pretty much left me out there to tirelessly tap-dance - all alone - with *his* guests.

Frankly, the night seemed to go on forever, as both Higgins and his associate wanted to make the most out of their Los Angeles evening with Marlon Brando.

When it finally ended, Marlon was laughing hysterically as he got into the car with Avra and me, chortling, "Oh, man, Joe, you really know how to keep the shine rag moving! Good God!" He went on, "There you were, on the edge of your seat, letting those guys think they were the most fascinating men since creation began. Your act was incredible! You *had* to know about Ireland! You *had* to know about their potato-eating lives! Oh, God! I wish I had a camera rolling!"

As we drove away, I tried to laugh along with him, but after his rib went on too long, I had to ask, "Well, why didn't you say anything? Why *did* I need to do all the talking?!" After a moment, a typical Marlon response arrived: "Look, what should've been said early on was simple: 'Hey, Michael, good to see you again. It's clear this tax thing isn't gonna work out, but I hope you have a good trip back'. And then we could've ended all this a bit earlier." As we were then pulling up to his house, I said, "Yeah, maybe you should've said that earlier, huh?"

He laughed, "Oh, hell no! Then I would've missed you doing that wonderful routine. I was impressed. But seriously, I worry.

You don't need to work so hard to have people like you. It was exhausting to watch." This wasn't that funny to me anymore. I was trying to stay calm. I knew he had had a few drinks, and for Marlon, this was not fully rude, in as much as it was his constant, sometimes irritating "over-observation" mode; always figuring you out and then telling you about yourself. Avra and I often had to remind one another - He does this with people he cares about. You can't get mad; you just need to understand that this is Marlon.

As he got out of the car, he said, "Tell Tony let's meet this week - I wanna talk about Chirac." I said, "Yeah?" He said, "Yeah. Let's do it this Friday." After he disappeared into the house, Avra then turned to me and asked, "Tony?" I could only shrug, thinking of what I was going to say to my best friend about finally meeting Marlon Brando.

When Friday arrived, I think Tony was a bit nervous, as most people seemed to be when they first met Marlon. Tony had met so many of the biggest people in the world, and he always handled himself with perfection and grace. To some extent, I think part of Tony's unease was due to my then longstanding relationship with Marlon; Tony wanted to "measure-up". I understood that completely, as I knew when I first met Marlon, in a sense, on Avra's behalf, to see if I was worthy of living with a young lady Marlon considered to be a cherished daughter. Tony also knew of the famous Brando "Anti-Hollywood" attitude, with Tony being the son of one of the industry's greatest champions. As we were driving up to Mulholland on that Friday, even I was getting somewhat nervous, never knowing what to expect with Marlon.

After telling Tony of the "Higgins" evening, I explained the whole "Chirac" and "tax" stuff. I then told Tony, "Don't take it all too seriously - I mean, let Marlon know you're taking his ideas seriously as he's explaining them, but when this meeting is done today, don't feel you have to go to Greg so he can ask Chirac for a 'Marlon Brando' tax break." The conversation itself was so absurd, by the time we were in Marlon's driveway, Tony could only ask, "What are we doing?" All I could say is, "You're gonna meet Marlon."

Knowing it was unlike himself to be having even the slightest jitter over such a meeting, Tony said, "Don't worry, I know what to say."

Entering the house, I could see Tony's gears turning. He's incredibly perceptive, taking in every household item, kitchen product, furniture piece and ceiling fixture. Tony's like a detective in that way, sensing the decorating tastes, financial priorities and eccentricities of someone's home. It's always obvious when we are writing, as he insists on certain props, colors and design schemes in important opening location descriptions. I used to find such details excessive, until I heard readers of our scripts say things like, "I knew this character right away by that peppermint 'cult' soap bottle you had in her shower." Seriously, Tony's amazing with all those observations.

In Marlon's house, visitors were often confused on all those observational levels; the design of his Polynesian-style home was a mishmash, the quality of the construction was, area by area, to say the least, questionable, and the furnishings were not the items you'd find in the home of a Hollywood legend - say, within the home of Gregory Peck.

I brought Tony into the living room. We waited and whispered for a bit as I heard Marlon getting ready down the hall, which basically meant he was getting out of bed, rubbing some water on his face, using the toilet and tossing on a bathrobe. I had seen him slowly appear into the living room from the hallway so many times, but I was now trying to see the sight through Tony's eyes. It's a strange thing to be in Brando's house... And now, here comes Marlon - and indeed, here he was. Marlon shook both of Tony's hands with a smile; they both knew so much about each other, both knowing that the primary education about the other man came from me.

As we all sat, Marlon's housekeeper brought Marlon a giant bowl of salad. I knew he was on a new diet starting today, this one around the idea that if he filled up on salad early in the day, he'd eat far less later in the evening. Well, that was the plan, anyway. Tony and I were sitting across from Marlon. We watched as Marlon leaned back with his salad bowl, swinging his bare feet up onto the glass coffee table, basically in our faces. I almost had to laugh as Marlon was giving Tony "The Full Brando," bathrobe, underwear, eating and shoving the soles of his beach feet directly at his new guest. Marlon told Tony that he was glad that they were finally meeting.

Some small talk about Greg came and went, and as the ice-breaking was over, I could hear Marlon wanting to get right to the heart of his "scheme". Moments into the talk, I used the topic of "Greg" to bring up Peck's friend, Jacques Chirac, the then President of France. I told Marlon that I had explained the tax idea to Tony; Tony nodded with a smile as conversation unspooled.

But first, here on this page - a few more words about the Pecks and the President:

By the mid 90's, Greg and Veronique of course had many big friends in high places, perhaps none as prestigious as the President of France, Jacques Chirac, a charismatic leader who it seemed would drop all he was doing when the Pecks would be in Paris for any of their many and frequent visits. Chirac really did love Veronique and Greg, and when I saw photos of the Pecks and the president, it often brought to mind something I truly believed when I'd see historic pictures of Greg or Marlon alongside revered leaders: when a world famous American movie star is in the group photo, nobody else in the frame is bigger. I really recall that when I'd often notice a framed photo on the grand piano collection at the Carolwood house of Greg, Frank Sinatra, Grace Kelly and her husband, Rainier III, Prince of Monaco. Of course, most people would look at that photo and ask: "Who's the guy there with Sinatra, Grace Kelly and Gregory Peck?"

Back to the "meeting" with Marlon and Tony: Brando was quick and blunt about his "Tax" idea, suggesting that he too could be a good friend to Chirac, laughing about how politicians like movie stars, perhaps an obvious idea that was also a nick at Greg as well. After a bit, Marlon was sounding a bit like Vito Corleone, suggesting Greg and Veronique "grease the wheels" for him, and in turn, he could then "grease the wheels" for Greg and Veronique - Over what? *For* what?

Marlon didn't really say. See, in a situation like this, Marlon's mind always went to a certain yet often undefined place - It was always about a "deal" that he somehow thought he was on the inside of; a unique set of pieces that fell *only* into *his* lap, and now he had to figure out how to get something out of it. He had just spent days dreaming of this Irish tax break that didn't pan out. With that still on his mind, here's this new situation with the French President and the Pecks.

The rather endearing aspect of this (to me) was the fact that he was Marlon Effing Brando! He could probably pick up the phone and call whoever he wanted and essentially get whatever he wanted whenever he wanted! But instead, Marlon loved this game, this "sly" and "clever" glide of connecting the dots - Even when he didn't fully know *what* he was trying to connect to.

Luckily, as previously spelled out, I had given Tony a great deal of education regarding Marlon, telling Tony what to do after all this went on for too long: smile, agree, stand, say you need to go, politely leave, and then know that this might all be out of Marlon's head an hour later. Tony eventually performed a version of that, but it was not out of boredom or irritation - Tony was fully engaged and in tune with Marlon; they hit it off wonderfully. Tony was actually excited to now tell Veronique about this unique meeting. Would he tell Greg? I wasn't sure.

We left as Tony told Marlon that he wanted to set up a dinner with Marlon, Greg and Veronique at Carolwood - *That* got me a bit unnerved, as I pictured some scheduled night all in order and then Marlon not going. As Tony and I drove down Mulholland, Tony was very excited; he enjoyed the meeting, shouting, "The man showed me the soles of his feet - a total insult in many countries - and I loved it!" I warned him about how quickly these sort of "tax" ideas flew in and out of Marlon's mind; Tony told me not to worry - He'd plant the right seed with his mother; if Marlon came back to Avra or me with a want to follow through, perhaps the Pecks could take it from there. Maybe. I couldn't picture Greg being part of one of Marlon's foggy notions. Sure, I could see Veronique arrange a perfect meal with one of Greg's fellow actors, an old acquaintance, but the whole French tax thing? The amorphous "Grease the Wheels" thing?

That was so Marlon. Veronique? Perhaps. Greg? Not even slightly.

Of course, as I was explaining more about Marlon to Tony, I realized that I was being a bit ridiculous: Tony had spent his life dealing with people as big as Marlon, people who might want something from Greg, Hollywood people who were perhaps even more filled with fantasy than Marlon. Tony would know what to do no matter how this was going to shakedown - or not; he was a master with big personalities, big ideas and big stars like Marlon.

As we were now zooming into Hollywood, Tony said, "There's only one thing I know for certain with this guy; he loves you Joey." As I brushed that off, he reminded me, "He said you're a son to him; you're family." I recall that being said, but I didn't think much of it at the time, only because I was probably still a bit nervous over the whole get-together. Thinking about that as Tony reminded me, I do recall how nice it was for Marlon to say. Tony followed that up with, "That's it, we have to do it." I asked, "What? Have a dinner at Carolwood with Marlon?"

"Maybe. But I'm thinking it's time we finally did it - time that *you* finally do it."

"What?"

"Ask him to play 'The Swede'." And it was that day with Tony and Marlon that finally started the ball rolling for *"Free Money"*. Without that, the film would never have been made.

The brilliance and the bravery of Tony, as you might recall, was displayed by the way Martin Scorsese became the Executive Producer of *"Doctor DeMott"*. When Tony saw a legitimate opening for something, along with a situation he could understand, he took action. Before this day, Tony had not been in Marlon's presence. Spending this time with him, along with seeing my relationship with Marlon - *Plus* hearing for years (from me) about how Marlon picked movies, how he sometimes "needed" to work for the money, etc. *All* that together soon had Tony out and about with our script and the possibility of "Brando". Tony knew it would be hard for anyone to offer Marlon *any* movie without real cash and production behind it, but now, Tony felt he had two huge things that were "factual" as he entered the gambling world of film financing.

The two huge things: *One:* a script Tony and his partner believed in. *Two:* Tony's partner is close to *thee* actor almost everybody in town wants to work with. Before long, Tony had "real" people with actual money lined up, *if* Brando would do *"Free Money"*. All this just as Avra was telling me that Marlon's accountants were getting nervous about his need to get back to work.

One night, thanks to Tony and Avra, I handed the script to "tax-cheat" Marlon. He loved the title.

PHOTO GALLERY

BOTH YOUNG - BOTH HAVING NO IDEA OF WHAT THE FUTURE WOULD BRING

Left: Greg, a happy California kid with English and Scottish roots.

Raised Catholic and in military school by age 10, he disliked his actual first name, "Eldred", opting to shift his middle name of "Gregory" into first position.

He'd go on to attend UC Berkeley, and later The Neighborhood Playhouse in New York City, becoming a student of Sanford Meisner.

Right: Marlon, the little wise guy, the kid who knew how to play monkey with a camera lens from a very early age.

A midwestern mimic who was fortunate to have a mother with a love of theater and the arts. But her issues with alcohol and her troubled marriage to Marlon's father shaped the young boy's dark humor, pain and extreme want to act out.

After years in a Minnesota Military Academy, young Marlon went to New York and became an acting student, guided by Stella Adler. She taught Marlon the "realistic" techniques of the Stanislavski method.

Both Greg and Marlon performed on the Broadway stage, work that earned the attention of Hollywood. Greg was offered the lead in *"Days of Glory"* in 1944, while Marlon's success in the 1947 Broadway production of *"A Streetcar Named Desire"* brought him west to star in the film version of the play. But not before he performed a lead role in Fred Zinnermann's *"The Men"*.

THE 40's - TAKING THE WORLD BY STORM

Look at these guys - Women must've literally fainted and dropped to the floor when they walked into the room.

About seven consequential years separated their arrivals into Hollywood, years when both filmmaking and "acting" changed significantly. Greg and his contemporaries bridged that gap between the "Golden" age of Bogart, Cagney and Tracy and the "New" era of Clift, Dean, and of course, the designated Leader of the Pack, Marlon Brando.

They both achieved the same unprecedented feat: four Best Actor Oscar nominations within their first five years in the industry.

As the years and films stacked up, Greg was often seen as the strong and fully confident man one would turn to with a problem, a war battle or a flat-out crisis brewing in the storyline, all while Marlon was constantly the rebellious mystery - sometimes heroic but never predictable.

To me, that's pretty much how they were in life as well.

THE REBEL AND THE VOICE OF INTEGRITY

THE 50'S, THE 60'S AND ICONIC HITS

After giant films such as *"A Streetcar Named Desire"* and *"Viva Zapata!"*, one of Marlon's most memorable roles turned out to be Johnny Strabler in 1953's "The Wild One" *(left)*.

Months later, Brando would score even bigger with the Elia Kazan classic, *"On the Waterfront"*, a film that gave Marlon his first Academy Award.

Below: Greg in the role of his lifetime, a part that some reports claim was first offered to Rock Hudson; attorney Atticus Finch in 1962's *"To Kill a Mockingbird"*. The film brought Greg an Oscar and became one of cinema's most enduring classics.

THE 1970's - HUGE "COMEBACKS" - HUGE BOX OFFICE

Above: 1976's "The Omen" brought Greg his biggest payday and true popularity in the modern era of 70's cinema, a rare transition for an actor who began his stardom in the 1940's. Greg treated the material as an actual story of parenthood, good and evil, insisting that it never be considered to be a "Horror Movie". The result revived A-grade "thrillers" for every major studio.

Below: What's left to be said about Marlon and 1972's "The Godfather"? It wasn't a big payday for Marlon (since he was coming off of years of films considered to be flops). He famously had to audition for the role, take an epic pay cut and create his own make-up for the screen test. He was only 48 years old when he convincingly played senior citizen Vito Corleone, a reality that often confused certain filmgoers, with young people thinking he was already "old" in the 70's.

THE 80's & 90's - THE MEN I KNEW WELL

I met Greg and Marlon when they only had a few film roles remaining but were looking for those great final projects.

Tony and I wrote the final starring roles for both men - One that was commissioned by Greg, the other was an original script I convinced Marlon to do. Greg optioned the story of *"Wild Strawberries"* directly from Ingmar Bergman himself. Tony and I created a contemporary adaptation with project producer Martin Scorsese and Marty's hand-picked director, Sean Penn.

Even with all that fire power, we couldn't get the proposed mass art film made.

Marlon's final starring role was in 1998's *"Free Money"*, a dark midwestern comedy that Marlon had a great time doing. Tony and I wanted to have Greg in the film as well, but as it was with so many projects, it turned out to be something Greg declined to be a part of. Maybe because of Brando.

Marlon and Greg: I saw them as "The Odd Couple" in my life. Greg was clearly no fan of Marlon's love of "anarchy" - an example of which is illustrated in the incident below.

Right: 2001 - Marlon was told to just happily introduce the event at a NYC concert honoring close friend of both Greg and Marlon, Michael Jackson. Instead, Marlon took it upon himself to discuss bloody, murderous world atrocities, getting booed off the stage. It was all supposed to be taped for a CBS special. Avra and Molly went to NYC with Marlon for the appearance. I called from L.A., asking Avra, "How did it go?" She said, "Don't ask." I said, "I guess I'll see it on CBS." She said, "You won't. He's cut from it."

MY BROTHER AND MY GUIDING LIGHT

Tony Peck *(above, with his sister, Cecilia, at Greg's memorial service)* and Avra Douglas *(right, with Marlon)* are the reasons I met those men, but they are also the best parts of my life. Tony is my writing partner, my sounding board and the quickest way I have of getting a badly needed laugh.

Avra is the mother of our daughter, Molly Rose and she became one of the few people on Earth who Marlon could trust without fail. Today, she runs his estate for one very good reason: Brando knew a solid, honest person when he met one. Avra is exactly that.

SIXTH CHAPTER
NAVIGATE
(GREG & MARLON ESSAY VI)

Greg was essentially allergic to conflict. He really didn't like it. And reportedly, his first marriage with Greta Kukkonen was filled with it. In simple conversation, you'd see him clearly defuse elements of a talk that might lead to angry debate, argument or even at times, a spirited discussion. Given all that, that is why I would delight when he would let himself get carried away with a heated political rant every now and then. I think he felt that his typical rules of non-conflict and social decorum had no place when important policies were at stake, when human lives were being shaped by politics, and government needed to be held accountable.

I recall a couple times when I'd almost randomly (deliberately) inject Ronald Reagan (as an example of a feeble-minded individual) or Richard Nixon (as an example of a crook) into a conversation - any conversation - just to watch the fire get started in his eyes when he heard those names. Sentences or moments later, an opening line would come from Greg, something like, "And why you've dragged Richard Nixon into this conversation, I'll never know, but a crook like that" - And he was off and running. With age, Greg did speak his mind more than in his previous years, but it also seemed that he spent more and more time alone with his thoughts.

Greg was so much more complex than he allowed the world to see, but he was reluctant to share all that for a number of reasons. Greg's private life was just that - Private.

As I've written many times here, Greg knew his image, knew the value of maintaining it and felt that it would be a boring "Hollywood" exercise to open himself up regarding his personal thoughts, desires and goals. In the 80's, if someone interviewing him for a TV movie still wanted the same old stories about how he disliked his real name of "Eldred," or how executives at Fox hated his mustache in *"The Gunfighter,"* he'd politely re-share those chestnuts with elegance and charm, knowing he was going through those motions for the sake of promoting a project.

Marlon, on the other hand - he had a whole different approach to interviews by the 1980's. It's almost as though he would only give a rare interview just to set a forthcoming project on fire. *"The Freshman," "A Dry White Season,"* and other titles, prompted Marlon to go to the press and trash the projects before they were even screened. In some of those cases, Marlon was hoping for a different edit before a film's release. He'd see a cut, find it to be lacking, and his only recourse: do a bit of hostage taking until the film could be fixed. Studios soon had to threaten Marlon legally before signing him, making it clear that he couldn't do a search-and-destroy on a project that had cost so much and had given Brando himself such great paydays.

And of course, this is the exact kind of behavior that Greg abhorred. Greg respected the filmmakers, his fellow cast members, and most of all, the people who paid to see his films. Greg felt, "Well, if the film turns out to be less than we all expected, we all know we tried; we did our best. They all don't work the way we want." Marlon often saw matters differently. There were times when it was pure rebellion from the ground up - If the writer wrote it, it was wrong. If the director wanted it a certain way, that was the wrong way to do it.

Marlon would almost always create his own dialogue, walk west just because the director asked him to walk east - You name it. As his character was asked in *"The Wild One,"* "What are you rebelling against?" Marlon's answer, "Whadda ya got?" Greg would also change lines, suggest his own blocking and do many of the things that stars do on film sets, but it was Brando you'd read about when the tabloid topic was "Temperamental Divas Out of Hand."

Context is everything and so is the messenger who delivers his own demands. I don't fault Marlon for having the passion and the want to shape his characters, and performance-wise, many never understood that he did indeed know his limits regarding "character" behavior. He told me once, "You wanna shock the audience; how far can you go before you break it? I'm not saying you hang a pumpkin on a gladiola tip and expect it to stay standing, but you push it, you try it."

And his want to push and "try" matters - all matters - did come from a few certain places: he knew that audiences always expected "Something" from "Brando," and there were films in the late 50's and early 60's where Marlon did the script as written and took the direction as ordered, only to end up in a forgettable movie - "forgettable" but for the fact that it starred Marlon Brando. That was the very thing that truly got under his skin. Even into the 80's, he was still discussing the burden he had to bear on lousy movies that - he felt - ignored his "non-acting" contributions. He said to me once, "Say a picture's DOA; all everyone says is that it's a 'Marlon Brando' movie! *My* ass gets kicked! Even the director skates clear of the smell!"

Of course, a successful film is key to the career of any star, and in those rare cases where "Classic" stars had to transition into "Comeback" stars and then into "Contemporary" stars - like Greg and Marlon - well, as I keep saying, that is a decade-spanning journey that few actors can accomplish. It takes a mammoth success to carry an older performer into the next few years of a career. And if *another* mammoth success doesn't come along...? Therein lies the problem. It's safe to say that the giant success of *"The Godfather"* carried Marlon all the way through to *"The Formula"* - maybe even to (for obvious reasons) *"The Freshman,"* with Marlon playing a version of his Vito *"Godfather"* character.

But after *that* set of films, it was perhaps a new starting point for Marlon. Yes, he was a legend, yes, he had *"Streetcar," "Waterfront," "Godfather"* - all that behind him. *But,* those were projects that were respected by fellow actors, filmgoers and society in general. They really didn't mean all that much to the grubby money guys of Hollywood in the 90's.

For Greg, the burst of industry pull he received from *"The Omen"* lasted all the way up to the failure of *"The Sea Wolves"* in 1980. After that, he did a couple TV films, produced an Oscar telecast and began to think about what his final years would bring.

Unlike Marlon, Greg was quite open and common-sense when it came to knowing what he needed and wanted in this last chapter; I'm certain he wanted a hit, both artistically and commercially. Marlon, of course, wanted these things as well, but he never wanted to be caught seeking them.

By the time Marlon agreed to play "The Swede," the evil prison warden in *"Free Money,"* he and I were "re-writing" his old screenplays less and less. By then, I think he was seeing the difficulties of getting a production going from the ground-up, a conclusion that Greg had arrived at when we finally stopped trying to get *"Doctor DeMott"* in place. Of course, this didn't mean that Marlon didn't feel the want to "re-write" all of his remaining and upcoming projects, *"Free Money"* included - I'll get to that down the road here. But aside from the writing, Marlon told me that he was looking to "Have a good time" with the final projects he'd do. He liked the fact that as dark as it was in places, *"Free Money"* was first and foremost a comedy. Just before doing the film, he had played a snuff film producer in *"The Brave".* As a favor to Johnny Depp, he took the role of McCarthy, a sadist who pays Depp's character, Raphael, $50,000 to be tortured and killed on film. A Native American living in poverty, Raphael accepts this deal, convinced that he has nothing left to offer the world, other than the snuff money that could help his wife and children.

Of course, it would be hard to think of a project more bleak than *"The Brave,"* a film that star, writer and director Depp first decided not to release after something of an early unwelcome reception. This was when Johnny was clearly on the rise to major stardom, and *that* was another clue to Marlon; proof that all the rules of stardom, distribution and independent filmmaking were once again changing. By 1997, Marlon wanted and needed a successful film, but there were two things he tried to stand firm on: as stated, he no longer wanted to wallow in dark drama, and he wanted the creativity he felt he could have without the "rules" of a producer-run "studio" production.

I was so hoping that *"Free Money"* could be what both Marlon and I were looking for: a future.

THE STORY RESUMES: FREE MONEY (1997)

When Tony and I wrote, *"Black Sheep,"* as I mapped out, we began with a story that was wandering around in my mind for quite some time: my sisters always half-joked that as a child, I was some sort of "White Sheep" favorite of my Mother's. Being that I was a non-drinker, non-smoker and therefore essentially Designated Driver To All, I would laugh at their gentle ribbing over that perception. In the Peck family, Tony would constantly suggest that his sister Cecilia was the "favorite" of both Greg and Veronique. Seeing the four Pecks together - Mom, Dad and the kids - I saw where Tony got those thoughts. We put that script together and took it to market.

After *"Black Sheep"* sold to 20th Century-Fox and we were still rewriting it for the studios, Tony and I sat down to write something new. He said he had a story that was rattling around in his head; well, perhaps, not a full story, but a notion that he felt could be pivotal to a new film we could write. He talked about how he liked prison films; I did not. No matter, I asked about his idea. He said, "Pretty simple, really: two guys commit a crime. One guy needs to confess - The other guy can't confess." I liked that; seemingly familiar yet immediately profound.

At the same moment, I had the want to write something that had yet to be done in film at that time: I wanted to make a dark comedy about where I came from, Minnesota. I didn't have a story yet, but I knew the tone I wanted to work with. Tony took the "Vibe" lead with our "Bluebloods meet the Mafia" characters in *"Black Sheep,"* two cultures Tony loved to discuss and I knew nothing about. Tony allowed me to paint the Midwestern tone of this new piece as we worked on his "confession" plot, complete with the landscape of a maximum security prison.

Using our "Two Guys" structure (as we also did in our first film, *"Tie You Up,"* and our second script, *"Black Sheep"*) we began writing, knowing that two guys like us knew how to write two guys in a movie. Our two guys in this Midwestern film again had aspects of us: back then, Tony would often voice the guy who had been around, had a plan and knew how to get both in and out of trouble. I would often voice the calmer, at times innocent voice. These two in this film were named "Bud and Larry," later to be portrayed wonderfully by Charlie Sheen and Thomas Hayden Church, in the movie titled *"Free Money"*. Thanks to Tony's deal making and Avra's knowledge of how to work with Marlon, I got Brando to star in the film, and with all due respect to Charlie Sheen, my first job after signing Marlon was to get Sean Penn for the role that Sheen ended up doing; I wanted to get Penn as Marlon's co-star for the picture.

It's hard to explain how many levels, paths and crossroads brought me to a few places where I was lucky enough to work with and interact with Sean Penn. To me, Penn's both the conflicted, difficult creature you think he might be, just as he is also the brilliant, dedicated artist you *also* think he might be. Complex, unique and totally original, Sean really is in a class by himself.

He had a great working respect for Greg during *"Doctor DeMott,"* and an absolute Actor's Fan-Boy Fetish for Marlon, a mindset regarding Brando that was, of course, common in the world of acting. Sean had a dream of working with Marlon; either as someone directing Marlon or getting to act alongside Brando. The acting opportunity was offered to him and as I'll explain, he turned it down. I begged him to play The Swede's son-in-law "Bud" in *"Free Money"* - The role was the co-lead of the film and he had many scenes with Marlon.

Sean turned it down for a number of reasons, first telling me that I had the unknowing misfortune of dealing with crooked money guys on this project. He said that years earlier, this very same company (that was co-producing *"Free Money"*) completely stiffed his brother, actor Chris Penn, on a film - Sean warned me to expect the same. Sean turned out to be right about that, but ironically, Sean would later work with these very same people when he needed someone to finance a Jack Nicholson film Sean wanted to direct. Ah, yes, Hollywood. Someone can be a complete crook - and your enemy - until you need them to get your next movie made.

Quick note: I'm not exaggerating when I again tell you that, often, there's nothing fictional about the criminal clash of some "Indie" Hollywood guys and the underworld (as seen in films like *"Get Shorty"*). That's a long way to tell you that there are indeed crooks in The Industry, especially in the low-budget world, where the search for money, the longing for legitimacy and the need to impress attracts some of the most corrupt guys you'll ever meet. One of the main producers of *"Free Money"* turned out to be a certified crook. That's not just *my* judgment; he was basically driven out of the industry by way of lying, cheating and court judgments. Within these pages, I'll simply refer to him as "The Hollywood Guy". Those in Hollywood; they know who he is.

Returning to Mr. Penn: the night that I was to have my first real "talk" with Marlon about his now-committed participation in *"Free Money"* was odd in the ordinary world, but quite ordinary in The Brando World. Luckily, I was initiated when it came to the twists, turns and challenges that Marlon would bring to any project. Granted, it's not as though there is ever a clear and straight path to a one-of-a-kind multi-million dollar endeavor; and that IS the definition of every major feature film. Still, I knew Marlon would throw me a curveball or two along the way.

With this "night" I'm referring to, I'm jumping to a moment in my timeline where Marlon had firmly agreed to do the film and I was set to direct the picture. While the aforementioned Hollywood financier was someone few trusted, an Old Guard Canadian co-producer was brought in to make everybody happy - *and* to guarantee the needed money that would come from the shoot in Montreal. Canadian Nicolas Clermont of Filmline International was a sweet, elfin soul who balanced-out the crook and brought a great deal of stability to what I knew would be a rollercoaster of a production.

Weeks earlier, Marlon had a good talk with Nicolas when I first brought the project up to Mulholland, and as early as matters were, it seemed that things were finally on course and that the film was going to be made. Marlon was the only real "cast" performer at that time, but that was as planned, as the obtaining of "Brando" would then force a number of name performers to simply fight one another to do the film - or so that was the semi-calculated strategy.

Yes, as always, I digress - Showing up at Brando's that night, to discuss the project Marlon had agreed to do; back to that. Well, who was there to meet me as I arrived? Once again entering my life, none other than Sean Penn. He was out in the driveway, satisfying a nicotine fit Marlon wouldn't allow in his house. After we made some small talk about our somewhat recent, somewhat frustrating adventure with Greg, Scorsese and *"Doctor DeMott,"* I talked about how much I wanted him to co-star with Marlon in *"Free Money,"* the dark comedy about an aging, murdering prison warden and his slacker, hapless, criminal son-in-law: Marlon and Sean: it would've been great casting. I assumed that's why he was here, even though, uh, I had not invited him tonight.

Of course, at that moment, all I could really focus on was the script in Sean's hand.

What is that script? Oh, I understood immediately, I had figured it out instantly: Sean heard that Marlon was ready (or needed) to do a movie again - Clearly, his thinking: "Marlon, why do Joe's odd indie flick when you could do *my* Oscar-caliber studio-level Potential Best Picture?"

When I asked why he was here, he said Marlon had told him how much Tony and I wanted Sean for the son-in-law role of "Bud," which was totally true. That was an early conversation that Marlon and I had even when I first asked Brando to give the script an initial read weeks ago. But the too-thick script in Sean's hand tonight was clearly not *"Free Money"*. As I squinted down at the cover, trying to look as though I was not squinting down at the cover, I could see that it was an adaptation of the classic Gabriel Garcia Marquez novel, *"One Hundred Years of Solitude"* - Pure and shameless "Oscar Bait" if ever there was such a thing. However, my heart rate changed for the better after he answered my casual question: "Oh? Who's making this?"

Penn shrugged, "Nobody. Yet."

I instantly had the whole picture clear in my mind and I felt better about all of it. I knew that Marlon needed to work soon, quickly - like, last month. At least, that is what he was hearing from his accountants, a few of his children and various people in Tahiti. At this moment, Sean did not have his Marquez film remotely lined up or ready. As experienced as Penn was in the business, I do think his "Marlon Fever" was stronger than his common sense at that moment.

To clarify, I think he felt that any studio would whip a film shoot into instant shape and operation if Sean Penn walked in the door with Marlon Brando and that script. By the way, if I were a studio head, I would do that in a second, but maybe that's why I am not a studio head. When a film is not a comic book franchise sequel or some other crass commercial piece of bubble gum, these studio-head guys are more often than not frustratingly cautious, slow moving to the point of time wasting, and not all that thrilled with "Art Films" starring aging stars, as *"Doctor DeMott"* starring Gregory Peck showed both Sean and me time and time again.

But to make his point about wanting Marlon in *"Solitude"* clear, Sean muttered a quiet threat as I knew I was in for an odd evening of unique battle; he sighed, "It's time Mar got back into 'The Real Game'." I knew what he meant, but I really didn't care to hear it from him, and not tonight. What was he saying? Perhaps correctly, he was saying that Marlon Brando needs to be doing "important" films, probably with studios who will finance yet stay out of the way for artistic reasons; studios who can get a film both properly made and distributed. *"The Godfather"* with Paramount. *"Apocalypse Now"* and *"Last Tango in Paris"* with United Artists - This is the kind of work many felt Marlon needed to be doing in his final years. Maybe Sean was right.

But as a constant eyewitness up at Mulholland, I saw what Marlon was offered in those days and what he was turning down. And as experienced as Sean was, I had to wonder how he thought he could get Marlon to agree to a "Real Game" film and then retain him for the next few years as that film would come together. I could only figure that, as Marlon once was, Sean was at *that* moment a big star in his prime. He was getting great parts, constant offers, awards and maybe, at times, not always seeing the filmmaking world as clearly as others might; tonight, those "others" being a desperate writer/director like me, and an aging, financially challenged icon like Marlon.

Seeing that his script rattled me a bit, Sean said, "Hey, I hear your script is pretty funny." I could only nod as he finished his cigarette and we went into the house. We found Marlon in the TV den; he hit the "mute" on the television as we entered. He rose his large frame off the sofa with a spinal growl as he grunted, "Let's do this in the living room," letting us know that this conversation was to be of "Living Room" caliber; not just mere casual "TV Den" chat.

As the three of us were still getting situated in the living room, Sean tossed the Marquez script down onto the center glass coffee table with a "slap". This was followed by Penn telling Marlon, "There's your next movie, right there." I thought to myself, "Wow, he's really just going for it. Jesus Christ!" Marlon picked it up, stared at the cover and then asked, "This is ready to go?" Sean shrugged, "I can pull it together - *We* can pull it together." Marlon's face said it all: that movie script presently in his hands - that script *might* - if all the stars align - *might* get filmed in about a year. Sean could see that *that* was the look on Marlon's face.

As earlier in the driveway, I suddenly felt better again, knowing *my* world and *Marlon's* world better than I believe Sean knew his own, at this very moment, in this very living room. Movies take so long to line up and go into production. Of course, I knew Penn knew this; up to that point, he had obviously worked hard to line-up and direct *"The Indian Runner"* and *"The Crossing Guard"* - two movies I loved. But even with Jack Nicholson in Sean's most recently directed film, I'm sure the picture took a while to get made. So, yes, I knew Sean understood the long path to a fully financed start date. Still, I'll say it again, I think as a constantly hired star, always having a project to do, turning down films left and right, having money in the bank, I think Sean didn't quite see Marlon's need for immediate work. Frankly, I don't fault Sean for trying. He saw an opening to finally work with his idol (on a "Directed by Sean Penn" passion-project) and he wanted to try and make it happen. All the more reason for my frustration when I was handing Sean the opportunity - maybe his *only* opportunity - to work with Brando on *"Free Money"*.

So after Sean said, "I can pull it together - *We* can pull it together," Marlon said, "Well, Joe's *'Free Money'* thing - we shoot this at the end of next month." I had an extra copy of *"Free Money"* and I handed it to Sean. Penn asked about the director - Marlon pointed to me. Sean then asked about the producers and the money people - I named them; he didn't know Clermont, but regarding The Hollywood Guy, as I mentioned previously, Sean said, "You know he's a crook, right? I know this. My brother, Chris, he did a movie for him; 'couldn't get paid." I had heard such things, quickly saying, "This is why we have Nicolas Clermont - He's working the money and the Canadian side of things; from Montreal." Sean blinked, "Canada? Then how are *you* directing? Their tax break is gonna come from using a Canadian director."

I said, "It c*ould*, or if they do enough Canadian casting, and they bill everybody a certain way - " Sean interrupted, "I don't even know the script, but you're gonna be handed Donald Sutherland or Christopher Plummer or Genevieve Bujold in there somewhere, and nobody's gonna give them billing over Marlon, I can tell you that." Sean wasn't being difficult or even negative; as usual, he was being smart and informed. At that time, a large part of "Canadian Content" money in Montreal would start with either a Canadian director *or* the top-billed actor being Canadian. Preferably for the budget - both.

Yes, when it came to the Canadian Content System of 1990's Film Financing, Penn did indeed know his stuff. He was mentioning things that I had thought about since the deal memos were being made for me at William Morris: Star casting and above-the-line talent required a number of Canadian hires, to trigger the massive tax breaks that Canada would give Hollywood filmmakers, along with production costs that were a fraction of American fees. Putting all that stuff aside, Sean soon got to a point that seemed clear: he really didn't care to be in the film unless he was also directing it. Once that was out in the open, Marlon did the strangest thing.

He stood and told us he was going to the kitchen for food, saying as he left, "I love you both - you two fight it out."

Oh, a quick side story on that script Sean brought that night - Years later, I'd learn that Penn never even had the rights from Marquez to make the film. Whether it was before the actual shooting of *"Free Money"* or after, I'm not sure, Sean had a production company fly Penn and Marlon to Mexico City, so they could totally shock Marquez with the unannounced arrival of a legend: Brando. Sean would pull this giant rabbit out of a hat; then the rabbit was supposed to personally beg Marquez for the book rights; rights Marquez had already refused to give to Sean.

When I learned of this plot years after *"Free Money,"* I was not shocked that Marlon would go along with it; he clearly would've loved the half-assed unplanned nature of the scheme, and most importantly to Marlon, he would've been sensing just how determined both Penn and his studio backers were to make a difficult, Oscar-bait project with Brando. Marlon would've been already envisioning a scenario where he'd probably see a big advance payday and not even have to do a movie; even on paper, it was a fragile project with a number of land mines to navigate.

So, to finish this side story: Sean flew Marlon down to Mexico, to pounce on an unaware Gabriel Garcia Marquez. When they learned that Marquez was not even in town for the surprise begging (Good God, how perfectly "Marlon and Sean," the kings of seat-of-their-pants thinking), they hung out in a Mexico City hotel room for a few days until Marlon was bored. Before long, Brando was torn between wanting to be back home and suffering a trip into a crowded airport.

As Sean seemed good at, he used his "Marlon Ticket" to get a plane pilot named John Travolta to drop everything and fly his own small plane down to Mexico, so John could finally meet (and provide a private flight for) someone he always wanted to be introduced to: that actor named Marlon Brando. (Sadly for John, Marlon always thought of Travolta as a dreadful actor.)

The story frustrates me somewhat, only in that it shows the difference between what struggling independent filmmakers (like I was at the time) go through just to get a film made, while at the very same moment, studio level performers can gleefully piss away tens of thousands of dollars (or more) on what can be - essentially, in this case, a total and unsuccessful vanity lark. Hey, Marlon and Sean were incredibly successful artists; I can't say they hadn't earned the right to do whatever the hell they wanted when it came to trying to get a film made.

But here I was with *"Free Money,"* thanks to Marlon, seemingly in direct competition with a studio, a star filmmaker (who would go on to win a pair of Oscars) and Gabriel Garcia Marquez. Okay - back to that tense night up on Mulholland with Sean, Marlon and *"Free Money"*.

Frankly, with Marlon now eating in the kitchen and being out of the living room, with so much now out in the open, it was suddenly easier to talk to Sean one-on-one. He asked, "Do you know Mike Medavoy?" I said I knew him well; he had been Tony's good friend and he gave us Culver City "Tri-Star" offices when I directed our first film, the unreleased independent feature, *"Tie You Up"*. By the time I was having this conversation with Sean, Medavoy was no longer at Tri-Star and he was running his own "Phoenix Pictures" not far from his former Sony/Tri-Star offices. "Phoenix" is also where Sean had his production office. Sean went on with, "Look, whether I'm in your film, directing it, both or neither, whatever the case, you should have a real producer attached, at least to make sure that Marlon gets paid. This is why I mention Mike." I explained how long I had been putting this together, how difficult it was to engineer; he understood all that. I also told him that Clermont and The Hollywood Guy did not want another partner, and that a real studio type like Mike would just slow this down. He asked if I would take a meeting with Mike - I said of course.

Then, after an odd moment of silence, he asked, "What's wrong?"

He was right about something being wrong, but I wasn't even sure what it was. As I thought for a bit, I muttered, "I want to direct this. But I'd rather have you direct it instead of some Canadian I don't even know, especially if you'll be in it. You and Marlon will be great together in this." Penn asked, "You *do* think ultimately, they're not gonna let you direct this."

Actually, Sean said that as a statement, not as a question. I shrugged, "Do I think they're telling me what I want to hear about directing so I continue to get Marlon into the movie? Of course."

I then added, "But with you *in* it, *and* as a director - They're gonna mess with *you* a lot less than they're gonna mess with *me*." He laughed, "Don't count on that. Look, let's talk to Mike." I nodded. He then said, "Oh, and just as an exercise, tell them I wanna direct this; see what they say. Then I'll tell you if *you* or some Canadian director is gonna make this." A bit baffled, I asked, "What exactly do you mean?" Penn said, "If they say, 'No way is Sean Penn gonna direct this' - Well, then I have a pretty good idea that you're not gonna be directing this either."

The next day, I had a call with Nicolas and we talked a bit about my meeting with Marlon and Penn. But first, he discussed a good call he'd had with Marlon earlier that day; it was about Brando's money, his escrow account, etc. - all things relating to Marlon's money and Brando getting paid. It all sounded good. Marlon's first million (of his ultimate three million dollar salary) had just been put into escrow that morning. When I brought up Sean directing, Nicolas said that that was a non-issue, as I was set to direct. Talking about my want for the best film possible, I said how much I wanted Sean Penn in the movie, and if *that* meant he would also direct - Well, that is something we should all think about. Nicolas said he'd run all that past The Hollywood Guy, but that, "Perhaps it's best to just get Sean out of the picture."

Huh? I thought that was an odd notion, especially coming from Clermont, who, I believed up until then, had an artistic soul and wanted to make good movies. But his thinking was actually quite practical: he felt Sean was already complicating things - or about to, especially since both Marlon and I liked Penn a great deal. Going back a few steps here for the sake of Clermont's figuring, again: getting any movie to an actual start date is incredibly hard - getting it there with Marlon Brando attached: very few have ever done it. And many have famously failed at it. In short: the less complication, the better. Clermont's equation without Penn was also about the exciting streamlining that just might be possible now that we had Marlon Brando; Nicolas felt that any actor of

Penn's age would jump at the movie - without directing aspirations attached - Tom Cruise, Brad Pitt, you name it. We get our pick. So thought Nicolas Clermont on that day.

An hour later, Clermont called back with an angry message from The Hollywood Guy: "No way in hell is Sean Penn to be considered as the director of this movie. *'Indian Runner'* was arty shit and lost money, *'Crossing Guard'* was arty shit and lost money! No way, no how!"

Clermont said he didn't personally feel this way, but this is how The Hollywood Guy financier felt about matters. After more discussion, the final word on Sean seemed to be this: he can be in the movie, but he will not direct it. I hung up, pondering what Sean had said. Yes, I was starting to think: when the time is right, they will tell me that a Canadian director - for the sake of the "Canadian Content" budget issue - is directing this. Not me.

Why did this stuff regarding Sean have me thinking all this? Maybe it was because I had great respect for Sean, both for his acting as well as for his directing. I was starting to feel that we would be lucky to get Sean in this movie, no matter what his demands about directing. Yes, I knew that people like The Hollywood Guy only looked at box office and budgets, and that works of passion and art such as *"The Crossing Guard"* and *"The Indian Runner"* were way over his small brain. But I do believe that even a bottom-feeder such as The Hollywood Guy could see the value of Sean Penn, directing, acting or both. And yes, my thinking again went to a place where I told myself, "Announcing the Canadian Director, doing that kind of switch-a-roo and rug-pull - When the time comes, that's gonna be a lot easier to do to *me* - than it is to Sean Penn." And with those thoughts, I went off to Culver City, to meet with Sean Penn, Mike Medavoy and their associates.

Cutting to the chase, so to speak, there were no great surprises at the Mike Medavoy meeting. In fact, it was so much of the "Hollywood" trail that I was accustomed to by then: I was handed the usual set of brakes: this project was moving too fast, it was going to be a major investment that didn't even have a distributor yet; with the high cost, what distributor would even want it after it was completed? Etc., etc., etc. The chatter and warnings went on for what seemed like an hour, until one unexpected thing happened to stumble out of my mouth in the process of all this talk.

I said, "Marlon got his first million this morning."

As you read a moment ago, that was true; Nicolas had told me that. That brought total silence to the room; a room filled with Sean and his team, Mike and his team, and me - with no team. They all knew: Marlon's not giving that money back. No way, no how. His remaining two million is based on the film happening by a certain date. Nicolas Clermont and The Hollywood Guy were not going to piss away their borrowed million just because "Real Game" players like Sean Penn and Mike Medavoy are now having conversations around the perimeter of this project.

After a silence that seemed to ask, "Then why the fuck are we wasting our time here?" - Mike, ever the quiet realist, uttered, "Well, Joe, looks like you're making your movie. Good luck."

Not long after that, Sean locked-in his decision to not act in the film. And *yes*, somehow, gee, the producers *did* need to have a Canadian director; I'd learn this after the project was getting underway. Another issue: the flood of A-List actors for the role of "Bud" never took shape. In the eleventh hour of casting, Charlie Sheen became available, thanks to a party-hearty-driven friendship with The Hollywood Guy. This was back in the days of Charlie being fully and solidly synonymous with bad direct-to-video movies and severe drug addiction, before his TV comeback era with CBS and *"Two and a Half Men"*. With frustration and anger, I felt this wild imbalance constantly throughout the production and with the ultimate reception of the film: I brought the project The World's Greatest Living Actor. The Hollywood Guy brought a washed-up, fall-down drug addict who then starred *only* in films premiering on VHS. I know, that sounds harsh, but that was the absolute industry view of that exact moment, told to my face time and time again.

And one last bit of casting business: Tony and I so wanted Greg for the role of the evil Judge Rausenberger, a character who would have many scenes with Marlon - Two issues with that: we weren't sure if Greg would do it, and more to the point, by way of Nicolas Clermont, the role was already given to that standard Canadian Content Master, Donald Sutherland.

More on Greg and *"Free Money"* ahead.

As for Sean; even after *"Doctor DeMott"* and *"Free Money,"* it would not be my last experience with him - Hollywood is a small town. And the Brando Universe was even smaller.

Before shooting *"Free Money,"* as all the initial deals were being put together to make the picture possible, Nicolas Clermont warned me, "My company has never paid three million dollars for a single actor, ever. I want to pay you and Tony what the script is worth, but the only way we can do this film is to first pay you a part of the script fee, while we then pay you two for other writing assignments, other projects I am doing in Canada. Then there will be the full back-half of your money down the road for yet another project from my partner."

At the time, it all sounded good, but even then, I knew that was all a long way to say that our final money would be coming from The Hollywood Guy, the man that many in town, including Sean Penn, had said was a crook who doesn't pay people. But I didn't really have a choice at this moment in time. Nicolas was here with some real money for me now, and more importantly, I already got Marlon involved, and he *would* be getting paid in full by Nicolas. So - as you may be asking: why would a "nice" guy like Nicolas work with a crook like The Hollywood Guy?

That's easy: say a "nice" guy wants to make a movie. But it costs a lot. So this "nice" guy gets a scumbag to find money. But the movie tanks. Still, the "nice" guy wants to make another movie. But it costs a lot. So this "nice" guy gets a scumbag - Okay, you're starting to see a cycle here.

In the worlds of thieves, addicts and gamblers, you'll probably have no trouble finding a "nice" one next to a scumbag.

Rome (1997)

When Tony and I sold our *"Free Money"* script to Nicolas Clermont's Filmline International, the contract was complicated, layered and filled with both potential and pitfalls. Part of our deal included a rewrite of a drama titled, *"States of Separation,"* a psychological sexual triangle that was set to be directed by *"Night Porter"* director Liliana Cavani. Cavani was a bold, sharp and imposing presence, from the Italian director generation of Bellocchio, Pasolini and Bertolucci.

With weeks before the *"Free Money"* shoot, Nicolas wanted Tony and me to start work with her. Tony and I flew to Italy to write with Cavani for a week; we'd then go back to L.A. to do the full Americanized rewrite for Nicolas. Arriving in Rome, Liliana did not disappoint when it came to intimidating me down to my small-town Minnesota roots. Even my time at Juilliard mixed with years in both New York and the Hollywood film industry didn't really prepare me for this steely-eyed director. The woman never smiled in our presence, she spoke no English, she actually wore a cape, high boots and she carried a walking stick - for clearly no medical reason whatsoever.

Tony and I worked our week with Cavani speaking through a team of interpreters, at the coolest cigarette-smoke-filled foreign-movie-set of a retro Euro-office I'll ever get to experience. At that time, we didn't have much of a track record as successful screenwriters, but she did know that Tony was Greg's son and that we had just landed Brando in a film we wrote. I was often at my wits end, seeing Rome for the first time and wanting to do a great job for both Nicolas and Liliana. Tony in contrast was such a complete and fully relaxed world traveller, returning to a city he loved, to a place he wanted to show me, eager to serve up the sights and acquaintances he knew quite well. Singer Tony Renis was a good friend of the Peck family; we went to his home and he sang his 1962 hit, *"Quando Quando Quando,"* something I saw him do for the crowd at a party in Cecilia Peck's L.A. apartment months earlier. His gag "party" version of the song was a rendition where he'd perform it as different singers, including Elvis, Sinatra and Jerry Lewis.

By the time the week was over, I wasn't sure how Tony and I were going to do a rewrite that would fully work for Cavani. Before leaving Los Angeles, I had watched her movies, read her shooting scripts from those films and even studied-up on her non-cinema projects; she was also a renowned opera director, getting ready to mount an upcoming production of Verdi's *"La Traviata"*. I felt like the script we were about to rewrite was essentially a TV soap opera at its core; a somewhat silly idea about a schizophrenic bombshell who has secret torrid sexual affairs with her two therapists, two doctors who also happen to be a seemingly happy heterosexual married couple. And yes, the bombshell has no idea about one of her "personalities" having a lesbian affair with the bi-curious "wife" therapist, and - okay, yeah, I think I'll just stop here.

It was all a pretty crazy idea, oddly enough, sounding better here at this very moment than it did as a potential screenplay back then. In fact, the script version we were starting with was already heavily rewritten, all in attempts to make it more deep, more dark and more brooding for Mega-Diva Liliana Cavani. *But* - we were also to make it "Made in the USA" commercial. At the time, the project was stalled at Filmline and Nicolas warned Tony and me, "Don't make your Americanized rewrite too serious. While it's not a comedy, it can't be bottom-of-the-well tragedy either - Think moody, think sweaty Tony Scott, think 90's Hollywood, think anything other than crying-from-the-gut Italian opera." I'm usually an "Anything can work when done right" screenwriter; optimistic and excited with a blank first page. With this, as stated, I really wasn't sure.

By the time we left Rome, we had struck up an almost smiling relationship with Liliana. At our last meeting, through our interpreters, she had a question or two about both Greg and Marlon; nothing fan-like or pedestrian - simply professional, filmmaker-based and artistic. The short discussion about Greg dealt with *"Behold a Pale Horse,"* the few questions about Marlon included talk of *"Last Tango in Paris"* - Perhaps the two darkest projects from those men. I left liking Cavani a great deal, feeling bad because I did not have a large amount of confidence regarding this project. She was so hoping that these two young American screenwriters could finally crack the code of a shop-worn script that just couldn't find a green light.

To cut to that chase; no, we couldn't and we didn't. We did a number of rewrites, but the film never did get made. Still, I actually learned a lot about the industry with that project. Your agent gets you an assignment because it's part of another deal; you do your best - like the many writers before you - but the story doesn't work, or the script can't get an A-List star attached, etc., etc., etc. So much of the equation is luck - in a thousand ways, taking a thousand shapes, all unspooling in a thousand unknowable moments. But I got to meet an inspiring film director. I got to see Rome, and Tony showed me a few of the places where Greg had filmed *"Roman Holiday,"* one of the truly perfect films of all time. Without a doubt, that was a project that had more luck going for it than *"States of Separation".*

Flying home from Rome, when I wasn't thinking of the *"States of Separation"* rewrite, my unease returned to *"Free Money".* I knew I'd soon be dealing with the "new" Canadian director for the upcoming shoot *and* with Marlon - I'd be dealing with *"Everything* Marlon" during this delicate period: between Marlon having said "yes" to a film, to him arriving on the set to *do* the film. I was lucky; most producers didn't have full access to him during this precarious period.

Fortunately, I knew the rare drill of Brando-wrangling. Believe me when I tell ya: it wasn't easy.

FREE MONEY REWRITE (1997)

Once I got Marlon to say "yes" to *"Free Money"* and he received that previously mentioned first payment of one million dollars, there were still many weeks before the film production; weeks where I knew that a number of things could go "Marlon" wrong. Of course, I had seen so many of his moves and tactics up close; times when he would look for a way to *not* do the project. In some cases, ways he would try to live out his constant dream of still somehow getting all of the money and then somehow *not* having to do the film. He was like the kid who prayed for an earthquake on the night before the school test, somehow engineered an actual earthquake, missed the test and then still expected an "A" on his report card. Something a bit like that.

One thing I knew for certain: he'll wanna go through the motions of "rewriting" the *"Free Money"* script. Always, always, always. This as I was already rewriting the script (for real) with the film's Canadian director, Yves Simoneau, a director I grew to like and respect. Simoneau was an accomplished director who understandably disliked the perception that certain films came his way only thanks to "Canadian Content" requirements. During these "rewrite" weeks, Yves was often up in Montreal, getting the production organized. We'd talk each morning and he'd tell me what he thought was possible, impossible or needing to change in the script. The original script had an active, younger "Swede" in mind, more so than what the character would be with Marlon, at his then weight and age. The sold-written script also had a number of elaborate set pieces; a few things Yves thought we should cut back on, even though we *were* keeping the giant centerpiece of the comedy adventure: a full-blown actual locomotive crashing through a for-real giant, deluxe, luxury pick-up truck, right before a botched train robbery by our dim-witted heroes, Bud and Larry, who as you know would be played by Charlie Sheen and Thomas Hayden Church.

So, yes, I wanted to keep Marlon focused on making this movie. I'd spend afternoons "rewriting" the script with Marlon while I was also rewriting it in the morning with Yves. But I knew there was one thing that I simply could not do: tell either man about the "other" rewrite. The reasons were actually quite simple - by now, I had learned how things work. Yves needed to make the script work for his shoot - Marlon wanted to stay busy and engaged before the shoot. If Yves knew Marlon wanted the kind of rewrites Brando and I were doing up at Mulholland, Simoneau, a realist, would've had true and legitimate concerns about directing Marlon and the script itself; more than he was already having. Those concerns might've trickled down to the money people - their fears would've been obvious: "Brando's rewriting the script we're already paying him to star in - What the hell?" This is the kind of thing that can delay or derail a film project. Given all that, please know this, fully and completely: I knew exactly what I was doing.

To be clear, Marlon's changes were huge - *and yet* - not things I took all that seriously, even as he moved the storyline from the Midwest to south Texas, made all the characters cowboys instead of Swedes and Norwegians and made the comedy script into a dark drama about race relations. So what *was* I doing? I was keeping Marlon engaged right up until the moment of getting him on a plane to Canada for the filming. Yes, I can hear your questions: wouldn't he want to know why we weren't doing the "rewritten" Texas script when that time came?

Details-*Schmetails*. He had just received a million dollars thanks to my involvement - I'd deal with those bigger problems as the shooting day arrived, already thinking of how I would ultimately tell him how those darn production company folks wanna do the "other" script (the one that I was rewriting with Yves). Also, through the years, I had seen how quickly Marlon's mind changed on things; while it was risky to lead him down the path of a "rewritten" script, it was far, *far* riskier to leave him to his own devices weeks before a film shoot without activity; a shoot where I was an Executive Producer and writer who had to get him to Montreal on time.

I had seen other Brando projects fall apart as Marlon clogged actual rewrite processes into un-workable places. Was I worried that director Yves and star Marlon would one fine day just pick up the phone and have a chat about the "rewrites"? Perhaps crazy to say, but, not really. They had already discussed the original script the initial deal was made over. Yves recommended that I *not* discuss rewrites with Marlon; Simoneau felt he was smart enough to know the fragile nature of working with Brando - *but* - he did not know Marlon as I did. Anyone who had paid attention to "Hollywood" in general through the 60's, 70's and 80's knew of the difficulty of just getting Brando to the film set. The rewrites I did for Yves were drastic to Tony and me, yet probably not all that impactful to anyone else - line changes, scenes merging, locations shifting; again, Yves was a smart filmmaker who was looking for good ways to streamline production.

Marlon's changes, on the other hand, were giant, epic and totally "Marlon" - turning a quirky comedy into a message-heavy cross between *"The Chase"* and *"One-Eyed Jacks"*. As nervous as I was, I knew if he wanted that remaining two million that would be coming his way (to actually do the movie), he'd have to show up in Montreal and do the quirky Midwestern comedy of the original script. While all this might sound a bit devious, underhanded and even flat-out crazy, please know, this is how things were often done regarding the last few films of Marlon, with the full support of his staff, his family and mostly, his accountants.

See, almost everyone who really knew Marlon seemed to know the "Brando" drill by then: If Marlon arrived for any given shoot, everyone knew that he would want a number of costly changes, perhaps on a daily basis. On the other side, those of us who really knew his temperament knew there would be a time when he would accommodate what the filmmakers were asking for; perhaps not with a smile, and perhaps not giving the director *all* that they wanted, but there would be a middle ground that might be reached. People have asked me for years, "Why was he such a trouble maker?" Frankly, most stars want to have a lot to say about the films they headline.

Think about it: your name isn't just above the title, it's often bigger than the title. In many cases, it's the reason the entire picture is getting made. And that's because, for many in the audience, it's the entire reason for paying money to sit in a dark room and watch.

Yes, Hollywood has decided that true "stars" are worth the trouble.

And a few have spent years being no trouble at all.

But others - They don't like showing up just to be told what to do and what to say.

To state the obvious, Marlon was definitely in that second category.

Oh, and how *did* the whole "rewrite" thing finally shake-down with Marlon? I got lucky, even though I was actually setting things up for this certain sort of conclusion all along. As we were rewriting our now "Texas" movie, I constantly mentioned how the exteriors to be shot in Montreal might not look as "Texas" as "we'd like." One day, weeks-deep into the "writing," he looked up with a squint as he asked, "Wait, where the fuck are we shooting this again?" When I mentioned Montreal once more, he paused. He then had yet another question: "What the hell are we doing here?" With a straight face, I shrugged. His third question: "When are we doing this?"

"We leave at the end of this week."

"The hell with this script; we'll do the old one. It'll be more fun anyway. Let's go get a burger."

He stood and then left the den to go get dressed for that burger, to get out of his usual daily robe and underwear. Yes, I breathed a sigh of relief, but by knowing Marlon, I had pictured a conclusion to this exercise weeks ago; one that would be some variation on the one I just witnessed.

His project after *"Free Money"* - It's a few pages from now. But trust me: you'll see I was right.

I was right to go through this whole "rewriting" corralling with Dear Marlon. Yes. You will see.

Greg, The Beg and Free Money (1997)

The role of The Swede in *"Free Money"* was written in a minimal, hidden fashion, meaning: he was created to be a quiet, hairy monster behind a giant beard, dark glasses and a winter hat; Tony and I saw the man as scary, threatening and mostly silent. To underline it fully: The Swede was devised as a man of few words. We always thought that Clint Eastwood or Robert Duvall would be great for the role. We never dared dream that we could get one of cinema's most famous shadowy, barely-speaking monsters - the guy who played Captain Kurtz in *"Apocalypse Now"*.

As a dark, Midwestern comedy, we knew we were ahead of the curve, writing *"Free Money"* long before *"Fargo"* came out. In fact, while writing, as I explained those loopy accents and these odd Midwesterners to Tony, I constantly said, "Somebody is gonna do a film about people like this; it hasn't really been done yet, but it will be." I'm not saying I was brilliantly clairvoyant about all this, or that *"Free Money"* can stand next to *"Fargo"* - Not at all. What I *am* saying is that as a Minnesotan from Brainerd, I knew these quirky voices, rhythms and oddball types had yet to be features in a major motion picture at that time. And growing up in all that ice and snow, with all those cheery-yet-dreary Minnesotans, I knew that a film that captured that region had to contain off-beat humor, unpredictability and a full degree of bleakness. *"Fargo"* arriving in 1996 probably helped get *"Free Money"* sold, but our film would also suffer by comparison.

Marlon did not want to play the role as covered-up or as "Kurtz"-like as The Swede Tony and I created. He wanted no sunglasses, beard or winter cap. He did want a big mustache, red hair on the fringes of a balding pate, and an amateur tattoo on that shiny scalp. It read, "Jesus Saves".

He'd wear all black, and even with Marlon's large size, he would have extra padding to appear still larger. As it was with *"The Island of Dr. Moreau,"* he truly was something of his own costume designer, with all due respect to (and with great assistance from), respectively, *"Moreau"* costume designer Norma Moriceau and *"Free Money"* costumer Francois Barbeau.

As I've explained, while Marlon's participation did not open the anticipated floodgates of "A-List" actors for the co-lead role of "Bud," his presence did bring in a great cast of people who indeed did want to work with Brando: the aforementioned Donald Sutherland, Mira Sorvino, Thomas Hayden Church, David Arquette and Martin Sheen. As I've told people for years, I was wonderfully pleased with the surprisingly solid performance Charlie Sheen delivered as "Bud," but after the chase with Sean Penn and the rest of that adventure, Charlie felt like a compromise; one that came with the challenge of his widely known personal problems at the time.

So as the cast was assembling in Montreal and Marlon was working with the film team to figure out his costume and make up, Tony and I were both thinking of a very key plan that meant a great deal to both of us: how do we get Greg into this movie as well? We had saved this tough task as an eleventh hour assignment, making sure that everything was lined up in this fragile parade: Marlon was actually in Canada, on set to do the film, the movie really was on, this was all finally happening, and whatever we were going to present to by-the-book Greg, we wouldn't be crying wolf.

The hard part was not about the lead producer or director; both Nicolas Clermont and Yves Simoneau nearly expected us to deliver Greg for a small role; to a degree, how could we not? Working as the film's executive producer and re-writer of the script at the time, I felt a bit overwhelmed to be dealing with such a personal situation. I got to Montreal before Tony, and prior to his arrival, we had calls about the matter, neither sure on the best move to make it happen. First - the role? In the weeks before filming would start, there was nothing still un-cast in the existing script that was worthy of Greg. Remember, by way of the Canadian Content rules, Donald Sutherland had the role of The Swede's partner in crime, Judge Rausenberger. Given all that, Tony and I talked out a scene on the phone that could be important, impactful and self-contained.

In the story, "The Swede" is Warden Sorenson; he runs a small town prison in a fully corrupt fashion. When our dim heroes, Bud and Larry, impregnate and marry The Swede's pretty twin daughters, dark hilarity ensues. They all end up living with the murderous Swede, with Bud and Larry later robbing money off a treasury train to escape from the warden, and eventually, ending up in his jail - Bud as a convicted train robber and Larry as an about-to-crack, yet-to-be-indicted kitchen worker who still lives in The Swede's house. Yes, quite complicated but it all works.

In our original script, we never see the parents of Bud and Larry; they are not brothers, but they quickly bond given their situations with the twins and The Swede. Basically, Bud and Larry are a couple small town losers who live for TV watching and beer drinking. Tony and I grew to love the character of Larry, especially after the casting of the hilarious Thomas Hayden Church.

Larry was a sweet, guileless Midwestern soul, with none of the clever craftiness of Bud. As dark as the overall story proves to be, the first half of *"Free Money"* is essentially carefree: Bud, Larry and their beautiful young twin brides hang out in local bars, watch

TV, make love - All is somewhat tolerable for the characters and even served up to us as full comedy - until harsh reality sets in. Once the train robbery and prison half-of-the-film takes over, the story takes a distinct turn. With Bud's marriage essentially dissolved and Larry's hanging by a thread, both men ending up in "The Swede's Prison" - Bud behind bars and Larry working in the prison kitchen like a slave, Tony and I had an interesting wish for Greg onscreen: let's have him arrive and confront The Swede. Who would Greg be playing? Larry's strong, imposing Mennonite father, Pastor Linders.

The proposed scene: Larry's semi-estranged father arrives from out of town. By way of regional small town gossip, he's caught wind of his son's odd, sad, difficult situation. But his son is a grown man and Larry fled from the strict faith of his upbringing years ago. Tony and I pictured Greg stalking into The Swede's office with a cross between the oddity of Captain Ahab with the wisdom of an Atticus, telling The Swede that while his son may have somehow sinned in the eyes of God, "fornicating" with The Swede's daughter before marriage (therefore possibly deserving punishment), there is also another truth: if The Swede hurts, wounds or does damage to his son, Larry's father will return and seek Fatherly Vengeance - "So Sayeth Thine Lord!"

The Pastor then exits, but not before The Swede has *his* say on the matter, nose-to-nose, with quiet, real threats. Scene. No need for any follow up. No need for a scene with Greg and Thomas Hayden Church. Just this intense confrontation between two fathers and two Hollywood legends. The best part: it does get The Swede thinking; maybe even scared. Yes, this powerful character played by powerful Marlon, who will surely dominate every other scene that he is in - he will be confronted by perhaps the only actor who could be on that equal or higher footing with Brando.

Tony and I wrote up some good pages, but we knew that there were bigger issues than the script: Greg and Marlon. We both knew of the years of odd, silent, irritated and totally standoffish behavior from both of them whenever the topic of The Other Guy would arise. We talked about bringing Veronique into the plan, of bringing Avra into the plan, of me talking to Marlon first, etc., etc., etc. We checked Greg's schedule - he was free, then only between weeks-apart bookings of his stage show, *"A Conversation with Gregory Peck"*. I checked with Nicolas; while it would not be the million-dollar fee Greg saw for the short time he was on Scorsese's *"Cape Fear,"* it would be substantial and all of the accommodations and related elements would be, of course, ultra-first-class.

Yes, and of course, all that stuff was just noise around the real issue about whether Greg would do it and whether Marlon wanted him to. Tony had the optimal idea: "Joey, if Marlon called Greg, 'says it would be great to have him in the picture; that would go such a long ways with Greg." I could only flip the script, "Tone, it's really not up to Marlon - Martin Sheen just signed on this morning; Marlon doesn't even know. By the way, we gotta come up with a role for Martin. No, I just don't want Marlon to say 'no' about Greg, to something that technically isn't even his call. Then it just becomes one more 'thing' with Marlon."

Over the phone line, Tony asked, "Martin Sheen? If Greg doesn't do this 'Pastor' thing, what about Martin?" I said, "He'd have to be Bud's dad then, that's for sure (because of Charlie), and I don't know why, but that kinda 'Mennonite' thing doesn't help Bud's character at all - It works well with Larry." I went on, "Anyway, back to Greg; *you* co-wrote the script: Marlon's not gonna be shocked to see your dad here if Greg shows up on the set."

Tony explained, "But that's just it; Greg doesn't wanna be just one more actor who shows up because he wants to work with Brando." I said, "Right, and he won't be - he'd be showing up for *you*." Tony sighed, "Yeah, I get what you're saying, but *because* of that; maybe all the more reason for his resistance: he doesn't need me to get him a role. On top of that, you know how careful and cautious Greg is about material; he'll know we just microwaved this up for him."

That was a point I knew to be true. By then, I had to get on the set to meet with the director. I told Tony, "Look, if possible, just tell him: it's a great two person scene with Marlon, one, maybe two days of work - The director wants him in this film, the producers want him in this film, we as the writers want him in this film

- Nothing could make all of us more happy. Nothing." I then had to hang up and go through storyboards with Yves. I felt bad putting Tony in that spot; I knew how Greg could be, and yes, Tony being his son only complicates matters. As I've often stressed throughout this book, Greg was a calculated, complex actor. He had great pride, an immense ability to analyze and a lot of caution, fully combined with megawatt intelligence. All that on top of his constant distance when it came to "Brando," a man Greg saw as a wildcard who, in Peck's eyes, often displayed a willful lack of all the characteristics I just listed above regarding Gregory.

Also - and let's be clear: this was not a "studio" picture that was occupying famous sound stages on the Paramount lot. This was a Canadian production, independently produced, no distribution yet attached - I could go on and on. It was a risk; I learned this as I tried to get Sean Penn involved. Greg spent a lifetime as a "studio" artist; he respected the organization, the rank and the well-oiled machine that a studio could deliver; he believed in an industry that had been very good to him. At this age, even with a script written by his son, was he going to show up for something that just might turn out to be one more oddity on the current list of Brando's follies? *"Dr. Moreau"?* The unfinished *"Divine Rapture"?* Only Marlon could help create a train-wreck that later might - maybe - be deemed as either a mess or as art - That was the chaotic magic of Brando.

And unlike Greg, Marlon thrived on it. A studio to Marlon simply meant too many people telling him what to do. In turn, a studio to Greg meant that intelligent people with huge resources and an investment at stake; they were all going to do everything they could to make a motion picture work - from prints to posters to promotion. And no, by the 80's and 90's, Greg wasn't all that thrilled with how modern studios packaged, made and publicized his recent films, *"Old Gringo"* and *"Other People's Money,"* as two examples. *But* whatever it was in current Hollywood, whatever that system still *was*, it was a system Greg understood. A system that tried to do more than just bet on a long shot. Of course, I fully believe that *all* of filmmaking is that kind of betting, from the biggest studio blockbuster to the lowest brown-bag indie.

But studios with money, distribution and ad dollars, they do have a distinct advantage over the independents, whether you have Marlon Brando and Gregory Peck in a picture together or not. This is also why Greg did some TV movies rather than "Indie" work in his later years: he knew the television networks were dependable - Whatever might've seemed sub-standard regarding TV films compared to major studio theatrical releases in the 90's, TV network movies got done, they were polished and they were presented as class acts, especially with major movie stars attached. Greg was incredibly shrewd; by watching all of his cautious moves during our *"Doctor DeMott"* adventures, I was certain he could envision a project all the way through: from the earliest paperwork to the possible reception of the finished, presented project - good or bad. He had years of experience with both hits and flops and he was truly aware of how studios, independent films and distribution had changed. While I - at that moment - was dreaming of major studios literally fist-fighting one another to pick up *"Free Money,"* Greg could've been self-narrating a mental picture from a then-hypothetical future of my film that went like this: "There's my name on a VHS box; my first premiere in a video store - Good God."

I thought about all this as I waited to hear back from Tony. When I checked my voice mail later, Tony had left a message that he did indeed talk to Veronique about the prospect before going to Greg. Veronique talked optimistically about the possibility, but Greg had yet to be approached. I felt this was a good sign; I was certain that she wanted Greg to work with Brando, and with her influence, maybe that could happen.

But just after I then passed on my own optimism on the topic to Nicolas Clermont, Tony called and said that this was not something Greg wanted to do. Greg was told about it. He listened. He thought about it. He decided it was not for him.

My heart sank, in a way I did not fully expect. Those two toe to toe - I really wanted to see that.

I was in a production trailer on the Montreal studio lot when I got that call from Tony. Seconds later, a giant semi-camper-rock-star party bus pulled up next to my production trailer; out jumped a good-sized entourage led by a somewhat spooky-looking Charlie Sheen, grinning behind dark sunglasses, along with a wobbly demeanor. I watched from the open window as Nicolas Clermont came out to greet the now-arriving Charlie and his "team". Sheen introduced Clermont to "LaMaSheen," the nickname for the deluxe party bus "machine" that was to be Charlie's headquarters, playground and home. Charlie seemed shocked and even a tad uneasy when gleeful Clermont told him that just this morning, his father Martin signed on; he'd be doing a small role in the film. This was news to Charlie. He kinda shrugged it off with an odd twitch.

Sensing the slight unwelcome shock in Charlie over that, Nicolas then quickly glossed it over with, "And it looks like Gregory Peck will be in the film as well." This created an instant burst of chatter in Sheen's gang, as Charlie slapped his hand to his heart, gasping, *"You are fucking kidding me!"* At the moment, I didn't want to go out there and break the bad news about that whole situation. Perhaps I was even hoping that in an hour from now, Greg might change his mind and we'd be getting him into the film after all.

But as I stared into space while Clermont disappeared into the soundstage with the Charlie bunch, I could only smile, knowing that Greg was not going to change his mind. That wouldn't be Greg. And arriving to be in this film - That wouldn't be Greg. I loved this project, I loved the fact that it was finally happening and I loved that I was able to get dear Marlon here to do it.

But getting Gregory in on this as well? That was just a greedy dream on my part.

I then realized how much I loved Greg - this absolute "Un-Marlon". For all of his correct procedure and orderly decorum, he was always so much his own man. I smiled, thinking back on a relatively heated moment Tony, Greg and I shared during one of our many *"Doctor DeMott"* writing sessions. About to hand yet another new draft to Scorsese and Sean Penn at that time, we were having a long day, as so many stage directions, performance cues and dialogue lines were being discussed, analyzed and debated. One didn't "win" all that many debates against Greg, but now and then, I felt the want, as a screenwriter, to hold my ground. In an exceptionally traumatic moment for DeMott in the script, he's forced to physically run from an emotional scare from his past. The story is filled with psychological ghosts, haunts and memories. Earlier drafts had him "running". Greg had changed that to "rushing". Upon reflection, he felt even that was too "fast" for his elderly frame, insisting he would now be "hurrying". I was tired and frazzled at the time.

I said, "I'd like to make a case for not watering-down the 'read' for others!" Then, a bad silence.

Seeing me sigh, he loudly laughed, "Joe! By now, you know how stubborn I can be! I'm *Irish!*"

"THE DEVIL'S OWN"
(During the "Free Money" Shoot: 1997)

I enjoyed the performance of Penelope Ann Miller as she was playing Greg's stepdaughter in the 1991 film adaptation of *"Other People's Money"*. Just the year before, she had played Marlon's daughter in *"The Freshman"*. She was quite good in both movies, and even then, I wondered where her career would be in a few years. Hollywood really has no idea of what to do with all those talented young actresses they over-cast at That Unexplainable Golden Moment, and then somewhat discard, seemingly in a blink. If everyone thinks that the exact same thing happens just as often with every young male actor as well, they're not fully paying attention.

Hollywood is a tough, harsh town. And sexist, absolutely, almost blatantly by its open addiction to male power and sexy young women. So much of the product is entirely about beauty, youth and sex appeal. And while both male and female performers know the score before getting into the game, it doesn't make it any easier to stomach when leading men in their 50's somehow have leading ladies in their 30's or even 20's. This type of thing seems to be getting better, but there's still a ways to go. In 1999, I was directing a film from a script Tony and I wrote, *"Diary of a Sex*

Addict" for Sony Pictures. My stars, Rosanna Arquette and Nastassja Kinski. On a particularly difficult shooting day, the three of us were sitting on set; it was the workspace of a therapist's office (Nastassja's character) and at a rare moment when there wasn't heated discussion about the script, talk somehow got around to how all three of us had just arrived at the age of 40. The moment hit me hard; they were both so talented and so accomplished, both having been part of so many films that inspired me through the years. It also hit me that we were all on this low budget film, and while I was lucky and grateful for the opportunity, they were now supposed to be directed by me - performers who used to take direction from the likes of Martin Scorsese, Francis Ford Coppola and Roman Polanski. No wonder this job was proving to be so difficult.

Writing this book that, in its own way, analyzes the sustainability of careers in film acting, I continue to see why Greg and Marlon so strongly represent the core of what Hollywood began as, what it became, and ultimately, what it continues to be today. It's a profit-making, costly business that constantly attempts to be an ever-changing, "current" art form, with the emphasis on "art". Many will dispute that "Hollywood" tries to be "art" at all, but those within the industry, and fans, will defend that label. As filmmakers, we all want to make something that moves people, that resonates, that has lasting value. As fans and viewers, we all know when we've experienced such "art" - It's cosmic collaboration, it's unique, and most of all, it's rare.

Both Marlon and Greg struggled to bring art to everything they were a part of.

As I talked to Greg about filmmakers like Alfred Hitchcock, or with Marlon about Charlie Chaplin, it often made me recall that Hitchcock, like Chaplin, also created back when film was just being formed; Hitchcock was shaping ways to tell film stories before the arrival of sound, having directed over two dozen silent films, some that can't be found today. So there it was, on some days, hitting me hard as I was in my 20's; I was working with two men who had worked with those who created the whole art form. What kept those thoughts from being so "lofty" during those conversations: neither Greg nor Marlon retained any sort of false reverence for men like Chaplin or Hitchcock. In fact, they simply saw them as fellow filmmakers - personally flawed ones at that. Of course, being Peck and Brando, they were somewhat entitled to those attitudes, both often laughing at me for being so analytical and interested in "Old Hollywood".

To be honest, I often tried to hide that interest when I was around Greg and Marlon, wanting them to see that I was not one of these industry geeks who simply lived for the business. Still, as they both knew of my enthusiasm and deep interest in our industry, like Walter Matthau did at the Carolwood parties, they'd both ask me questions regarding film history, current film trends and other questions that surprised me when asked. More so than Greg, Marlon sometimes woke up on any given day feeling that he knew nothing about "current" Hollywood, convincing himself that when he actually made an effort to stay current and "market" himself, he could end up doing films like *"The Godfather"* and *"Last Tango in Paris"*.

But were those projects (not his performances) thought-out pursuits and well-planned "business" approaches on Marlon's part? Or were they lucky rolls of the dice that were just opportunities of the moment? With Marlon, you never knew. In that exact pairing cited above, I still say that many - film critics included - would never have stopped to see the brilliance of the daring, abstract *"Tango"* without first re-finding their Brando love by way of *"Godfather"* the year before. Whatever the case, by the 1990's, those two films were a while ago. Now and then, at around that time, he'd sometimes grow anxious, feeling he had to be more aware of the rest of the industry. He'd think back to the years in the late 50's and through the 60's, doing mostly whatever he wanted to do, too often without commercial success.

That's because no matter what some in Hollywood might say, filmmaking is an art without rules. And once somebody *does* create a "rule," well, that's the time to quickly break that rule. By the 90's, as the look, feel and sound of films changed, evolved, devolved or simply got reinvented, iconic stars such as Greg and Marlon often knew that they were being asked to be a part of any given picture to lend class, history and, in some cases, attract other actors to get onboard the film. That fact would often frustrate Marlon. He did not want to be a mere "lure" for actors; when he'd finally get the itch to actually work, he wanted to take new chances in this modern age of cinema, but sometimes, we'd both question what the hell this "modern age" was supposed to be. He recognized that bold "new" wave with *"Tango"*... but what were the 90's?

One such conversation of "Contemporary Awareness" centered around Marlon one day asking me to sit down and watch *"The Devil's Own"* with him, a film he knew almost nothing about. I didn't know all that much about it as well, but I certainly knew more about it than Marlon. Why did he want to see it? We were in Montreal, both having the day off from *"Free Money"*. I was touched and moved when he said that he was really enjoying the film shoot - this film that Avra, Tony and I brought to him. Nearly shocking himself, he said he was feeling that he was really "going to get back into it" - film acting, but mentally, in these past few years, his mind had really dropped out of "current" Hollywood. He said it was all a foreign language to him at this point.

I asked, "Why this film? *'The Devil's Own'*?"

He shrugged as he handed me a VHS of the film. "I was told this stars the two biggest guys out there; to be honest, I don't know who the hell they are." He wanted to watch it and then talk about the "Hollywood" of that day in the late 90's. It reminded me of when I first wrote with him years ago, when he had schooled-up on the fame of Tom Cruise and Robert De Niro, wanting them in *"Platinum Toenail"*. So, we watched *"The Devil's Own,"* a somewhat strange wannabe thriller that seemed to collapse under the weight of obvious rewrites, big budget bloat and star power that seemed out of place, all in a movie that tried to have grit, reality and textured nuance. Oh, yeah, and it starred those guys Marlon didn't know: Harrison Ford and Brad Pitt. After the film, Marlon's first thoughts on those actors: About Pitt: "That kid's too pretty to be believable." And about Ford: "That guy has only two faces: one where he smiles and one where he don't." I recall the dread I felt as the film was ending. I could tell Marlon didn't like the movie, and he was always The Ultimate Grand Inquisitor. I knew that once the end credits rolled, I would have no magic notions, thoughts or ideas regarding his place in "Current Cinema" - or any thoughts about "Current Cinema" whatsoever. I could only discuss why I felt that film didn't work for me.

And frankly, whatever that film was, it was pretty much how "Hollywood" had been doing it for years, even in Greg's and Marlon's days: Pay "A-List" actors a lot of money, script-ready-or-not, dive in and make the movie when everybody's schedule allows (because these "A-List" people can get booked end-to-end for years) and hope that the shoot can ultimately be edited into a hit. Whatever it turns out to be, with names like Ford and Pitt, the film is then promoted as though it is gold. Again, a lot like the same stuff Marlon and Greg agreed to do as well-paid stars: Greg in *"How The West Was Won"* and *"Marooned,"* Marlon in *"Guys and Dolls"* and *"Superman"*. I'm sure all the filmmakers involved with those films had noble intentions, but at the end of the day, they were business-making ventures, no matter how much "art" and passion went into them.

Of course, ultimately, I had no valid "90's" insight for Marlon, but aside from his earlier stated want to "get back into it," his focus that day was probably more like that of some once-popular 60's rocker, one who one day woke up Rip Van Winkle-style and realized that rap was here, and it was something he knew very little about it. Frankly, nobody could've brought such a fictional old rocker up to speed on rap. How does one explain the simple progress of pop culture, current movements and, basically, however one might want to categorize "New Stuff"?

I believe that the magic of Marlon's more rewarding eras was not something he could have necessarily planned, hatched or choreographed, any more than his 70's *"Godfather"* renaissance was. Of course, when legends like Marlon had that *"Godfather"* rebirth, or in his own way, the immensely profitable *"Omen"* luck that hit Greg in the 70's — well, these were occurrences that let artists at their rare level feel that it's never too late to "make" it happen again. For some of their generation and fame-level, the answer to that quest was simple: just say "yes" to every single thing that is offered, feeling that at least one of these projects will "hit". Both Greg and Marlon knew that such a path would be pointless, and perhaps in their cases, damaging to their careers; careers often based on the fact that they both gave "rare" appearances.

Passion-wise, at times like that *"Devil's Own"* screening, I wished both Marlon and Greg still had the want, desire and strength to perform theater. As someone who had done a great deal of theater, I certainly understood their dislike of the routine, the tiring schedule and the sheer grind of stage, but still, I knew they both loved acting, and back then, any top-level professional theater producer would've moved heaven and earth to create a stage project for either of them. Greg did enjoy the level of stage performance that came with his touring Q&A mixed with film clips presentation, *"A Conversation with Gregory Peck,"* but was it a play? Of course not, even though he'd often compare the night of casual chat with an evening of theater. Whatever the case, I often think that theater can - yes, I'll say it: feed the soul of any actor, even if you happen to be a legendary Hollywood icon who is now more comfortable with a camera than the live audiences of your younger days. My sister and I sat front row as we saw Katharine Hepburn in a Broadway play when she was 75, and she was truly something to watch - energized, intense and far more interesting to us at the Ethel Barrymore Theatre than she ever was as a film star. Did all her years as a movie legend play into our love of watching her up on that stage? Of course! But as Juilliard actors in-training at the time, we could see that she was thrilled to still be up there in front of an audience and practicing her craft.

But even though they never returned to the stage in that fashion, both Greg and Marlon did love acting. Career management was a whole other ballgame. This is perhaps why I am still - to this day - so fascinated by my years within their final decades. Their first atomic bursts onto the movie scene were long before my time, and like all things phenomenal, not fully understandable or subject to analysis. Their middle years - Again, before I knew them, but both well documented enough for me to understand how they sustained themselves, how they grew and how they both fully stayed (and thrived) in an elite game that mixed Hollywood *and* International filmmaking.

Their final years - *This* is where I got to watch, analyze, participate and even personally question them. I got to see how two brilliant men tried to figure out triumphant, and yes, dignified final acts.

Oh, and as for some of my final thoughts to Marlon that day regarding *"Devil's Own,"* I recall concluding with, "Look, a movie like this - This is proof; in some ways - as a business that will never fully figure things out, 'Hollywood' will never change."

Pause. He then looked at one of his watches; he wore one on each wrist at that time in his life.

He muttered, "So, you're saying this was all bullshit. Good. 'Cause it's time to eat. Let's go."

That evening, we had a scheduled dinner with some Chinese diplomats who were in town. They were big shots, and like those earlier stories about the possible tax rates of Ireland and France, yes, Marlon wanted to look into somehow saving money by working with the Chinese. I don't know how the evening came about, but there we were in an elegant Chinese restaurant, speaking through an interpreter with three men thrilled to be having dinner with Brando. After a lengthy meal, someone across the big room shouted, "Hey! Buddy! Do ya wanna do the cab scene?!" Marlon sighed with misery as he recognized Rod Steiger coming our way; he was also in Montreal, doing a small part in a very low budget boxing film. Marlon tried some polite chat, as Rod wanted much more than a "Hi-Bye". I guess they had not seen each other since *"Waterfront,"* and while Rod was thrilled, Marlon was not, mostly because of the attention-grabbing approach Steiger just performed there in the restaurant. After Marlon finally got Steiger to leave, Marlon turned to me and muttered:

"See, example: ya gotta stay current, or that's what happens to you - nobody wants ya around."

SEVENTH CHAPTER
The 70's & 80's
(GREG & MARLON ESSAY VII)

Not long ago, I caught an old interview where blockbuster film director Richard Donner discussed his first meeting with Greg regarding *"The Omen,"* the movie Donner directed into a great success, ushering in a new era of "Studio A-Level" horror film, as well as a new career era for Greg. The interview I saw was one of those "Hollywood Conversation" YouTube videos that I really like; quite a time in tech and pop culture history when we can just click away and watch so much; anyone who's ever made a film or TV show is on YouTube talking to someone about it. I think that's great. What hit me is how a then admittedly star-struck Donner discussed meeting Greg, saying, "It's like meeting Marlon Brando - Gregory *Friggin'* Peck!"

And, of course, this comes from someone who has met and worked with both men. It's also the kind of line that reminds me as to why I am writing this book - It's not my imagination or a personal "willing" of stray thoughts: they really are two rare men who were both at singular levels, as I will never stop saying in a thousand different ways. For Donner - who has certainly met his fair share of stars - to cite "Brando" as he discussed meeting Greg, well, that's my exact point - There's very few of these film actors that actually fall into this stratospheric league.

Donner would go on to tell the interviewer of how rich *"The Omen"* made Peck - Greg was later able to buy the Carolwood house because of that very film.

I had heard that Greg had a contract that gave him five percent of the film profits. The movie initially grossed around sixty million. His 5% turned out to be $3,000,000. No actor anywhere in 1976 was getting a salary of 3 million per film, ironically - not until Marlon would (a couple years later) in Richard Donner's *"Superman"*. Three million in 1976 was probably a bit like 15 million today, maybe more. 20th Century-Fox simply didn't envision it making that much money, so whatever money Greg got subsequent to the film's release, the studio was more than glad to pay. *"The Omen"* wasn't expensive; maybe around 2.8 million. Greg's base salary was probably, I'm guessing - somewhere around 300,000 dollars. It was a smart move on his part; the film was a giant hit, he made huge money, and to an extent, it fully re-launched Greg's career in the 1970's.

As noted a few lines back, a couple years later, Marlon got roughly 3 million upfront for playing the Man of Steel's father in *"Superman,"* another record-breaking salary for the actor, something he had been doing throughout his career: being the highest paid of all - by miles. Of course, that was another reason many of the older Hollywood stars grew to resent Marlon - The way they saw it, he always misbehaves, percentage-wise, he's turned out mostly bomb films, and then, after a "lucky" break by way of something like *"The Godfather,"* he's back, and, once again, making much more money than anybody else in town. Of course, it goes without saying, with their respective three million dollar paydays, both under the direction of Richard Donner, both men did very different things with their money. More on that in a moment.

Director Richard Donner is a good point of reference as I yet again go on to compare and contrast my two friends. As I continue to mention, both Greg and Marlon broke into an industry that was still quite young when they caught fire - *silent* films were only about a generation into the distance when Greg showed up. And if we can say that the sound era really started at the beginning of the 30's, and Marlon arrived at the beginning of the 50's - well, you adult readers - like me - sadly know the shortness of 20 years. Again, there were no rules to being a legendary international film star; perhaps there will never be "rules" for such a singular job. Both Greg and Marlon were rebels in their own individual way; you don't go into acting without being one. But as we know, Greg always respected the boundaries of established rules, even when he would occasionally rail against them in the name of creativity. Marlon, of course, openly railed against any and all rules, even when he knew he had to have (and needed) them.

By the mid 70's - another 20 years into this ever-changing experiment called commercial cinema, both Greg and Marlon were still looking for those big scores, artistically and financially.

Both Donner films, *"The Omen"* and *"Superman"* gave Greg and Marlon, respectively, that financial cushion that launched them into their final years, and it's safe to say that both films were ultimately genres that neither man cared to embrace fully - for Greg, the horror film. For Marlon, the superhero film. *And* - let's be very clear: both films became the full re-launching *("Omen")* and launching *("Superman")* of their respective genres. *"The Omen"* brought back the A-List horror film. There would be no *"Avengers"* or DC Superhero films today without *"Superman"*. But neither Greg nor Marlon saw that coming. In fact, when both actors were approached for those films, it's been well documented throughout Hollywood history: you had to talk more "mythology" than "comic book" with Marlon, and with Greg, you were never to use the word, "Horror". Still, in the end, those films are what they are, and thanks to Greg and Marlon, they are both pure genre movies that have rare weight, quality and integrity to them.

With those success stories under their belts, Greg and Marlon got right back into the swim of working - Greg went for the flawed-yet-heroic historical figure - the *"Patton"* route, with *"MacArthur,"* followed by the against-type Nazi villain in *"The Boys from Brazil"*. Marlon reunited with the director he helped to make a star; Francis Coppola was looking for a very special name performer - Someone worth waiting for, worth confronting after a long ride up a dangerous river. It could really only be Brando as Captain Kurtz in *"Apocalypse Now"*. Marlon followed this with a somewhat small part in *"The Formula,"* alongside fellow Oscar refuser, George C. Scott. I think Marlon saw both films as good paydays for small amounts of work.

Of course, as he always did, he got much more involved than he first anticipated. He created an entire character, voice and new demeanor for his villainous role in *"The Formula,"* broad to the point of Scott asking if Marlon was serious with his costume buck teeth, funny voice and odd timing. Marlon didn't have an answer for him; he just lost himself in the character and Scott had to go along for the ride. As for Coppola's film, the 1991 documentary, *"Hearts of Darkness"* shows how *"Apocalypse"* became a set of unexpected experiences for Marlon, Coppola and the entire film team. With the ever-shifting schedules, stories and bleeding budget of the epic production, some might argue that by now, the challenging eccentric here was no longer Brando - instead, it was Coppola himself.

Whatever the case, Coppola ended up having to use Marlon in an abbreviated way; some might say a masterful way; the minimal appearances, the barely-there lighting, Marlon's improvs before a terrified and still Martin Sheen before the murder of Marlon's character.

It's one of those odd films that has become legend; the impression of the picture has improved over time, I feel much to the credit of the "Brando Mystique". I saw it opening weekend in New York City at The Ziegfeld Theater. I really don't know what that giddy, film-fan audience was expecting, but within the packed house where I viewed it, it was literally booed off the screen by the end. Marlon never talked much about the movie, but I do know that after he finished filming and left the Philippines, he was once again, someone who claimed to be no fan of Francis Ford Coppola. *But* - in typical Hollywood fashion, they'd work together yet again years later, with Coppola executive producing *"Don Juan DeMarco"*.

But a few years before *"Don Juan"* it's worth noting that both Greg and Marlon made their exit from the 70's and 80's as not just legendary stars, but also as sought after names; a feat incredibly rare for men who found fame in the mid 40's and early 50's. That's a long stretch of time to be on top. As the 90's began, Greg clearly decided to do less and less work; he had managed his income incredibly well and it was easy for him to be selective about his roles and appearances.

Marlon, on the other hand was a few years younger than Greg and a few dollars short when it came to being where he wanted to be at this stage of his life and career. So Brando had a few films still in him at the start of the 1990's. He also had some ideas he wanted to pursue. Ideas that he hoped would allow him to avoid a very certain job: acting in movies.

As I've discussed throughout these pages, many of Marlon's film-acting frustrations in his later years came from wanting to personalize the entire project; the studios wouldn't let him, the independent productions had to grapple with that. He didn't want to necessarily direct the films, he didn't want to necessarily write them, but he knew he was the "Reason" for it all happening, so he wanted it all to be "His". A good example of this happened during the filming of *"Free Money"*. The center and turning point of the film story was written and designed to be presented as a dark, stand-off at gunpoint in the town bar, involving all the leads in the story. Marlon's "Swede" character is about to attempt a double murder; he wants to kill the shiftless men who married his daughters, just as the returning local girl - (now) hot shot FBI agent (Mira Sorvino) intervenes. A lot happens and many exposed truths instantly change every character from this point forward. The scene was complicated and important.

And the morning we were to begin shooting it, Marlon wanted it all to be different, redone and restructured, to the point of new sets needing to be built. In short: instead of a dark, violent shoot-out on the floor of a bar, he wanted to fall head-first into an un-flushed toilet while chasing his sons-in-law, be knocked unconscious, and the story would try to move on from there. When I told the director Marlon's wishes, there was this instant and understandable want to "Set Brando straight" so he'd do the scene as written and we could all stay on schedule. I said I'd talk to him.

When I asked, "Why the change?" Marlon's answer was oddly hard to argue with. He said, "I've been playing the guy for a week now. I couldn't've known before, but I know now: this early in the film, he's not the kind of guy who is gonna get into a gunfight with this woman; maybe later in the film; let's save that. At this stage, he's the kind of guy who is gonna fall into a toilet stall while he's chasing these two bums he hates. That's who he is at this stage of the story. Okay? Trust me: it'll be funny, it'll be original and it'll be something that people haven't seen before."

I went back to the set and made my case - My case for Marlon. In fact, I put it this way: "We're lucky; he knows what he wants to do. We're not guessing. If we want to shut his ideas down at this stage, we lose him. We lose his passion and his drive." I think everyone got it. Everyone here on this ten million dollar production; they were here because of Brando. Hell, the ten million arrived because of him. Funny; people can resent stars, but like it or not, they make stuff happen.

Of course, as I watched him climb over a restroom stall and fall in that toilet later, I already envisioned some lame film critic's review; one that actually *did* come to life and actually *did* exist months after the release of the film. Jesus! Just as I predicted, it contained the following:

" - *And the nerve of the screenwriters, having the great Brando falling head-first into a toilet -* "

THE STORY RESUMES
FINISHING FREE MONEY (1997)

On a cold day in Montreal, Marlon and I sat in a small diner and happily stuffed our faces, celebrating his completed time on *"Free Money,"* a film that turned out to be his final starring lead vehicle. I recall it being cold because just before that meal, Marlon sat out at a card table at his final outdoor film location and autographed (with personal messages) "Brando" headshots for every cast and crew member. After the hours-long signing, as I was waiting to go eat with him, he ran his frozen hands under his star-trailer's steaming hot water, telling me, "Damn, 'fingers are ice, but I got 'em all signed." The picture signing was his idea, and I thought it was an incredibly nice thing to do for all those crew members and performers; he knew how much those individually autographed photos would mean to everyone involved with the film. He didn't always end a shoot this way - He truly liked those people and the project. Yes, there were hiccups along the way, but for a film with Marlon, it was a home run when it came to smooth shooting and how Marlon felt by the end. As we sat in the quaint diner, there were no talks of lawsuits with the producers, no bitterness or anger - as there had been with many of his previous projects. No. Instead, he was pitching the sequel to me, telling me the next one would simply be titled after his character, *"The Swede"*.

I was so glad that he was happy and filled with glee about the project; I'll never forget his enthusiasm when I compare it with the eventual outcome of the film. Of course, much of Marlon's pleasure with the shoot had to do with the production allowing him a lot of freedom, along with the fact that this was not a film with studio interference involved. Years later, his actual final screen appearance would be a supporting role opposite Robert De Niro, in Frank Oz's heist thriller, *"The Score,"* an expensive studio-level production that would again bring Marlon to Montreal. Prior to filming, Marlon asked me about Frank Oz - Marlon knew nothing about the man or his work. Loving the perfection of Oz's puppeteering work with both the Muppets and the Star Wars films (Yoda), I discussed Frank's artistry, as well as his work as a film director.

I'll never forget sitting in Marlon's den, hearing his stunned howl of a laugh, claiming that I must be joking about this guy also being the actual "Miss Piggy". Already knowing a big studio film would put reins on him (boy, did they), he chuckled about how he would be ready for a fight with a director who was also a puppeteer, pre-writing his insults about Frank putting his hands up the asses of actors so Oz could manipulate them better. Yeah, sadly, that's how it was filming *"The Score,"* when then pregnant Avra helped De Niro play ref between a frazzled director and a legendary actor in a final supporting film role. Marlon so hated the project and the finished film.

So, oddly, whatever *"Free Money"* turned out to be, it was Marlon's final "happy" film shoot.

CAA, CBS AND THE WORK (1998)

As only diehard TV trivia buffs will recall, the short-lived 1989 CBS sitcom, *"The Famous Teddy Z"* was an 80's version of a 1949 legend, featuring characters based on the true story of Jay Kantor, a Hollywood agent who, as the tale goes, was plucked from the MCA talent agency mailroom by Marlon, just as Brando's career was getting underway, only to become the agent of the (soon to be) famous actor, much to the shock of that day's industry and established agents. Of course, for years, so many people loved these "Lotto"-like stories about powerful, unpredictable Brando - You'd hear that he'll star in a movie written by his gardener, he'll make his immigrant housekeeper a millionaire, he'll let his non-industry pals direct his films, on and on and on.

Not all true - for the most part - but that was the mystic appeal and charm of "Crazy" Marlon.

And what an epic appeal it was. Strange to think that an actor who had emerged in the early 50's could still have that level of legend, inspiring a TV series that could attain a precious prime-time network slot, just as U.S. pop culture was about to enter the 1990's. While there are details of Kantor's story that seem to vary as others "Who Were There" convey it, evidently, the heart of the tale was true: Brando was such a power, such a disrupter and such a rebel, if he wanted his giant Hollywood deals to be handled by a kid previously from a mailroom, that indeed *was* going to happen.

Marlon aside, that type of story resonates to this day for so many reasons; the attractive elements are many: someone can receive a random fluke-filled payday in nutty Hollywood, the rules of "The Industry" aren't really "rules" at all, and perhaps, most pleasing of all, the feeling of a Big Wrench thrown into the works run by the "Business as Usual Suits" - those filthy rich "villains" within the high towers of the studio executive suites. For whatever reasons, the many stories of Brando calling his own eccentric shots as he elevated "The Lowly" became legend.

I mention all this as change came to Brando in the 90's. Up at his Mulholland home, Marlon would feel a definite shift in his "power" in his later years. While some people were even more enchanted (as time went on) by his legend, thus wanting to perhaps become The Last Lion Tamer (the last director or producer to "deliver" a great final Brando performance), others had no choice but to pass on Brando, feeling that the challenges he'd bring to a costly project might play into the risk of not just perhaps the quality of the project, but maybe, even the possibility of it not getting finished at all. While much of that rap had been around since his days of *"Mutiny on the Bounty,"* I again make a strong case as to how unfair some of those notions were to Marlon.

If Marlon had just stayed within the studio and talent agency system and did what he was "told to do" time and time again, he'd have a longer list of completed, maybe even better-known films. And, of course, he would not be Marlon Brando. As straight-an-arrow as Greg was, he too knew that *that* kind of studio film trap was something he needed to avoid as well; he had no interest in becoming a cookie-cutter star who just kept churning out assembly-line product.

But unlike Greg, Marlon took part in a number of essentially independent films (even some backed by studios). Sometimes these were experimental productions - sometimes for friends (George Englund: *"The Ugly American,"* Christian Marquand: *"Candy,"* Johnny Depp: *"The Brave,"* me: *"Free Money"*). Sometimes for daring artists he barely knew (Bernardo Bertolucci: *"Last Tango in Paris,"* Gillo Pontecorvo: *"Burn"*). Some of those precarious productions would almost fall apart before completion due to their own faults, irrespective of Marlon's behavior, with the production cost increases later pinned on him by way of his "chaotic" contributions.

So as Hollywood kept track of the failed or unfinished films (*"Divine Rapture"*) with Marlon attached, the industry began to assign a new form of "blame" onto him; a blame that was different than the kind of attitude that dogged him during the "Just Before 'Godfather'" era. By the 90's, many thought Marlon was simply too impossible to predict - more so than ever before. That was unlike the "Box Office Poison" label of his 1960's Universal Studio days. During the years when Avra and I were up at Mulholland, his film projects were on a unique case-by-case basis; not always through agencies, rarely through studios and in a surreal way, occasionally considered by Marlon no matter where they came from. He'd pass on most of these projects.

But as his accountants would nudge him regarding his "need" to work, he'd occasionally ask me to read or recommend something that would find its way to his Mulholland office. While I didn't necessarily feel like Jay Kantor or even Jon Cryer's fictional *"Teddy Z,"* I occasionally felt the weight of knowing it was up to me when it came to connecting some (often) unknown artists with their idol. I also kinda hated that position, knowing that as an actor, writer and director myself, all of *my* efforts were often up to one single person who could possibly be the life-changing "yes" or "no" in my own career. Show business - That's just the way it is.

I grew to hate those often nameless and faceless decision makers, and as I occasionally became that kind of gatekeeper for Marlon, I so wanted to be "right" on all sides about things. As written about in Susan Mizruchi's book, *"Brando's Smile,"* I did indeed convince him to do *"Don Juan DeMarco".* He first shrugged the project off as a firm "no," mostly because he harbored years of bad feelings against the project's executive producer, Francis Coppola.

But as an avid filmgoer at that time, I sincerely felt that the star of *"Edward Scissorhands"* and *"What's Eating Gilbert Grape"* was a gifted actor. I was already hearing great things from industry friends about the then upcoming *"Ed Wood,"* and it was clear to me that Johnny Depp was much more than just a handsome young actor, looking ahead to some very big films and years. Like a younger Marlon, Depp saw himself as a serious character actor who just happened to be ridiculously good-looking as well. After Marlon issued a definitive "no" on *"Don Juan"* and did not want to discuss it further, I wrote up an essay for him, explaining the story and artistic possibilities of the project, leaving the pages for him in his TV den.

He called the next day, wanting to talk about the script and my writing on it - and of course, he had the question that I knew he would have: "Why can't I play the other role?" Quick rough spoiler for those who have never seen it: the story is of a delusional young man who believes he is Don Juan, treated by a mature psychiatrist who finds his own winter-of-life inspiration by way of this passionate young patient. Yes, Marlon asked me why he isn't being considered for the *"Don Juan"* role. His next question: "What the hell kinda name is 'Depp'? German?"

To be fair to Marlon's first question, this conversation was long before there was an actual *"Don Juan DeMarco"* that any of us could've had in our heads; a film starring Johnny Depp. And Hollywood has done that kind of flip-around casting, especially when stars are involved. Hell, amazing rewrites happen with stars involved. (Related side note: check out 1989's *"Family Business"* - Sean Connery, his "son" Dustin Hoffman, HIS son, Matthew Broderick. On what *planet* are these three related like that?!) Anyway, as I've discussed throughout this book, I've often thought the following: the most horribly miscast films in the world are more than likely star vehicles. I know firsthand as a screenwriter and a director - When a "name" is put into a script that was created for someone else entirely, the filmmaking becomes nothing but an exercise into trying to make the mismatch work. Many studio executives would disagree with me simply because they are star-crazy, seeing only the star, knowing the star is the insurance for the budget, and fully convinced that the star is actually bigger than the casting, and even the story itself.

Hearing the story within the script, it was perhaps natural for Marlon to relate to the *"Don Juan"* role; as written, it was the perfect part for a younger Marlon Brando, filled with quirky lines, erotic interludes, neurotic behavior and perhaps most obviously, it was the lead cited in the title. Without specifically discussing his own psychoanalyzed past and his troubled children, I did work my way into a long discussion about what he could bring to the role of the psychiatrist.

I now mention his past and kids because Marlon, of course, had a famous interest in analyzing mental health, from both his own history and as a parent.

We had many talks about those matters previously, but I knew Marlon; he wouldn't care to get that personal when being sold on a movie script. *But* - along the way, he *did* want to be sold. He knew he had to work, he turned down almost everything that came his way, and he saw that I felt there was some potential in this project, more so than much of what arrived at his Mulholland doorstep. The talk went on and I felt he was persuaded. But just when I thought he was won over, he stared quietly and said, "No. This sounds like some role for Gene Hackman."

I was tired by then. For whatever reason, I sighed and shrugged, "Yeah, he would be great in this." The room was now quiet. I didn't really know if I had said anything wrong or not, but as it was with Marlon at times, you'd often reach that point where you knew that the game was over. After a moment, he picked up that essay I had written. "But thanks for the letter, though. Geez, you didn't need to go to so much work; you really got the steam shovel out on this one." Again, I shrugged. I made some excuse about having to leave. After a few more words, I started for the door. With the essay still in his hand, he said, "Go get the script. Let me see this thing. Maybe we can rewrite it." I almost laughed as I left to go get the printed screenplay from his office.

As film history shows, Marlon ended up doing the picture, and in the process, became great friends with Johnny, a wonderfully gifted soul I'd later exchange thoughts with after Marlon's passing. We'd reflect and laugh over Marlon's wit, character and complete uniqueness. We'd both watch Depp's children and my daughter on the playground of their school, The Hollywood Schoolhouse on McCadden Place, along with another father with kids in the school, Al Pacino.

During one such "Marlon" exchange with Depp, after we'd laugh, Johnny simply stared, tearing up as he quietly muttered, "What a gift he was." Almost hilariously, Depp and I shared the rare experience of actually getting The Great Brando to do our passion projects - Johnny with *"The Brave"* and me with *"Free Money"*. I say "hilariously" because I guarantee that we both knew the similar difficulties Marlon brought to our beloved projects. And in spite of how those projects may have been received or not, I'll bet I speak for Johnny when I say that neither of us would trade either of those film shoots with Marlon for anything in the world.

While Marlon's acceptance of the *"DeMarco"* film was a twisting journey for me, other projects he threw my way had even more surprises. One day, he was thrilled that a hit TV show was going to give him a crazy amount of money simply to walk through a door. Or so he was told. As the original run of NBC's *"Will & Grace"* had become a big hit, the producers had the idea of having Marlon arrive as some sort of much-talked about but never before seen character, some large, heavy man from the life of Megan Mullally's character - or something like that. The companies "KoMut" and "3 Sisters Entertainment" sent Marlon a memo and appearance description that they clearly saw as hilarious, but I didn't quite get the premise of the joke. I never really watched the show, and that was for a personal, perhaps some might say petty reason.

One of my very last auditions as an actor was for that show, for a lead role that ultimately and deservedly went to the brilliant Eric McCormack. And as I vividly recalled, thanks to the mean-spirited behavior of the casting people and those I was reading and taping for, it was truly an unpleasant, horrific yet eye-opening experience. It was one of those rude situations that every working, auditioning actor can sadly discuss, the kind of indignity that has actors telling themselves, "I really cannot subject myself to this anymore. Better to be delivering pizza full time."

Years later, as I was up at Marlon's house, reading the proposal that came to his house from the *"Will & Grace"* producers, I recall trying to put that long-ago casting matter out of my head. But while my brain was forgiving, my gut was not. I would always change the channel when the show came on, even as I heard that it was a truly great series. And how could it not be? Such an amazing cast and team of writers - and of course, the greatest sitcom director of all time, James Burrows. Still, I couldn't watch it. *And yet*, on that day up on Mulholland, I could see that Marlon wanted that big payday just to walk through a door, and more than likely, have a shocked studio audience gasp, followed by endless applause. So, I did what I thought I should do: I told him he should do the walk-on. We had a talk about it; he knew nothing of the show and nothing of my past bias; I was completely positive, endorsing and supportive of this job, centered around by what the proposal stated - a special appearance in a special episode of a special hit series.

But oddly, that Brando antenna must have gone up. After I made my case for why he should do the job, he sat there for a bit. He then said, "You don't like these people." I was stunned. I had said *nothing* of the sort. He picked up the phone, called his agent and said, "Tell Grace and Bill to forget it." It wasn't the first time his perception amazed me, and at that moment, I can't pretend I wasn't pleased. Oh, General Industry Warning: Be nice - You never know who or when.

By way of many casual conversations, I talked to Marlon about many of his films, both recent movies and early classics, but for no particular reason, I never talked to him about his Emmy-winning appearance on the ABC sequel to *"Roots"*. I knew it was a rare and singular thing for Marlon to do what was essentially a mini-series episode, but, of course, *"Roots"* and its sequel: these were not "ordinary" miniseries episodes; at the time of their creation and airing, these were the biggest things on earth. And so was Marlon. He had one scene in the epic mini-series and the entire project was promoted, understandably, as though he was starring throughout. For whatever reasons, even though I had never discussed *"Roots"* with Marlon, I could see that for the most part, given a choice in the matter, he had no real want to do television.

Both Greg and Marlon often suggested that "The Work" was all that mattered - Acting. They both *did* love the craft of working as "The One Who Creates a Character". But whether they liked it or not, they both became international film stars, and since both of them saw the invention, advent and evolution of network television, neither seemed particularly in love with the medium. As I've discussed a few times, when the projects clearly interested him, Greg took roles in television - but not many. At the apex of the original ABC *"Twin Peaks"* fever, when the trial regarding the killing of Laura Palmer was a huge pop culture phenomenon, show creator David Lynch asked Greg to play the judge who would preside over the court proceedings involving Laura's murder.

Greg had no interest; he did not know the show all that well and its current popularity meant little to him. Tony and Veronique told

Greg that it would be a great, current event for him to be a part of. No matter. Greg saw nothing of interest in either the project or the role.

But when television projects arrived with "True Weight" in Greg's eyes, he would consider participating. He brought immense gravitas to the WWII drama, *"The Scarlet and the Black,"* to *"Moby Dick"* (the television version that starred Patrick Stewart as Ahab), and to *"The Blue and the Gray,"* where he was able to fulfill a lifelong dream of portraying Abraham Lincoln reciting the Gettysburg Address.

It was a screen moment that is almost bizarrely redundant by way of a singular moment in the world of typecasting.

It was the model of integrity played by the model of integrity.

Going back a beat or two here with Marlon: after I was helpful when it came to getting him to do projects like *"Don Juan DeMarco"* and *"Free Money"* - projects that he enjoyed doing while getting his three million into the bank, he would often toss scripts my way - scripts that were offers he was unsure about - so he'd say. More often than not, I know he didn't want to take the time to read them, and no matter what the case, he did not want to get back to work.

In 1998, when the *"Free Money"* footage was then in edit, CBS approached Marlon with a dramatic TV film, *"Behind the Mask,"* an earnest tearjerker that had many of the elements of *"Don Juan DeMarco"*: a mature doctor who deals with the mentally challenged receives unexpected life lessons from a young patient. The production company and the network must've met his asking price of his relatively new agency, CAA, because as I took the script home that night and started to read it at his request, Avra asked me, "Is that the one he's doing tomorrow?"

I could only ask, "Huh?"

At this moment in time, Avra and I were very busy on two different tracks - While she was working with Marlon up at Mulholland, Tony and I spent every day rewriting and organizing a film we would later make for Sony Pictures, *"Diary of a Sex Addict"*. After a series of meetings on *"Addict"* that day, Marlon had called me, asked me to swing by his house to get the script, and here

I was, hearing this odd question from Avra, "Is that the one he's doing tomorrow?"

What the hell? After getting more information from Avra, I called Marlon with my own question: "What's going on? You said 'Read this' like it was something you might think about doing someday." He explained that he was set to shoot tomorrow, but he didn't know if it was any good. As the call ended, he suggested, "Read it tonight and call me; I'll be up late - the sooner I know, the better." I asked Avra if she had read it; she said she had. "It's a nice little story," she said.

"Jesus, is that the way you explained it to *him*?"

"No. I didn't even get to talk to him about it. I brought it up but he changed the subject."

We both knew that he was probably looking for a way to get out of this project; any way possible. As previously noted, the only TV film he had ever done was that epic *"Roots"* sequel for ABC many years back, and even with his casual attitude toward film and TV in general, he of course inherently knew the difference between theatrical feature films and television movies.

Yes, it's an easy distinction to make, but I was sometimes surprised to see Greg getting over those hurdles in ways that Marlon could not. More than the "TV" aspect, I knew that Marlon simply did not want to work on any movie right now, especially so soon after having done *"Free Money"*. I quickly read the script as I tried to remember all the words that got him to do *"Don Juan DeMarco"*. I knew by now how to be legitimately sincere about a project without having him turn cold on it. If you pushed something too hard on Marlon, he'd see right through you.

If you failed to use the perfect subtle endorsement, he'd quickly shrug, "Sounds lousy. I'm out." I was a bit nervous because he was now a recently-signed client of CAA.

This was after years of being something of a freewheeling star who would have one of his accountants or attorneys field independent offers. With "cops" and "gatekeepers" at the level of CAA, I sensed a new era for Marlon - for better or worse. The better: studios and networks would step up and now feel "safer" with wild Brando. The offers coming to Marlon would be solid, bonded, real, etc. (unlike a crumbling, unfinished *"Divine Rapture"*). The worse: the offers would be like this one: potentially plastic TV movies, empty studio projects he would hate (i.e. - his final supporting role in *"The Score,"* a glossy production of a job that made him miserable). But most of all, I could see Marlon getting himself into a lot of trouble with an entity as powerful as CAA. You don't wanna mess with these guys or make them look bad. Even if you are Brando.

For all those reasons, I knew it was best to tell Marlon that *"Behind the Mask"* was a worthy project. And it was. Years back, I was an actor in a TV film about Alzheimer's called *"Do You Remember Love?"* It could've been relatively lightweight "TV 'Affliction' Move-of-the-Week" fare, but for the performer at the center of it, the great Joanne Woodward. Her presence elevated the project into an Emmy-winning, important piece for CBS. I envisioned something similar with this project. I called Marlon after reading it and gave him my endorsement. He looked at one of his two wristwatches and said, "It's not late. Come over here and tell me all that to my face."

As Avra was already falling asleep, I tiredly got in the car and drove up Mulholland. Finding Marlon in his TV den, I said, "You should get some rest. What time is your call tomorrow?" He laughed, telling me that my "approach" of assuming he would actually go to work tomorrow - he found that funny. As I settled onto the sofa, I again reminded him of my endorsement of the script. He said, "Sounds dull to me." I asked, "Have other people read this? Have you talked to other people about it?" He mentioned one of the producers on the project, a woman I knew. He also mentioned a reader at CAA - They loved it. He found those endorsements to be red flags.

It didn't take long to see just how strongly he did not want to go to work tomorrow. As I made great cases for both the project and his role in it, he resorted to conversational tactics he liked to torment people with, remarks such as, "I always know you're struggling with the truth when I see you make that one particular gesture with your left hand" - God! A Perfect Marlon Maneuver - he always knew how to throw you off balance, even if he was just making something up in the spur of the moment. Moving the story along here, yeah, it was a very long night.

After what seemed like forever, I felt I was actually winning him over on the project. My steps were somehow both precarious yet focused. I talked about the strength and experience he would bring to the role, about the wisdom of his knowledge - How he knew this story of mental health more so than any real doctor. I also brought up that CBS movie I did years ago, with Joanne Woodward, an actress I knew he had great respect for ever since they worked together in 1960's *"The Fugitive Kind"*. He asked, "She did one of these things?" As I told him a bit about it, I felt I was getting closer. But perhaps most impactful, he knew and occasionally respected the fact that I was an industry nerd, so I brought up the money and power of CBS and CAA - not as threats, but as strong financial entities he should firmly hitch his often needy little wagon to, actually getting him to end the conversation with, "Yeah, this could be the start of something good. Okay."

Feeling better, I left the house, under the darkness of a mountain sky. I drove back to my Hollywood apartment, tiredly crawled into bed with Avra and pondered the unique strangeness that just took place, realizing that I had become numb from this kind of Marlon-created chaos.

Early the next morning, all of the phones in the apartment started ringing around the same time - My cell and landline, Avra's cell, our dedicated FAX machine - all of them. It was a mess of different calls, all frantic, all panicking and all frazzled. Who was calling? A producer we knew from the *"Behind the Mask"* production company was calling. An agent from CAA was calling. An Assistant Director from *"Behind the Mask"* was calling. An executive from CBS was calling. And yes, a call was coming in from the office of the President of CBS, Les Moonves.

It seems Marlon had dropped out of the project early that morning, telling the film's producer that two people he works with, Avra Douglas and Joseph Brutsman - these two recommended he not do the film. The *"Behind the Mask"* producer we knew and liked had our phone numbers and those numbers were somehow given out to all these other people. Avra and I called Marlon - no answer. Beyond frantic, we got dressed and started driving up to the house.

Zooming up Laurel Canyon, I suddenly felt horrible for all those people who were ready to start their workday today - with Marlon Brando. Yes, this *was* the first shooting day of a project that probably took years to put together. I absolutely knew that every person on that project had told everyone in their lives about their upcoming "Brando" film - a once in a lifetime event.

Of course, I knew this from my *"Free Money"* experience. *And* - remember my "rewrite" days? Read on:

These TV movie producers, CBS and even CAA - none of them knew that they had to wrangle, harness and chaperone Marlon weeks, days, hours and even minutes before the first shoot day! They signed papers weeks ago, got his measurements and then thought he would just - what?! Just show up like any other actor on the start date?! But why should they think otherwise? He had clearly agreed to something. I was certain that a million of his three million had already been handed over to him via escrow. Why would they think this would or could possibly happen?

Of course, when we got to the house, Marlon was sound asleep after a long night and early morning of troublemaking. We found a way to get him up by way of our shocked shouts, yells that were along the lines of "Hey!" "Marlon!" and "What the fuck?!" When he was finally up and awake, he waddled in as he tied his robe, laughing, "You both thought this thing was a turd, don't bullshit me! Avra, you couldn't even talk to me about it; it's gotta be pretty bad for that." More conversation led to Marlon being a bit more honest; blaming us wasn't really working.

Before long, he said he felt completely railroaded by "greedy" CAA over this whole thing. Convincing him that we couldn't just leave everything in this present broken state, especially now that *we* were dragged into it, we soon had everybody on the phone together: CAA, CBS and the *"Behind the Mask"* producers. On the open speaker phone in the den, after the initial, opening layers of smoke getting cleared, Marlon was charming to everybody, somehow able to quickly turn himself into the victim regarding all this. It was masterful. His voice was soft, old, quivering and tearful. He soon had the entire group in the palm of his hand, telling everybody that he just couldn't go through with it. Not at this age. Not at this stage in his career. Not ever.

He then added the cherry on the cake - One that would change our lives for the next few months.

Marlon assured them with, "I will write something better. And I promise, we'll do that."

That remark created a gaping pause in the conversation. Marlon, Avra and I looked at each other during the silence.

All the call-parties who were not up here in this Mulholland TV den quickly found a semi-polite way to end their part of this unique conversation and get the hell off the line: *Click x 3!*

I'd later learn that they all immediately talked together right after Marlon, Avra and I were off the line, and that talk led to a call that reached Marlon about ten minutes after the full group conversation. Avra and I watched as Marlon picked up the ringing phone from the very positions we all still manned from the previous call. It was CBS on the line. Marlon looked at us, clearly not wanting to put the call on "speaker" this time. Instead, looking slightly rattled, he grabbed a pencil and paper and wrote down an address and a time, all as he was muttering a few "Uh huh"s and "Okay"s. After he hung up, he asked, "Who is Les Moonves?" After I explained that he ran the CBS Television Network, he asked, "What kinda name is 'Moonves'?" Avra and I shrugged.

Marlon then let out a yawn as he informed us, "We all have a meeting with him this afternoon. He wants to hear about this other movie we're gonna write." He then groaned as he stood up.

There was then a strange silent moment as Avra looked my way. I felt absolutely no thrill over this "news". Only panic. He handed Avra the slip of paper, muttering, "We'll talk on the way over there; 'figure out a story. I gotta get some sleep." And with that, he disappeared into his bedroom. Avra and I looked at each other yet again, totally at a loss over what to do next.

We went to "Swingers" on Beverly for breakfast and tried to talk out a strategy, but we both knew that *that* was a bit like writing on water when dealing with Marlon. I went over some of Marlon's favorite projects - scripts I had written and rewritten with him: *"Platinum Toenail," "Tim and His Friends," "Jericho," "Fan Tan," "Skuzz," "Bull Boy"* and others - none of them would make good TV movies, or maybe even good movies, period. After too much conversation, we both agreed to let Moonves do as much of the talking as possible. And Marlon? Well, there would be no controlling him: he'll say what he wants to say; we'll just try to fill in the blanks.

We went home, I cancelled some *"Diary of a Sex Addict"* meetings I had lined up with Tony, I got into some good clothes and we went to go pick up Marlon that afternoon.

Arriving at the Mulholland house, much to our surprise, he was showered, shaved, dressed up and ready. Was he looking forward to this? Or perhaps, just a bit (rightfully) scared over the whole thing? On the ride over to CBS, I asked about "the new project," in case Moonves wanted to actually hear a pitch right then and there. He started telling a story that was ridiculously close to the movie he had just walked out on, complete with the mental hospital angle and other identical elements. Knowing Marlon as well as we did, Avra and I started to shift the characters and story into places and pieces we knew Marlon liked. By now, we knew that he liked the idea of his character being some sort of eccentric loner, a drifter, arriving at some rule-tight organization only to then break all the rules - not with anger, but with charm, whimsy and humor. This mysterious man would probably arrive on a skateboard (no, that's not a typo), perhaps with a large dog as his only companion. He'd be something of a reformed con man - or *was* he reformed? *Hmmm?*

Even though this mysterious man had no roots and was totally freewheeling, he'd need to end up at this rule-tight place for a while - this hospital, this school, whatever it was that needed some shaking up and some waking up. He'd end up charming and wooing some single, mature, sexy woman of color, and he'd also befriend some troubled younger man, a guy who had a horrible, tight-assed father - the father probably being the very creep who *ran* this tight-ruled hospital or school or whatever - in Marlon's mind, to be perfectly played by Charles Grodin.

And yes, *that's* why the young man was "troubled" - his tight-assed authoritarian Charles Grodin dad! Before long, the troubled young man would feel that this odd stranger on the skateboard (somehow on a skateboard), *he* was more of a father to him than his tight-assed "Grodin" dad! That dad would be justifiably publicly scorned by the son and humiliated, cast aside by all in the story, just as it was time for this old ex-con man to get on his skateboard and be a' movin' on . . . along with his only real friend, that giant dog. Probably as a beautiful sun is going down.

We arrived at the Television City parking lot just as Marlon was liking this story. Avra craned her neck, hoping *not* to see her father's car - This is where he was one of the stars of *"The Young & the Restless"* - She didn't want to run into him, convinced that her dad would grow ridiculous when finally meeting the man he always wanted to meet, Marlon Brando. Parking the car, I asked Marlon, "Quick, if there's a pitch for this, what is the name of your character? That'll be the title." Marlon shrugged, "Jimmy." He then added, "But back in his con days, his nickname was *'Saint Jimmy'.*" As I helped Marlon out of the car, I said, "Even better!"

Walking into the building, I saw Marlon take special note of the giant fenced-off satellite dishes that occupied some of the parking lot space at Beverly and Fairfax. He kept pointing and muttering something about them as we coaxed him into the building, knowing we were a bit late.

As the three of us walked down the halls lined with cast photos from past and present CBS shows, word seemed to get out that Brando was in the building. Quite a few workers stepped out of their offices and cubicles, all wanting a peek, a glance and a gawk. I had to laugh as we passed a giant cast photo that featured Avra's smiling dad in the soap cast - She rolled her eyes as we made our way to the office of Les Moonves. Once we got to Les's reception area, we had a large mob of people quietly following us, with another large mob that was waiting for us with the receptionist.

It really was certifiably crazy, and just as I thought I was about to lose my bearings in this ocean of observers, I turned to see that blinding white smile of Les Moonves, who came out into this reception area to personally usher in Marlon Brando. Les whisked us into an office that was more Beautiful Giant Apartment than Workspace. In fact, it really *was* an apartment, complete with a bedroom, bathroom, bar, dining room and living room. The coolest part for TV-Nut-Me: there it was up on an epic wall: a giant, elegantly done, mile-long "Schedule" that showed all the nights, times, shows and networks. Jesus, this really is where it all happens!

With the door finally closed, Les stood back and looked at Marlon with kind of a "Jeez, you're really here" sort of stare. The three of us took in the massive office, with Marlon and I taking special note of that giant overhead schedule. As overlapping small talk moved us to the living room area, Marlon started laughing to Les about those satellites out in the parking lot. I was only now learning what Marlon was thinking as he was staring at those broadcast fixtures outside: he wrongly thought those satellites were the network's "new" way of *now* competing with - HBO (?) - Yeah, Marlon had some of his facts wrong, but through his babble, he did manage to blurt out something that triggered Les, saying that (from what Marlon had heard) award-wise, CBS was now becoming obsolete when it came to the "prestige" of HBO. That *was* true.

We had only been in the room for a moment, but this coming from Brando set Les off into a speech that I absolutely loved, me being an old school fan of the classic three networks. Les said, "'HBO'? Oh, Marlon, I would *love* to have the critics worship us before we even show them a show! I would *love* to have the critics *not* hate us just because we're 'network'! I would *love* to call two episodes of something a 'season'! I would *love* to start a 'season' whenever the hell I felt like it! I would *love* to not worry about a single Nielsen rating! I would *love* to not worry about a single sponsor! I would *love* to not worry about a single censor! I would *love* to not worry about a single affiliate! I would *love* to have a 'schedule' that has no shape or structure whatsoever! I would *love* to *not* have to program news, sports, weather, late night, mornings and daytime! I would *love* to show non-stop, uncut, unsponsored recent hit theatrical blockbuster features all day! Oh, Marlon, all that, believe me, *I would so love!"*

Les brilliantly blurted that whole phenomenal list with good cheer and fun, but I could tell that Marlon's HBO "prestige" crack hit Moonves in a very direct way. Again, I so loved that speech, especially hearing it in *this* office from *this* man. He was so right! I grew up loving network TV, and as Les was making the list, I was reminded of what I always knew but rarely thought about: yes, while the three major networks are *broad*-cast relics in an evolving *narrow*-cast world, face it: the Old Big Three were flat-out miracles. Perhaps they still are.

If you look at the world before cable, satellite and internet, you need to remember that ABC, CBS and NBC were beyond amazing; they blazed every trail. Nothing that exists today in "media" would be here without the methods, models and examples set forth by those pioneering companies. Yes, you can point to radio, motion pictures and even publishing as related partners and predecessors, but in the end, it was network TV, for better or worse, that changed nearly every aspect of our lives. Guys like Les clearly understood and appreciated every bit of that.

Shifting gears, Moonves introduced us to a couple other CBS executives who joined our talk; one was an attractive woman who Marlon took an instant liking to. As all six of us got comfortable in the living room, booze quickly flowed and Les assured Marlon that there were no hard feelings for backing out of the TV movie. These assurances were followed up with a very direct question from Moonves: "So, tell us about this other movie we're all going to be making." After a cold moment, Avra and Marlon turned to me. Marlon then said, "Okay, Joe, you're on." Luckily, by then, Tony and I had a few years of feature film pitching under our belts - There were those who were far better at it than us, but we had become pretty good at leaning in and telling the story. Because of that, I now found the words and tone as I proceeded to tell Les and his team about *"Saint Jimmy"*. Marlon interrupted every now and then, but even his clumsiest additions were greeted with thrilled laughter and giddy excitement by the CBS folks. Of course they were; think about it: these network people were having a TV movie pitched to them by Marlon Brando!

When I ("we") finished the pitch, Les smiled and nodded, "So who's gonna write this?" He pointed at Avra and me with that question mark still in the air, seeming to forget that this all started when Marlon, on the phone earlier that day, said that *he* was going to write the script. When Les asked the question again, Marlon pointed to himself, Avra and me as he said, "Three-way split." I then added that I had written Marlon's previous film, now in post. That clearly made an impression on Les. After much more chatting and laughing, Moonves stood and told us that he now had to get to the *one* meeting that day that he could not get out of - whatever that was. It was obvious that he had already cleared a busy schedule for this single get-together. As we left, Les said that the network would be in touch with CAA and that we should all be happy to be moving forward on a project.

Leaving CBS, Marlon was thrilled. He took Avra and me to an Italian restaurant for dinner. As we ate at our cozy corner table, he warned of how little the "writing pay" was probably going to be. We shrugged. Avra and I lived in a world where a "little" to Marlon was "a lot" to us. As the evening went on, we could only laugh over what this day had become. It started last night as Marlon asked me to read a script. And now, here we were: writing a Brando movie for CBS.

But I can't say that the meal was a "celebration" of any kind - it was all too strange for that. Well, "strange" was far too weak a word for what was about to unfold.

PART TWO

Avra and one of her many friends, occasional writing partner Beth Flatley, wrote a horror movie back in the late 80's called *"Teacher's Pet"*. It was a Demon Child From Hell thriller that was sold to and produced by German TV network RTL Television, under the very German title *"Klassenziel Mord"* which brokenly translates to *"Murder Class Goal,"* which I guess meant that the goal of this teacher's class was murder - or something like that. In short: Marlon knew that Avra was a produced screenwriter but rarely introduced the idea of collaborating with him.

I believe he saw Avra as his most beloved and trusted friend, his most rock-solid dependable employee, and he knew that he kinda ended up brutally fighting with everyone he ever tried to "co-write" with. I knew that Big-Time. He never liked a fight with Avra. Avra is the kind of person that doesn't get in fights, and if you're fighting with her, it doesn't take long for you to realize that you're the one who is wrong; trust me, I know this. Marlon never liked that sort of thing. On the other hand, occasionally, Marlon did love a good battle - over anything, really, and if you were truly in his universe, you were bound to have a doozy with him every now and then. All this is leading up to how the three of us started "work" on *"Saint Jimmy"* for CBS.

That night at the Italian restaurant with Marlon after the whirlwind CBS day went on for a while. As I indicated, Marlon was already getting a bit odd over the whole deal. He knew he was now on the hook with both the network and CAA, and that this new script and the first pay that would come with it would be big issues. When work and money were ever involved with Marlon, nothing was easy, and matters always, quickly became combustible. Avra and I were not looking to get rich over this deal, but by now, we fully deserved to be a part of it if a salary was involved. Mind you, this all popped into our lives in a blink. It felt as though we got sucked into this whole shit-storm in the strangest of ways - even on The Brando Scale. One moment we're minding our own business - A few hours later, we're telling the head of CBS that we're writing a TV movie for him that will star Marlon Brando. And one final note on that moment: I assure you: Moonves knew to a certainty: he knew full well that these two younger people with Marlon were going to be the ones writing the script - doing the *real* writing - not The Movie Star. At the end of the network meeting, I watched as one of Les's associates wrote down my name and Avra's name on a CBS notepad; she then asked for our phone numbers.

That night at home, Avra and I talked a great deal about the possibilities - good and bad - over this project. One thing seemed certain: after the whole mess with a stranded ready-and-waiting film crew, CAA scrambling like mad, and maybe, just maybe all of it getting ironed out simply because Les wanted to meet Brando, I understood something that I knew Marlon knew as well: there would be no grand payday for this TV script - Marlon was just lucky that this whole thing panned out as it did. Frankly, considering all that had happened, he was getting off easy.

Again, no "epic" "Three-Way-Split" salary was fine with Avra and me - Marlon sharing large numbers with anybody was always problematic; he'd get real *"Treasure of the Sierra Madre"* over stuff like this. *But* - somehow, simply because this was such a Marlon adventure, I was already doubting Avra and I seeing money at all, and there was no way that I could afford to work on this if I was not getting paid, and I of course knew that Avra should be paid as well - At least WGA minimums for each of us; we were both members. This sounds like simple common sense, but again, with Marlon, you never know.

He was so used to me writing for free for him - perhaps my mistake, but it was what it was.

Now with money involved, and us actually being deep in the action when it was all coming together, it was different. It's different when you know someone is paying for a script. And again, while I knew Avra should also get her share of the CBS money, I took into account that she was also an employee of Marlon's. If I was already thinking about my former free writing for Brando and Avra's existing salary, I knew Marlon was as well. But mostly, I knew that with the three of us, only two of us would actually be "writing" the script; again, Les Moonves knew that as well.

The day after the long, exhausting CBS day, Marlon wanted to lounge about and bask in the sunshine of not having to do *"Behind the Mask"*. As we brought up *"Saint Jimmy"* and suggested a few good ways to start, he changed the subject, joked about "not doing it" and became irritated as I pressed him on it further.

Having dinner without him that night at the Hamburger Hamlet on Sunset, Avra and I were both starting to have thoughts similar to one another, knowing Marlon as well as we did.

I said, "My guess as to what's gonna happen: we're all gonna split the writing money and he'll make it impossible for us to get a script done. Then *we'll* be in dutch with CBS and WGA."

Avra shrugged, "I don't know. It would be more like him to just blow the whole thing off; the money, the writing - all of it. Then he'll gloss it all over with one fancy public dinner with Les."

I disagreed with, "I don't think so. There are too many 'cops' on him this time - Remember, this is *after* he's already 'committed the crime' with the TV movie - *That* production company might be involved now, too, after this whole screw-over. How could CBS not give them first shot at this *"Saint Jimmy"* thing? Whatever *that's* gonna be. And then there's CBS and CAA" -

"I heard they got Donald Sutherland for the *'Mask'* movie; that was fast."

"It had to be. My guess on Marlon - and don't ask me why - You wanna hear this?"

Almost fearfully, Avra nodded, "Yeah. What?"

"He's gonna keep all the writing money, tell us we're not on the project and either *not* write a script or get some stranger to write it for free."

Avra stared. She then sighed her nervous giggle, knowing there was every chance of that scenario. We had a somewhat similar experience on a Marlon project years back, the comedy called, *"Tim and His Friends,"* an un-produced script that had Marlon bringing-on and shoving-off writers throughout, all as Avra and I were putting together actual scene pages that he would eventually give to Whoopi Goldberg and other stars he wanted in the film. As things got "real" for that project, we struggled to stay on it, even though it had slim chances of getting made.

Remember, all this with *"Saint Jimmy"* - this was after I had already gone on the whole Marlon rollercoaster ride of screenwriting, production and money issues with *"Free Money"*. Oddly, I felt I was now joining a club of guys like Elliot Kastner and Francis Coppola, guys who would go through hell and back with Marlon over projects, get into flat-out wrestling matches with him, and, somehow, always patch things up, perhaps ready for the next film down the road with him. Reading this, you might feel that Marlon was someone who would cheat people out of money, or worse. That really wasn't the case. I knew Hollywood people like that - Marlon wasn't one of them. So what was he? He was crazy different - both Crazy Difficult but Crazy Great.

As we all know, Marlon was a giant star who played by his own rules. He starred in a feature film I wrote, but if you were his friend, he could also spin all your wheels for quite a while and assume that you wouldn't take it personally. By the way, all this is exactly why Greg was always so careful, so cautious and so disciplined. Peck knew the weight of his stardom and of the dream-power Hollywood brought; he never wanted to lead people on, under-pay people or *not* do every bit of filmmaking aboveboard. I think that's why Greg let few into his world; he did not want to disappoint or disillusion. And here's the nuttiest part of the industry and the methods of these two men: Hollywood is one of the few arenas were your product can be made *either* by the rules and by the book - OR - it can a big free-for-all - and either method just might succeed.

Back to *"Saint Jimmy"* - Avra and I got home that night and I had a message on my phone machine from CAA's Bruce Vinokour, a very nice agent who then led the agency's activities in TV mini-series and movies-of-the-week. He too had my number after the whole blow up with *"Behind the Mask"*. He was asking about who represented Avra and me. I had just come off of a horrible situation with William Morris and was between agents. Avra did not have an agent, but we had a mutual longtime friend in Mark Mazie, a super smart entertainment attorney who we first met through Avra's father. I called Mark to ask if he'd work with us over this CBS deal.

Mark knew Vinokour, praised Bruce's work and said he'd be happy to help, getting hold of CAA immediately. This was all good news to me. We did not instigate any of these proceedings, we were simply doing exactly what professional people are supposed do when they are dealing with entities as massive and legitimate as the CBS Television Network and the Creative Artists Agency. Actually, I was then feeling the slightest bit of shame, only hours before harboring such paranoia over what Marlon would or would not do. With Mazie contacting Vinokour, I felt relief.

But, of course, my relief vanished the next morning as I listened to a voice mail that came in from Marlon. He wanted to know who "Mark Mazie" was and who "Bruce Vinokour" was.

Oh, and he also wanted us to know that we would not be needed on the project; he felt it would be best if he would write the script himself. I sighed, oddly smiled and shook my head.

Yes, given that this was Marlon, so much of this was predictable - in fact, I had pretty much pre-called this exact outcome. Given Marlon's dark tone on the phone message machine, I didn't want to call and get into it with him at the moment. In fact, rightfully, I was angry. Again, Marlon pulled us into this craziness, we were actually helpful when it came to dealing with a network he had essentially stiffed on one fine morning, and here we were, now dealing with *this*? And no, I wasn't dumb enough to think that Avra and I meant anything to CBS, but still - dragged into this we were. Was he angry that "our attorney" had talked to one of "his agents"? Probably. Anytime "real" people were involved with matters, Marlon would grow tense, angry and even hateful.

I called Mazie and he had an idea, telling me that he first wanted to make what he called a "careful" call to Vinokour. Whatever that was, he did that and called me back, asking if I could meet him for a bite as he explained a way forward.

Finding Avra still home, she said that Marlon had left her a voice mail this morning, telling her not to come up today. After hearing it, she couldn't get him on the phone. This was always his method if you were "out" for a day or a week or longer. Those in the inner circle would often go through "Time Outs" with Marlon, his way of expressing his anger, but also - on the bright side - sparing you his ugly mood while he was cooling down. I explained the whole Vinokour/Mazie thing to Avra and told her I was off to meet Mark, asking her to come along with me.

We met Mazie at a Beverly Hills coffee shop and he told us that as far as he knew, Marlon had yet to speak directly with Vinokour - Mark said he could tell: Bruce knew nothing of Marlon's "mood". In fact, to Mark, it seemed as though Vinokour at this point had yet to have one conversation directly with "new CAA client" Brando - ever, but Bruce did leave word on Marlon's office phone machine that he had made contact with our representation: Mark Mazie.

Mark then asked us more about how all this mishegas came about; we explained the crazy *"Behind the Mask"* story, the even crazier Les Moonves story, the whole thing. Given the unique, fragile situation and our friendships with Marlon, Mark suggested that we write a very carefully worded letter to Vinokour, but let Marlon see it first; see how he responds, and then we'll take it from there. Since it sounded like Bruce knew nothing of the whole CBS visit - (and why would he?) - or who the hell WE were - (and why would he?) - Mazie thought we should drop the name of Moonves on everybody's toes by way of this "letter," and see if this might help Marlon understand the "fairness" of our position. We asked more questions. Mark, smart guy that he was, gave more suggestions, and hours later, Avra and I sent this to Marlon via FAX:

Dear Mr. Vinokour,

Thank you so much for reaching out to us so quickly after the great meeting we had with Mr. Moonves at his CBS office. We are thrilled to begin work on Marlon's new TV film for CBS, "Saint Jimmy". We have worked with Marlon on a number of projects through the years, always grateful to be working with an artist of his talent, accomplishment and kindness. We were also thrilled by the enthusiastic reception Mr. Moonves gave our pitch of the project. Of course, knowing that this story will come to life thanks to Marlon, we're sure Mr. Moonves could envision it all before him.

Again, Thanks! Please feel free to contact us or Mark Mazie if anything else is needed.

Very Best Regards, Avra Douglas and Joseph Brutsman

Every word of it was true and from our hearts. So what were we up to? Nothing nefarious whatsoever. We knew at this moment that Marlon was not talking to us. Why? Only Marlon knew. We were tossed into this *thing*, trying to make the best of it - trying to make it as "real" and as "safe" for us as possible. We quickly wanted to create a distinct form of communication with this busy, important CAA agent - a player who now seemed key to this situation. Were we even going to send it to Bruce? That we were unsure of. First we wanted to shake Marlon loose from his anger, while, yes, staking our rightful claim to what had already transpired in all this.

Of course, we also knew there was a good chance that this "letter" could infuriate Marlon.

Yeah. It did.

An hour after it was faxed into Marlon's hands, a "counter-fax" from Marlon was trying to come to us through our home machine - our fax machine was out of paper. The phone rang. Avra picked up - It was Marlon's giggling housekeeper (she often nervously giggled). She said she was trying to send a fax from Marlon. Avra said she'd put paper in; Marlon could try to resend in about a minute. Avra hung up. She looked at me with big eyes, both scared and laughing.

Avra said, "Oh my God, he's so pissed off. He wants to send us a fax. He'd only be doing that if he's really, really mad!"

I sighed as I shook my head. Frankly, I was getting more and more angry about this. Avra stood there as I reached for the fax paper. She stopped me.

She said, "No, this will be funny. Let him keep trying to send. This is ridiculous." A minute later, a fax tried to come through. But still, no paper. The phone rang again. Egged-on by Marlon, the giggling housekeeper was now getting angry through her giggles, wondering why the fax wasn't going through. This time I was on the phone, telling her our fax was "working fine; try again."

Ring! With no paper in our fax machine, of course, no fax came through. This went on for over a half hour, with many attempts up at Mulholland, with the now furious, now *not* giggling housekeeper continually calling to yell at us (for Marlon), with the two of us telling her, time and time again, that it was "working now! Try again!"

As ridiculously crazy as all this was becoming, Avra and I grew silly with laughter, knowing that Marlon had to be pulling his hair out, incensed that he could not send whatever masterful insult he had concocted. And yes, I knew Avra was correct; he was not sending something benign or friendly, not within this situation, not with this feverish "fax" obsession currently in play.

Within that very time frame, I received a call on my cell phone from Bruce Vinokour, saying that he had our contracts ready, he'd send them to Mazie, and that he had just received a "glowing" letter about us from "Mr. Brando". He seemed somewhat puzzled by the letter, feeling it was perhaps unnecessary to send to CAA, but still, sent by Marlon it was.

Uh, okay. (???) Politely, I asked if he could fax us the letter - he agreed, we had a pleasant sign off and that was that. "A glowing letter about us from Mr. Brando"? What the hell?

I hung up. I was confused. I told Avra to quickly load the fax - CAA was sending something Marlon had sent them - about us?! Beep! It came through - we stared at it, long and hard.

Dear Mr. Vinokour,

Thank you so much for reaching out to me so quickly after the great meeting I had with Mr. Moonves at his CBS office. I am thrilled to begin work on Avra and Joe's new TV film for CBS, "Saint Jimmy". I have worked with Avra and Joe on a number of projects through the years, always grateful to be working with artists of their talent, accomplishment and kindness. I was also thrilled by the enthusiastic reception Mr. Moonves gave Avra and Joe's pitch of the project. Of course, knowing that this story will come to life thanks to Avra and Joe, I'm sure Mr. Moonves could envision it all before him.

Again, Thanks! Please feel free to contact me or The Great Mark Mazie if anything else is needed.

Very Best Regards, Marlon Brando

At that time, I understood Marlon - say, 90-some percent; I had him "figured out" to that fuzzy set of math. Avra knew him *over* 100 percent; better than he knew himself. I could only ask:

"What? I don't quite get it."

"Wow. Oh my God. He's furious!"

"He is? Really?"

"Don't you see? He thought this would be the greatest 'Fuck you' he could give us! Turning around our words and names like this! I've seen him do this before. No, if he really thought he was saying something 'nice' about us, he would've written something himself - it would've been beautiful. He wouldn't've tried to shit all over *our* letter like this."

"But why send it to Vinokour?"

"My guess - He was so pissed off over not getting through our fax. He thought he was going full scorched earth, sending it to CAA."

"Expecting CAA to think - uh, what? They don't know us. And they don't have *our* letter."

"You know Marlon. He doesn't think these things through in the slightest when he's angry."

"Bruce thought it was a 'glowing' letter. He doesn't know it's a - What? 'Parody' of another letter" - ?

"He doesn't know Marlon's 'sarcasm' yet. And maybe Marlon thinks we already sent our letter. *If* we had done that, yeah, maybe *then* Bruce would sense the friction at work here. Maybe."

After too much silence, we both sorta just laughed, shaking our heads and sighing. What now? Moments later, Mazie called and said that this quick deal already went through. It wasn't a lot of money, but it was something. So we had a CBS deal made by CAA. With Marlon mad at us.

For the rest of the day, Avra and I tried to figure out a next-best move. As smart as she was about Marlon, she kept reminding me of a certain belief she was sure about: "There's nothing we can do now but wait for him to come around." Of course, she was right. Later that night, Marlon left a phone message, telling us, "Get up here tomorrow; *now* we have to write this fucking thing!" Did we know this was how it was gonna go down when we sent the fax of the "letter" to Marlon? Not a chance. Did Mazie know? Of course not. That's the essence of Marlon; you *never* know. *But* - we *did* know the drill now that we were once again about to face Marlon; and that happened the next day. *The Drill:* we would act like the bad stuff never happened, we would never speak of it again, and mostly, as the "new writing" starts, we would know that this is gonna be a very long slog to get from "Page One" to "The End".

For the next few months, Avra, Marlon and I did a few versions of *"Saint Jimmy"*. Thanks to Marlon's insistence on bizarre plot points, unfocused characters and strange dialogue, each draft was worse than the next. The process of writing was the same as the other scripts I'd create with Marlon - He'd record our conversations about the material, the tapes would be transcribed, I'd try to shuffle elements of those transcriptions into a script, adding stuff I thought could make it work, he'd insist on horrible additions, and by the end of it all, well, I'd simply hope for the best. Eventually, both CBS and CAA cried "Uncle" and said "Enough! Stop making drafts of this dreck!" By then, Marlon's attention had moved onto other things, Avra and I had done all we could, and, well, we were actually incredibly relieved to be done with this epic adventure.

From that point on, Avra and I really did what we could to *avoid* ever giving Marlon "Project Advice". It never was something that we instigated ourselves to begin with, but after the *"Behind the Mask"* and *"Saint Jimmy"* craziness, we were determined to not get into the jam again.

But alas, nobody can make history repeat itself quite like Marlon. Years later, in the Mulholland den one day in 2001, Avra and I explained the Fox network TV show *"In Living Color"* to Marlon, along with discussion of that show's creator, Keenen Ivory Wayans and his first *"Scary Movie"* motion picture; a hit comedy. After a bit of talking, Marlon asked, "So, you're saying, this guy made a black *'Sid Caesar Show'*?" After we clarified the differences, telling him that it was a bit more like the African-American *"Saturday Night Live,"* we made a strong endorsement of Wayans for a very simple reason: CAA had already set the whole thing up: tomorrow was Marlon's first day on the set of *"Scary Movie 2"*, and Marlon was clearly having reservations about wanting to work on the comedy feature.

By then, Avra and I knew well: Marlon might sometimes need to take jobs like this for the money, and we already had our dreadful experience, where he would use even a perceived shrug from us as a signal not to do a job. Of course, we never believed that our actual opinion was the basis for him walking away from any potential employment. No, we knew that the real situation was this: by now, Marlon did not like the process of most forms of filmmaking, looking for a reason, *any* reason to pick up the phone and say he was out of a project. By this time, we knew that we did not want to be seen as even being remotely responsible for Marlon Brando being "advised" to *not* follow through on an agreement.

The next morning, like a pair of prison guards, Avra and I brought Marlon to the set of *"Scary Movie 2"*. He didn't have a large role, playing a parody of the Max von Sydow "Father Merrin" priest from *"The Exorcist,"* but of course, the production was thrilled to have Brando for a few-day shoot. As we sat in a "Star" trailer with Marlon, he was appearing tired and pale. He didn't look well. By the time he was in costume and make-up, it seemed as though he was about to faint, throw-up or both. Avra was going to read Marlon's lines through an ear piece during the shoot; she went to the set with him as I waited in the trailer. With Marlon in that condition - or whatever was going on with him, I had no interest in visiting the set of *"Scary Movie 2"*. I also had screenwriting to do on the laptop I brought. I just wanted to steer clear of The Marlon Show today - I had done my part: I helped Avra get him to his high-paying job and that was that.

In what seemed like no time, Avra and Marlon came back to the trailer. Stagehands were helping Marlon along as he limped up the trailer steps. He looked at me with glowing red eyes. Drool was leaking from his pained grimace. Something unfortunate was also dripping from his nose as well. I looked at Avra - She was nearly in tears, fully horrified by Marlon's near-death appearance. The stagehand said something about "pneumonia" as Marlon was gently put onto a sofa in the trailer. Avra said, "He's really sick. They said he should go to a hospital." After the stagehands were gone, Marlon quietly muttered, "Let's get packed and get out of here. Please." Avra and I got everything put together, pulled our car up to the trailer and helped Marlon into the car. He collapsed onto the backseat as Avra put the car in gear and we pulled off the studio lot.

Down the road, Avra asked, "Marlon, do you want to go to the hospital?" He painfully uttered, "Turn left, up here." For the next few miles, he choked out various directions, such as, "Go right at that light, please." Avra asked, "Are we going to a pharmacy? What?" He'd groan, holding his belly. Before long, by way of Marlon's directions, we arrived at that same Italian restaurant that we went to after our CBS meeting. Not wanting to just blurt out a laugh, he instead kept the pain and agony game up for just a wee bit longer, quietly coughing out, "I think I'll feel better if I get something to eat."

He got out of the car as I asked Avra, "Did we really just fall for that?" She shook her head, "You should've seen him on that set! He terrified that entire film crew. They thought he was dying." I had to ask, "Wait, are you in on this with him?" She said, "No! I thought he was really sick! And so did you." Neither of us wanted to believe that he pulled one over on us. Getting out of the car, I grumbled, "Why do we forget? He's a great actor - That's, like, pretty-much his thing. Jesus!" With the longest of sighs, we walked into the restaurant. There he was, sitting at the same cozy corner table we shared after that meeting with Les Moonves a few years back.

He smiled.

We sorta smiled.

As we sat, he muttered, "Just like my videotape project."

I asked, "What's that?"

He chortled, *"Lying For a Living"*.

Yes, as he had been chatting-up for quite awhile, Marlon was thinking about a series of acting instruction tapes that he wanted to create and market - *That* epic adventure is coming up. But first here on the horizon (as we now leave 2001 and go back to 1998 in our timeline) was the release of *"Free Money"*. Would it be the hit-worthy-of-a-sequel he was hoping it would be?

We were about to find out.

WATCH IT (FREE MONEY 1998)

The French film editor Yves Langlois was known for cutting together many great action films, as well as the fascinating prehistoric art hit, *"Quest for Fire"*. He worked for quite a while on the edit of *"Free Money,"* along with Robert Redford's favorite composer, Mark Isham, who did a great score for it. By the time *"Free Money"* was ready to screen, the financial people behind the movie booked the largest theater on the Warner Brothers Burbank lot and threw a big event to unveil it for potential distributors, the cast members in L.A. and for - if he would attend, Marlon. I loved and knew that Warner theater and that entire area of the lot quite well, having played Agent Efrem Beaman alongside Kate Jackson and Bruce Boxleitner in the final two seasons of the Warners/CBS series, *"Scarecrow & Mrs. King"*.

While this screening of *"Free Money"* was not going to be some red carpet, paparazzi-lined evening, it was exciting - and nerve-racking - for me. I invited many friends and members of Avra's family. I hadn't seen much of the final edit and I was getting mixed reports from both Yves Simoneau and Nicolas Clermont, but they were chalking up their uncertainty to too many weeks of staring at it for too long, certainly something that can happen as you form raw film footage into a feature film; after a while, you really don't know what the hell you're looking at.

I was almost surprised to see how accommodating Marlon was regarding his want to go to Warners and view the film with an audience. He did make sure that he could just slip into the back unnoticed as the lights were going down, but nonetheless, he went to Burbank and watched the film. I was so frazzled, I don't even recall if Greg went to the screening or not. I know he was invited, but by then, I also recall that Tony had become quite frustrated with the project, having strong disagreements with the director, certain that the final edit would not at all represent the script we wrote. I certainly understood all his concerns (and he's always been - and still is - much better with these perceptions than I am), but between Marlon and my ongoing dealings with both Yves and Nicolas, I was trying to keep a certain set of blinders on and hope/pray for the best.

In that theater on the Warner lot that night, the film received a nice enough reception. People laughed in the right places, took the fun ride regarding the vast adventure of it all and marveled over the bold audacity of Marlon's performance. To some extent. It really depended on your age.

Older viewers almost universally hated seeing Marlon so heavy, so crazy and so comedic, while younger viewers with no investment in *"Streetcar," "Waterfront"* or even *"Godfather"* - it seemed they found this strange fat old man to be wild, funny and, at times, flat-out hysterical. One little kid was giggling as the end credits rolled, "The Swede! The Swede!" That's the way Marlon's character's name was shouted out, quite a bit by other characters throughout the film.

When the lights came up, I wasn't at all certain about any of it - It all kinda worked and a lot of it didn't. But like Yves and Nicolas, I was way too close to the whole thing. I was hoping my doubts were all about that. Still, I was unsure. Tony and I always knew that the tone of the piece was key. The plot had wild twists and a number of surprises, but I felt it always needed to be grounded in an exact form of Midwestern drollness. Again, we wrote it before *"Fargo,"* and now it looked like something that was trying hard to be*"Fargo,"* a very tall order for any film. On top of that, we had "Brando," and as I just mentioned, the man is a true generational controversy.

That hit me hard as I spoke with Avra's uncle after the screening, Alan Douglas. Alan's brother - my father-in-law, soap actor Jerry Douglas (as you'll recall, "John Abbott" for years on *"The Young & the Restless")* was also here. Jerry said he liked the film, jumped into his sports car and sped off the lot. That was fine with me; it was Alan's opinion I was interested in. Between the brothers, Alan was always the deep, incredibly hip intellectual of the two, having spent his professional life nurturing abstract projects on Lenny Bruce, Miles Davis and Alan's one-time best friend, Jimi

Hendrix. After Jimi's death, Alan was made producer, protector and arbiter of all things "Hendrix," until a series of legal battles with the Hendrix family in 1995. I loved Alan. We always had open, honest, intelligent sets of exchanges - on any topic, project or idea whatsoever.

"I hated it." Yes, those were the first words from Alan's mouth. The discussion quickly became an essay on Marlon, his career and what an audience would make of Brando playing such a broad, comedic role at his present age and weight. All that set me off. I immediately became defensive and combative, telling Alan, "This is so much like all of you from your generation. It's like you're all still defending this radical young rebel to your father because he put Clark Gable out of business, as if he's not allowed to be anything other than what all you old beatniks think he's supposed to be!" Alan had never seen me like this, but then again, I had never before just come off a multi-year battle as a producer and a writer trying to get an epic feature film completed starring Marlon Brando.

As for what Alan was saying, I had heard it all for years and I certainly heard it during the production of the film: "You can't have 'Brando' do that! 'Brando' would never do that!" This kind of stuff from possessive fans who don't seem to know that nobody tells Marlon what to say, think or do. On top of that, it's as though they feel that he must be shielded from - Who? - Himself?! As though the "Brando" they're still in love with should be protected from this old, fat, nutty "Brando" they're not so crazy about?! Jesus, these people gotta look inward at their own loss-of-youth problems or just go and get a shrink!

Staring at me ranting that type of anger, as though I was someone he had never met before, Alan shot back with, "Hey, you're right! You don't put clown make-up on Bob Dylan and expect me to like it!" I said, "Jesus Christ, go watch 'Candy,' go watch 'The Freshman' - Hell, 'Bedtime Story'! He's allowed to be funny when he wants to be! People here tonight, they brought some young kids - they were laughing like crazy; they're not hung up on 'Cool Brando' like you are!"

We were soon having this long, loud walk-and-talk as we were getting far away from others at the theater, now finding ourselves under the iconic Warner Brothers water tower, having passed parking spaces, office doors and assorted signage all citing various mentions of Clint Eastwood and his Malpaso Productions, all reminding me of the constant branding, lionizing and industry worship of superstar names. After more argument, Alan and I both took a breath. He then said, "Look, maybe you're right; I have a certain view of all this. I hope the thing hits. What do I know? It's kinda 'country bumpkin' humor; it's not for me, but that doesn't mean a fucking thing. I'm an old Jew from Chelsea, ya dig?" That got me to laugh. We shared a warm hug but I was rattled, feeling that there was more wrong with the film than just an old hipster's view of an overweight Brando. Yeah, as Alan walked away, I was having more than a few bad thoughts about *"Free Money".*

I was also having thoughts and questions I sometimes did harbor regarding Marlon - and Greg as well. The two of them acting at this age - was it a bit like asking Muhammad Ali to put on his boxing gloves in his later years? Making Sinatra sing when he could no longer hit the notes? (and that indeed was the case in his final concerts). In many ways, acting is a skill like any skill. Is there a time when some just can't do it as they once did? Of course, the answer to that could very well be "Yes".

The next day, Marlon told me that he wasn't thrilled with the film. He called Nicolas and told him that Joseph Brutsman would do an edit on his Avid and try to fix it. This was news to me, but Nicolas quickly called me and asked me to give it a try, or at least to go through the process, to keep Marlon - for now - from speaking to anybody about how he did not like the film. Clermont was mindful of Marlon's behavior after Brando became disenchanted with either the film or the producers of projects such as *"Christopher Columbus: The Discovery," "The Freshman"* and *"A Dry White Season"*. By differing degrees regarding those films, Marlon let his dissatisfaction be known to the press before the products were released, many say doing damage to the first impressions of those movies. It was indeed a pattern of his. With this film not even having a distributor yet, Nicolas was quite scared of Marlon's next move.

Long story short: after a little more editing, a little more thinking and some shopping to distributers, Clermont couldn't get a major studio to bite. But he was able to unload the film market by market, country by country, all without a U.S. theatrical distribution - which, of course, is what everybody wanted: an American theatrical release. Instead, the film made its cable debut on the "Starz" movie channel, played for quite a while on "Comedy Central" and then landed into home video by way of "Lionsgate Entertainment". Simoneau and I were asked by Lionsgate to have a real-time, running-time taped conversation in a recording studio as we watched the movie from start to finish; this became the commentary "extras" track for the limited-run blu-ray. And there we were. And are. Yeah. That is the story of *"Free Money"*.

Between The Hollywood Guy's now defunct company and whatever eventually went on with Clermont's Filmline Productions in Canada, it seems that *"Free Money"* is a hard find when it comes to syndicated runs, free film channels like "Movies!" and other streaming or cable outlets I wish it could still be seen on. I'm not expecting it to break out into cult status, but with that cast, the laughs it offers and - of course - Marlon Brando's last starring role, the film deserves more than the odd graveyard it now sleeps in.

When I find myself feeling somewhat negative about the whole endeavor, I remember a few things that make me smile: the joy and giant laughs Tony and I shared when writing the original draft in Cheryl's screening room. The fun I had watching the brilliant Thomas Hayden Church perform his role as written, and how his "Larry" was exactly what the writers envisioned. Paying off all my steep bills from Montreal, when that first check arrived from Nicolas for the script purchase. And most of all, Marlon's participation, and how much he loved the role. When I *first* gave him the script, he smiled as he stared at those two words that created the title. He then muttered, "In our lousy business, there's no such thing."

Marlon was right about that - and I'm not just talking about "free" money. As I mentioned earlier, (and as Sean Penn had warned about) The Hollywood Guy totally fucked me out of big money that was contractually due me; the giant top agency that made the deal between us did *nothing* to help, saying, "Hey, that's just the way he is - don't take it personally." It rocked my world: a producing partner legally owed me thousands of dollars - survival money due to me, and according to a major agency, there was nothing I could do about it? I had to get a lawyer, who got me a fraction of what was owed me. It shook my financial life for years, forcing me to rethink my entire career as a freelance artist living project-to-project.

Especially as Avra and I were about to enter a totally new phase of our lives together as parents.

Molly (2000)

As much as I somehow became the Designated Driver, non-smoker, non-drinker of my immediate family, it's my sister Pam who was The Real White Sheep of the Brutsman family. Well, my mother was the pure, snow-whitest of white sheep - so pure, she is not even allowed to compete in this arbitrary "sheep" competition. As for the rest of us: my dad was a 7-night a week nightclub musician, my younger sister Laura went to New York City to become a performer. I did that as well. That leaves Pam: a hard working communications worker who stayed in Minnesota. She went from - yes, literally - a beautiful young phone switchboard operator - with those ancient cords, plugs and hoses and all - to a high-ranking media executive within a series of mammoth, always-merging communications and tech companies.

All her professional life, she's worked for those kind of epic, always-swelling concerns that went from being big-yet-friendly "Ma Bell" phone companies, to later becoming those satellite-driven planet-sized walls of essential data I will never understand: the sort of mega-corporations that have become more vital to us than the standard utility companies; they somehow keep all the wireless working, the smart-phones humming, the internets running and the screens glowing as technology continues to change, enlighten and/or destroy us on a minute-by-minute basis.

With all this, she's had financial success, the stability of owning a nice home, and many other things that come with *not* thinking she was born to share her "creativity" with the world. I phrase it like that because I often half-joke to her that she was lucky to have more common sense than "creativity". To explain that, ask her accountant and my accountant (if I could afford one) - You get the idea; Pam is quite stable in business and work. Which is why in the other areas of her life, she's wonderfully animated, colorful and more so than her siblings, full of volume and life.

Like many sets of brothers and sisters that are close in age, Pam, Laura and I all started becoming parents at roughly the same time. I mention Pam's animated, colorful volume because her tone and excitement level is drastically different than the shy, quiet, near-scared qualities that I know I share with my younger sister, Laura. As we both always knew, the two of us became actors *because* we were, I'll say it again, shy, quiet and perhaps, socially awkward - like our mother. Pam, like our club-entertaining father, is good with strangers, always speaking with real volume and always knows how to express her feelings freely. So between the mid-90's and the year 2000, when my sisters were having children, Pam one day began crying about something that I had been reading about in the news - I was seeing many articles about an epidemic of newly diagnosed American children with autism.

And while I never really thought that those stories could ever be about members of my own family, Pam's tears and her strong voice told me otherwise: her young son Mark was diagnosed as being autistic. Conversation I had with my parents and Laura had us all not wanting to believe this. We felt (prayed, hoped) that this was all an overreaction to some possible mention some careless doctor had made to Pam, along with all that was in the news - and *boom* - Let's say Pam's overacting.

Our hopeful thoughts: within a few months, certainly within no more than a year, Mark would be "on track" regarding his growth path and that would be the end of all this "autism" business. Laura, my parents, and I were not being heartless; we were just so wanting this to be a case of Pam being, just as she occasionally can be, emotional with too much volume, all about something that will go on to solve itself. But then not too long after that, Laura had her children diagnosed - they were all born close together and they were all moving from babies to toddlers fast - one, two, three of Laura's four children - All three diagnosed with autism. My parents were soon the grandparents of seven grandchildren - four of which were diagnosed as autistic.

Five- once my only child, Molly, was born in 2000, and was also diagnosed with autism in 2003.

And there it was. Me and my two sisters. All special needs parents.

All deep into massive therapies: hourly early intervention, numbing, draining debt and complete depression beyond measure. That is how the new millennium began for Avra and me.

However - as we move forward here within these pages, please allow me to step back to the joyous year of 2000, when Avra and I married in March, and later, Molly was born in October. Her arrival dovetailed with the final few years of Greg and Marlon, obviously forcing my attention to shift in large and significant ways.

The three years just before Molly's diagnosis were the happiest days of my life. As I'll get to within these forthcoming chapters, Molly's year prior to her diagnosis was a year when Avra and I both worked for Marlon full time, with Molly essentially living up at Mulholland for over twelve months. Avra, Molly and I would have hundreds of dinners with Marlon, who often liked a great deal of attention during any given meal (not that he would ever admit to such a desire).

I'm biased, but I'll say it: Molly was an adorable, charming baby; she stole Marlon's spotlight.

As she giggled at the dinner table, Marlon would sigh, "Okay, how the hell do I compete with *this?*"

WHISPER (2001)

From the 60's through the 90's, William Hanley was an award-winning stage and TV writer with a keen sense of character and dialogue. While he was perhaps best known for television films such as *"Something About Amelia"* and *"The Attic: The Hiding of Anne Frank,"* Bill was also known by theater students throughout the world, mostly for a pair of short plays that were and are more than likely performed on a daily basis: *"Mrs. Dally Has a Lover"* and *"Whisper into My Good Ear"*. These two small classics are poignant character studies from the early sixties, perfect for theater training, acting labs and scene classes. I knew of the plays from my days at Juilliard, never thinking back then that I'd later have a long and intimate connection to Hanley's work - as well as to the writer himself.

My mother-in-law, actress Arlene "Tasha" Martel, did the "upkeep" that most aging performers rarely do: she never stopped seeking out acting classes, training sessions and theater coaches, right up until the time of her passing in 2014. As someone who knows acting and the world of theater, I admired that greatly. Arlene wanted to constantly be performing, learning and growing as an actor. We had our ups and downs as family members - and of course, as in-laws - but I loved her dearly; she was an eccentric, beautiful original. Just after the 90's had ended, in one of her many Los Angeles classes, she and actor Raphael Sbarge performed Hanley's *"Mrs. Dally Has a Lover"*. It's the story of a mature woman finding reawakened passion by way of a sensitive younger man. I never got to see their rendition of the short play, but knowing both Arlene and Raphael well, I can't think of better casting at that time.

Within their scene class and circle of actor friends, their rendition was incredibly well received, successful enough to prompt Arlene to a "Next" very bold step - It was bold even for her, a woman who was as fearless as they came. That step: she somehow tracked down the private, secluded writer William Hanley, to obtain the film rights for *"Mrs. Dally"*. Hanley was surprised, even a touch honored by the perseverance it clearly took for her to find him and make an offer. Bill was not what you might call a public individual, and he knew (in those days just before "absolutely everything" being on the internet) that it took some doing for Arlene to unearth his personal contact information and whereabouts in Connecticut.

Once Bill learned of Arlene's long career as a known actress, he could see that she was a legitimate, respected performer with scores of network and studio credits to her name. But even with all that, Hanley had bad news for Arlene: the rights to the project she was asking about were sold and locked up years ago, by some producer, studio or media entity. Still, impressed with her tenacity, he suggested, "What about the other one?" He assumed she had the Dramatists Play Service script edition that contained both short plays: *"Mrs. Dally Has a Lover"* and *"Whisper into My Good Ear"* within the same volume. She recalled thumbing through *"Whisper,"* knowing that the play was the story of two elderly male New Yorkers who have entered into a suicide pact; on the day of the story, they go to the park to see the ultimate deal through.

As disappointed as Arlene was regarding *"Mrs. Dally,"* she figured, "Hey, I tracked down this wonderful writer, he seems to be offering me a chance to work with his time-tested material; why not?" But she had to tell Bill, "I can't pay you for the rights until it's sold as a screenplay." After years in the business, Hanley was good at creatively working within that margin between firm money and a potential collaborator's enthusiasm — without spinning his own wheels by supplying free writing work or - let's call it what it can be - getting royally screwed.

And he was a realist, aware that he was having a talk about an ancient one-act play; one that never *did* get a deal like *"Mrs. Dally,"* so his next questions were key: "Who is going to write this? Who is the professional writer who will adapt my play into a film script?" Unbeknownst to me, she blurted, "My son-in-law is a professional writer! He's sold scripts to studios! 20th Century-Fox! Universal! He's written for Marlon Brando! He's written for Gregory Peck!" Between Arlene's perseverance that brought about this conversation, and maybe, because of my odd yet possibly impressive-sounding resume, Hanley created a legal option for the adaptation of his play. And it was this project that taught me, perhaps, the most about "aging" in Hollywood.

It also brought me front and center to the kind of job I began to call my *"Sunset Boulevard"* projects - projects featuring elder principals looking for that great final hit. *"Whisper into My Good Ear"* is the story of Charlie and Max, two elderly men who are facing the end of their life journeys. Charlie is loud - both grouchy and full of good cheer, while forever missing his late wife, the love of his life who passed away years ago. Max is quiet, reserved and thoughtful. He's also a closet homosexual who comes out to Charlie on this day; the day that they've both agreed would be their last. Both living in near poverty at a rundown hotel, they made a deal a while ago: if life did not improve for them within the next few months, why stick around at their late age? They would pick a deadline date, buy a gun and they would serve as the enforcing presence for the other; no backing out of this. While that brief description sounds like a dour little theater piece about two old guys on a park bench contemplating death, know that thanks to the talent of Bill Hanley, it's much more than that.

My different drafts of the adaptations stayed close to Bill's version as I worked to open it up a bit, expand certain themes in certain drafts, and even try the story in different decades — as a story in the 50's, the 70's and in the then contemporary 90's. During my adaptation stages, Hanley flew to Los Angeles a few times for other writing projects; he took the time to have meals with me and discuss the script. During these years, Bill was quite busy with adaptation assignments, having recently then shaped the *"Gone with the Wind"* sequel-novel *"Scarlett"* into a 6-hour miniseries for CBS, and he was currently adapting Edith Wharton's *"The Reef"* into a television film, a project CBS would later air as *"Passion's Way"*. In short: this guy knew his way around the literary world. He was generous, gracious and encouraging, always suggesting *"Whisper"* improvements in the most subtle and helpful of ways.

When there was a draft that finally had the approval of both Arlene and Hanley, my mother-in-law broke down doors to attract actors, producers and directors to the project, and being that this was a story about two old men, the list of people who agreed to discuss it all was impressive — meaning — many of the great elderly men of Hollywood felt a connection with what would soon be nicknamed and short-handed as - you read it there above: *"Whisper"*.

Marlon and Greg? They would enter this particular story much later. Why later? Well, let's just say that working with family is always a tricky thing. Working with family on a Hollywood film project - Even more so. While both Avra and I loved Arlene, we knew that the origin of the script, along with Arlene's participation, was not something Avra initially cared to push up at Mulholland, just as I at first felt the same about Carolwood. Even with writer William Hanley's blessing on the script, and even after Arlene had "name" directors involved, early on, Avra and I were squeamish about putting Greg and Marlon in the uncomfortable position of dealing with such a "family" project. What would it take to approach them? A *"real"* production.

If it was already a green-lit studio film? Maybe. Probably definitely. But as it was, Greg and Marlon would both clearly see their early participation for what it would be: they would be the "lures" for a then un-financed film; a film that was not a passion project of their own. As I explain that type of scenario to those who have never worked in the industry, I usually hear the same questions: "Wouldn't Greg and Marlon have read it as your friend? What if they would've loved it right away and then *wanted* to have signed on from the start? Why would they not take the time to read a script?" - On and on. I believe the answers are obvious - Marlon and Greg spent the full extent of their careers being led around on projects, used name-wise as financial bait, and of course, often frustrated as films *they* wanted to do could not get financed.

And at their iconic positions? Well, I believe I've been making this clear: filmmaking at a high level is complicated. It's money, it's egos, and it's timing within an incalculable set of odds.

Even big studios end up with huge disappointments and layers of egg on their faces all the time; they don't have the answers as to what works. And when I say "big studios," never forget that the green-lighting of films, these are just the decisions of a few individuals - individuals who live in a revolving door of "power" *in* one day and *out* the next. Even when you see "Giant" studio guys finally out on their own, producing without the money and resources of the studio, you'll often see failure and even desperation. People give Robert Evans so much deserved credit for the successes he had as he ran Paramount. But without the clout of the studio, he was actually involved with courtrooms and alleged crimes just to get a film like *"Cotton Club"* made as an independent producer.

Tony and I worked with "Spielberg Discoverer" Sid Sheinberg as he pulled the mammoth levers within Universal Studios. But we saw a very different story as we watched Sid running his own "Bubble Factory" productions with his sons over in their offices on Wilshire. Mike Medavoy running his "Phoenix" pictures after he was out of Tri-Star — The same, and frankly, none of this is to pass judgment on these men; all incredibly smart producers who knew how to get films made. But the studio world and the independent producing world are two very different places, even as they can often work together at times.

Think of the amount of money it takes to finance a film; millions of dollars. With that, as I'll never stop saying, you could build a skyscraper with office and apartment rentals, or a large business, probably with guaranteed returns. Instead, you are rolling the dice on a few reels of film - a block of data these days; something that may have no future whatsoever; a gamble no matter how you look at it or who is involved - Yes, as we all know, big stars and big star directors "bomb" almost every week in the industry. That leads me to a great "Third Act" life story.

As an extended side note, please allow me: One of my favorite "Industry" timelines involves a man who was never about the movies, only about TV - and man, was he ever - TV through and through: let me to take a moment here to talk about Fred Silverman. He ran all three networks at one time or another, deciding what America would watch in a pre-cable "Three Network" world. He had huge successes at all three networks - Yes, even at his last stop at NBC, where he planted the seeds for quality like *"Hill Street Blues,"* the franchises that would come from David Letterman, the continuation of the "post-classic 70's" *SNL*, and many other innovations.

I mention that NBC stuff because he's often wrongly referred to as a "failure" at NBC, after the "magic" of shaping the CBS "Tiffany" network and taking third place ABC to first. In short: he was a successful, shrewd programmer with a lifetime of immense power at all three networks.

So after all three of his mighty network reigns, he's an independent producer, putting his own TV projects together, and then selling them to networks, like any other producer. So what does this brilliant "innovator" do? Ground breaking stuff like the grand rule-breakers from his past: *"All in the Family"? "Roots"? "Hill Street Blues"?* No. Actually, he does something that actually *was* brilliant: he gauges the then maturing age of the network audience, he reaches back to three former CBS stars all looking for their own third act, and he creates *"Matlock"* with Andy Griffith, *"Diagnosis: Murder"* with Dick Van Dyke, and *"In The Heat of the Night"* with Carroll O'Connor. Today, those shows are all considered TV for old folks, yet they were also all long-running hits of their time, all still constantly running today in reruns.

They're also all great examples of how aging Fred Silverman was - to me - a brilliant creative mind when it came to a truly impossible job: figuring out what millions of people want to watch.

I go off into this Silverman story as I discuss *"Whisper"* because I was often dealing with "age" and "What an audience wants" as I dealt with Greg and Marlon - And I certainly dealt with these very same issues as I was writing my screen adaptation of *"Whisper into My Good Ear"*.

SO - Returning to *"Whisper"* — After I finally got it into presentable script form, Arlene was able to get the pages to people I was thrilled to meet - and for a time - work with. And nobody was more fascinating than the man who handed me his Oscars when I first walked into his office.

How Arlene got the script to Robert Wise, I'll never fully know. But I do recall when she called me one day and said, "You must get yourself to New York! Now! Tomorrow morning, I have a meeting set up with the man who directed *'West Side Story'* and *'The Sound of Music'!"*

Of course, I knew who she was talking about, and I also recalled that he had directed the first *"Star Trek"* film - Even though Arlene wasn't in that, she had played Spock's wife in the original series - a classic performance and episode. She was tight with all the *"Trek"* people, through conventions, live appearances and all that revolved around that fanatical *"Trek"* universe of that time. Could she have met Wise through that network? I never asked and I'll never know. All I knew at the moment of her call: I was somehow going to New York City to meet Robert Wise.

Somehow getting there from Los Angeles, I (today) vividly recall the incredibly brief New York meeting. I also recall that Arlene and I were both broke, and yet we made the air travel happen. Arriving in the early morning, I found Arlene at the midtown Marriott hotel where Wise and his wife, Millicent, were staying. Years later, I'd learn that Millicent was a longtime "Trekker" who convinced Bob to do the first *"Star Trek"* feature for Paramount, so maybe she did have that *"Trek"* connection to Arlene.

L.A. residents, Bob and Millicent, were in New York as he was receiving yet another film honor at some event; a very common situation for Wise in his later years. In those days, Arlene would get back to her hometown of New York as often as possible. She had somehow tracked down Bob days earlier, put the *"Whisper"* script into his hands - and here we were.

Let's back up a step or two here: In a mad dash, I was able to fly out of L.A. on a night-flight after I got the call from Arlene, arriving in the city by morning, and getting to the hotel just as Bob and Millicent were leaving, on their way back to Los Angeles, to their Century City condo. Given all that, yes, there *is* a natural question here: why make the trip? Simple: to show the commitment, to try and lock him into a Los Angeles meeting, and most of all, to *not* leave matters with a casual, "Well, Arlene, maybe we'll look up your son-in-law once we get back to California." No. I was there in New York City like an actual Big Shot Bicoastal Filmmaker: to get in his face, make an impression and do what I could to create a future for this infant project.

Literally, as Millicent and Bob were about to step into their car for Kennedy Airport, they were certain that there just wasn't enough time to take even a minute at the hotel lobby bar for a chat. Frankly, moments before, as I was *running* to this "meeting," I didn't think any sort of encounter would occur; the schedules were too tight and I assumed that Bob certainly didn't have the "absolute need" to meet; not with the frantic passion for a meeting that I shared with Arlene.

Actually, I'd later learn that it was Millicent who wanted to make sure that, at the very least, a live "hello" would be exchanged for the efforts of everyone involved; like Veronique Peck, Millicent Wise was always aware of a certain Industry Fact: it's only a good thing for your aging icon husband to meet with younger up-and-coming talent, especially when there might be an actual project at stake. Somehow, at that time in my life, I passed for "up-and-coming talent".

As I ran into the hotel, up to the lobby bar and over to Arlene, Bob and Millicent, in a matter seconds I heard Millicent insisting on just how "short" this "meeting" needed to be. In this mad rush, I first had to adjust as I caught sight of a smiling Robert Wise. Here was a filmmaker I had studied all my life. For me, meeting legendary filmmakers was different from meeting legendary stars - In a sense, those directors are also stars, but to me, just a bit bigger. I recalled when Tony had first introduced me to Scorsese, or when, of all people, Walter Matthau first introduced me to Billy Wilder at a Carolwood party, and then Wilder and I discussed film editing; well, it's hard to explain the excitement you feel, meeting those artists. When I met Wilder, I was dealing with difficult film editors on my first feature as a director. I told Billy, "They yell at me." With his Viennese accent, he barked, *"Joe! You should be yelling at them! Repeatedly!"*

Returning to my Wise story - At that moment in the hotel lobby/bar when I first met Bob, I also saw a worn copy of my *"Whisper"* script in his hands. Robert's handwriting was scrawled about in a few written blocks on the cover. I immediately knew that the handwriting was about the script, not something he was writing on for other purposes because it was handy paper - the character names from the script of "Max" and "Charlie" were seen throughout the handwriting. He indeed said that he had read it, he liked it and he had notes. Wow! I was thrilled - this crazy sprint across the continent was worth it just for that information coming from Robert Wise.

Interestingly, I also had that "click" that I felt with a number of older performers, writers, directors and producers; that "click" that told me that perhaps, maybe, there were not all that many people with major film projects today who were looking to hire Robert Wise. Maybe. I really didn't know at that moment. It's a hard "click" to figure. The most positive moment of this entire drive-by was when their airport chauffeur approached with a look that told everybody that this "meeting" was over right now. That's when Millicent, as she was leaving, handed me a card, telling me, "We'll all have dinner at our place next week: Friday at six - here's our address." Great! It wasn't "maybe" - It was a set invitation. And with that, the Wise couple was off to JFK.

Whew. There was an odd silence as Arlene and I sat there, somewhat stunned, watching the limo disappear up 3rd Avenue. It had all happened so fast. Was the whole flight and its expense put on assorted credit cards worth it all? Absolutely. And as many can tell you in Hollywood, that is often how movies get made. Slowly. Then quickly. Then slowly. Then quickly again. One desperate, often unpredictable meeting - or choreographed "chance" encounter - at a time.

True to her word, a week later in Los Angeles, Millicent greeted Arlene, Avra and me into the stylish Wise condo in Century City. It was as beautifully retro as one might expect from a man of Robert's era: 1960's Lincoln Center; somehow both gilded and groovy at the same time. As dinner was being put on the table, Robert gave us a tour. It wasn't a big place, but it was quite nice. I couldn't help but to speculate as I looked around, wondering if there had been - and perhaps *still* were - other "Wise" properties; those money-draining monsters in Bel Air or Malibu; the Hollywood homes you get to have when everything is going great; places that cost thousands of dollars a month just to maintain, along with a true fortune that goes out each year for property taxes. This small, beautiful condo just off Pico Boulevard and Avenue of The Stars; this is where Robert Wise was living right now, and knowing what I knew about him as a smart craftsman and filmmaker, I thought it was perfect. Was this a "down-sizing" situation? I didn't know. Whatever it was, it was still incredibly expensive, given its location and quality. But being that it was Robert Wise, my mind was reeling with all those thoughts of what *"is"* and what *"was"*.

See, when I was a kid, Robert Wise was as big as it got; some could argue bigger than any movie star; to me, the American David Lean. Within the mid-60's flux of an industry on its way to becoming the "adult" cinema of *"The Graduate"* and *"Midnight Cowboy,"* he was able to steer Broadway adaptations into must-see "Event" pictures. This, after a lifetime of being an editor and craftsman alongside the likes of Orson Welles. Yes, Wise held a unique place in film history.

I was reminded of all that as I entered his home office, seeing his Academy Awards up on a high shelf. He caught my glance, and it seemed he knew the drill at that point. With the laugh of a leprechaun, he asked, "'You wanna hold 'em, don't you?" Of course I did. Don't ask me why, but that's exactly what you want to do. As high as the shelf looked, Robert was able to reach up and hand them over in one, smooth motion. Without being too obvious, you first want to see which award is for what film; which one of these was shared with Jerome Robbins? Which one is heavier? No, they both weigh the same (eight and a half pounds) and, yes, as many have noted, the Oscar is always heavier than it looks. When seen on TV, it must be the exuberance of those holding it that makes it seem lighter than it really is. I loved that Bob shared these with someone he had just met, someone he barely knew. How generous of him, I thought at that moment.

I had seen Greg's *"Mockingbird"* Oscar next to his honorary Oscar in his office, but I never thought to touch them, and no offer was made. Marlon had no Oscars at Mulholland, and it really wasn't a discussed topic in his house. Even when playing "Trivial Pursuit" one night with Marlon, a few of us flinched as he received an "Oscar" question: "What is 'Oscar' standing on?" Looking back, it's funny to think that we thought the question would bring him anger, even rage. Instead, he just pondered and then shrugged, "A pedestal?" (The answer is a reel of film.) Whatever was in his head, I always thought that he liked *not* knowing the answer - or liked thinking that he had fooled us into pretending that he *didn't* know the answer. "Oscar" who?

Marlon's "Missing" Oscars made for great guessing games in Hollywood. Did he give his *"Waterfront"* Oscar to his father? And where was it for years? The *"Godfather"* Oscar? Was it given to Sacheen Littlefeather that night in 1973 when she refused it for him on worldwide TV? Did the husband of Brando *"Bedtime Story"* co-star Shirley Jones - Marty Ingles - really have that Vito Corleone Oscar? And how? That became an odd legendary story as well. Funny how everything about Marlon - especially Oscar related - has the feel of Tall Tales on steroids.

As for the Academy Awards of Robert Wise, I knew exactly where they were that night in Century City, and after a meal with him, I was convinced that we were going to make a movie together. With dinner soon ready, we joined the women in the dining room as Bob told me that we would talk about *"Whisper"* later.

Returning to his home office after dinner, Robert told me what he liked and didn't like about the current script. He was a masterful classic storyteller who appreciated straightforward character arcs, instructive pacing and a resolution that would clearly leave the audience with "something". As I did with everyone I would work with, I re-studied their previous films. More than most, he was something of an enigma given his large body of work - work where he was not exactly the author, originator or creator of the initial materials; he was a director who most often adapted the work of others, something common with many film directors to be sure, but few in that "non-auteur" category leave their marks as well or as mysteriously as Robert Wise.

He had done so many different kinds of films, but the more I'd watch, the more I'd feel his touch on all of them, even his earlier work as an editor. He was editing talkies when that art form was still quite new, cutting together everything from early Ginger Rogers pictures to the best films Orson Welles would ever make - therefore, some of the best films ever made, period. As he and I were speaking that night in his home office, he had not had a real success for quite some time, so as we discussed the script, he would now and then toss out an occasional, "But what do I know? I could be wrong about something like that these days." It's not that he doubted himself, but he was aware enough to understand how cinema was an ever-changing game.

I thought about that as I recalled then recently watching what was perhaps his last real artistic success, *"The Sand Pebbles"* with Steve McQueen. Made in the 60's, with a story set in the 20's, the film was clearly anti-Vietnam-war in its tone, just as other war films made a mere four years later were as well: *"M*A*S*H"* and *"Catch-22"*. I mention those movies as I ponder an era of Robert Altman and Mike Nichols versus the mood, feel and tone of a Wise picture.

The changes in Hollywood that took place between 1966 and 1970 are in full view when one compares those two 70's war films with Bob's *"Sand Pebbles"* from '66. And here I was, talking to him about making a film in the 90's. It's something I very much wanted to do. But I also knew the challenges of getting people with money to invest in a film with Wise at his age.

Bob had it much tougher than Greg or Marlon in these later years; stars are stars - They can impress you just by still being alive and walking into the room, and if the role you need to fill is an 80-year-old man, hell, you get an 80-year-old man. But the energy, drive, workload and force of directing is different, especially if you are associated with mammoth films as era-distinct as *"West Side Story"* and *"The Sound of Music"*.

Frankly, young Hollywood in the 90's could not even begin to fathom how films that perfect even got made - I'd watch them a number of times and I couldn't figure it out. They were locked in a certain elegant moment of epic filmmaking, where art, technical achievement and overall Hollywood craftsmanship came together in a totally singular way. The equipment Wise used in his glory days was state-of-the-art by way of military scale - giant cameras, fleets of helicopters, and machinery more suited for building a city rather than creating art. I think it was Bob who once said that movie making in that era was a bit like signing your name with a construction crane. Go take a new look at both *"Sound of Music"* and *"West Side Story"* - try to put your head around every shot, each angle and set-up - You quickly see the perfection of what his key era was about.

After that evening with Bob and Millicent, I started the rewriting of the script based on a few ideas Wise had. Over one of our phone calls, he told me not to go *"too wild"* on changes yet, feeling that the current script was quite presentable, and as he put it, "They'll be rewrites down the road that are gonna drive you buggy; it always happens. Before long, you'll be reaching for the arsenic." I assumed, in his wonderfully arcane fashion, he was telling me that the volume of the forthcoming rewrites will eventually drive me to suicide. I had to laugh. He was such a great presence. But weeks later, while his attachment helped to get older actors interested, it was clear that Bob's age and recent track record created problems when talking to early investment types.

While I was having calls and meetings with Karl Malden, Martin Landau and Anthony Quinn about the roles, Arlene was learning that merely getting Wise insured for a film shoot was going to be incredibly challenging - if not impossible. While that type of thing might sound wildly premature - planning-wise, in the scheme of legit film production, it's quite key and in this case, primary. Producers and insurance folks we consulted with told us to quietly talk to other directors as well; it's not that anybody was signing anything at this stage, but, just in case it was *not* going to work out with Wise, we were advised to have other directors in mind. With that, Arlene and I did our best to move forward with the more positive aspects of the project.

Unfortunately, the "more positive aspects of the project" included full rewrites all the afore-named actors wanted to see, as well as rewrites from directors who were on deck to replace Wise if it didn't work out with him; directors such as *"The Empire Strikes Back"* helmer Irvin Kershner and Edward James Olmos, whom I first met on the set of his series, *"American Family"*. I'll never forget that meeting with Edward because I arrived on a soundstage and I accidentally bumped into one of the cast members; I apologized, walked on, stopped and thought to myself, "Jesus Christ, that was Raquel Welch?! And she's still gorgeous! She could melt your teeth!" And as I did the math later on the drive home on Sunset Boulevard, it hit me: she was 62?!

Returning to Irvin, meeting Kershner at his house, I was warned by Arlene, "Don't talk about 'Star Wars' - He doesn't like to talk about 'Star Wars'!" So, of course, the first thing I did was ask him about "Star Wars". Like a grumpy old Rabbi, Irvin said, "Now, why would you ask me about that? You have a decent script here about two troubled men, guys with big problems, life and death stuff, and you sit there as you are and you bring up 'Star Wars'?!" I smiled and laughed, "I was told this would happen. Well, let me ask you about something else."

I brought up performing and Juilliard, knowing he occasionally worked as an actor. I recall he did a small part in Martin Scorsese's *"The Last Temptation of Christ,"* and man, does that make sense - nobody has a "Bible" face like Irvin. I discussed having worked recently with Marty on Greg's *"Doctor DeMott"* project. He lit up, "Well, let's get Peck into this *'Whisper'* thing. And your mother-in-law tells me you're pals with Marlon Brando, too; they'd both be great in this thing. In fact, you're gonna need that kind of wattage to get this thing made." After that, we had a good, long meeting, but I could see that he was letting me know that the project needed to be on a more financially solid "real" footing before he'd put anymore time into it - a perfectly legitimate wish - if not demand on Kershner's part. Still, he sent me out the door with ideas he thought could make the script better, saying as I left, "Get a new draft, maybe I'll have a look."

By now I had oddly different "rewrite" marching orders from too many different elderly actors and too many prospective elderly directors. I stress the "elderly" aspect because day after day, month after month, this project was showing me the ageism and kooky "Youth" obsession that Hollywood is almost always driven by. I was constantly being told that the problem with this very good and very worthy project was that it had no unifying production core that was realistically approaching actual "funds" at this stage, and *that* was because it was a film about two old guys - to be played by two old guys - to be directed by an old guy.

End of story.

Well, "End of story" or not, I persevered.

Arlene and I kept feeling that the right two actors with the right director could change the course of the project. But younger "name" directors were not interested in directing two older actors (yes, unless they were at that rare "God" level of say, a Marlon Brando or a Gregory Peck - And if those two were together? Wow! - I'll be getting to that) - and even as my many rewrites created younger roles to be added to the cast of characters, the project became years of challenge.

Robert Wise eventually left the project as funding failed to form and that insurance issue did indeed become a problem, but many of the others, both actors and directors checked in every now and then (and some, often) to see how the project and the "rewrites" were going. It became a situation that I would encounter again and again and again: a difficult film project tries to keep the ball in the air for years and years, and only *one person* is doing work on it - for free: the writer. There is this illusion of the constantly "rewritten" script getting stronger, better, more fundable, especially when somebody with a name contributes some "notes" to the endeavor; notes the writer must install. But there's quite understandable reasons for this whole "rewrite" practice - The "old" script isn't bad - it's merely "shop-worn" after a while, it's possibly been rejected by "others" - this *new* rewrite, hey, it must be better! Fresher!

Yeah, as understandable as the facelift on the aging Hollywood performer.

And I fully get it: people who have earned reputations, industry vets who are star names; they want "new" material. And note-wise, they want their "say" on a project they might be involved with. And you might also say that the producer is working at this time as well, making contacts, organizing meetings, etc., etc. Yes, Arlene - God Bless her - she was doing this constantly; it was her sole daily job. But during all this, I was also working and writing with Marlon, writing and producing other projects with Tony and creating my own projects and films as well. Rewriting *"Whisper"* for free, time and time again was becoming a strain on my household - with Avra, with her mother and with me. Eventually, I was finally realizing that I couldn't keep rewriting a "new" script for the sake of every "new" old actor or "new" old director Arlene might be able to make contact with. One night, I just snapped over it all.

Before I would tell Arlene that I was done with the project, I first had separate talks with Avra and Tony, for good reason: time and time again, as I met producers, directors and money folks, I'd hear very much the same thing I heard from Irvin Kershner: to paraphrase him:

Here you are, actually knowing Brando and Peck, knowing them well, and they might be the only two "elderly" names - together - who could make money people sit up and truly listen.

As always, Tony was gracious, understanding and eager to try and join in, but he also reminded me of how organized, legitimate and monetarily fair Greg was throughout the entire *"Doctor DeMott"* adventure. Tony was quite clear: at his then semi-retirement age, Greg might entertain a real and solid studio offer, but he probably would hesitate when it came to being part of a beg-for-funds attempt, a "Damned Goose Chase" as I could just hear Greg calling it, especially with Marlon, a star who by then was quite famous within the industry for a number of damned goose chases - and proudly so.

While Tony was doing his best to politely keep a door slightly open, Avra was far less flexible on the matter; she already saw the friction the project caused between her husband and her mother. Avra knew Arlene was a passionate woman who was beyond passionate about this project. Avra reminded me of how we finally got Marlon into a film like *"Free Money"*; with real upfront funding and real people. Also, Avra had true love and respect for Greg, Tony and the Peck family; she could not picture the freewheeling natures of Arlene and Marlon thrust into what she saw as that oh-so orderly Carolwood atmosphere. She knew Greg well by then and she couldn't envision him happily dealing with an unproduced producer such as Arlene, and, of course, Wild Card Brando. Avra loved Marlon, but she fully knew his flaws better than anyone.

She also reminded me of all the wheel-spinning and time-wasting that went on as I was then trying to work with Marlon on *his* own dead-end passion projects. How many off-the-wall rewrites would Marlon want with *this* picture? I suggested that Greg's stabilizing presence might calm and assure investors, as well as industry suits who really *do* want to work with Hurricane Marlon. She could only giggle with a sigh, "Listen to yourself; you sound just like my mother." She was right. I was under the spell of the project. It's such a unique Hollywood syndrome; you can't let go of that unmade film. And when you take it out of the drawer years from now, that spell that got you into the chase years ago will probably still be there. And yes, old, dead projects *can* get made years later. That of course is why those nutty dreams stay alive.

Short of having a major studio picking up the project and creating a large fund to start pre-production, I saw no way to approach Greg or Marlon on the project. I signed a document for Arlene that gave her my blessing with the then "current" script, but left my rights in place in case the produced script retained much of my work. Even though she had done none of the writing, she asked if she could put her name on the script as the writer; the project meant so much to her, and she felt that billing would help her as she now went out into the world alone with the project. I told her, "Of course" she could do that. Hours after that, she already had a meeting set up with her old friend William Shatner, about his possible participation as the director of *"Whisper"*.

As the years went on and the various copies of the script passed through Hollywood, from one elderly set of hands to the next, Arlene was struck with cancer; she died on August 12, 2014. Family friend Marianne Williamson spoke beautifully at Arlene's service, where her fans showed a vast montage of Arlene's film and television work. She had done so many parts, so many roles, so many projects; the volume of work was astonishing. To see her on screen in her youth was an exercise in taking in absolute beauty and charm. She was one of those skilled performers who really was just one audition or role away from being a star. These days, I'll see her pop up at least once a week on "ME TV" reruns. I can only sigh and smile. She was such a dynamo.

Marlon had died years before that memorial service for Arlene, but I couldn't help but to think of him as I was watching young Arlene in her film and TV montage. Because there's a sweet twist to this story. Totally unrelated to Avra, much younger Marlon and much younger Arlene had a rendezvous that ended with a kiss or two, and reportedly, not much more than that. This was in Brando's *"One-Eyed Jacks"* era, when every glance the actor made became an invitation - and he glanced and invited a lot in those days. He remembered the encounter well, but I don't believe he talked all that much to Avra about it. She was aware of it, but I think Marlon never felt it was comfortable conversation with Avra. Frankly, it wasn't all that comfortable between Avra and me as well.

Marlon brought the Arlene rendezvous up to me a number of times, loving to have "Guy Talk" that included classic "A Mother-in-law is Hell" material - not that I could ever picture Marlon having to seriously deal with in-laws. He liked to poke me with the stick of it because he knew that Arlene was colorful, quite talkative and often a lot to deal with. He wondered how I dealt with that as a son-in-law. I'd often joke, "Sometimes, with as much patience as I can fake." He told me that the infamous rendezvous ended when it did because she was "too chatty". Arlene's version: she told me that she simply "Made my exit from his presence," not wanting to be just "one more" on his epic list. Whatever the case, she did stick in Marlon's mind, as years before cancer took her, during the fury of her *"Whisper"* chase, Arlene was rushed to the hospital in need of heart bypass surgery. Arlene had no insurance and Avra and I had no savings for the hospital bill. Without the slightest hesitation or ask, Marlon picked up the phone, called the hospital and took care of the entire matter for Arlene.

Marlon did many things like that throughout his life, for many people; gifts none of us will ever know about. He was so generous. But as he'll say, he also knew that he was fortunate. Lucky.

Perhaps luckier than some of the great older artists looking for that final score with *"Whisper"*.

EIGHTH CHAPTER
LUCK
(GREG & MARLON ESSAY VIII)

Continuing on here with "Luck" - a word you will hear time and time again in Hollywood. Often, it's a word people don't like to talk about: ("What *'luck'*? It's my *talent* that did it all!") At other times, people in the industry cling to it, as though it's their excuse - "I never made it big because the 'luck' wasn't with me." Those people are often laughed off, but guess what - they can of course be correct as well. If you work in film, TV and theater enough, you meet dozens of people with incredible talent, looks and skills - and yes, the "luck" never blessed them.

The right casting never came along, their screenwriting is ahead of its time, not *of* its time, whatever. We know this is true because we all recognize that performer, writer, director, producer or whatever role - that struck gold, made a career or at least earned a lifetime of residuals by way of that *one project*, that one opportunity and sometimes - much harder to define - that one indefinable moment in Hollywood history.

Sustaining that "luck" once attained is another thing, but even *that* is hard to define. Within the industry, "Luck" can lead to more "Luck," and that's because Hollywood is a scared, confused place. It clings to those with momentary "luck". Example: say a relatively unknown performer is signed to a big movie; it happens more often than you might be able to recall at this moment. Yes, it took more than "luck" - that performer probably showed the skills to get cast - *but* - the "luck" of *that* project being there, at that moment, needing *that* individual - ?

Anyone who has been cast in anything (or attained *any* job) knows all the impossible to define elements at work here - when did the project get a green light after years of development? If "luck" is with you, when *you* were just getting to the right place, the right time and the right physicality (and talent level) to be cast. Again, too many variables to even imagine.

Okay, so within mere hours of that big movie signing mentioned above, thanks to that one bit of "luck," that unknown performer (with the right agent) can immediately be signed to many films; projects that will take the next few years to create. Why? Because, as screenwriter William Goldman taught all of us, Hollywood knows nothing - to paraphrase that brilliant author.

So, as a producer, why would I participate in the insanity of the instant "sign up" of a seemingly unknown performer? Simple: that upcoming performer might "Hit" by the time "My" project is on his or her schedule - and it certainly won't be for lack of trying; Hollywood will do all it can to promote *"my"* new "investment": that yet to be successful or unsuccessful performer.

To cut to the end of this strange chase, this is why you might see a newcomer bomb in a debut, followed up by possibly five more bombs in a row after that. And guess what? Often, the bombs won't matter a bit - That performer is now in the Famous Club, probably signed up for even more failure, becoming a household name to people who have not even seen this person in a single failed project - but this "star" is all over the internet, constantly on the entertainment news shows, the talk shows, dating the right people, and seen in all forms of Hollywood promotion.

I know, some readers will say this might sound like the sour grapes rant of someone who never "made it" in the business. But during those times when I was squarely in the show-biz trenches, I did indeed see versions and variations of this game. Once I was a "known" actor in TV casting circles, I'd be given parts without reading. ABC had me on the publicity circuit when *"Slap Maxwell"* was on; I took part in that exhausting racket, even flying to London to promote the show. Once Tony and I sold our first script to a major studio, doors opened, meetings were set up for us, deals on top of deals were made. At my own level back in "The Day," I did indeed see how it works. But even giant names who have truly "made it" big know this is all true.

These were conversations I often had with Greg and Marlon. Were these conversations I could only have with them when they were in their later years? I often wondered. When these men were in the thick of their fame, work and superstardom, did they see the business in the same ways? Of course, the question could also be this: was the business the same when they were both younger, more in demand and both absolute Kings of the World? To be clear, unlike many others, Greg and Marlon were on huge pedestals right up until the days they died; perhaps even more so as Hollywood saw both of them as rare aging treasures in their final years.

  Still, they both knew the difference between their Glory Years and their Later Years, and they both had plenty to say about the business, their careers and the entire aspect of "Luck".

When pressed about their success, their lives and their respective legends, both Marlon and Greg would ultimately shrug into the mention of "Luck" - I heard Greg use the word as he was being sincerely humble during one of his live *"A Conversation with Gregory Peck"* theater evenings. And during a taping of Marlon's unreleased acting classes (*"Lying For a Living"*), Marlon finally shut down the Brando-Fawning of Edward James Olmos with the phrase, "Stop, it was just luck." Of course, when men like Greg and Marlon used the word, everyone just smiled it away, as though it was a sweet crowd-pleasing gesture of their (possibly false) "modesty".

After all, this is Gregory Peck and Marlon Brando; no mere "Luck" can possibly be attached.

But of course there *was* "Luck" - time and time again. But that fact takes nothing away from those two giants. They were talented, dynamic and totally *of* their time and moment. That perhaps is a key definition of fame and stardom - being *of* your moment. Take a star - place them in a hypothetical time machine, place them somewhere else in history - Hollywood newcomer Charlie Chaplin in the 1980's? A just-off-the-bus Clark Cable in the 1990's? Do they "Hit"? Some would say, "Of course not - stupid exercise - stupid series of thoughts." Perhaps. But I think that is *why* we bask in the power of "Stars". It's all somewhat fluke-related, all impossible to explain, and perhaps, the real definition of "Miracles" on Earth. Seriously.

To me personally, I have no better definition of the aforementioned type of "Miracle" than The Beatles. These four guys, coming together, *when* they did, *how* they did, mixing their talents *the way* they did, for *that* generation at *that* time, leaving behind so much joy, emotion and love; magical music that will last forever - Or, at least, until some unforeseen generation says, "Who cares about those guys?" That ending sounds impossible to some; likely to others. And so what? That's the march of time at work; we can't fight it, stop it, or at times, remotely understand it. But still, while they were here, while their music still lasts, The Beatles - those four individuals - who they were and what they did; they make me believe in "miracles" far beyond any Scripture in any existing religion. Yes, I know John, Paul, George and Ringo were mere mortals, but "The Beatles" - C'mon, nothing short of "4-planet-aligning" miraculous. (Of course, generation-based opinions can differ; whenever Marlon heard me praise-on about The Beatles, he would sneer, "I don't get it - *One good song: 'Rocky Raccoon,'* and that's it!")

The way I thought of The Beatles - stars like Brando and Peck had that very same effect on others. Perhaps surprisingly, I can't fully share that view of them because I was lucky enough to know the real men: their actual faults, their ongoing fears, their often ordinary realities and their never-dying dreams. I was lucky to have been there when they talked about such things as "Age," "Time," and, yes, "Luck". They both allowed me to be a part of it - sometimes even asking me to help them, in situations I never could've dreamed of back when I was a young film-nut growing up in small-town Minnesota. Back when, from my remote distance, I *then* surely saw those two "Stars" as living, breathing and walking miracles.

Getting to know them *when* I did, *how* I did, *the way* I did - that was *my* "luck". Leading me to this: luck-wise, by 2001, Marlon was finally understanding the true "Luck" that had landed in his life decades ago: the world had long thought of him as "The Greatest Living Actor".

"Luck" or by way of his own doing, that *was* the case. And he now wanted to cash in on that.

THE STORY RESUMES
Tony Kaye ("Lying For a Living" Part 1) 2001

Greg liked talking about "acting" even less than Marlon. After I saw Greg's wonderfully strong, compassionate performance in *"Other People's Money,"* I had questions about the film, his co-stars and the production. He was happy to discuss. But when I got around to asking about his great performance, he froze into an icy Peck pause, arched a famous eyebrow and said, "Joe, just shut up." (I loved that; you had to know Greg well to get one of those.) We had a laugh about that, but it brought me back to the differences Greg and Marlon had regarding talk of their craft.

To the shock of many, Marlon often found a way to embrace such a discussion, bringing *your* human behavior into a talk about *his* skill. It was actually a somewhat modest approach. Long ago, Marlon grew tired of this constant "Greatest Actor" burden he had been given. But he never stopped being confronted with it. Along the way in life, he'd boil down the idea that we all *act* throughout life - as we try to be "social," as we attempt to be "polite," as we "oil" our challenges, trying to get rid of the friction - or in some cases, *create* friction, whatever the situation might be - romantic, work related, or perhaps his favorite region: the lies we all tell ourselves. Ah. Yes.

All this led to his final attempt to shape a financially successful project, *"Lying For a Living"*. It had a long road; I'll start when he finally found a way to put the unformed notion on videotape.

Stay with me - Here goes.

Having a soul that overflowed with empathy beyond measure, Marlon had a fully mystified fascination with Nazis. He could not remotely understand the type of monstrous thoughts that built death camps, ran gas chambers and somehow believed in a Final Solution. As he was with every aspect of his life, Marlon was fear-less about having conversations concerning all forms of a topic that interested him. And as history shows, Marlon also recognized a distinct type of evil and draconian thinking when it came to race relations in America, and of course, the United States' treatment of the Native American. His fascination with man's-inhumanity-to-man led to Marlon viewing films and TV projects on the Third Reich and all the remnants of its wreckage.

"American History X" was a 1998 film about neo-Nazi skinheads in L.A. It starred Edward Norton and was directed by a true character of a creative soul, the eccentric, self-proclaimed provocateur, Tony Kaye. Marlon was impressed with Norton and would go on to work with him years later on *"The Score"*. Diving deeper into an appreciation for *"American History X"* and those who made it, Marlon soon found himself face-to-face with Kaye. They forged and retained a friendship that lasted until Marlon was ready to go through with a project he had been kicking around; he talked to me about it often and he had discussed it with Avra for years: *now* he was finally going to make it: a series of how-to acting tapes. In reality, Marlon wanted to try anything other than making acting tapes. But countless nights of watching TV infomercials made him settle on a core idea: his name on anything other than *"acting"* would not resonate with the public.

He had tried and failed to lure vacationers to his beaches in Tahiti just off the "Brando" name (years after his death, once he was not around to call the shots, all that would change), and he had no idea of how to shape his version of "Newman's Own" and that level of marketing. Besides, as mentioned earlier, he did not want to create a non-profit - He wanted an income that he could enjoy that did not include acting. But over the years, not only did he confront all of his own challenges with self-marketing his own famous name, he also saw others in the industry fail and have damaged names in the process: suits, restaurants, wine, neckties; some perhaps having a giddy moment of good luck but then ultimately failing with various celebrity names attached.

Yes, for every celebrity-named product that "works," there are many more that fail. Late in life, Marlon finally accepted that the world connected him with "acting," and in an era of VHS, DVD, home school courses and 1-800 infomercial orders, he saw his potential series of acting tapes as his retirement. Almost a strange thought for someone who was still being offered a 3 million dollar pay day a number of times throughout any given year. But frankly, it was also a testament to the big life he maintained for so many family members and properties, from Mulholland Drive to Tahiti, along with a number of other excesses and unseen generosities.

Again, I heard him talk about wanting to do acting tapes for years; we'd often discuss how they could be shot and what might be a good way of putting them together. But frankly, in my heart, I really didn't think he would get around to making them. He had an ambitious plan, envisioning a dozen hours of instruction, lectures and guidance. We had long discussions about my years at Juilliard Drama and his years with Stella Adler, because he said he wanted to make something completely different and "real" - He saw the audience that would relate to where he and I were trained as "elite," "boutique," and "limited" - especially when he'd discuss his Life Theory that he says had always connected his common "truth" with his remarkable "art": *acting*, he'd insist, is, "Merely lying, and we all lie, all the time. Every moment of every day." Perhaps true.

And perhaps cynical sounding to some, but to Marlon, it was also the connective home run he wanted that would bring together his "acting" tapes with a paying mass audience - This would *not* be "Stella Adler" or "Juilliard"! As he saw it, "The World's Greatest Liar" will teach *you* how to lie like a pro! Get that job! Impress that boss! Flirt masterfully to your heart's desire! *(Yes, get laid!)* Talk that cop out of giving you a ticket! And perhaps most lucrative of all, sell anything to anybody!

By the time Marlon was actually going to make the tapes, I was neck-deep in post with a film I directed and co-wrote for Sony Pictures, *"Diary of a Sex Addict,"* a story about lying if there ever was one. It was a small feature film project Tony Peck and I were doing to get back into the creative production world after the epic, international filmmaking challenges of *"Free Money".*

Returning to Tony Kaye working with Marlon as I was off making my movie and Avra was caring for our new baby, I'd hear that

Kaye and Marlon had a plan, and that Tony had plenty of ideas on how to get Marlon to actually shoot the videos. By the middle of 2001, Marlon, his son Miko, Sean Penn and Kaye were meeting to put the shoot together for acting videos, lining up star pupils, homeless street pupils and theater-school-type friends of Tony Kaye. Marlon would fund the shoot; they'd do it at a studio in Hollywood, and for reasons only Kaye might know, they would shoot it on seven mis-matched Hi-8 pro-sumer cameras straight out of Best Buy.

As Miko was lining up stars for the "class," like his friend, comic SNL actor Jon Lovitz, and Miko's boss, Michael Jackson, Kaye put the word out to Brando-loving celebs, and along with Sean Penn's help, they soon had Robin Williams, Jon Voight, Leonardo DiCaprio, Edward James Olmos, Whoopi Goldberg and Nick Nolte. Marlon called Harry Dean Stanton, and there they were: Marlon, ten stars, along with amateur actors, Tony Kaye, and Tony's crew of cameramen, sound guys and assorted lookie-loos eager to see Marlon Brando teach professional "lying".

To give you a broad picture and a big teaser before the details are filled in: Tony and Marlon parted ways three days into the shoot - (much more on that later) - but Kaye's video team stayed on to shoot for another ten days. When it came time to post the project, Marlon called Avra and me. By late spring of 2002, Avra and I had both worked hard on "Lying For a Living," having spent a full year up at the Mulholland estate. She had transcribed all of the spoken words from the many hours of the long 13-day shoot and edited the text into a book worthy of a coffee table.

Avra did that as I was busy logging, syncing and editing the footage into a series of 12 "How To" tapes, complete with a one-hour documentary on the day Tony Kaye decided to blow the whole thing up by insulting a pair of amateur actors in the class - Yes, more on that in a moment. As far as the final "products" that were to come from this exercise, I had contacted home video distributors, Avra had started discussions with Harper Collins for the book, and in spite of Marlon's stops and starts, we did have a series of products in both video and print, along with leads on who would want to distribute the stuff. To dress matters up,

I made professional looking video cases for the few VHS copies Marlon allowed me to duplicate, and now and then, he'd ask me to show them to someone for "feedback". Frankly, nobody really knew how to react to the videos, mostly because nobody knew what to expect from Brando to begin with, especially when it came to this kind of exercise with this particular eccentric: 12 hours of "acting lessons" from a man who had been declared as The World's Greatest Actor decades ago - a title he hated; a title that nobody could ever live up to, and here he was: to some, trivializing it all. To others, not living up to an absolutely impossible aura. To almost everybody who saw the tapes: confusion, disappointment and a loss as to what to say to Marlon - and at times, to me - about the videos.

To clarify: looking back before the initial video shoot of the project: Marlon had no real plan when he went into the production regarding the "lessons". Kaye set up the shoot, had his seven mismatched video cameras, a room of amateur actors, a few famous guests and some semi-pro "ringer" actors he had brought in. They did improvs that Marlon commented on, and after a few days, Tony lost his patience by merely being one of the seven designated cameramen. He saw himself as the director of the project, but not knowing Marlon incredibly well before the shoot, he only learned as the taping began (and far too late) that this was Marlon's project to direct.

Jumping ahead again to the finished edit: I showed the finished tapes to friend and one-time Judy Garland and Streisand producer Gary Smith, the genius who puts together all those great "AFI List" shows - "*100 Greatest Heroes,*" etc. This was the first time I showed the tapes to anyone.

To me, this was a testing of the waters. After taking a while to watch all of the *"Lying For a Living"* tapes, Gary called me into his Hollywood office and said, "Joe, I don't know what to tell you - Maybe this: perhaps call it '*The Marlon Brando Experience*', cut it down to a couple hours, add music and effects - maybe even some funky animation. See if it can find a cult following."

I could only sigh as I laughed, "Okay, Gary, I'll let *you* tell him that. *He* sees this selling bigger than Jane Fonda's workout video." But I wasn't laughing much as I drove up Sunset after leaving Gary's office. I couldn't tell Marlon I had shown Gary the tapes; this was an early trial where I did not run this "viewing" past Marlon. I knew the tapes needed work. I'd need to edit more. But sometimes, after doing a lot of cutting on a project, an editor can feel the truth in his stomach.

The truth here was pretty simple: with this material, I felt I had already done what could be done.

Okay, that's the short version; allow me to elaborate further on the details of this bizarre journey.

TALK (2002)

Stepping back to the time when I was starting to edit *"Lying For a Living,"* I arrive at a moment where I must discuss Avra's immediate family, a unique set of five distinctly different people. When I met them all, they were very much separate islands: as I wrote about in the previous *"Whisper"* story, her stunning, colorful mother was a once successful but later-to-be struggling television actress. Avra's older brother was a happily married man with a sweet wife and a beautiful young son. Avra's younger brother was a college student, bright and seeming to always be changing schools and majors as he was always searching for just the right fit. And all that school changing and major switching was being paid for by Avra's newly-crowned soap star father; an actor who got incredibly lucky late in life by landing the kind of then-rare job that could never exist today: a 25-year run on a network daytime drama. Avra's father Jerry Douglas was soap patriarch "John Abbott" on *"The Young & the Restless,"* and hard to believe, in certain circles, Jerry was bigger to some people than Marlon and Greg combined. You'd need to go to a Daytime Drama Convention or a Soap Expo to understand how that oddity could be true.

Avra had a complicated set of relationships with both of her divorced parents. Again, Mother Arlene, sometimes known as "Tasha", was a free spirit who often looked to her responsible, level-headed daughter for an "adult" figure and a voice of reason.

In her youth, Arlene had beauty and charm at a level that attracted James Dean, Cary Grant and even, as previously mentioned, Marlon Brando himself. In turn, after years of perseverance as a part-time actor, Avra's insurance-and-water-softener salesman father finally got that wildly lucky late break with the long-running CBS soap, thus allowing him to start a whole new life once he got the daytime drama: new houses, new half-his-age wife who-was-once-a-soap-fan, new son, new everything.

Avra's older brother, Adam, was the son of Arlene's first spouse; a husband before Jerry. And Avra's younger brother, Jod, was at a young, difficult stage of life when Arlene and Jerry split. This put him at the center of legal battles, custody fights and other painful family challenges. In short: it was easy to see why Avra's family was separated, not always together and once again, all five, often each on their own solo island. Driving, Avra and I "Made the Rounds" on holidays.

Constantly treating Avra as though she was the responsible and centered daughter he wished he had, Marlon was always interested in Avra's family; if Avra had troubles with a certain family member, Marlon then had those troubles as well. If Avra "vouched" for a certain family member, Marlon also loved that family member. It was an incredibly endearing aspect of Marlon - He trusted very few. But once he *did* trust you, he could - within reason - have your back for life. Through that path, Marlon grew to trust and like Avra's younger brother, Jod, for a number of reasons; reasons beyond Avra's endorsement. Young Jod was bright, fun and intelligent. After graduating college, Jod decided that he would try his hand at writing: magazine articles, pop culture journalism and other forms of taking real life and putting those true stories into words.

He was extremely good at it, and before long, he was published in both print and online.

Through Avra, Marlon had met Jod when Jod was quite young. As Jod matured and became a published writer, Marlon had an idea one day as we were all putting together *"Lying For a Living"* up at Mulholland. After the reminder presented by the "New-Acquaintance-Now-Banished" Tony Kaye, freshly cautious Marlon insisted on keeping all aspects of this project firmly "In Family" as he called it. As I mentioned previously, Avra worked on the book version of the project as I was editing the video versions, both of us, along with Molly, up at Marlon's house day in and day out for over a year. But early on, before that year passed, with Jod's recent writing successes, Marlon thought it would be good to have him write up the forthcoming publicity releases for the book and videos; he asked Avra to invite Jod up to the house for a meeting.

When Jod arrived, Marlon explained the project, probably being his usual vague self about what he wanted, how he wanted it and what the "rules" were for the watery assignment. Already working in media, Jod knew much more about the then "current" state of publicity than Marlon. I don't know exactly how the whole thing was presented to Jod by Marlon, but even with the "Marlon" experiences Avra and I had shared with her brother, Jod might not have been prepared for how little Marlon actually meant it when he would say things like, "Let's do this." Or "Use your own judgment." Or the always Brando classic, "I'm leaving this whole thing up to you."

I had heard all these things when Marlon and I would start different projects, scripts or even invention-based schemes. Why would Marlon use phases like that? For one very good reason: he wanted you to go off and do some work for him. Of course, you would feel that you should indeed do that work. *But here's the deal:* Marlon always had an obvious "safeguard" when the time might finally arrive for *his* participation *or* for the presentation of the work:

The "safeguard"? Very simple: he wouldn't do it. Or he would say that the work wasn't ready.

Say you write and "sell" a film with Marlon, at his direction and with his guidance? His plug-pull on the project was always easy and most effective: he wouldn't do it. Product endorsements, gadgets he'd say he wanted to put his name on - Almost always: in the 11th hour: Marlon decides not to take the meeting he asked you to set up, he wouldn't show up on the set, he might not get into the car or get out of bed - Take your pick. Avra and I had seen it all. *But* - could there be a version of a "Marlon Project" (back when he was alive) that could reach the public *without* Marlon? Well, in a sense, that happened weeks after Marlon and Jod met, as Avra and I learned one day that Jod was days away from having an article about *"Lying For a Living"* in Tina Brown's then relatively new magazine, *"Talk"*. Avra was livid, panicking, furious, telling Jod he couldn't sell the article - *any* article on the project just yet; Marlon had not approved such a thing! I did my best to stay out of the family argument as the incident blew up into a loud and ugly affair.

As the family fight turned into a stalemate, it soon became clear that the article was indeed going to go to press. Was it a "positive" article? Would Tina Brown *want* a piece that wasn't typical "Crazy Brando" stuff? Avra and I didn't know; we were not allowed to read what was sold to Brown. And frankly, it didn't matter. Marlon would go ballistic over the fact that it was being printed at all. This was when Avra and I were working at Marlon's house every single day. By then, our financial lives as new parents were tied to both Marlon and his project of acting tapes.

Avra became a nervous wreck, wondering how she would or could break this to Marlon. We had seen it when Marlon would find out such things after-the-fact; "friends" writing articles, books, or citing the wrong thing in an interview or documentary about Marlon - We saw him cut these people out of his life forever - close relations, longtime employees, etc. Through all that, Avra knew Marlon well enough to know one thing: tell him *before* it comes out. Don't let somebody else call him and introduce the problem - "Hey, Marlon, I read about your nutty acting tapes in 'Talk' magazine." Yeah, we could hear the whole thing before it even happened.

The day before the article was to go to print, Avra nervously, tearfully, went to Marlon and told him about Jod's writing and the Tina Brown magazine. Marlon listened. He was hurt. Things got quiet. Too quiet. He had experienced a lot of situations like this throughout his life, especially by way of journalism (many say "Gotcha" journalism was born when Brando trusted Truman Capote to write a "nice" *New Yorker* article in 1957). But Marlon didn't see this coming from a direction near or originating from someone as trusted as Avra. He sent Avra home, telling her he'd call her when he felt she could come back to work. As cited in the CAA story, this was his occasionally used system of probation, punishment or in some cases, final banishment. Again, I was still up at Marlon's with my editing system in his office, putting together the acting tapes.

Coming home that night from Marlon's, I held Avra, feeling so bad for her. Oddly, I kinda understood Jod in this as well. He was a young, brilliant writer. A legendary man tells the young journalist that he can write a story about his forthcoming project - Hell, Jod was asked to do it. Before you know it, a person like world famous publisher Tina Brown is listening to you about your work. Yes, because of Marlon Brando, but still - it's a frustrating, heady, confusing place to be. I had been there in very similar circumstances when Marlon had sent me out into the world as his "representative" for different projects, only to then have egg on my face in front of others as Marlon decided to lose interest-in or slam the brakes-on the very thing *he* personally instigated.

So coming home that night after Avra was "dismissed," we were both frustrated and depressed. But turning on the TV that night as I sat there with Avra, something beyond amazing happened.

Incredibly, Avra and I saw an *"Entertainment Tonight"* report that we thought might change everything. It seemed Tina Brown, the magic touch behind the then current re-births of *"Vanity Fair"* and *"The New Yorker" magazine* - It seemed her two-and-a-half-year-old venture - the one that was her own, original creation, *"Talk"* magazine - It seemed this was already, after only a few issues, a big fat failure. The issue that was to go to press *tomorrow:* cancelled.

And that was the end of *"Talk"* magazine. The ET report felt like it was created only for us.

We were stunned. I said to Avra, "You didn't need to tell him." She tearfully shrugged, "He might've found out anyway. Better that I did." I knew she was right. But my gears were turning.

The next morning, I got up early. It was dark. I was determined to have a talk with Marlon about this, no matter what his thoughts were. I felt so bad for my beautiful wife and I wanted to tell Marlon about the magazine going under; there was a good chance he would know nothing about that. I was going early because I couldn't sleep and I wanted to plan what I was going to say; it wasn't the kind of talk I often had with him. This was just plain odd from every angle.

Interestingly, from the light shining up in the TV den, I could see that he was up very early - Or had stayed up all night; that sometimes happened as well with him. Few things got Marlon as emotional as incidents involving Avra - He really did think of her as his daughter, and I'm certain he was as upset over the whole thing as she was. I went to my editing studio, the Brando "office" building that was out in his large parking lot. I phone-called up to his TV den, asking if I could come up there. He said the strangest thing - strange for him: "I'll come down there to you."

I started to wonder if I too was banished from the house by way of association. After a few minutes, he arrived. In his underwear, bathrobe and slippers, he pushed the sliding glass door open and entered the office, then finding an uncomfortable chair to squeeze into. After we had both settled, I told him that Avra was very upset. He sincerely sighed, "Of course she is, poor thing." I then told him about *"Talk"* magazine folding - just last night!

He stared. Silence. More silence, Marlon then muttered:

"He'll publish it somewhere else."

"Oh, no way, man! Not a chance," I angrily laughed. I explained how much this tore Jod and Avra apart, with Jod being the only member of her immediate family that she (once) had a good and open relationship with. No, I was certain - Jod caught a break on this one; he got lucky.

Still angry, Marlon almost smiled, quietly telling me, "If he wrote it, he'll publish it somewhere else. Don't argue with me; I know these things."

I asked, "Why would he do that after all this?"

Brando shrugged, "He's got a 'Marlon Ticket' - he's gotta cash it in."

Marlon then tried to laugh. But he didn't. He rubbed his face for a moment, until he was simply holding his head in his hands.

After too much silence, I thought he might cry. He didn't. But he was upset, sighing, "You think you know people, you think you can trust people."

"You're not talking about Avra?"

"Of course not! That little shit brother - He better not show his face around here again."

After barking that, he stared out the window, into the darkness for a while. He then asked:

"Do you know what it's like? To know that you can't trust a single person on this planet?"

His words made me think of something I had often thought about regarding Marlon. Something I thought he would not want to hear. And yet, at this moment, I thought maybe I could say it.

I thought to say it now, because I could not think of anything else to say.

I asked, "Can I tell you something I think you already know?"

"Shoot", he said. So, I then just went for it.

"You're an amazing survivor. You know I'm a movie nut, so indulge me. You've been burdened with this ridiculous fame in entertainment - I mean, it's really not on any sane level whatsoever. It's maybe on a level that a handful of people have ever experienced. And look at some of those others and how they dealt with it: your friend, Marilyn, Elvis. Even Chaplin couldn't get his head around it when he got older; you saw that in person. They let it get to them. And here you are. You're still here. You're a singular survivor. You have to be proud of that. That's an accomplishment, beyond any movie."

Silence. He stared. Yes, I was realizing in this pause: I was not comparing him to world leaders or historic figures, even though his name was as big as perhaps any in history. No, my short list was by design: creative souls who never could've known they were signing up for "Legend".

I was always aware of how Marlon valued his own place in humanity over his career. But even knowing that, I didn't know if I had just said the dumbest thing that anyone could ever say to Marlon Brando or not. And never in my life did I think I would say such a thing to him, but I did.

Stone-faced, he sighed, "The key is knowing what *is* and what *ain't*. That took quite awhile."

When he spoke those words, I immediately thought about the tragedies with his children.

Those were events that grounded him into a reality he barely knew in his wild glory years. After more silence, he stood, telling me, "Tell Avra to come back tomorrow. And believe me when I tell you: that rat brother is gonna sell that article to some other magazine; 'wanna make a bet on it?" I shook my head "no," laughing, "You claim to know what *is* and what *ain't* - not me."

Still not smiling, he slid the glass door open, stepping into the cold darkness as he left the office.

Days later, Jod's "Nutty Brando" article on *"Lying For a Living"* was printed in *"Rolling Stone"*.

Of course Marlon heard about that. But he was good enough to never bring that up to Avra or me.

Jesus.

That survivor.

He really did know what *is* and what *ain't*.

George Englund ("Lying For a Living Part 2")

Marlon had a massive era one might call, "A Legend in Search of a Career". I believe those were perhaps his most interesting years. In fact, I consider that entire stretch between *"On the Waterfront"* and *"The Godfather"* to be his most fascinating, when the film business itself was in a stage of flux, far more scattered than the "mess" that many considered Marlon's life and career to be. Even with occasional projects as commercially successful as *"Guys and Dolls"* and a few others that were incredibly interesting (such as *"One-Eyed Jacks"* and *"The Fugitive Kind"*), that often-described "Dry Spell" for Marlon was really just a degree of expectations; the actor at the center of both *"A Streetcar Named Desire"* and *"On the Waterfront"* - How the hell was this performer supposed to stay within *that* zone of quality, innovation and newness? Impossible.

Given his want for control, and given the way Hollywood was then reshaping itself, it was inevitable that Marlon was going to become some form of producer, complete with multi-picture deals, on-the-lot offices, and all that was arriving with major actors all becoming more powerful.

As we continually study: with the double victories of *"The Godfather"* and *"Last Tango in Paris,"* Marlon was back on top by the mid 70's. And with the commercial glow of *"Superman"* followed by the artistic glow of *"Apocalypse Now,"* the public once again - and perhaps for the final time, felt passionate about the man who had changed film acting back in the 1950's.

But back to that Difficult Era before Marlon's 70's renaissance - Marlon worked in the 60's with a man who considered himself to be Brando's creative partner, George Englund, an occasional writer and director who somehow made something of a career out of knowing Marlon Brando.

One day, when I was editing *"Lying For a Living"* up at Marlon's house, Englund drove in from Palm Springs to have a look at my continuing cut. I met him and he watched for a while in my Avid suite in Brando's office complex, securely separate from Marlon and the house. After viewing a bit, disappointed George sighed as he hit "pause" on my console, muttering, "Jesus."

George of course knew Marlon well. As we spoke, even though we had just met, he could see and hear that I had earned the right to be his absolute peer, fully knowing and understanding the good, the bad and the beautiful within the Brando Universe. He looked around the room and then unplugged the phone lines from the wall. Our eyes met with a pained smile. Most people often "joked" that Marlon had his property literally "bugged" - George clearly still had those feelings, even though he had not been part of Marlon's in-person world for quite some time.

He then asked, "Do you have anything that happened that was interesting? Unexpected? All this here - What is it? People do scenes; Marlon approves or disapproves - No direction. He either looks mean criticizing or looks out of touch being too nice over mediocre work, especially to the black students - That's glaringly obvious. Did something weird happen during the shoot? Something that would be worth watching? Usually, when he's around, eventually, it does."

I had exactly what Englund was asking for. As previously mentioned, on about the third or fourth day of the 13-day shoot, I believe Tony Kaye was frustrated by both his apparent demotion from director to mere cameraman and by the lack of dynamic footage. During all these improvs, there *was* a clear pattern to Marlon's criticism and praise of the improvised scenes: Marlon was wonderfully supportive, nurturing and caring when it came to the work of the African-American performers - to an uncomfortable and beyond obvious extent. And vice versa with Caucasian performers, especially young, attractive Caucasian women, some who were often in tears over Marlon's criticism. And while many of the African-American performers were quite good, some were as dreadful as any of the amateur performers in this lot, irrespective of race or gender.

So - on *that day* in the autumn of 2001, early on, perhaps the first scene of the day, a pair of female African-American amateur performers began an improvisation. Marlon didn't know their names yet, but he liked both of them immensely. In their 30's, they were both quite large, had beautiful sunny smiles and they would giggle with glee when Marlon would talk to them "off camera" (remember, as the editor of all this video and always-on audio, I saw and heard everything) - Being Marlon in 2001, aged, charming, "Brando," and years before "Me Too," he'd coo some casting-couch-type lines to them as they'd make small talk; "young, hip" material (in his mind) such as, "Baby, you got back." Mind you, I was not putting exchanges such as these in the edit. Seeing Marlon as the overweight 78-year-old legendary womanizer that he was, both women seemed to get a legitimate kick out of him, talking off camera about his wit, warmth and appeal. Perhaps most key to this Tony Kaye story I'm taking a while to get to: As amateur performers, these two wonderfully sweet women felt *safe* in Marlon's class; free to express themselves in improvised scenes.

Well, that day, they started their scene. It was neither good nor bad. Yet. But from behind his camcorder, Tony Kaye yelled, *"Cut! Cut! Ugh! That was awful!"* Long pause. Marlon almost fell off his chair. Before he could take charge, the whole room became a loud encounter session about acting, honesty, courtesy and even about Marlon, as he sat there stone-faced and let the younger people have it out with one another, with most people attacking Kaye as he would be occasionally defended by the small group of semi-professionals he had brought to the class. Bottled-up thoughts erupted about the way all this was going after these first few days of confusion.

Eventually, after about 55 minutes of group anger, Marlon spoke up, telling Kaye to leave. Tony did, along with many of those who Kaye invited - But not all. Some of them clearly made a decision right then and there: Yes, Tony Kaye got them in here, but the following thoughts had to occur: "I'm leaving Marlon Brando's once in a lifetime acting class over Tony Kaye? Tony the Provocateur? Who seems to be fighting with someone everyday in the press? Uh, I think I'll stay." Marlon fully took charge of the class and they lurched forward for the next ten days or so.

From the moment that fateful "Tony Kaye" shoot-day started: from the moment everyone gathered for the class, through to the interaction and the argument, to the moment (Post-Kaye) when Marlon said to the two women, "You gals were doing gangbusters - Start it again" - *that* was all about an exact hour. It became my one hour "documentary" of the class, cut to real time with seven-camera coverage and lower-third I.D. titles on everyone on screen. This "hour" ended with a strange, cold feeling; discomfort, confusion and no real conclusion. And George loved it.

Englund exclaimed, "What the hell? Why didn't you show me this first?" I told George, "I haven't really shown it to anyone. I made it once I finished the Marlon-requested 12 Volume Set; I'm not sure who this is for." George asked, "What does Marlon think?" I shrugged, "I told him I might edit *that day* together; he said, 'Don't bother.' So, no, he hasn't seen it." Englund laughed, "So, you cut it together for the same reasons Kaye did what he did, for the same reasons I liked watching it." I nodded, "Yeah. Because it's interesting; Kaye knew he was lighting a fire. But what does this video say?" George sighed, "I think it says Marlon's not much of a teacher."

I liked George well enough in those hours up at Mulholland, but like so much that happened up at Marlon's house, I can't say I wasn't uneasy. I was unsure about George. Maybe it's because Marlon seemed to have seemingly mixed emotions about Englund; sometimes pleasant when George was mentioned; often not. But I knew that that type of stuff from Marlon was not always a true barometer of the real story; to know Marlon well and for a long time - that was a guaranteed road of ups and downs. And if you were a betting man, you'd often need to wager that any falling out with Brando - within any given friendship, romance, work relationship or even momentary exchange; well, the fault could often and rightfully be considered to be Marlon's. Of course, I say this from my own biased view of the ups and downs I myself had with him.

No, I think what I felt from Englund was his own sizing up of *me* - perhaps understandably so. Marlon always had a small, loyal circle of friends. *But* members of the circle would change. Those from the "Older" eras would wonder about the "Newer" people, while those of us in the later years had heard a great deal about some of those "Older" members; even read about them in books. And Marlon often felt that there was nothing wrong with turf wars over him, especially when female employees were involved. After all, wasn't everyone working together for Marlon?

That's the way George seemed to be approaching things when he came into my editing bay that day. Given all that, I still wasn't shocked to learn that years later, after the project was in one of its many stalled limbos, after I was done with it, George Englund drove back in from Palm Springs to (ultimately unsuccessfully) revisit, revitalize, re-edit and redo *"Lying For a Living"*.

Frankly, I was actually forecasting that very day when George first wanted to see the videos.

But back to that first session with George; before long, after a visit with Marlon and a final "goodbye" to me in the edit bay, he was leaving. He wished me luck. As he was driving off, I plugged the phones back into the wall, just as Marlon was trying to call me. He asked me to come up to the "study" - AKA the TV room. He said he had a great new idea for the tapes. When I arrived, he was hanging up the phone, telling me he had just turned down Avra's

Harper Collins deal; he saw bigger offers on the horizon. He saw book sales as "small potatoes," even claiming that the "biography" he wrote with Robert Lindsey had failed to provide a real income for him. This news pained me completely.

Avra had done an amazing job getting Harper Collins involved, and signing off with them would've solved a great deal. Because of Avra's work, the publishers had sent a smart representative to Los Angeles and Avra and I had dinner with her; she saw the potential of *"Lying For a Living"* as a big glossy book, with still photos from the class, Marlon's best "instructions" and quotes in print, and perhaps most importantly, this Harper Collins exec knew marketing, sensing that the "Brando Acting Mystique" might play better on paper and in photos rather than video. She was absolutely right, and if the book deal would've been good enough for Marlon, both Avra and I knew that a difficult next move might be to tell Marlon that the tapes should not be released, allowing the giant glossy book to be the real and final "documentation" of those rare and special classes.

Oh. Yes. *More* "news" Marlon had in his TV den after turning down Harper Collins: he wanted to show the tapes to someone he didn't care for - A guy he had little regard for but he *did* trust his judgment; interestingly, not the oddest criteria combination in Marlon's world.

This not-all-that-cared-for guy with the trusted judgment; he lived a short ways down the road, and Marlon wanted me to get a set of the tapes over to him right away - Now.

This guy was eager to view the videos and offer an opinion, over a dinner at his home tomorrow.

He happened to be Warren Beatty.

BEATTY ("Lying For a Living Part 3") 2002

By now, through a series of Brando-connected introductions and other Hollywood networking moves, producer Mike Medavoy was getting deeper into Marlon's circle. Even though Medavoy and Marlon had worked in the business for decades, Mike arrived late in Marlon's life, only getting to know Brando around the time of *"Lying For a Living"*. Interestingly, through Tony, I had known Mike for years. Like Sean Penn, Medavoy crisscrossed throughout my career. He was part of the evening that brought Beatty and Marlon together; Mike was longtime friends with Warren. The day before the dinner with Beatty, I brought the 12 VHS set of *"Lying For a Living"* to Warren, so he could watch as much as he could before the epic dinner meeting.

Marlon insisted that Avra and I come to the dinner that would be hosted by Warren and his wife, actress Annette Bening. Medavoy of course wrangled an invitation to the dinner, not wanting to miss a conversation between Marlon Brando and Warren Beatty. As I mention a number of star-chasing individuals in this volume, I'd be remiss if I left Medavoy off that list.

While some might say that *that* is the very job of an ex-agent turned producer - that job being to chase stars - Mike was a very special breed of fan when it came to the mega-famous. As mentioned, I first met Mike years back through Tony. Years later, I remember Medavoy's name coming up on the set of a series where I was doing a few days as a director. A star actor on this set struck up a conversation with me as he learned that I - like him - knew Mike. I'll never forget this actor laughing as he said, "If Mike's at a party, and he sees Jack (Nicholson) walk in from the north door as Warren (Beatty) walks in from the south; poor Mike. He's gonna wet and shit his pants just as his head explodes, not knowing which way to crawl so he can start to toady."

Avra and I had to get a babysitter for Molly on the night of the dinner at Warren's. We then took one car over with Marlon to the Beatty house. Medavoy was driving himself over and he arrived as the three of us were getting there. The house was beautiful. I'd later learn that it was a rental as their "real" house (a few doors down) was being remodeled. I had met Beatty a few times previously; Tony and I were guests on the set of *"Bugsy"* (thanks to Mike, who once ran Tri-Star), and often, when Tony and I would grab lunch up at the Beverly Glen restaurants, we'd occasionally see Warren having very quiet, in the corner, one-on-one lunches with highly unique guys; men like Mort Sahl, Dick Gregory, Buck

Henry or Scott Rudin. Tony and I would say "Hi" and quickly be on our way; you really had to know Warren well to get into real conversation with him. When first meeting him years back through Tony, a few things seemed clear about Beatty: he's quite guarded, he's very discreet and he exudes a distinctive brand of powerful intelligence.

It was no different that night as he answered the door and let us in. He showed us around a very white array of entrance areas and living rooms, featuring a very white fancy staircase, until we eventually arrived at the very white dinner table, where one thing was immediately clear to Marlon: this was not going to be some steak and potatoes meal; even the small set-out dishes and stylish utensils previewed exactly what it turned out to be: an elegant macrobiotic vegan grazing with very small portions and only healthy selections. I knew Marlon was having these immediate thoughts because I was having them at the exact same time; our junk-food-loving eyes met, knowing we'd both probably be going to a burger joint together a bit later after this meal.

Annette came out, and yes, even in her casual around-the-house attire, she's positively stunning - very much like Warren; instant intelligence and immediate laser observation; the two of them together create some mutant form of cosmic sunlight. I had met her a few times before; the kind of meetings where I'd remember and she would not, and I mean no disrespect in that fact; through Tony, Ed Begley and others, I recall brief introductions at various parties, functions or other crowded gatherings where she was clearly one of the shiny objects in the room. Tonight, she could not have been nicer, immediately making extra effort to talk to Avra and me while Mike was doing all he could to split his manic fan-boy attention between Brando and Beatty.

Before long, all this pre-dinner chat featured Marlon staring across the room at Annette as he was being cornered by Warren and Mike. He broke away from them as he sauntered over to our circle, where Avra and I were talking with Bening. "Old Hollywood" is an amazing thing; you could see the absolute shifting face and posture on Marlon, as this former leading man was approaching a world class beauty. The smile, the arch of the brow

- he was still "Brando," but then again, not quite. He had already met her at the door, but he knew little about her.

I'm not sure if Marlon had seen even a single film Annette had been in, but he certainly knew of the legendary "Beatty" womanizing prowess, and Marlon was wildly curious about The One That Finally Got Beatty - The woman who converted Warren from Super Stud to Family Man.

Marlon was an immediate flirt with Annette, but he quickly learned that all those moves that might've worked so well with Marilyn Monroe; well, maybe they weren't working as smoothly on Annette Bening; she was polite but clearly unimpressed with Marlon's aggressiveness. Yes, of course he knew that she was a married woman and this was her house, but that kind of thing never slowed him down in his past. And no, while he wasn't looking to get sexual with her, he definitely had a fully reflexive approach and demeanor that clearly once conveyed immediate attraction and instant invitation. I only noticed because Marlon was not like this with every woman; he could easily see that Annette was one of these rare beings from his past - the kind of elite person he liked a lot - and almost always won over: a famous, beautiful female movie star.

The stilted conversation ended as dinner was eventually served at the small circular table, with Warren at 12 o'clock, then to his right and around: Mike, me, Marlon, Annette and Avra. Marlon showed me the small plates and little bowls before us with a giggling grin, and I was on edge as I would be with my own father in such a situation, hoping he wouldn't say something rude, impolite or flat out mean to the gracious hosts. The very healthy small-portioned meal was quite good, but it went down fast with Marlon; he asked for another serving rather quickly.

Certain small talk during the meal was already telling me that Beatty and Annette did not like the acting tapes, and they clearly wanted to save that conversation for the upcoming time when all the food was off the table. Talk between Marlon and Annette caught my ear as I heard him proudly tell her, "Not everyone has an editor who went to Juilliard." Introductory exchanges in the living room earlier had me telling Annette that I was Marlon's video editor, so now putting that together, she leaned around Marlon to ask, "Joe, you went to Juilliard? Theater?" I nodded, recalling her recent work, particularly *"American Beauty,"* somewhat randomly uttering, "Uh, yeah. Kevin Spacey was one of my classmates."

While the mention of Spacey received nothing more than a vacant blink, she did have her gears turning, still stuck on the confused collision of "Juilliard" and "editor". She asked, "So you're a Juilliard trained actor, and you edited Marlon's acting tapes?" Her tone was not rude when she asked, but I got the *entire* picture right then and there. She was really asking this: "You're a classically trained actor, and the way Marlon teaches acting in these tapes - uh, you're okay with this?" I knew that Annette had real stage training by way of San Francisco's American Conservatory Theater; she did understand what Juilliard and actual acting training was all about.

But just as I was about to get into a deeper conversation with her about all this, she flinched! Big! Hard! Her face snapped into a glare at Marlon. Avra noticed it to Annette's right. Annette moved her chair closer to Avra. I looked at Avra. Marlon quickly put food in his mouth. Well, it seemed that under the table, Marlon had possibly put his hand on Annette's knee? Or something within that general area of behavior? As I had mentioned earlier: totally unacceptable but purely reflexive behavior, from the Wild One who used to get away with absolutely anything on Earth.

Hey, maybe it was all some spacial accident; the table *was* small and he was a very big guy, but whatever it was, it went unnoticed across the table; Beatty and Medavoy were deep into "Mike Ass-Kissing Warren" conversation. But on this side of the table, it was - to put it mildly - an awkward beat. Avra quickly started a new subject, reminding Annette that cute little Molly was our daughter; as we were still working up at Marlon's at that time, Avra had taken Molly to a nearby Mulholland Drive park recently, where Annette was strolling; she stopped to introduce herself and coo at our two-year-old. I recall this because just days before this dinner, Avra told me of the encounter, saying, "Molly looks more like Annette Bening than she looks like us."

After the dishes were cleared and it was finally time to talk "tapes," Warren decided to stand as he began to open the discussion. Haltingly, he muttered, "I'll start with what I saw, what I remember: Robin Williams, yeah, funny guy. We learn nothing, but, absolutely, a highly talented individual." (Yes, Robin performed in the tapes.) "A fair amount of 'casting-couch' behavior." (Yeah, Marlon displayed some of that with the actresses in the tapes.) "There was the trashing of a dead man, a great teacher, I don't know why." (Lee Strasberg was a hero of Warren's; a man who spent his life saying he taught Brando when that was not at all the case; Marlon wanted that clear in the tapes; he always thought this falsehood was a great disservice to Stella Adler.) "I remember some improvised scenes; some good, many bad, but no clear direction or assistance from the instructor on those." (Pretty-much true.) "Michael Jackson was sitting there watching it for some reason." (Michael was in the "student" audience, motionless behind dark sunglasses.)

And then Warren Beatty said *it* - "And my biggest take-away, if I might move from what I *saw* to what I *think*: you can't release these tapes. If you do, you'll ruin the franchise."

Silence. Marlon was burning with anger. Avra and I had a feeling things were going to go this way, but still, we were not prepared for the moment: we hadn't seen many people this bold and honest with Marlon. Medavoy was squirming in his seat. He could feel both Warren's discomfort and Marlon's rage; Mike clearly is uneasy when stars are not happy. Annette broke the silence with, "Joe, what do you think?" In a bizarre moment, Medavoy blurted, "Who cares what *he* thinks?!" Those were words that everyone else in the room understood purely from a guy like Mike Medavoy: in a gathering where we have three giant movie stars, two of them legends, you're asking a *nobody* what *he* thinks?! Annette immediately read Mike's tone, sharply snapping, *"He's a Juilliard trained actor who cut the tapes together! Yes, Mike! I'd like to hear his thoughts!"* She said it fully in my defense, but frankly, I was kinda sorta with Mike on this one - I *really* didn't want to be dragged into the conversation at this volatile point. Still, my mind was spinning, stuck on Medavoy's "Howard Rosenman"-style bark. Good for Annette. So - I began. I talked about the, uh, tapes being "different, unique, unconventional, just like Marlon." As she sensed me hedging, Annette pushed back with, "But this is being presented as 'Acting Instruction,' and we both know it's not that." I could only counter with, "No, Annette, it's not what you had at A.C.T. or I had at Juilliard, but - " Marlon then interrupted, quietly growling with an evil giggle to Warren, "You'll ruin the franchise? - What the hell does that mean?"

Warren went on to openly discuss the "Brando Mystique," the fascination around the world of Marlon's hidden nature. He presented a "Less is More" theory, saying that the tapes showed too much of him, carefully trying to indicate delicate "age" and "weight" elements, feeling that certain exposure at *this* late stage in Marlon's life could jeopardize the way audiences might view his earlier "classic" work. Beatty's words were very much like the argument I had with Avra's uncle Alan that night on the Warner lot after the *"Free Money"* screening - Alan Douglas and Warren Beatty were both from the True Brando-Worship Generation, both wanting to keep their *"Streetcar"* through *"Apocalypse"* Brando powerful, virile and most of all, mysterious.

It was hitting me now just how cautious Beatty was as a performer, a filmmaker and even as a celebrity. A lot like Greg. To Warren's credit, when he finally became a force in Hollywood, he made few films, often spaced out for years. When he'd finally come through with a *"Heaven Can Wait," "Reds"* or even a *"Dick Tracy,"* they were events; carefully calculated and wonderfully crafted films that kept him on the A-List for quite some time. But when he'd take chances on comedies like *"Ishtar"* or *"Town & Country"* and he'd get burned, he'd disappear for awhile, not wanting to be seen in the losing column again - ever again - at least not for a few more years.

As Marlon again fumed about the "Franchise" line, Beatty went into a talk about his current project of that moment: a careful set of negotiations he was presently in the middle of, trying to get a number of studios together to release a full collection of "Warren Beatty" films, with many of his hits scattered across studios such as Paramount, Columbia and Warner Brothers. This was the era of DVD "collections," and studios and production companies rarely felt the need to split profits for the sake of an actor's desire to see their work "packaged" together. It really was the perfect kind of Beatty project - making a nice presentation of, yes, "The Franchise," trying to do something that few actors could put together, and, of course, it was all about him. As he went on about it, I could see Marlon getting both more bored and more angry at the exact same time. Talk of DVD releases of old movies; this was one of the *last* things ever to be on Marlon's mind.

With my brain swirling, I wanted to bring the topic back to the tapes - *but* - for Marlon's sake, I also wanted to perhaps take a defensive poke at Beatty. I said, "I hope *'Ishtar'* will be in that collection; I love that film." Marlon giggled, *"Ishtar,"* prompting Warren to grow louder as he exclaimed, *"That* is a very funny movie! Joe, you're not the only one who loves that film!" Full disclosure here: all that went exactly as I had hoped, because: A) I really like *"Ishtar"* B) I had read that Beatty was notoriously defensive about *"Ishtar"* C) I knew Marlon would giggle at the mere mention of a word like *"Ishtar"* and D) It led me to talk of how I wanted Beatty to perhaps re-think Marlon's acting tapes. I boldly brought up the "unfair" treatment of *"Ishtar,"* comparing it to a Brando film I recently wrote and produced, *"Free Money,"* talking of how we can't let critics be the final judges of what might work and what might not. Warren said, "Look, you wanted my opinion; I think these tapes could hurt the franchise - I know you don't like that word, Marlon, but that's how I feel." It was all getting uncomfortable. Avra quietly said to me, "We should pick up Molly from the babysitter." I was glad she said that, but Marlon pulled me back down as I was standing, telling me, "We have more time." Understanding our car situation (the three of us drove here together), Warren told Avra, "I'll get Marlon back if you two need to go." Brando grumbled, "I get it; Avra needs her baby; Joe, you stay." Avra smiled sweetly as Annette referred to Molly, "She's so adorable." That led the women to the door as the conversation then went to Mike asking Warren what a "solution" might be regarding the tapes. A new edit? A new framework for what Warren watched? What? Beatty was a smart guy - Maybe he had an answer. As Avra went out the door, Annette used that shift in the evening to make her exit as well. She gave the four of us a quick "Goodnight" and vanished up that long flight of very white fancy stairs.

Mike was looking dog-tired, but he really didn't want to miss conversation between Marlon Brando and Warren Beatty. As talk dragged on with the four of us, Mike was hoping to end the evening, twice asking, "You ready to go, Marlon? I can drive you." It was clear that Marlon was finally comfortable in that chair. Beatty soon muttered, "You look tired, Mike; I'll get these guys back." Mike reluctantly stood, telling us all that he *did* have an early day tomorrow, one that involved a morning call with Terrence Malick, a great name-drop to Beatty if ever there was one. After Medavoy left, Warren re-organized the conversation, getting personal, friendly - actually, wonderfully helpful. The three of us talked for another hour or so, about the editing of the tapes, the possibility of some of the "lessons" coming off better in book form, maybe even shooting more footage. Marlon talked about wanting to have zoologist Jane Goodall and some of the apes she worked with in a segment. Warren listened as Marlon talked about our human instinct to "Lie" and call it "Acting," our primal need to be "Liked," thus another form of "performance".

Beatty could only smile, muttering, "I hear you. I understand what you're saying. I just didn't see any of that in your tapes. I'm sorry." When talk about the tapes grew too tense yet again, I watched and listened as Warren asked Marlon about their mutual friends (and Marlon's neighbors), Jack Nicholson and Jack's longtime permanent assistant and house-sitter-of-sorts, former actress and former club owner Helena Kallianiotes. Warren hadn't seen or talked to either of them for a spell; the same went for Marlon. After more talk about more mutual friends and non-friends, Warren looked at me and asked, "Juilliard? You still act?" I shrugged, "Once in a while. But I don't chase it. I got tired of running all over town with my picture in my hand." Beatty nodded, "I hear you." Actually, it was kind of nice of him to even *try* to relate to a thought like that. This is a guy who hasn't had his picture in his hand for quite a few years.

When Warren and I finally got tired Marlon up and out the door, Beatty disappeared for a moment to get a car, only to drive up in the most compact two-door, two-seat foreign sports car I had ever seen; a tiny hardtop with a fastback. Where the hell was I going to sit? Frankly, where the hell was Marlon going to sit? Beatty got out, assuring us, "I know it looks tight, but I think we can do it." I crawled into an "area" behind the seats that wasn't big enough for a briefcase. If that wasn't bad enough, Marlon then got in. The entire vehicle dropped quite a ways, the back of his car seat squished me up against the rear windshield and by then, even Beatty's driver's side was pretty-much filled with overflowing Brando. It kept getting worse for both Marlon and me as Beatty worked gingerly to carefully get Marlon's passenger door shut. Once that was finally accomplished, Warren ran around to his side, struggled to get in, and eventually got his door shut as he threw the car into gear. We zoomed through the driveway gates as they opened.

In actual pain with the back of a car seat literally making a denting impression into my chest, I looked down at the lights of Hollywood as Beatty steered the small vehicle around the curves of Mulholland drive - *This* stretch of it famously known as "Bad Boy Drive," in honor of this area housing Marlon, Warren and Jack; and I was in the car with two of them. Of course, it felt surreal - What in the world was I doing in a tiny car with Marlon Brando and Warren Beatty?

How strange was my life? The two men seemed to have nothing left to say. To kill what had now become an awkward silence, I brought up how great it was to have talked with Annette. Marlon graciously took the cue, telling Beatty, "Now I see what all the shopping was about. Man, you have got yourself a winner." Of course, he was directly referring to Warren's famous marathon dating years; an era when nobody thought that Warren Beatty would ever really settle down with anybody. Warren sighed to Marlon, "Yeah, she is something. I'm a very lucky guy. She's much smarter than I'll ever be." His remark was very heartfelt and revealing; throughout the evening, I could see that Beatty *was* both very smart *and* in need of *looking* very smart. He values intelligence, and his thoughts on Annette did seem to me to be warm, sincere and generous.

When we finally got up to Brando's house, even through his rapidly-arriving exhaustion, I could sense that Marlon was truly upset. He had put off making those acting tapes for years. He dreamed that once he made them, they would bring in millions for his family and his retirement. "Acting Instruction from Marlon Brando" - how could that miss? Tonight was one of the first real judgments made on the tapes that was said directly to Brando, by a man that Marlon did trust, even though, as he liked to say, he wasn't crazy about. And I knew Marlon - I knew it didn't take a lot to make him quickly shy away from any project. I sensed that Beatty's words tonight about the tapes did indeed start to put the nails into the coffin of *"Lying For a Living"*.

Arriving at Brando's, Warren struggled, eventually getting Marlon and me out of the small car. I grabbed Marlon's arm; he was practically falling asleep, barely standing upright here in the dark driveway. Warren asked, "Joe, you can get him in okay?" I nodded, thanking him for dinner and his time. Marlon's eyes were closed, he was muttering something, but neither Beatty nor I could make it out. I said, "He's tired." Warren nodded. He stared at Marlon. After an entire evening of being a commanding host, Beatty suddenly looked sheepish, nervous, like one of his 70's jittery film characters; that stuttering handsome enigma who's not sure of what to say or how to say it.

After more awkward glances, Warren got into his tiny little car. Rolling down the window as he put it in gear, he said, "Oh, and hey, Joe, I'm glad you liked *'Ishtar'* - You *get* it!"

As Warren Beatty's taillights disappeared through Brando's gates, Marlon opened his eyes with a forced-awake, "Is he gone?!" I laughed, "Are you really tired or are you faking it?"

He muttered, "Both." The old railroad ties that form the steps up to his house were before us. He *was* tired. I took his arm and slowly helped this very large and very tired old man up his steps.

Halfway up the stairs, Marlon quietly wheeze-chuckled, "Oh, I really hate that guy." I laughed a bit myself, not knowing if his harsher-than-usual remark was years in the making or suddenly formed after tonight. Marlon then asked, "What do you think of him?" Unsure of how to respond, I said, "Well, I think he really does want people to think of him as smart."

Marlon quietly mooed, "Ooooooh yeaaah."

Once we got up to the sliding kitchen door, he asked, "Why the hell did you want his advice on our project anyway?"

I laughed, "You put this whole evening together. Not me."

He growled, "Next time I have an idea like that, stop me."

He then asked, "Aren't you hungry? For some burgers?"

I said, "After that meal? Of course."

He smiled, finding a totally new energy as he started heading back *down* the stairs.

He chuckled, "No wonder that wife of his is such a skinny little gal; they eat rabbit food!"

We arrived at one of the pearl-colored Lexus sedans he had in the driveway, immediately wishing that Warren Beatty had owned such a spacious machine.

As I got Marlon into the passenger seat, I recalled, "Oh, and don't tell Avra about this; I told her I was starting a diet."

As I got into the driver's seat, reached for the keys above the sun visor and got the vehicle started, Marlon muttered one of his pure Brando lines regarding my "diet".

It was one of those absurdly funny remarks that has you feeling fortunate at that moment, reminding you that Marlon considers you to be his friend.

"Don't worry, man. You can afford another pound or two. If we're ever in the woods and the bears are chasing us, I'd rather be you."

Later that night, sharing a laugh and a meal at "Fatburgers" with Marlon, along with his newest far-fetched ideas on how to "save" the acting tapes, I recall again feeling fortunate. Avra and Molly were in my life. Marlon was in my life. And we both agreed that the burgers were great. In my mind, even Warren Beatty didn't have it this good.

This evening in its entirety was one of the last epic events I was able to share with Marlon. As I will cover in the forthcoming chapters, between Molly, her soon-to-be-diagnosed autism, and the aging of both Greg and Marlon, I was seeing less and less of those great and dear friends. I didn't know that at the time, but those conclusions were fully underway without any of my awareness.

Avra's uncle Alan loved a quote from his friend, Miles Davis. It pretty much says it all.

"Time isn't the main thing. It's the only thing."

Passing (2003)

After *"Lying For a Living"* faded into that figurative Big Dream Drawer that held Marlon's other unrealized ideas, inventions and projects, Avra and I now had two separate jobs - She needed to care for our infant child and I needed to secure and maintain steady employment - in an industry that served up mostly freelance work on a sporadic basis. More on all that coming up. The end of *"Lying For a Living"* also coincided with the failing health of both Greg and Marlon. Greg was rarely seen in those days, and Marlon had a housekeeper who moved her family onto the Brando property and did what she could to keep people from seeing Marlon.

These were sad and difficult times, of course, especially after Molly was diagnosed with autism, an event that occurred between Greg's death in 2003 and Marlon's passing in 2004. So even though there is much more to tell here, please allow me to momentarily move to their exits; I'll get back to more "story" shortly; a more joyful, appropriate place to ultimately end.

Yes, jumping ahead here, with more to come on each event, I'll painfully get this out of the way: Greg passed away on June 6th, 2003. Roughly, a year and a month later, Marlon died in 2004, on July 1st. Marlon's death came with layers of illness that, when combined, were as complex as every aspect of his totally non-ordinary life: diabetes, along with respiratory failure, liver cancer, pulmonary fibrosis, congestive heart failure; all that led to pneumonia that ended his life at the age of 80. Over a year before, at the age of 87, Greg had a stroke followed by bronchopneumonia.

So like them: I saw very little of Greg's private demise, while I held Marlon's frail hand not long before he was gone. As they both left the stage, my usual over-analysis of both of them kicked-in to an even higher gear, especially when I felt that their published obituaries barely scratched the surface of their industry, political and cultural impacts. I'd often see shrugged blather about *"To Kill a Mockingbird"* for Greg and *"The Godfather"* for Marlon and that seemed to be that. Given that occasional short-shrift, in my opinion, I found myself boiling down the essence of their lasting impressions and their professional legacies: some of my simple reductions below.

As I often do, as you've already witnessed, I first needed to use yet another Industry Timeline for perspective. When Hollywood filmmaking *finally* reached a certain pinnacle, what seemed (at the time) to be The Ultimate Evolution, from crude, silent-film "Primitive Invention" to sophisticated storytelling a few years after *"Gone With The Wind,"* Greg was clearly the biggest "Last to Arrive Star" of that blossoming era, just before "The Big Shift" of cultures and attitudes within filmmaking took place. And *when* that "Big Shift" *did* take place, without a doubt, Brando was the biggest "First Star" of that era; an era that stretched into The Full Demise of The Old Studio Heads. It was also an era that went on to include the creation of the film rating system, the advent of the American art film, the ushering-in of the 70's revolution and the short-lived Hollywood Moment where Director's Creativity over-ruled Studio Greed (safe to say, *that* moment perhaps ended with Michael Cimino's *"Heaven's Gate".)* There: "Last Star" and "First Star" - A somewhat complicated examination of what I feel is a rather simple breakdown of that transition. And what I find perhaps most remarkable: Greg's most famous and iconic role came long after his Burst-Onto-The-Scene successes of the 1940's.

Of course, Greg's death made obituary writers speak of his gentle dignity, his quiet heroism and his talent for displaying compassion, all writing about *"To Kill a Mockingbird"* first and foremost. We were also reminded that for almost six decades, Greg was an industry giant, one who broke onto the scene as a young actor in the war years, somehow, almost immediately, racking up four Best Actor Oscar nominations within the short span of half a decade.

When comparing the better, more extensive obituaries of Marlon and Greg, the list of Greg's awards, honors and tributes seemed endless. And while that same list regarding Marlon was shorter, many were aware that Marlon was quite famous for literally turning down awards, honors and tributes, with his *"Godfather"* Oscar not being the only one he walked away from. I remember when someone called him at Mulholland about a possible "American Film Institute Lifetime Achievement" award (one of a few calls he received on that matter). He laughed it off as he hung up the phone, then asking me, "What kind of award is that? You gotta *be* there or they won't give it to you? How the hell is *that* about your work?"

When put in that context, it's hard to argue with Marlon's point. Still, as one of the creators and founders of "The American Film Institute," Greg rolled his eyes with a gasp when he heard me telling that story to Tony; again, reminding me of how Greg and Marlon were on such different planets within The Industry universe.

Another thing that struck me as I read their tributes was how they both single-handedly elevated the industry in totally different ways. In shorthand: Greg brought status, while Marlon brought art. Because collaborative studio filmmaking had already become so costly, risky and commercial by the 1950's, nobody could've envisioned a leading man like Marlon, one who was more rock star than cooperative studio team player. Yes, even back then, those in the industry and within the workings of pop culture knew things were always changing, but nobody could've forecast "Brando". Nobody. Along with that, he brought a double whammy: Marlon wasn't just an immediate movie star, he was also deemed, just as quickly, the medium's "Greatest Actor," a heavy burden of a title for a young man, to say the least. Always remembering that as I dealt with him, I recall joking with Avra, "No wonder he's still so erratic: before Marlon, movie stars were movie stars and great actors were great actors - he really was the first to be told he was both."

As written about for decades, Marlon and his "artistic" behavior eventually became something of a headache to The Film Industry, all while Greg was bringing just the opposite to a business that longed for prestige, respect and perhaps most of all: dignity. Going through Greg's obituaries, the constant tributes to TKAM were lined with phrases like "friend of President Lyndon Johnson," or "led the campaign that kept conservative Robert Bork off the Supreme Court," a SCOTUS public awareness campaign that had never been tried before. Greg also fully grasped the pure power ties between Washington and Hollywood, understanding epic backstage players such as Lew Wasserman and Jack Valenti - guys who mixed the two worlds with ease.

In short, more than any famous figure of his generation, it's safe to say Greg literally connected Hollywood power and Washington power, in ways that made both towns swoon with admiration. Hollywood felt they had their own perfect President, just as Washington was blown away by this occasional visitor's presence, his charm, and yes, what they so respect in D.C.: his dignity. Of course, Marlon was always incredibly political as well, but unlike Greg, he was a proud yet sometimes reckless grenade thrower, not a diplomat whatsoever. For decades, many Native American leaders credited Brando for singlehandedly putting their cause on the map for many white Americans who had never given their plight a thought until then.

But to leave Marlon and Greg out of this political conversation for the moment, I believe it's worth noting the strange regional hypocrisy at work within a few certain facts: even the highest level of "Hollywood" pretends that art comes first and creativity is key, all while wanting to act both aloof and even anti-establishment when it comes true power, vulgar money and high finance. Oh, they love shouting out good box office numbers, but they'll often swear it's all in the name of artistic success and creative achievement.

At the same time, Washington poorly attempts a somewhat odd version of a reverse ruse, often claiming that appearance, vulgar show business and popular shiny objects do not interest their "serious" populace; a community involved with governing, the economy, world markets and global issues. Pure bullshit on both counts. Washington is positively giddy and star-struck with

Hollywood, just as the black-tied money guys of Hollywood are in drooling awe of Washington power and prestige. Again, I really do leave artists like Greg and Marlon out of those mindsets. As I've stated before, they were creative souls who were legitimately passionate about people, causes and justice, both having much to lose and little to gain back then as they constantly put their names, their fame and their reputations on the line. And, as I've stated often, politically, to me, Greg's genius was all about how he fully kept his dignity as he swam with sharks on both sides - of politics *and* show business. Marlon's political genius was all about a raw, passionate, world famous artist giving a voice to groups who needed a voice at the time, whether those communities were African-American, Native-American or Hispanic. I hope they passed on knowing that they both had moments that really did make a difference when it came to important matters beyond filmmaking. You simply had to be there to know that Gregory Peck actually did change the make-up of the U.S. Supreme Court. And you simply had to be there to know that Marlon Brando brought true public awareness to the plight of the Native-American, at a time when most Americans were not giving it the slightest thought. Their voices were huge, in eras long before bloggers, vloggers, social media and 24-hour news.

You simply had to be there. Today's fame-hungry politicians in the House and the Senate (call them what they are: dog-catchers who own 2 suits) can only dream of having Peck's and Brando's influence and sincerity.

But this is not to say that political movements or events in Washington mean more than the impact of art. Both Greg and Marlon proved that a film can be as powerful as any social action or even law; the influence of a film can be vast and lasting. That's why Greg was so upset when he started to feel that cinema that meant something was vanishing. I think his words at his American Film Institute Lifetime Achievement honor in 1989 say it best. He saw the corporate nature of "New" Hollywood as the problem, and he put his thoughts into words, as only Greg could do.

"There's been a lot of glamorous financial news in the papers lately: multi-media conglomerates. It may be that, in a few years, all pictures and all television will be made by two or three of these behemoths who happen also to own magazines, newspapers and cable stations, and to manufacture and distribute video cassettes. If these Mount Everests of the financial world are going to labor and bring forth still more pictures with people being blown to bits with bazookas and automatic assault rifles, with no gory detail left unexploited, if they are going to encourage anxious, ambitious actors, directors, writers and producers to continue their assault on the English language by reducing the vocabularies of their characters to half a dozen words, with one colorful but overused Anglo-Saxon verb and one un-beautiful Anglo-Saxon noun covering just about every situation, then I would like to suggest that they stop and think about this: making millions is not the whole ball game, fellas. Pride of workmanship is worth more. Artistry is worth more."

That's the way I remember Greg. He felt pride and meaning in filmmaking. So incredibly rare.

NINTH CHAPTER
EXPECTATIONS
(GREG & MARLON ESSAY IX)

Before getting to the final stories (stories years before they passed) that I want to end this book with, I'd like to offer a bit more perspective on these two guys. If I may - consider the following: maturity versus adolescence. Wisdom versus innocence. Conformity versus rebellion. Sometimes I thought of phrases like these when I was comparing Greg and Marlon. It made me think of how we are all wired. Of how some of us reach a "peak" in life later, while others see their younger years as their "best". With stars like Brando and Peck, you can sometimes take measure as to who they were from their casting and how their performances were received. Sometimes. But not always with "Stars". As I keep stating within these pages, "Stars" can be the most miscast actors in a film. They are often cast only because they deliver a box-office number, first and foremost.

When stars like Greg and Marlon were in their most sought-after eras, their names were often far more important than the film titles. In a knee-jerk way, on any evening, we all might go see that (insert star name here) picture, rather than going to see (insert "star-less" movie title). Brando's name certainly enticed people to see a then unknown, original passion project (of Elia Kazan's) such as *"On the Waterfront,"* while *"The Godfather"* still might've had a large initial audience merely on the strength of a widely read bestseller. The same goes for *"To Kill a Mockingbird,"* a huge novel with a built-in audience pre-movie. But in both cases, try to think of those films without those stars *now*. Basically impossible - AND - it's possible to say that the popularity of their performances have surpassed the popularity of the actual books (and yes, I'll make that claim even with TKAM, as mandatory school readings recently declined due to various "PC" issues.)

While the Academy Award is not always given to the "Best" whatever in any given year, whether it be Picture, Actor, etc., there are times when they seem to get it "right," for lack of a better word. With three acting Oscars between them, that trio of honors still seems as "right," rather than prizes given out of sympathy, political correctness or any other thought process. *"On the Waterfront"* was awarded "Best Picture," and it would be hard to separate that story without the performance of Brando. Marlon was still in his chameleon stage, bouncing from Tennessee Williams to Shakespeare to whatever felt the most challenging to him. He was already given this "Greatest Actor" burden after only a handful of films and he seemed to be testing himself as to what he could and could not do, operating more as a hungry actor rather than a movie star.

When Greg finally got his acting Oscar for *"Mockingbird,"* it was almost as though he had then grown into a comfortable place; comfortable for the audience and the very man himself; a place steeped in integrity, justice, humbleness and devotion to fatherhood - all that really was who Greg WAS. Was Peck's real life that "established" before that? Were things that "clear" for Greg and his acting roles *before* that? To his credit (and probably to his more youthful pleasure as a younger actor), not really. He was quite versatile and adventurous in his youth, taking on a variety of parts. It's often difficult to compare the different characters in much of his earlier work.

Take three 1950's pictures that opened nearly back-to-back-to-back: *"The Gunfighter," "Captain Horatio Hornblower"* and *"David and Bathsheba"* - a psychological western, a swashbuckler in the 1800's and a Biblical epic in the classic Hollywood tradition. Greg's common role throughout all these? Typecasting? Not remotely. Here's what it was: He was a huge box office star who also happened to be an actor who could pull off all these types of films. Those films (in that order listed above) easily could've starred other actors such as (in the same order) John Wayne, Errol Flynn and Victor Mature; all essentially being typecast in ways that Greg was *not* in all those films, making those movies today - to me, starring Greg - far more interesting. Face it: what would be unique today (or even remotely intriguing) about another old John Wayne western, another old Errol Flynn swashbuckler or another old Victor Mature Bible epic?

Perhaps the best thing about Greg's *"Mockingbird"* Oscar is that as a prediction, it was basically guaranteed to go to Peter O'Toole that year, along with the "Best Picture" of the moment, *"Lawrence of Arabia"*. My theory has always been that Greg's Academy Award was almost a second 1962 "Best Picture" Oscar, given the power of Greg's performance. Getting back to my previous thoughts, I also believe that The Industry recognized the "Atticus" that Greg had become. In that era of John Kennedy and civil rights, Greg represented more than just a maturing actor; he was a leader - with all of that being conveyed by a masterful performance.

Marlon's two Oscars paint his evolutionary picture in an even more vivid fashion. As I wrote previously, when he was the only key performer from *"A Streetcar Named Desire"* to go home without an award, Marlon wasn't thrilled. Yes, it was probably one of the final times to give the legendary Humphrey Bogart an Academy Award, but two other realities were in place: "Old Hollywood" went for the "Elderly Guard" over the "Young Upstart," and also, Marlon's Stanley Kowalski was a unique and complex villain for the cinema of that time. I fully suspect Marlon's "Stanley" lost the Oscar for the same reason his story lost "Best Picture" to *"An American in Paris"*; the Broadway play that *"Streetcar"* was based on carried the ugly elements of both mental illness and rape - not topics for the general mainstream "Hollywood" films of that time.

However - the high level of the acting in "Streetcar" was undeniable - thus three acting Oscars. *But* - Hollywood didn't want to give the Academy Award to the rapist. Especially at Bogie's possibly last Oscar party - (Even though it wasn't - Bogart still had the glory of *"The Caine Mutiny"* and a number of other successes ahead of him in his final six years).

Just a few years later, Marlon's Terry Malloy in Elia Kazan's *"On the Waterfront"* had many of Stanley's same qualities; the characters shared a lack of education, a similar brute force and a shortage of sophistication when it came to the opposite sex. But that's where much of the comparison ends. Unlike Stanley, Terry had a love for a trapped mob-connected brother, an endearing crush on a pretty neighbor girl (he took part in her brother's death; it's complicated), he cared for a flock of filthy birds, and best of all, when push-came-to-shove regarding right and wrong, he took a stand, both in a courtroom and on the cold docks of Hoboken. He was certifiably heroic.

Oh, a bizarre side note on that element of Terry Malloy "taking the stand": it seemed to take quite a few years for Hollywood to "turn" on the film, later seeing the entire production as Elia Kazan's naked justification to testify before the House Un-American Activities Committee, something he did *before* making *"Waterfront,"* the story of an "Honorable Stool Pigeon".

During the McCarthy-era red-hunting years, Kazan named names and careers ended because he did, as the U.S. government did what it could to ferret-out Communist Party influence in Hollywood. Decades later, those who assisted in the creation of Hollywood's blacklist (those like Kazan) lost much of their historic luster. Yes, that reexamination even took place with someone who was as revered in his day as Elia Kazan, a man who was key to the careers of both Greg (*"Gentleman's Agreement"*) and Marlon. Yeah, "Gadge" - Kazan's nickname as a "gadget" aficionado and repairman in his youth, - He was a brilliant director with a complex history.

End of side note. So - as I started this series of thoughts with the notion that Greg really grew into the mature man the world felt they knew by the time he played Atticus, that had me looking at the "mature man" Marlon grew into, looking at the roles that so defined him in the 70's and 80's. This is a time when the public had grown to feel they knew the men, beyond their acting performances. The perceptions may have been incorrect; nonetheless, they existed in the public, and sometimes, no amount of acting can make perceptions of "Who a star really is" go away.

When you look at three of Marlon's characters from that "mature" era, you could not think of a trio of men who could be less "Atticus" than Godfather Vito Corleone, Paul who danced the Last Tango, and deranged Captain Walter E. Kurtz, a man embracing an apocalypse right now. Think of Atticus compared to those guys: a trio of men with no actual sense of real fatherhood, sane justice or even faint reality. Three men who do things "civilized" men are not supposed to do.

For some, those three Brando roles might be hard to compare with one another; we do meet Paul and Kurtz in the most troubled, disrupted moments of their lives, but still, we are seeing what they are made of by the way they handle present existential upheaval. And yes - to add: Corleone is indeed a parent - but of what? Proud career thieves, extortionists and conscienceless killers.

Still, and incredibly, we believe Marlon in all of these nearly impossible roles - a military man fully off the deep end, a suicidal widower thrust into a final sexual odyssey, and a cuddly old Mafia killer - in the same way that we totally believe Greg as Atticus Finch. Years after TKAM, as expertly as Peck played a murderous Josef Mengele in *"The Boys from Brazil,"* it seemed audiences could not accept a man of Greg's character and caliber behind that scowling mustache. And that was not "stunt casting" - it really was a great actor playing an interesting part. But the strength of Presidential Medal of Freedom recipient Gregory Peck perhaps overpowered the portrayal of a madman who cloned Hitler. It might not have worked for a number of people. And that's because to many, Greg simply was a man who did what a real man is "supposed to do."

Yet a year after *"The Boys from Brazil,"* when a Marlon character in *"Roots: The Next Generations"* embraced that same swastika as Klan leader George Lincoln Rockwell, a man who enjoyed using the N-word on writer Alex Haley (played by James Earl Jones) as Rockwell threatened Haley at gunpoint during a *"Playboy"* interview - that role earned Marlon an Emmy. It's not that anyone thought Marlon Brando really had that kind of horrific streak within him. So why did it work so well? Great acting on Marlon's part? Of course. But when you're that famous and that well known for so long, I'm certain there's much more to it than that. It worked because by then, after decades in the public eye, Marlon Brando had made one thing clear to everyone in the world: something he had in common with all of his darkest characters:

"Don't ever expect me to do what you think I'm 'supposed to do.'"

But perhaps, when it comes to the two most iconic roles that today's audiences instantly name when it comes to Greg and Marlon, there's even a simpler set of personal equations: how many mafia dons do most of us know personally? None. What are they? Powerful. Mysterious. Someone you will never know. Yeah. Brando works; 'even has a last name ending with a vowel. For Greg: the opposite in tone, but even more rare casting-wise. Think this: we all know that person who swoons over their dad, yet few of us can ever really *get* what that person fully sees in that father they love so much. I guarantee: millions have made their case with something like this:

"To understand how wonderful my father is, think of Gregory Peck as Atticus Finch."

THE STORY RESUMES
GOODBYE CAROLWOOD, GOODBYE GREG (2003)

Stepping back to when Avra and I were expecting Molly Rose to enter our lives back in 2000, a rare crossover of our Brando/Peck worlds occurred as Avra's friend, Rebecca Brando worked with Tony Peck to hold our large baby shower at Greg and Veronique's Carolwood estate. As wonderful as all that planning was on both Tony's and Rebecca's part, I do admit: in the weeks leading up to the event, Avra and I both grew tired of the oft-asked question; yes, a question asked by nearly every invited guest: "Will 'he' be there?" - Of course, the "he" being You-Know-Who and/or You-Know-Who. To cut to the chase, neither made a showing, both knowing that their appearance would immediately make the event all about them, something they both knew a lot about regarding every aspect of their lives for a very long time.

With my Brentwood-based soap-star father-in-law then being neighborly friends with the likes of Chris Jenner and her family, we were happy to get gifts from the soon-to-be-famous Kardashian family; soon-to-be-famous for more than merely being associated with the strangely killer-less murders of Nicole Brown Simpson and Ron Goldman. Another unique thing about Chris; we were already hearing rumors that her second husband, Bruce Jenner, occasionally cross-dressed in private? The Olympics hero guy? We really weren't sure what to make of those whispers.

So while our little Molly had yet to make her appearance into the world, she was indeed at Greg's house that evening in 2000. That was her first visit - of sorts. Her next one would be days after Greg had passed away in 2003. This was shortly before her diagnosis of autism.

Part of laying Greg to rest was a massive gathering that took place at his home after the opulent service in downtown Los Angeles, at the Cathedral of Our Lady of the Angels. At the time, Molly was becoming quite difficult and hard to manage. She was still a toddler but her "Terrible Two" tantrums and fits were becoming a regular - at least hourly - challenge. As much as Avra wanted to go to the church service, I went alone as Avra stayed home with Molly. Later, when a nighttime gathering with friends and family took place at the Carolwood house, Avra wanted to go to pay her respects to the Pecks. We thought we'd need to chance it, taking Molly and hoping for the best. Her increased tantrums were now at a level where we felt they couldn't be entrusted to a babysitter, as we tried to imagine how anyone other than Molly's parents would deal with such sustained volume, wild self-injury and physical trauma, all from such a small child.

On the drive over, Molly seemed fine. As we pulled off Sunset Boulevard onto Carolwood Drive, we could see that valets were already lining up cars all throughout the residential streets of Bel Air. I had never seen anything like it on these small, ritzy roads; there was an actual traffic jam of both parked and barely moving high-end cars sprawled all throughout this exclusive neighborhood. As crazed as the situation seemed, it was even crazier: newly-posted temp signs insisted that everyone "Attending the Peck Gathering" first go to the valet station at Greg's house. In other words, don't *even* think you can just leave your car anywhere in this neighborhood and walk to the Peck house; threats of tow away zones, signs of "private" street fronts and curbs, notices to stay out of non-valet-run areas, etc. It was all part of the absolute chaos that was brought on by one very simple fact: so many people wanted to be a part of Greg's farewell.

As we inched our way to the valet station at the gates of the Peck estate, Avra and I were growing more and more terrified over the ticking time bomb that was our daughter. As random as her tantrums seemed to be lately, there were trigger clues that were becoming more obvious; loud crowds, commotion of any kind, unfamiliar environments - all these things had been setting her off these days, and as we were finally able to arrive at Greg's packed house, I could see that this might be every horrible Molly trigger rolled into one.

Sure enough, just as our car was being whisked off to God Knows Where by some valet and the three of us reached the house on foot, Molly broke into a siren's wail of a tantrum. She was at the toddler age where she was hard to carry (especially while throwing a fit) and would not cooperate with walking if she simply decided not to. The upside to our situation: there was a giant mob of people here - So many. I always saw the Carolwood estate as vast, epic, spacious - not at this moment; everywhere you looked, it was simply jammed with far too many human beings. The downside to our situation: this was no "party" - I had no idea that so many people crammed together could be so quiet - Everyone was hushed, silent, respectful. Everyone but little Molly Rose Brutsman. I recall trying to carry her, actually hoping that people would interpret her tantrum cries as extreme sorrow over Greg. Spotting Veronique, Cecilia and Tony, I told Avra, "Say what you wanna say to them; meet us on that deck where we had the shower!" Avra understood; she didn't know the full property all that well, but she remembered where Tony and Rebecca Brando had hosted our baby shower thirty-some months ago. I nodded a frazzled nod to Tony as I ducked into the shadows with loud Molly and headed to the dark side of the property.

Unfortunately, that dark space was packed as well; there were far too many people jammed onto this property, and yes, you couldn't turn your head without seeing someone you knew, either personally or from the famous side of the world. I was shocked to find an iron outdoor patio chair to plop into - shocked that it was not being used. I tried to quiet Molly but it wasn't working well. My eyes darted to a dark window on the sub-level of the house; I knew every inch of this place quite well. Avra soon arrived and had no trouble finding us in this crowd - she just honed-in on the endless shriek. I stood with Molly in my arms and said, "Follow me!"

Using one of the many backdoors to the estate, I led Avra and Molly down to that dark sub-level room. This was the very den where Greg and I watched and laughed over the opening of The Reagan Presidential Library, over a dozen years ago. Keeping the room dark, I put Molly on the floor, right where Greg used to do his back and leg exercises. Being on the cool floor, away from the crowd, in the dark; all this was starting to agree with Molly. As we caught our breath, Avra marveled, "This place is huge. Where are we?" I explained this funny little living room-den-bar to Avra, recalling how well Greg seemed to like this often overlooked space. Glancing around, Avra had a confused squint as she noticed a framed photo of Tina Turner behind the bar, lit by the outdoor lights. I said, "Yeah, they were good friends. We should stay here until Molly calms down." Avra sighed, "There was a wait to see the family; I think I jumped the line, right in front of every Sinatra."

Just as Molly was calming and we were getting our escape and valet parking plans in order (we had a plan to tip the valet super-big if he would just *tell* us where the damn car was), a *light* turned on in the room - *Molly screamed!* Our heads turned to see Rachelle Begley at the staircase. I yelled, "Shut that off!" The room went dark again. I knew Rachelle. Two years earlier, I had directed her (and her husband, Ed Begley, Jr.) in *"Diary of a Sex Addict"* for Sony Pictures, and I loved her wit, honesty and humor. "Sex Addict" was a very difficult shoot with very difficult people involved, and I recall a lunch Rachelle and I had on the set, where the two of us discussed the problem of working with true assholes. Months after this very night, Rachelle and I together would create her "Green-Eco" reality TV show, *"Living With Ed."* Rachelle had become a first-time mother not too many years before this moment, having a beautiful little girl named Hayden. Avra recalled meeting Rachelle at the *"Sex Addict"* wrap party, and as we all worked to calm Molly in the darkness, we talked about parenthood, Greg and this epic gathering.

Here in this room, I first laughed over the fact that Rachelle simply took it upon herself to wander the sprawling Peck estate alone. Growing to know Rachelle so well years later, it was perfectly like her: daring, perhaps uninvited but fully and positively don't-give-a-shit. That night, she claimed that she couldn't keep up with her husband Ed out there in the vast mob. She expressed what I knew: everybody loves Ed Begley, Jr. Everybody wants to shake his hand, give him a hug, ask an "Eco" question. Ed, Ed, Ed. I recall back from our on-set lunch; she said she sometimes gets tired being this invisible "thing" next to much-loved Ed. She claimed that even after countless introductions to Veronique, the name of "Rachelle" still failed to register or stick with Mrs. Peck, to the point of Veronique still introducing herself repeatedly, as though they've never met. Knowing both women so well, I still find myself laughing about that to this very day. Rachelle is a beautifully dynamic woman who will not be ignored. And Veronique; well, she was Veronique.

Molly would go in and out of tantrums as we three adults sat on the floor with her in this dark room, trying to figure out a little girl's pain, seeing all those people out there on the property. They couldn't see us. They were all out there for Greg. Rachelle talked of how she wished she had known Greg better, how kind he was during their few exchanges. I talked about some of my times and experiences with him, discussing how singular and special he was.

As Molly's screams would flare up again, Avra and Rachelle talked about Hayden and what she was like at Molly's age. As new parents with our first child, we both had questions.

Rachelle was attempting to be supportive and helpful as she was watching Molly gasp, writhe and cry between full-blown tantrums. But I'll never forget when Rachelle Begley quietly, reluctantly uttered a simple phrase.

"This isn't normal." And Rachelle was right. Not long after that night, Molly was diagnosed by renowned Pasadena Developmental Behavioral Pediatric Specialist Diane Danis.

Absolutely everything changed after that.

Oh, back to the night in that lower-level living room in the Carolwood estate. Molly's tantrums finally drove Rachelle out of the room; she eventually felt that there was little she could do to make things better, also feeling that Ed was not in the mood for a lengthy stay here at this very sad gathering. For what seemed like the longest time, Avra, Molly and I remained on the floor of the dark room. It took awhile for Molly to cry herself asleep. Before long, I felt the best move was to simply outlast the crowd outside, and then, hopefully, just carry a sleeping child out to the valet parking, get into our car and drive to the Burbank home we had recently purchased.

And all that is indeed what happened. As I carried Molly off the property, I had a feeling that I would probably not be back to this house again. I couldn't picture Veronique living here without Greg. I was correct about that; she would later move to another home in nearby Holmby Hills.

That night, in spite of the challenges, I felt so incredibly fortunate to have known Gregory. He was a Complex Enigma and a Common Citizen, somehow combined into one singular human being.

I believe my "Pop" Dabney Coleman said it best: "Gregory Peck. Goddamn. That is a man."

GREG'S SERVICE REVISITED (2004)

As I and many others can recall, the downtown Los Angeles memorial service to say goodbye to Greg was an epic event, even more so than the packed reception at his Carolwood home. It was a religious mass, a packed celebration of a life, a farewell to a saint. I really can't do justice to it merely by explaining who was there at the cathedral, what people were feeling, etc. But if I may,

I'd like to express its impact by way of a roundabout, totally singular story.

Here goes. Please stay with me on this for a bit.

Like many cable networks, "TV Land" grew up fast. And incredibly, they first did it on the sustained model that the rest of basic cable quickly abandoned - showing old TV shows. Once the rest of basic cable learned they could actually thrive by pretending to be "creative" networks, "producing" cheap, lousy reality TV, they all stopped showing reruns of *"Andy Griffith"* - something it seemed they all first did when "Basic Cable" was born - seemingly overnight.

Not giving up on Mayberry and Hooterville even when they were finally up on successful feet, "TV Land" perfected their model of presenting old stuff in new packages. But they too eventually caught the "bug" of thinking they were creative. Actually, I say with all due respect, there *are* some bright people at places like "TV Land," and a few years back, they grabbed onto the clever notion to both create new shows and honor the old ones. Loving old TV as I do, I liked it when they were giving respect to shows that have stood the test of time.

One such moment of respect was when "TV Land" honored the surviving cast and creatives of *"The Dick Van Dyke Show,"* one of those rare, perfect collisions of talent, historical timing and complete brilliance. As he was receiving the award from the network on the evening built around the tribute, *"The Dick Van Dyke Show"* creator Carl Reiner essentially announced that he'd like to create a brand new episode of the series. Would it be a pilot? One of those dreadful "reunion" shows? Who knew? Frankly, I only knew one thing: if Reiner, Dick, Mary and the others were going to put Rob and Laura back on the tube for even a moment, I was going to watch it.

Not that I was fully keeping track of things such as TV shows at that time, but when *"The Dick Van Dyke Show Revisited"* eventually aired, many things had changed in my life. My daughter had been recently diagnosed with autism, Marlon was gravely ill and Greg had passed away. My daughter's situation threw me into a whirlwind of depression. That whole period of time is a pure blur to me. I didn't really bother with things that once interested me; things like a brand new episode of *"The Dick Van Dyke Show"*. But one late night, when I couldn't sleep, I turned on the TV and caught a re-airing of that show I had missed in its recent premiere, *"The Dick Van Dyke Show Revisited"*.

More on that in a moment - First, a recollection about the man who was Rob Petrie, leading me to yet another roundabout tale - Don't worry - I'll be back on track momentarily.

Here we go:

Dick Van Dyke is perhaps the only known star that I feel I actually fawned over, with no shame or hesitation about it whatsoever. As you know by now, as a kid, TV was my medium, my religion, my God, my oxygen. Dick Van Dyke was a huge part of all that. One night in L.A., my friends Ed Begley, Jr. and his wife, Rachelle, took me to a benefit dinner supporting The Los Angeles Midnight Mission. The gala was at The Beverly Hilton, and we hung with Ed's pal, the hilarious Larry Miller. There were many big names there, but just as the evening was ending, Dick Van Dyke kinda pretty much surprised everybody as he took to the stage to the opening notes of Randy Newman's *"You've Got a Friend in Me"* — an instrumental version of the song began to float into the air from the overhead speakers. The *"Toy Story"* tune fit the grinning, Disney-esque Van Dyke well; he smiled and waved as the instantly charmed audience then witnessed what we were only hoping for as we heard the first song notes - Yeah, unannounced and in the most unexpected fashion, Dick Van Dyke just started singing and dancing to this song. Of course, he was skilled, graceful and, well, perfect. Even at his advanced age, he was flawless.

As I watched, I realized what an inspiration he had always been to me - and so much more. As a one-time young, gangly, mostly comedic actor, he was a true role model to me. Later that night, as he was waiting for the valet to bring him his car, I had to do it. I had to do something I never would've done years back, back when I didn't wanna meet Greg or Marlon, always hearing my mother as she told me not to "bother people". I walked up to Dick Van Dyke, took both his hands into my hands, and I said, "You are a national treasure." He asked me, "What's your name?" I told him. He said, "Thank you, Joe. You don't know how much I appreciate that."

He said it as though he meant it, even though I'm certain he had heard that a trillion times before. I knew my courage to do that came from Greg and Marlon. Before meeting them, before getting to know them, I never wanted to even approach such people, and certainly not for something like my encounter with Van Dyke. But so often - even today - I think, "Thank God I had the nerve, the courage and the opportunity to connect with someone I thought I would mean absolutely nothing to - and that maybe, just maybe, I could be wrong about that."

Ah, oh, yeah, back to his "TV Land" reboot - I watched it that night. And, yes, as I was expecting, it was one of those somewhat creaky nostalgia trips displaying too much age and a high degree of evidence as to why this type of thing rarely works, *but - the plot* - The plot caught my attention: old Alan Brady (Carl Reiner's variety show "Sid Caesar" star character) called his old show writer Rob Petrie out of the blue - He wanted Rob to write his eulogy; Brady wasn't dying, but he wanted to get started on "producing" a true tear-filled epic; the kind of giant show-biz industry funeral Hollywood would always remember.

And what was it that gave Alan Brady/Carl Reiner this idea? Well, according to Alan (as he talked to Rob on the phone), Brady had just been to the Los Angeles memorial service of Gregory Peck.

Alan had never seen anything like it. It was a huge event, like no other, cloaked in a massive sadness that vain Alan Brady so wanted to begin choreographing for himself.

Alan Brady wanted to be as loved as Gregory Peck. Greg's passing was the plot of the episode.

I smiled as I watched. Carl Reiner (who, by the way, *all* of Hollywood also loved) - he clearly loved Gregory Peck; Carl couldn't have chosen a better or funnier idea - his Brady character was an egotistical showman who so wanted to harness the emotions of others at the time of his eventual demise. Just mentioning "Gregory Peck's funeral" was the wonderfully comparative punch line. And the TV audience didn't need to have attended Greg's service to understand - They knew the emotions connected to Greg and they loved the absurd plan Alan Brady was hatching.

And yes, Carl Reiner was right to use Greg's service as the basis for the entire plot of his reboot - as Reiner saw himself that day in Los Angeles, as the entire film industry said good-bye to Greg in downtown Los Angeles, it truly was a massive event of epic sadness.

Like one I've never experienced before or since.

And what a strange and perhaps appropriate thing: Greg's death was the actual, literal plot of the very final episode of arguably Hollywood's Best Loved Television Show.

And let's face it: who doesn't love Dick Van Dyke and Gregory Peck? (And Carl Reiner, too!)

Lastly, by the way - Could there be a better tribute to a life seen as well lived? I don't see how.

REGRET (2004)

A year after Greg had passed on, I was thinking about a few of the final emotions and thoughts I believe he had - some thoughts harbored, some shared - shared unwittingly perhaps; he was quite guarded.

Going through some files, I went back and reread an interview he did a few years before his passing, a New York Times piece that feels as though the publication caught Greg on a very open, very honest and, perhaps even, very cantankerous day. While the piece was mostly pleasant, cheerful and filled with pure Greg "Legendary Actor Aging Beautifully at Home" charm, it also had portions where he discussed sharp regrets he had regarding certain aspects of his early-to-mid-career work; years when he felt he was far more concerned about presenting himself as a dependable Hollywood performer, than he was about delivering performances he felt could've (and should've) been more "daring". One example: he discussed his performance as Ahab in John Huston's 1956 *"Moby Dick,"* saying he'd deliver a far more daring performance of the captain as a mature actor; he'd give a performance that he felt would be much closer to what author Herman Melville was envisioning when he created the maniacal, obsessed character.

I felt for Greg as I read the interview; one could see that he was often torn between being uniquely bold and being consistently dependable. Of course, both aspects served him well in Hollywood - particularly *his* younger era of Hollywood, before edgy films required a rating system, back when severe censorship was ever-present and when studio heads could make or break a performer simply by not liking an actor's attitude. But even with all that to contend with, he was able to make himself into a daring star who was also a respected artist and a team player, doing what he could to make a big budgeted film work. To sum up that *NYT* interview, I felt the artistic regrets of Greg, spoken at a time when I knew first-hand that he felt he had one or maybe a couple opportunities remaining - opportunities to deliver a performance that would shock those who thought they knew exactly what to expect from Ol' Lovable Gregory Peck.

And perhaps, therein sat Greg's views of the "Free Pass" Marlon Brando was often granted, when Greg saw young actors fawn over even some of the most phoned-in Brando performances. I won't name those films or performances - one filmgoer's "meh" is another filmgoer's "wow" - but even Marlon sometimes laughed at how Brandophiles could find the gold in even some of his most tossed-off roles. Marlon chuckled about this once and I could only end my part of that conversation with, "Hey, audiences like you." He suddenly got serious, closing the topic with, "Look, if someone doesn't know the difference between *"Burn"* and *"Candy,"* they should put down the popcorn." As I've stated before, any talk with Marlon about filmmaking was rare, and by the end, I don't believe Marlon had the slightest regret about anything regarding his acting, body of film-work or craft - He never stopped loving the exercise of acting, but the final film products and the reception they earned: I think all that stopped having earth-shattering meaning to him years ago. No, I'm certain Marlon's final regrets were all personal and private, all based on family and friends - something I'll get to in a moment.

While that *New York Times* interview was a few years before his passing, Greg talked mostly about his film work and not his personal life; not surprising as Greg was both quite private *and* nicely accommodating to a press that still tiredly wanted to discuss *"Roman Holiday," "Gentleman's Agreement,"* and most of all, *"To Kill a Mockingbird"*. Marlon's rare interviews of that era would speak neither to the professional nor the personal - Only to the political and the philosophical, as I've covered a bit earlier. He'd ask interviewers like Connie Chung or Larry King to recognize social injustices, as well as investigate their own compromised souls, to ponder their own journalistic reasons for asking questions he felt were pointless and trivial. Reading Greg's *NYT* interview a year after his passing, I somehow felt that Greg died with no regrets about his family, his friendships and his relationships - Only possible regrets regarding his work. Of course he never got over the suicide of his son, Jonathan, but when it came to being the good person that he was to others, I think Greg knew he had done well.

By the end, Marlon, on the other hand, felt that he wanted to reach out and make amends to those who felt they had been mistreated or misunderstood by the great actor. But by the time he was facing these thoughts, it was becoming too late. The last time I saw Marlon was on his final birthday, and he was a very different person.

The backstory leading up to that birthday gathering: from the early 90's up into 2004, together and separately, Avra and I had many adventures, misadventures and projects with Marlon. (Of course, Avra's relationship with him went back even further.) Together, we all had some big moments and even bigger transitions: Avra, who had known Marlon since her childhood, had now become a valued family member during Cheyenne's many tragedies. I convinced him to do *"Don Juan DeMarco"*. Avra suffered the crazy Australian shoot of *"The Island of Dr. Moreau"*. I wrote, Executive Produced and struggled with his final starring role in *"Free Money"*. Avra helped Robert De Niro wrangle Marlon on *"The Score"*. Avra and I were there as Marlon made himself sick enough to duck out of *"Scary Movie 2"* while he was already on the set. The epic, insane CBS project with Les Moonves and CAA. Avra and Molly in NYC on 9/11 with Marlon for the Michael Jackson concert. And of course, the sprawling, multi-layered, many bizarre chapters of *"Lying For a Living"*. There were so many ups, downs, lateral moves and changes, and as Molly was born within that time, our lives with Marlon would come and go in waves. Marlon was high maintenance, and when you have a new baby, well, time is time. I was still writing with Tony, and I was also constantly taking other writing work, as well as doing more video editing, illustration, acting and directing work, knowing that Marlon was not my firm source of income, even with feature films like *"Free Money"* and his acting tapes to work on.

Avra, while still an ongoing member of Marlon's staff, would often take time away from Mulholland, for our daughter's sake, and, as all things regarding Brando, to get a break from Marlon. It was also within this time that Molly was diagnosed with severe autism, something that turned our world upside-down. I went into the steady work of reality TV, as Avra went into the steady work of getting our daughter to as many therapies as we could afford - everyday, every hour; as much as Molly could stand and as many as we could pay for, with many of our early intervention therapists getting more than seventy-five dollars an hour. In short: it was a dark and expensive time for us. We'd eventually lose our twice-mortgaged house over it all. This occurred as Marlon was getting sicker, and those who cleaned his house and cooked for him decided to fully move into the Mulholland estate, closing off many visitors and "outsiders" in the process.

So, it seemed that there started to be a "shut down" at Mulholland as Avra and I were dealing with Molly. Soon, Avra was not working at Marlon's at all. And Marlon was not on the phone as often. Information about his health seemed more difficult to obtain. We knew he was on an oxygen tank by April of 2004, but when we'd have an occasional phone conversation, he'd joke about getting back on his feet and getting back into "fighting" shape. To keep my new job of producing and writing reality shows, I drove a collective three hours a day to Ojai, where the editor of the shows lived and worked. Again, these were difficult times, as money was scarce, our home was hanging by a financial thread, our daughter was in a constant state of tantrum, and both Avra and I knew that Marlon might be a lot sicker than his housekeeper was telling us.

Working on a Saturday up in Ojai, Avra called from our Burbank home and asked if I could come back early enough to go see Marlon before nightfall; today was his 80th birthday, and she was determined to give him a gift and a card, even if the housekeeper was making it difficult for us to see him. From the way Avra was talking, I did start to feel that this might be the last time we'd see Marlon. By the time I got home, it was clear that Avra had spent quite a day with Molly. This was a very difficult set of years for our daughter - her tantrums, fits and crying sessions could go on for hours. Avra was always so good, so patient and so understanding with Molly, dealing with the impossible on an hourly basis. In turn, I believe Avra felt sorry for me, working 24/7, spending much of my day sitting on the freeway, and together, drifting apart - becoming what parents of other autistic children predicted we would become: a totally independent constant provider living with a totally independent constant caregiver.

As Avra, Molly and I drove up Mulholland, she said we needed to stop at a pharmacy or gift shop - She had a present for Marlon, but she did not find time in the day to get a card for him. I don't recall the gift that year, but she always got him some small thing that never failed to connect; just the right book, just the right CD or small magic trick - whatever it was, she knew him so well and he clearly trusted her taste, intellect and gift-giving. Traffic-wise, we ended up running into an over-priced pharmacy for the card, the drug store up at the Beverly Glen center, a swanky little strip mall of sorts for the wealthy and elite off Mulholland in the Hollywood Hills.

Within the small selection of the store, the only card we could find was a schmaltzy, overly glittered pink missive about fully sincere "Undying Love" and "Eternal Appreciation". It was a far cry from the usually comedic "Fart Joke"-style cards we had always given him - The kind of crude humor cards he had always loved.

Getting back in the car, I laughed, "He's gonna ridicule us to the skies for this card!"

Always the truth-teller with the correct thing to say, Avra threw the car into drive as she muttered, "Let's hope so." I totally got her meaning. If Marlon is still hanging in there (health-wise) as "Marlon", he'll read that card, put his hands to his cheeks and rapidly bat his eyes like a cartoon "Sweet" Mary Pickford, letting us know what corn this birthday greeting was. Any other response? Who knows? That would mean that we had no idea of what kind of shape he's in.

Arriving, it definitely felt as though the housekeeper and her family did not want us there. She had moved her family into the main Mulholland house and she had changed the code on the main gate. Avra called up to her and said we were here, wanting to wish Marlon a happy birthday. After a tangle of clear reluctance and near argument, the housekeeper buzzed us in and we drove up to the house. Getting out of the car, I first poked my head into the parking lot office, the space where I had spent so many months editing *"Lying For a Living"*. The offices were overrun with bugs and in complete shambles; it looked like an absolute crime scene.

Making our way into the main house where we had been thousands of times before, it was a scene straight out of *"Grey Gardens,"* with the kitchen and the living room mirroring what I saw in the offices. The housekeeper we were once quite friendly with came to us with a shrugged greeting that was far from welcoming. She said that Marlon was probably sleeping and if we had any gifts or cards to leave for him, it would be best if we just put the stuff on the kitchen counter and then saw ourselves out. From a distance, Avra heard Marlon groan a confused noise from his bedroom; it sounded a lot like "Avra?" Almost immediately in tears already, Avra shouted "Marlon?!" as she zipped past the housekeeper and went to Marlon's bedside. I stayed with Molly outside the bedroom, wanting to give Avra a moment with Marlon; it was clear and it was thick in the air: things were not good. When I heard Marlon ask, "Where's Joe?" I felt it was a good time to go see Marlon. Holding Molly by the hand, I turned the corner through the doorway to see things I hadn't seen around Marlon before: rails on the bed he was on, a wheelchair nearby and oxygen tubes that ran from a tank to Marlon's nose.

Avra and I shared a quick glance, both looking away from one another, as we knew that we were both about to cry. I took Marlon's hand, trying to shape a lean-in hug from this now frail, unwashed and fragile man - a man I knew for years as the strongest, most dynamic lion I had ever met. At this moment, he was thin, pale and not fully mobile. But there was still some "Marlon" there; trying to be joking, attempting to be sarcastic and looking for a laugh as we shared a brief chat; a few words that kinda just hung there in a knowing, chilled atmosphere.

After more awkward small talk and moments of fighting tears - on everybody's part - Marlon decided to open his present and card. He went for the card first. Avra and I looked at each other and struggled to find our first smiles since arriving, feeling - perhaps trying to *will* into reality, that sarcastic Marlon would let us have it for our sappy card. As Marlon read the card to himself, he started to cry. I was so hoping he was pulling a well-acted gag, something he was so good at doing. But no, he was moved. Avra had to look away; she went to pick up Molly as a distraction as Marlon and I looked at one another. He put his hand to his heart and nodded, feeling that those words about undying love and eternal appreciation were written especially from us to him - and at that place in time, those words were exactly that. The moment made me reevaluate every bad or dismissive thought I had ever had about the entire Hallmark company and their subsidiaries. I had to touch Marlon's hand again. We both smiled.

A few moments later after the present was open, it was clear that Marlon was tired and that the housekeeper wanted us out of there. It was also clear that Avra was barely hanging on and that her fragile state was getting to both Molly and Marlon.

I suggested that we go.

Almost as though to end the pain she was clearly going through, Avra agreed.

She gave Marlon a long kiss on the forehead, tearfully picked up Molly and left the room.

I went to Marlon for one last time. He still had that card next to him. He again motioned to the card, put his hand to his heart and gave me a nod.

I touched his face, careful with those oxygen tubes, feeling that he badly needed a shave.

We both smiled as he closed his eyes for the night.

I turned and left the room, somewhat certain that I might not be seeing Marlon again.

As Avra, Molly and I arrived at the car out in the Mulholland estate parking lot, I could see that Avra was too upset to drive. I got behind the wheel as she got into the backseat and held Molly in her arms. I had a flashback of leaving Greg's estate with Avra and Molly - leaving Greg's estate for the final time. I had that same feeling; I felt that I was now saying goodbye to this bizarre, elaborate, yet strangely comfortable place. Inch by inch, it was the embodiment of Marlon - Every unorthodox design, every unconventional space and every stalk of bamboo.

We passed Jack's driveway. A mile down the road, we passed that opulent home where we had shared that singular evening with Warren and Annette; we were passing that home here on the *"Bad Boy Drive"* stretch of Mulholland. I was thinking, "Beatty can no longer be a member of the 'Bad Boy' club. Hang in there, Marlon - If you go, there's no way Nicholson can represent all that debauchery on his own." I then thought of a wonderful quote I had read from Marlon:

"People ask a lot, they say, 'What did you do while you took time out?' - as if the rest of my life is taking time out. But the fact is, making movies is time out for me because the rest, the nearly complete whole, is what's real for me. I'm not an actor and haven't been for years. I'm a human being - hopefully a concerned and somewhat intelligent one - who occasionally acts."

Thinking of that as we drove home that night from Marlon's, I was hoping that he would get some rest, while I was also hoping - hope against hope - that maybe in the future, he could take some "time out" to perhaps, possibly, do some acting once more.

Because whether he would ever admit it, those who knew him knew: he really did love acting.

SUMMER IN THE VALLEY (2004)

To fully explain some previously mentioned (yet now needed) facts: by 2004, with my three-year-old daughter diagnosed with severe autism, I knew I needed *only* steady, constant work, not the "Maybe" and "If" freelance work of feature filmmaking or network television that I had been doing since '83. In short, this is when I got *fully* into the less-paying but far-more-steady world of the then-just-arriving "reality" TV. My brilliant cousin Bud was an incredible salesman who was then breaking into that new realm of broadcasting; "new," as all those basic cable "networks" were pretty much young, confused and dependent on adventurous trailblazers like Bud, innovators who were figuring out how to do competitive programming on little or no budget - or unions.

And think about it: if you weren't there, try and picture it all: so many of these small half-assed wannabe "networks" popped up at the same time with nothing to show, not really having a clue as to who was going to make all this yet-to-be-invented non-union television. My friends in scripted union TV and film were absolutely laughing at basic cable, saying they should just stick to showing old *"Andy Griffith"* reruns, wanting no part of this nickel-and-dime amateur hour. But there was another big thing happening in media at that very same time: home video rental. People would wait around the block on a Friday or Saturday night at "Blockbuster" or "Sam Goody" just to get a VHS tape to take home. Home video was so popular, it spawned many "Direct-to-Video" features within the same rental stores. Those were mostly independent or Hollywood feature films that couldn't get theatrical distribution. Tony and I made a couple of these features.

This arm of home video became big enough to spawn VHS tapes that weren't just non-theatrical films - there were also tapes that were specializing in "topics" and not "stories" - topics such as guns, military history, cooking, line dancing, and anything you could think of. And of course, much of this type of low-rent, just-grab-a-camera production had a certain budgetary relationship to what may have been the biggest driver of home video at the time: pornography. In short: there was a lot to get at your local VHS video rental store just as basic cable was arriving.

But going back to those gun, military and line dancing tapes; that's the stuff that my cousin was making and getting into those video rental stores, right alongside major studio films. On some of his videos, I pitched-in as a director and writer. So when basic cable networks needed low-cost shows and real Hollywood was laughing in their faces, Bud was in the right place at the right time. He crossed over from home video to basic cable, becoming one of the first producers to get newly made "original" shows on The History Channel, The Learning Channel and others.

Creatively, Bud gave a great deal of leeway to his incredibly talented friend and editor, Steve Beebe, as well as to me. Together, Bud, Steve and I created the early TLC car TV hit, *"Rides,"* and this led to the long-running automotive makeover show, *"Overhaulin'".* It was a helluva difficult show to do. Early on, all three of us were directing, producing and writing the show, epic episode after epic episode. All to Bud's credit, he figured out how to finance and manage such a unique adventure; Steve first gave it shape and flair, and I was the original sleep-deprived director who actually stood there with my camera crew every night for 8 days in a row, watching automotive-master Chip Foose make a show car out of a junker. I also wrote for and directed our great hosts, Courtney Hansen and Chris Jacobs, dear friends today that Bud and I first plucked from the herds of all those many pretty people who auditioned for days when the show was born.

Months after *"Overhaulin'"* was on its feet, Marlon left a phone message about how I should come up to the house, so he and I could try to finally figure out *"Lying For a Living".* He had tried one last go of it with George Englund, but that went pear-shaped. His message included his condolences about Molly's diagnosis - something he had already discussed with me months ago. At this time, I hadn't seen him since that sad evening of his birthday. As he was that night, he sounded old and tired on the phone. I wanted to return his call, but the schedules of *"Rides"* and *"Overhaulin'"* kept me insanely busy, seven days a week. As stated earlier, I wasn't seeing a lot of Marlon after Molly's diagnosis. Neither was Avra. I felt Marlon thought that Avra and I were angry over how things had ended with *"Lying For a Living,"* when he told us one day that our work was done, not long after that evening with Warren Beatty. Marlon thought we were angry.

It wasn't anger - Avra and I both understood when Marlon had eventually spent too much money trying to make his acting tapes into something he'd be happy to market. His accountant warned him: he couldn't keep Avra and Joe working on the project endlessly. Of course we understood. But right after we were both done with *"Lying For a Living"* up at Mulholland, that is when we learned shortly thereafter that our infant daughter was never going to have an independent or "normal" life. I believe any parent in our position can tell you: for years after that first diagnosis, you feel like you're going through a series of funerals each and every day. So regarding Marlon at that moment: we had no time. Avra and I were told that the only hope for any sort of future for Molly was early intervention. To reemphasize and underline previous thoughts: this is a world of constant therapy, constant activity and constant spending. This made Avra a now-lifetime tireless caregiver and made me into a constantly working earner. In short: we really had no time or energy for high maintenance Marlon at that moment. And we certainly were not going to spend time battling his door-blocking housekeeper every time we wanted the opportunity to see him. We loved him, but we were in a tailspin and it was all about our love for our daughter.

So - on a day when I was directing a crucial episode of *"Overhaulin'"* - Oh, for those who might not know, here's the deal: the original *"Overhaulin'"* was a Learning Channel show where a beloved old junker car is "stolen" from an unsuspecting owner, and days later, that shocked owner gets an epic "reveal" - The car is returned as a beautiful, super-cool made-over ride. As wobbly as the first episodes were, the show was an immediate hit. The family of the car owner always secretly worked with us as "Insiders," telling Chip Foose what the car owner wants in a remake and guiding the clueless owner through the "sad" week of his or her "stolen" car. As insane as that kind of automotive build was in the short span of a week, often, remaking the car was not even the hardest part of the show. With all that "stealing" and "revealing" involved, each episode was also a tangle of hidden camera pranks, heists and fakery. Bud and I were quite audacious when the show was just starting, impersonating police officers, pulling off high-wire stunts and doing all we could to make sure that the car-owning "mark" never saw us coming.

Our first African-American mark had a 1970 Monte Carlo that Foose made into a beauty. I remember so much of that episode because Bud and I were at odds over how to "reveal" the car. We were always trying to do something different and clever, and sometimes, we had "gags" where the owner would be tipped-off as to the whereabouts of said "stolen" car. However the Monte Carlo reveal was going to go, we were by then already successful enough to have actual police officers in on the act. In one of the first proposals for the "reveal" for this episode, the mark was going to be "wrongly arrested" as he was going to pick up his now-located "stolen" car; he'd be handcuffed and detained, until the whole surprise would be revealed.

While the goal of the final "prank" was to always first create a true state of actual anger, confusion or even sadness (of "The Mark" (owner) just before the reveal, to *then* get a 180 degree whipsaw euphoric reaction to the unveiling of the remade car), I had strong doubts about this one. As I watched Bud and the real cops explain the "fake arrest and handcuffing" to the African-American mark's family, I saw they were quite uncomfortable with the whole thing.

Yes, the owner was about to get his "stolen" junker returned as a beautiful Foose show car, but for moments - far too many moments - there would be a reality here: a black man was actually going to believe that he really was being wrongly accused, arrested and cuffed by a pair of actual cops. After some debate, we decided that the mark's friend, one of our "insiders" would be the one "wrongly arrested" - this insider would know what we were doing; he'd arrive with the mark; the mark would witness this "arrest" just before getting his car. But however it all got sorted out, just in time as the mark was arriving, I was tired, frustrated and not happy to be arguing about all this, especially after many sleepless nights filming the makeover of the car.

There were other arguments that day as well, as there often were on this tense, multi-layered and complicated "Reveal Day" set. However it worked out, I was stressed out, getting call after call on my cell phone just as we were finally shooting the fragile reveal, keeping my ringer on mute with the phone in my pocket as I focused hard on the camera monitors that showed our "prank," our "mark" and his response to his remade car. Back then on these early *"Overhaulin'"* episodes, it was almost like a live show, in that you only got one shot at fooling the mark, surprising him or her, and then getting that actual response when the beautiful car is first seen.

Once the series was a certified institution, about a season or two later, we'd figure out many different ways to break up the reveal, keep it organic and still have actual responses for the video shoot. But at this earlier stage, we were still producing it in a much more compressed, actual, pressurized and "live" way. And it worked well, giving TLC and our audience a very unique and rare "legit" show; you'd watch it and know this "prank," surprise and makeover was all on the level - unlike a great deal of obviously phony reality TV trash (then and still now) on basic cable.

That evening, once we finally had our reveal, our celebration footage and everything else we needed in the can, I checked my cell phone, to see that Avra had tried to call dozens of times. This was unlike her, and as a father and a husband, I suddenly became terrified. I called back and was relieved when she answered immediately.

But my relief vanished as she quickly and tearfully told me, "Marlon died."

I guess I wasn't shocked. And I suppose I had been expecting this call for a while now; the last time I saw him was that night on his birthday, when he was hooked to an oxygen tank and had hospital rails mounted on his bed. Still, I was shattered to hear it. For the last 14 years of my life, he was such a constant presence, such a true force, and more often than I appreciated, such an absolute joy - even when he wasn't. As I told Avra that I had to take care of more production business before getting home, she told me she was being asked to attend a meeting tomorrow regarding Marlon's estate. I was surprised to hear that; she was surprised by that as well.

I told Avra: with all that I had to take care of on this wrap day on the *"Overhaulin'"* set, I'd probably be getting home a bit late. And tomorrow morning, I'd be leaving early; Bud, Steve and I were currently finishing an episode of *"Rides,"* a show I'd write and we'd put together up at Steve's edit bay in Ojai. After telling Avra that I'd try to get home as soon as I could, I hung up, watching the continuing party of crew, "insiders," "mark" and others all still marveling over a reborn Chip Foose Monte Carlo.

I stared, but my vision blurred into a series of thoughts. My mind immediately wandered. I was so sad to have lost my friend, a true artist, but in line with that, my own situation of that exact moment hit me hard. I trained and came to this town to work with legends like Marlon and Greg; not to struggle to get fake "drama" out of the painting of a car. I was struck with many thoughts about how I so hated this new form of crooked "storytelling" unfolding before me, this thing called "Reality TV" - No, I knew we all couldn't get to make *"A Streetcar Named Desire"* or *"The Godfather,"* but I thought about how this new form of "Cheap TV" was Neither-Nor; it had none of the truth of real documentary, none of the art of true storytelling; you could feel the lowness of it from the first shows made for basic cable, and trust me, those of us there back when it was all being created; we could actually smell the danger of it all from the first phony moment. We who came from real film and TV asked so many of the early questions: What's real here? What happens when an audience believes *this* but it's really *that*? Yes, let's jump *way* ahead here: would there have been a Trump presidency without *"The Apprentice"*? Over a decade of selling America a totally phony view of a total phony? Of course, without years and years of that shit, he *never* would've been in a "popular" position to win three swing states and then nearly kill democracy. Of course, obviously, my mind never could've gone that far into that type of future on that day, but my bitterness was there to be sure. Marlon was an artist - at storytelling.

So, I shifted my thoughts even more as I stood there that evening after hearing about Marlon. I thought back, to the wonderful day on *"Free Money"* a few years past, to that moment when I was in Montreal with Marlon and 10 giant film cameras were there to capture a "One Take" scene: Charlie Sheen's character, responsible for crashing an actual locomotive into a beautiful truck owned by the character played by Marlon Brando, in his final starring film role. And all this was happening that day because Tony Peck and I took some blank paper and created this wild scene. As storytellers. And it happened because a great artist agreed to star in our story.

Then I snapped back to present reality, directing a car makeover show for basic cable. I reminded myself: I was lucky to be earning - for Avra and Molly. That made me smile as I thought of an "Industry" joke Marlon told me a few times; he'd often repeat jokes and he liked this one a lot:

The Joke: A guy who was once a great movie star; he was now older, totally washed-up, mopping up filth and worse off the sticky floor of a dank strip club. When this man griped about his horrible situation and the history of his professional demise to some perverted, masturbating patron of the club, the jerking customer asked this janitor, "Why don't you quit this shitty job?" Halting his mopping for a moment, the former star answered, "What? And leave show business?"

TENTH CHAPTER OF TIME
(GREG & MARLON ESSAY X)

Unlike Greg's epic, definitive, and yes, literally famous funeral and memorial service, Marlon's series of farewells were, well - They were a bit like Marlon. While there was a quiet family gathering, there was also the sprinkling of ashes here, the throwing of ashes over there, some for Tahiti, some to places unknown. A few people had celebrity-packed gatherings where many seemed to be fighting to be the Designated Most-Grieving Widow. I was at one up at Mike Medavoy's house where the all-star cast of *"Meet the Fockers"* walked in together; maybe they all car pooled from the set that day? One small gathering I recall quite fondly; just a few of us, perhaps six, up at Yachio Tsubaki's home. I sat next to Sean Penn. We shared some of our best Marlon tales - there were so many. At one particular moment after we were both laughing hard over something Marlon had said, it quickly got quiet. I looked at Penn. He had tears in his eyes. I could barely hear him when he struggled to say, "To've known him; God, we were so lucky."

Sean was so right. After Marlon's passing, Avra was named as a Brando estate executor, in charge of keeping the image of Marlon alive. At the same time, Tony and the Peck family were only a few months into this same type of business regarding Greg, his estate, and his lasting "Image," for future audiences who will only know these men by way of films, photos and products.

The ongoing legacy of any deceased artist in this modern age is as mysterious and hard to predict as any aspect of their career. When I was young, revival movie theaters were just getting started in major cities. By way of this, I remember reading back then that Humphrey Bogart and W.C. Fields were becoming more popular than they ever were during their active, live careers. TV reruns, merchandising that catches fire, a renaissance of old ideas - There's really no way to know what will last, what will sustain or what will fade into the darkness with the ethers.

Today, Avra and Tony deal with these things on a daily basis. Greg left behind a legacy of dignity, grace and respect, and he also left behind a family that knows how to preserve all that in style; the Peck family represents Greg's career and interests in a number of ways throughout any given year, through film anniversaries, posthumous honors and occasional merchandising; one of the top sellers in the Oliver Peoples line of eyewear is the "Gregory Peck" set of frames, based on the glasses Greg wore in TKAM. Huntsman suits also promotes with Greg's image. Aside from these high-end specialty items, Greg is understandably a tough sell in the world of mass merchandising, a world where "The Three Stooges" are far easier to hawk than Atticus Finch. Both Greg and Marlon fall into a category that is perhaps far too esoteric for the crowd buying souvenirs on Hollywood boulevard. Running Marlon's estate, I see Avra deal with such matters on a constant basis - Marlon himself knew those limitations as well. As I've mentioned so often, when I was putting together his *"Lying For a Living"* tapes, he constantly wanted to make sure that I was not gearing the edit for "Acting Students" only; he'd watch a rough cut and grumble, "This isn't for Juilliard students; it's for every liar out there with a working credit card."

Today, putting aside the unique and complicated success of South Seas hotelier Dick Bailey's "The Brando" resort in Tahiti (a mega-high-end licensing deal with a number of international moving parts), Avra and the estate have found that the "marketing" of Marlon's legacy is often something of a challenge. Avra and her commercial teams have learned that the primal, most basic images of Marlon are the most - of course - duh - marketable. *"The Wild One," "The Godfather"* (which Paramount fully owns and controls) - This is how people want their "Brando" in the commercial world today - simplified, impactful and easy to figure out at a glance.

This theory is certainly understandable when you see Marilyn Monroe in the *"Seven Year Itch"* white dress (over the wind off the subway grate; fully risqué and yet fully innocent at the exact same moment - Skirt-up, she's exposing herself, but it's not her doing!), or when you see James Dean standing there in the red "*Rebel Without a Cause*" jacket. Think about that! Only three major films to his name and that *one* uncomplicated image still excites kids who have never even seen a Dean film in their life. Like that popular image of Che Guevara that thrilled so many young people in years past: very few probably knew the actual history, but it seems that youth can easily smell, spot and respond to "rebellion" when they see it, sense it or are peer-pressured into it. Of course, context of a star or one of their roles is everything when it comes to marketing, legacy and lasting appeal. John Wayne made films wearing WWII and Vietnam-era uniforms, historic non-western wear and even a cop or detective's suit and tie. Nobody really cares about seeing him in any of those outfits today. But display him with that tall cowboy hat, vest, neck scarf, rifle and boots - Man, you can sell anything to certain audiences - cook books, posters - even throw pillows. That "Duke" image resonates with more than a few people, and especially with emotionally attached Wayne fans who buy items such as those I listed above.

Perhaps an even better example of context: "Lucy"- I've come to the obvious conclusion that audiences, consumers and just the flat-out public today - They care far more about "Lucy Ricardo" than they ever cared about Lucille Ball - It's as though Lucy in color is a whole other thing; fans would rather see their favorite redhead in black and white. Probably the same with Jackie Gleason and Ralph Kramden - Of course, those characters, especially on constantly re-running TV shows, make huge and lasting impressions with people. Those from comedy and music have different "legacies" than those who brought forth primarily "drama" - artists such as Marlon and Greg. But given those limitations, time will certainly march on to show Greg standing in that courtroom with his Atticus glasses; a dated black and while image that probably only speaks to those who know the nuance, emotion and dignity of TKAM. And even those people will grow confused; I know fans of the film who seem to forget that he *lost* the case. Of course, that error speaks to the mythology that Greg alone created within the role. People see him standing there in that courtroom, and they see a victorious hero. Greg has many contemporaries who are both legendary and yet nearly forgotten or ignored by many. Some would say it's ridiculous to think James Stewart, Cary Grant or others of that ilk could ever fully fade away, but as I follow the legacies of Greg and Marlon today, I understand more and more about what it takes to make stars of their magnitude resonate into the future.

I'm sure that some reading here feel there's an apples and oranges set of comparisons when it comes to remembering the great performances of Greg and Marlon and whether or not their faces appear on enough Hollywood souvenirs one day. It is indeed a confusing mix of equations, and as I've learned when studying their careers along with the world of film itself, there are no real rules, reasons or even set expectations within all this. Perhaps I ask these questions because I grew up with Greg and Marlon being *names* as big as any I knew in any history books, news stories or pop culture events. Then I was so very lucky to know them both well. I was there when they passed away, and frankly, I had a hard time thinking of a world without them, both as legendary figures and as friends. I watched both my wife and my best friend go though transitions that are hard to face - Tony lost his father. Avra, only after Marlon's passing, learned that she was the sole "Family Member" in his eyes to be in charge of his permanent legacy.

It seemed that Marlon changed his will, post-life plans and estate matters a number of times. I sensed this because twice, he asked me to come to the house and officially "witness" some form of notarizing that was going on regarding all this. I never knew what he was signing or changing, but when the notary then needed my "witness" signature on some document, I knew that this was all some form of official legal proceeding. One thing I did learn by my presence: I myself was not part of any of Marlon's post-life plan - One cannot be the notarizing witness while also being in the will or in the estate plan; at least that's what the notary told me on one of these occasions. Hearing that, I shrugged, having two thoughts on that: given Marlon's large family, complicated life and bizarre orbit, I never expected to be any remote part of the Brando world post-Marlon. My second thought: I truly had immediate and sincere pity for those who would be enlisted for any of that. Between his children, ex-girlfriends, business associates and extended entourage, I could only imagine the green-envy free-for-all that would explode - from Los Angeles to Tahiti and beyond - once Marlon was gone. In fact, one of Marlon's old ex-girlfriends (who did odd jobs at the house now and then) contacted me after she had learned that I attended those notary "witness" signings - She had executed that very job a couple times for Marlon up at the house; she was now thrilled that she was not again asked, thinking that perhaps *my* witnessing work meant something good for her: *now* (she hoped) she was either in his ever-changing will or she was destined to be some part of his ever-changing estate. When Marlon died, much to her disappointment, she was part of neither scenario.

As I've fully established throughout these pages, artists like Greg and Marlon were complete and fully operational businesses onto themselves; certainly not the most "typical" of businesses, but absolute well-known products for decades. They were individuals who earned what some fully-staffed businesses could not earn within the same fiscal year. That of course is why their lives were so rarified, unique and, at times, flat-out strange. Of course, this is how it is with any major star, especially today, in this age of multi-million dollar salaries and extremely lucrative Hollywood deals. For the years that I knew Greg, an efficient, cheery woman named Victoria ran many of the matters up at the Carolwood house, especially when it came to Greg's business matters, correspondence and day-to-day bookkeeping. It seemed that she was no boss of any kind, but she represented the family well and she seemed expert when it came to doing what Greg and Veronique wanted and needed done. She was the kind of office worker who made and filed multiple copies of valuable documents, choreographed the maintenance on the vast property and did it all in a smiling and well-dressed fashion. I liked Victoria a great deal.

In turn, Marlon's Mulholland office was quite another story. When Avra was asked to be a permanent part of the "company," the operation was staffed by an odd mix of old girlfriends (of Marlon's), young secretaries who came and went, and Carlos, a handyman who had been up at the Mulholland home for quite a while. Avra knew all these people well, having been friends of both Marlon and his children for years. To clarify further as I come to so many conclusions here within these recollections, her real and permanent job started after she and Marlon returned from overseas, following the somewhat unsuccessful plan to keep Cheyenne hidden from the world following the murder. It was a sad and somewhat haunted Mulholland house that Avra was walking into when she returned from the Cheyenne caper in Orleans, France. And as Avra and I were living together in Westwood at the time, I recall how troubled Avra seemed as she would come home each night, dealing with all of the darkness, depression and gloom that was still up on Mulholland thanks to that fateful trigger pulled by Christian Brando. The "office" itself was that bungalow I've written about so much, that building out in the parking area, a multipurpose structure that had a couple main office spaces connected by a bathroom. The odd building often seemed to be visited by ants, and every new person hired to work there (and there were many) felt determined to "finally organize" decades of legal documents, letters, photos, screenplays and most of all, random miscellaneous papers. For many years, before Avra was there, Marlon had a well-known secretary, Alice Marshak. This was during the time when Marlon led a huge and always-busy life; major agents, studio heads and movie stars always knew that they had to deal with Alice if they were going to be working with Marlon.

During those heady years of the 60's and 70's, when Alice was actually a published author herself due to being Marlon Brando's "Super" secretary, nobody - and I mean nobody - could've pictured a world where, one day, anybody would ask, "'Gregory' who? 'Marlon' who?" I think back on the Mulholland office and the Carolwood office as the "Headquarters" that held the keys to the kingdoms; multimillion dollar projects that could either stop or move forward based on a "yes" or a "no" from Marlon or Greg. While it's great that today there's a profitable "Brando" hotel in Tahiti and a successful "Gregory Peck" line of eyewear, there's so much more to their legacies. With the studios then and now getting so many of the actual film profits, while the power of the original filmmaking was often out of their hands, both Greg and Marlon knew that more often than not, they had indeed become products for hire, and they constantly fought so many of the forces that made that so. As they were leaving this Earth, they both knew that their families should indeed do what they could to keep their voices, images and thoughts alive. Not just for the merchandising profits, but also for the filmed stories they worked so hard to tell.

A final bit about these men and what they left behind: During the years when I was seeing both of them on a steady basis, I learned to not bring up Marlon in front of Greg, to avoid an eye-roll, a groan and the rest of it. But during one of the last outdoor patio lunches I had with Greg, Veronique *did* bring him up: "So, Joe, how is Marlon?" As a shot at me, Greg chuckled, "Yes, let us hear directly from Brando's biographer." I laughed back, "No, I'm gonna be *your* biographer." Having finished lunch, Greg stood. While going into the house, he growled, "Joe, don't you even joke about that." Oh, and about that house; Marlon's also: you could not have known those guys without knowing them in their homes; that was simple logistics. After their deaths, when I heard both homes were demolished, I felt *such* a loss. Jack Nicholson bought Marlon's lot and leveled the house. And in the "Small World" category, one of my father-in-law's soap opera bosses bought a home next to Greg, then bought Greg's, leveling the house for acreage.

The Carolwood house and the Mulholland house *were* these men - Perfectly and privately so.

THOSE "FINAL" ROLES:
THE DOCTOR & THE SWEDE

There are many great moments featuring Greg in his daughter's wonderful documentary, *"A Conversation with Gregory Peck,"* a 1999 preservation of his touring stage talks with audiences, combined with a great deal of additional footage that looks into Greg's life, particularly his private days after the movies. Cecilia Peck put the project together with famed documentarian Barbara Kopple. I recall one scene that I felt so embodied Greg, just as it gave indication as to the world his family was fortunate enough to live in. In a telling docu-moment, Greg and Cecilia are in a New York park filming. They have a small dog (in a carry-bag) with them. A park worker approaches and says they can't be here with the dog; it's a violation of the park rules and they need to "comply". Away from the park worker, with a degree of both privilege and rebellion, Cecilia giggles to her father, "What if we *don't* comply?" Spoiled? Perhaps. But in Cecilia's defense - One: as the film's producer, she didn't care to lose a nice, quiet location like this park. Two: the tiny dog *was* in a small bag. And Three: her unquestionable lifetime auto-reflex: "I'm here with Gregory Peck." Whatever the case, Greg, looking at the put-upon park worker, led his daughter out of the park, sweetly assuring Cecilia, "He'll feel better if we comply."

Greg never lost his feelings or awareness for those who had jobs less rewarding or less glamorous than the job of being a film star. He saw a park worker who was given the thankless task of being on his feet all day, to monitor some grass, trees, stones and assorted bench-work. Greg also always thought ahead, probably thinking, "I don't care to have some park worker tell some press person, or anybody - that Gregory Peck is some kind of arrogant rule-breaking jerk."

Years later, Avra was a producer on a great documentary about Marlon that used all of his personal home recordings, interviews and even audio from his unreleased acting instruction tapes, *"Lying For a Living"*. The documentary, *"Listen to Me Marlon"* is in some ways the greatest Marlon Brando film ever made. It's his story told in his own words. I think of both Cecilia's *"Conversation"* film and *"Listen to Me Marlon"* as a pair of projects that are perfect representations of the men: *"Listen to Me Marlon"* is solitary, isolated, almost tragically lonely; it really is a man talking to himself, while *"Conversation"* is inviting, sharing - Family. But while these are great films, they are not the art of those men - In fact, let's face it, they only exist because of the skills Greg and Marlon brought to storytelling within film; they became great and loved actors; that's why we want to know more about their private lives - thus those documentaries.

Going through this whole set of "Greg/Marlon" comparisons, back and forth, this and that, one of the most solid personal facts for me boils down to this: Tony and I wrote the scripts that held the final starring roles for both of these legends: one script made the massive leap into becoming a film, the other did not. Greg's script did not become a film because Greg was Greg. Marlon's script became a film because Marlon was Marlon. That set of equations is far more complicated than you'll gather from an initial first glance.

The primary simplistic notions might be true but they're incomplete - Yes, Marlon was often impulsive, unpredictable and sometimes in need of money. Greg was cautious, selective and didn't need to work for the sake of his bank account. Given that, Greg also insisted that *"Doctor DeMott"* must be in good hands; we couldn't have gone higher on the food chain than Scorsese running the show. And when Marty brought in the likes of Sean Penn, Jim Sheriden, Martha Coolidge and Arthur Penn - all working off a story option from Ingmar Bergman himself - Greg knew this was a "real" project. But as the project lingered, and even that crew of professionals could not line up the adequate financing, Greg knew that settling for less might lead to an embarrassing disaster, one he'd rather not deal with at this stage of his life - and career.

The bigger the project, the more prestigious the project, the harder things can get in Hollywood. To be shaping a remake of Ingmar Bergman's *"Wild Strawberries"*? You don't want to look bad failing with that. And as other big names climb on board a project like this, they don't work for free; even their "Cut Rate for

'Art'" is a serious bit of money. Greg always had the clout to wrangle together a lower budgeted shoot of *"Doctor DeMott,"* but why would he want to do that? And as you read this, don't assume that Brando's name as *"DeMott"* could've been any easier - not that that was ever a consideration. But I mention it because some still have the assumption that Marlon Brando could've green-lit any film he got near. As I've explained all throughout this book, time and time again, that simply wasn't the case.

It's almost kind of funny how the film industry can end up spooking itself, especially in its eternal, positively schizophrenic chase between art-making and hit-making. A remake of an Ingmar Bergman film had many asking me "Why? It's a sacred classic! It's untouchable! Why?!" But an original comedy like *"Free Money"* is just that: an original comedy, written by a couple guys named Tony and Joe. The moment Avra, Tony and I got Marlon involved with it, it was an inverted version of the *"DeMott"* challenge, with some industry people feeling something lopsided about the whole affair - The Great Brando? Will participate in such comedic piffle?!

Yes, I knew with *"DeMott"* there was this daunting "Thing" under the shadow of Bergman, just as *"Free Money"* had this daunting "Thing" under the shadow of Brando in a contemporary comedy. Whatever those concerns were, whether they were sound or foolish, Marlon cared little about how he would be judged in a film such as *"Free Money,"* or whether it would truly be successful or not. Of course he worked hard on the picture, and of course he would've liked a commercial hit, but at the end of the shoot day, Marlon knew all that was out of his hands. Greg on the other hand, as star and producer, felt the pressure to make *"Doctor DeMott"* into a memorable, perhaps "Final Film" for himself; he had no want to make a cheap indie "TV-ish" feature out of it when big league financiers were turning out to be reluctant about the funding.

To elaborate more on this "producing" element between the two projects; *this* may illustrate the most dramatic differences between the men and those pictures: after obtaining the story option from Ingmar Bergman himself, Greg was more than just the star of *"Doctor DeMott"* - he was the Executive Producer and center of the entire operation. With *"Free Money,"* Marlon was a hired actor. Granted, once Marlon is your "hired actor" (as I've explained by way of my details of the film shoot) there's a lot more to it than that. But still, those positions tell a great deal of the story; a story of how one film got made and the other one did not.

Years before both of those projects, Greg and Marlon were "Big" enough to be handed producing titles - and even a directing title for Marlon - simply by acting in their films. I'm not saying they didn't earn the titles, but their status as superstars allowed them to become more than actors; Marlon was drafted-in to direct *"One-Eyed Jacks"* after Stanley Kubrick left the project. Greg produced alongside William Wyler *"The Big Country"* - on and on, picture after picture, in their prime, they were both so much more than performers. After those earlier projects, they both saw themselves as producers with production companies, doing what all artists do, fighting for more control of the final product. But by the 1990's, their careers, and the business, had changed.

As it turned out, Greg's role in *"The Portrait,"* the TV-movie version of the play *"Painting Churches"* would essentially be what one could realistically label as his final starring role, even though you can argue that the "story" firmly belongs to his character's daughter, wonderfully played by his own daughter, Cecilia. And given that situation, perhaps it was a perfect final outing for family man Greg, who more than likely did the project expressly for Cecilia. His role of Gardner Church was a man who was reaching an age where details in his mind were fading and time was running against him. His wife was played by longtime friend, Lauren Bacall.

As it was in Greg's life, Gardner had a near storybook marriage when judged on the merits of longevity, aging gracefully and love within the union. But it's the parenting that proves to be the hiccup, as an adult child starts to feel both the distance from her parents and the inevitability of their final years. To me, it's an elegant little story that frankly plays far better on stage with lesser-knowns rather than the in-your-face camera work attached to legendary names - along with the obvious nepotism casting, to boot. Don't get me wrong, *"The Portrait"* is a nice little film, but if you never felt the nuance and richness of the original off-Broadway stage production, you might watch the TV film and wonder how and why it ever got made.

The original New York stage version I saw of *"Painting Churches"* was the perfect union of weight, cast and intellect; the kind of near-chamber-piece-sized production that has you pondering it later, talking about it further and recommending it to your friends. Alas, that indeed *can* be the problem with any film version of stage material combined with movie stars; in this case, the epic presence of Peck and Bacall, along with Greg's real daughter. Now add the lack of that real-yet-unreal atmosphere that comes with an audience in a theater, replacing that with TV movie claustrophobia and "realistic" cuteness - Well, you probably get the vibe of my critique.

Having said all that, I'm certain that many might love the film for the very (opposite) reasons I've cited here: they've never seen the play, they loved seeing icons Greg and "Betty" together again, they loved that girl being Greg's real daughter, it's a good clean look at a good clean family that has just enough problems to be interesting - or perhaps, relatable, etc. Whatever the lingering reception today, I'm sure that someone will drill me with the possibility that *"The Portrait"* is still better received today than Marlon's farewell tour, my own *"Free Money"*. More on that in a moment. First, I'd like to think about what Greg's *"Doctor DeMott"* could've been.

Unlike *"The Portrait,"* *"DeMott"* clearly was an outright lead vehicle for Gregory Peck, that rare mass art film that dares to explore an imperfect man (with a respected facade) in his final years. Produced by Martin Scorsese and directed by Sean Penn, it could've been a successful, possibly important film, especially with that great cast we had that day at the reading. After a number of rewrites, I came around to the notion that Bergman's film was not a problem for us; it was simply a template that allowed us to explore the life, regrets and emotional journeys of an honored professor on one fateful yet seemingly uneventful road trip. When Ingmar Bergman first wrote to Greg about this being "The story of my father," I was as intimidated as any screenwriter would be. But through the rewrites, it became a story about Greg. As I learned more about Greg's challenging first marriage, and his son who committed suicide - These were far greater clues to the new script, greater than any books I read about Ingmar Bergman and his upbringing, books like his biography, *"The Magic Lantern".*

Of course, anyone can freely speculate about a "great" film that never got made, but few get to have the pieces, the players and the proven possibilities I saw in place during the long and ultimately unsuccessful journey of *"Doctor DeMott."*

As for Marlon's final starring role - Well, I've probably talked enough within these pages about "The Swede" and *"Free Money"* - It's still a fun little film that surprises those who stumble onto it to this very day. It's a unique country lark that aspired to be not much more than a series of laughs, some adventure, a victory for the good guys who learn along the way, a punishment for the bad guy who earns his ultimate lot in life, and in the end, a happy filming experience for a friend I loved dearly. As you'll recall, Marlon left the set giddy, convinced of a sequel. Well, it certainly wasn't the first or last time that Marlon would be totally wrong about something.

Look, as far as this "Final Starring Role" thing goes, here's the deal: these men could not have engineered their cinematic "Farewell" any more than they could've planned their first big hits or those few films they're still known for today. I fully understand when Sean Penn was dying to see Brando "go out" with something as potentially "respected" as a film version of Gabriel Garcia Marquez's *"One Hundred Years of Solitude"* - I get it. But in high-priced, ever-changing Hollywood, things rarely ever play out the way a beautiful screenplay might like to propose.

I was a 16-year-old film fanatic when I sat through *"The Shootist"* in a Brainerd, Minnesota movie theater. It was John Wayne's final film, a movie that had all the markings of a "Final Film" - Big stars showed up in some of the smallest roles, there was an entire "Good-bye" atmosphere (regarding Wayne) to the production and story, and of course off screen, people had read about John

Wayne's deteriorating health for many years. I saw it for the very reasons I always try to catch the final episode of a TV series - even if I don't watch the series - I can sense the personal and human elements attached, both in front of and behind the cameras.

As far as choreographed swan songs go, it would be hard to do better than *"The Shootist"*. Was it the pinnacle for Wayne? Over *"The Searchers"*? *"Red River"*? *"True Grit"*? *"Rio Bravo"*? *"The Quiet Man"*? Not even close to those great films. But here I was at 16; NOT a John Wayne fan, certainly not a fan of his politics, not a fan of traditional westerns - but I was moved, leaving the theater with an unexpected tear, along with a strong feeling that that was the last of John Wayne.

For Greg, *"The Portrait"* in no way diminishes *"To Kill a Mockingbird"* or *"Roman Holiday"*. *"Free Money"* will do little to dilute the impact of *"The Godfather"* tomorrow. Or *"On the Waterfront"*. Or *"A Streetcar Named Desire"*. You get the idea.

See, that's one of the odd things that often frustrates Hollywood and those who follow it: the artists who give us the best of structured, scripted, art directed, choreographed and produced "Hollywood" - They're rarely able to give us - or themselves - a true "Hollywood" ending.

THE ENDING

I saved this story for last. I felt it so embodies Greg, Marlon and my involvement in their lives, thanks to Avra and Tony.

Having a creative partner and friend like Tony, and having watched years of my wife dealing with Marlon's many children gives me a unique perspective on the difficulty of that life, of having that parent of immense fame. While all that has been discussed throughout this book, this final story is, to me, both touching and mysterious. Of course, notions of bothering to "understand" the "troubles" of those with a wealthy, famous parent irritates many. I know. As I've dared to have that conversation about this with fellow "ordinary" folks, I've found that it doesn't take long for someone to sarcastically blurt out something exactly along the lines of, yes, here's that phrase again: "Gee, we should all have such problems!" I'm sure there were difficult times when even I had such notions, dealing with the Brando and Peck families, as well as other such children of Hollywood. But if you stop to truly think of the actual life challenges, you get it.

As a related side-story to the recollection I'd like to end with, I return to the set of *"Free Money"* in Montreal - and one of the endings of *that* story. When making that film, Martin Sheen arrived late in the shoot to film the final scene of the picture. Within the movie story, Marlon's "Swede" is now in jail. The Swede's "new" warden is a man played in this final scene by Martin. It's a scene I was fully opposed to, protesting it every step of the way. More on that in a moment.

Like many big, star-packed yet rambling productions (especially a production with Marlon), *"Free Money"* scenes were sometimes new the day of shooting, to accommodate "Guest Stars," with scenes occasionally discarded and frequently re-written, often on an hourly basis; *that* - and wrangling Marlon, *that* was why I was there. The shoot had two other wild card issues that also made for constant changes: the two stars. Brando was Brando; previously cited; enough said. *And* - this film was shot in the depths of Charlie Sheen's drug days. Somehow, he always made it to set and knew his lines, but it was frequently a shaky high-wire and a struggle for everybody.

He'd sometimes shove ice cubes up his ass to get through a take, but get through those takes he did, only to crawl back into his Elvis "Star" bus the moment he'd hear "cut," to party-on with his friend and guest, rocker Bret Michaels. His father Martin arrived on set in very much the way that other stars arrived on this film: they had firm confirmation that Brando was actually *here*; therefore, they would then show up and be in the movie, essentially doing whatever we wanted them to do; they were there to work with Marlon, even if, like Martin and Donald Sutherland, they had worked with Marlon before. With an added, singular twist, Martin, of course, was also here to see his son, but given the circumstances, even that was not a certainty. While the Sheens were not estranged, it seemed uncomfortably clear that if Martin and

Charlie *did* have a moment to say "Hi" to one another, it might be odd. Especially if it took place in front of others.

At the time, as it seemed he had always been, Martin was the sweet, passionate, fast-talking Catholic activist Hollywood had long known him to be. He is a wonderfully inviting man who lets you in, immediately wanting to discuss faith, politics and the state of life on Earth. He treats everyone as a friend on a level field, listening to what you're saying, always responding with kindness and never dismissing your point of view. Seriously, Martin is a true force of nature. So much so, Marlon was not fully in the mood to meet with him before filming. When I told Marlon that Martin was here and wanted to see him, Marlon groaned, "Is he still talking a lot?" It made me wonder if Martin was indeed that same person back in the Philippines when a much younger Martin and Marlon shot their scenes under very different circumstances for *"Apocalypse Now"*.

When Martin arrived at the sound-stages, he saw Charlie's bus, that opulent semi-hauler-sized drug-den of a motor home that the younger Sheen lived in. We kept it close to the set so we would always have access to Charlie when needed. Martin decided not to knock on the door.

"Maybe he's resting," said Martin. Of course, I immediately sensed that Martin simply did not want me or any of the film crew to see him having to openly deal with his foggy, red-eyed adult son in real time, nor did Martin seem to want to go *in* there either. So instead, Martin and I stood outside the bus and talked for what seemed like an hour; discussions about me writing and producing the film, being close to Marlon, along with talk regarding the Pope, nuclear power, California government and drug intervention - Yes, he pointedly brought up that last one.

As direct and talkative as Martin was, I could see he was slowly approaching something of a question; perhaps - a request he was trying to ask of me? Along the way to this possible request, he mentioned that Clint Eastwood had a form of "intervention" for Charlie after the filming of *"The Rookie"*. I strongly started to sense that he was approaching the idea of Marlon talking to Charlie about drug and alcohol abuse. Through a lot of veiled language from both of us, I pretty much shut that down, only because I felt that Marlon would not want to get involved with the Sheens in this way. And through even more veiled language back and forth, I could hear that sweet, caring Martin understood that. Strongly sensing his disappointment, I found a roundabout way to say that *he* was free to discuss such a matter with Marlon when they would come together for filming. Martin suggested that that would not be such a great idea. He was right.

I felt horrible for Martin. Even with all of his positive energy, supportive ideas and deep faith, it seemed he was not able to straighten out his adult son. Of course, Marlon had these very same issues with his son, Christian. At that moment, I changed the subject with Martin, handing him the new scene my fellow producers forced me write for him. It was an ending scene I didn't want in the film, but I didn't share that with Martin. It was a "Gag" scene starring the two leads of *"Apocalypse Now,"* along with the added baggage of one of them being the actual father of our leading man - an ending with a gob of winks to the camera, and at that moment, I hated it.

I hated the idea of Martin Sheen, of all people, being the last moments of a film I had worked on for years. Why? Well, I believe any filmmaker will understand. As crazy as it might now sound given the eventual lack of success regarding the finished film, I had incredibly high hopes for *"Free Money"* back when it was being made. With all the attached elements, how could I not? I wanted this comedy drama to resonate at the end, not fade to credits with a "stunt" scene.

And by the way, all the gripes I'm about to go into: none of this was Marlon's fault, Martin's fault, perhaps it was all *nobody's* fault, but it *was* the reasoning of "The Money People" to end the movie this way. To paint the picture: Marlon's evil "Swede" is in jail. He was a crooked warden all during our story, finally getting what he deserves: life behind bars. A man walks up; *this guy* who hasn't been in the rest of this film; he is the new warden. Snap to black. What? I was "told" that "It works so well on two great levels!" WTF? I knew the *levels* "The Money People" were talking about, and they were the very reasons that none of it worked for me.

Level *One*: "The Money People" loved that when these men last shared the screen, the tables were turned. Or were they? Willard (Sheen's character in *"Apocalypse Now"*) was the assigned assassin of Captain Kurtz (Marlon's character in that film) - It was an assassination that was completed. No matter; in my mind, why the hell do we need to think of *"Apocalypse Now"* at this moment? And *Two* - and maybe worse yet: "The Money People" loved - get this: Marlon's been abusing Charlie Sheen all throughout the film, and *now*, who is Marlon's "new warden"? Charlie's real-life *dad! Ha!* Brilliant. I was told, "So many great winks to the audience!"

Yes, I know that the finished film didn't work for many people long before that scene came along, but still, at that time of filming, I just did not want the movie to end with a confusing muddled layered "gag". Okay, that's the end of my rant on the end of my film, *"Free Money"*.

Back to actor fathers and the difficulty of raising Hollywood kids; yes, the challenges are many. I am only now getting to the story that I find both touching and mysterious, all to the credit of both Marlon and Greg, two men who were outstanding fathers in very different ways. While it's easy to see Greg as the ultimate symbol of perfect fatherhood - And he was indeed a thoughtful and attentive father - there's often a misinterpretation of Marlon's fathering skills. Because Marlon was so private, and seen as so solitary, it seems his role as a father was often dismissed, and at times, even criticized. The number of children in his family *was* difficult to determine. Essentially, Marlon wanted to take care of all those around him. As he grew older, that became a challenging, costly, and at times, impossible task. While some would say that he created his own problems with all of his relationships, islands, moods - whatever you want to attribute to Brando - Nonetheless he loved his children and struggled to be there for them.

As we've discussed, like more than a few Hollywood stars, Greg had a son who committed suicide. Jonathan Peck took his own life in 1975. Right up until the end of Gregory Peck's life, he said thoughts of Jonathan would strike him all the time. Daily. Any parent would understand that; that way of thinking when something like that happens to your child. While the reasons are all different when the act is suicide, many wonder about the numbers involved with children of the famous; it's a list that I won't go into here, but it is extensive. And as many know, it happened to Marlon Brando as well. After watching his son Christian go to jail for the murder of the young Dag Drollet in Marlon's Mulholland home, Dag's girlfriend, Cheyenne committed suicide in 1995. I don't think Marlon loved anyone the way he loved his daughter, Cheyenne.

It goes without saying but it cannot be overemphasized: after Dag's murder, Christian's trial, his incarceration, Cheyenne's failed therapies, and ultimately, her suicide, there were days up on Mulholland when, understandably, it seemed that there was very little left of Marlon. The strongest force in the history of dynamic personalities was often reduced to a sobbing, wounded giant. Avra worked up at his house during this era, and she'd come home with daily sad stories of Marlon's mental state. She was often worried about him. We all were.

In a moment when he opened up to her about it all, Marlon said there was a "side" aspect of all this that he found both puzzling and unpleasant. He made it clear: this "thing" he was about to bring up, it was hardly an important matter in the scheme of things, but still, it bothered him. With all that had happened, from the gunshot in the den to the funeral in Tahiti after the suicide; he heard from nobody in "The Industry". Nobody. After a lifetime of filmmaking, performing, creating art with others - After all that, he heard from nobody from his Hollywood world.

Of course, some might assume that Marlon Brando had no Hollywood world, and this was something he brought up as well; his own legendary solitude, his self-shaped standoffish nature, his want to be left alone, now coupled with events that, to some, seemed too difficult for casual acquaintances to comment on, or even offer solace over. Whatever the case, Avra knew what he meant. Of course those near and dear to Marlon communicated with him after the tragedies. Those from the inner circle; we were always giving support to Marlon and his family. But Marlon also knew something else: when *he* saw situations like celebrity family suicides and deaths on TV, he had Avra send out comforting notes. He'd pick up the phone. He had been on the other end of it, and he responded, even to many he had never met. It was quite touching, knowing *he* himself knew the power of a surprising note or call coming from Marlon Brando.

Yet he was so big, it seemed many probably were indeed at a loss as to how to respond to him. Whatever the case, he felt alone in the industry town he worked and lived in.

That's when Avra approached me with an idea that was nothing like anything she had ever asked of me.

She wanted me to ask Greg to send a letter to Marlon.

And while that seemed so simple, so obvious and so loving in its nature, it was anything but easy. And when thought is given to it, it's plain to see why the idea of it all, given these two men, was not just difficult; actually, it was absolutely impossible.

Of course, I thought I could at least try.

I talked to Tony, who then spoke to Veronique. Before long, Tony, Veronique and I were sitting in the Peck house, discussing the possibility of the idea. They both understood and actually liked the notion, grasping what Marlon must be going through. They also knew that Greg was the exact kind of studio pillar and fellow legend that Marlon was discussing; Greg was *the* icon of the mainstream industry, perhaps the most respected, beloved icon Real Hollywood had remaining. Greg was in a very singular category, as unique as Marlon's solitary place.

And perhaps, this is why Tony and Veronique told me that they would probably be unable to get Greg to do it. They carefully explained the awkwardness Greg would feel by doing such a thing out of the blue. These two men were not close friends, they had always been in very different places throughout their long careers. I also had that uncomfortable feeling I had often when dealing with the intersection of these two men: something happened in their mutual pasts that left both of them saying, "The hell with him." That's just my speculation, but they had pasts that included so many intersections of politics, mutual friendships - I don't know. In an industry where it seemed that Marlon had way too many enemies and Greg had absolutely none, I was never sure with these two.

And maybe it was just that: They were just too opposite ever to be even friendly with one another. They both did their work together with civil rights marches and other liberal cause events back in The Day, but that was as far as it went.

As Tony and Veronique predicted, Greg was more than unreceptive to the idea, he was angry about it. He felt unfairly put on the spot over the mere possibility of it all, calling Avra and me, "two star struck kids with a silly idea." While that seemed harsh, I had to put myself in his place, especially knowing Greg as I did. Everything he did was always right, proper, justified, needed, understandable. Yes, again and always, that was all the opposite of Marlon. For Greg, the requested task would be beyond daunting: an iconic actor reaches out - out of the blue - to another iconic actor; icons who do not speak to one another - for reasons known only to them.

The actor reaching out would need to pen a sensitive, meaningful set of thoughts regarding people, events and emotions he's not a part of; yes, it's all possible to do, maybe, but why would Gregory Peck need to do this? And for Brando? Greg could easily have been thinking, "Crazy Marlon? Maybe he's still that odd, raging wild card who just might pick up the phone after I go out on a limb with a letter; he'll call and say something humiliating like, 'Uh, Mr. Peck? What the fuck is this about?'" As nutty as that might seem, *that* was often the incorrect yet exact idea people had of "cynical" Brando; he's just *that* strange, cruel and unapproachable.

So Avra and I dropped the idea.

Days after it was all put out there, I thought the smoke had cleared at Carolwood. I was back at Greg's house for some reason or other, but, uh, no, the smoke had not cleared. I ran into Greg.

He was avoiding me in a way that I had not experienced before.

No, not fully rude. Just clearly different, avoiding conversation with me as he made his way out to his greenhouse. My then-recent appearance at the house had been about wanting Greg to write Marlon, Greg wasn't going to do it, and that was that. In a somewhat rare moment for her, Veronique came to me and said she felt bad about how it all turned out. She said she wanted Greg to do it, but given all the unusual elements involved, cautious, proper Greg could not see a way to write the letter. I told her that I fully understood and that was the end of it. Tony had also approached Greg on the matter, feeling it was all a no-go. I'm sure Greg felt under siege by now.

It took Avra awhile to get over the "star-struck kids" remark. Perhaps it was a stark reminder of something we were always mindful of: No matter how much these famous people allowed us into their lives, and vice versa, there might always be a sharp divide presenting itself.

But also, Avra understood the openness of Marlon far more than she understood the guarded nature of Greg. I explained, as I had many times before, how different Greg and Marlon were - These weren't just public, created images - kind Atticus Finch-like Greg writing to reclusive, wounded Vito Corleone-like Marlon - No, this is who they were. She understood, reminding me that, of course, *this* is why she *wanted* such a letter to come from someone as dignified, respected, rarely heard from and well thought of as Greg. She felt it would have touched Marlon.

Anyway, whatever all of that might have been about, at this moment in time, it was over. Done.

Days later, Avra was working up at Mulholland. She went out to lunch off the property.

When she returned, passing the mailboxes, she saw that one of the other assistants had gotten the day's mail. She drove in, passing cranky Jack Nicholson and his car filled with golf clubs, as she had done hundreds of times, slowing down because cranky Jack liked it slow on this road.

When she got to the office, an assistant asked Avra, "Joe; he writes with Gregory Peck's son? Yeah? You've mentioned that?" Avra affirmed that, wondering why this was mentioned.

The assistant then said, "Marlon got a letter today from Gregory Peck."

"Uh, what's that about?" Avra asked, "Where is it?" The assistant said, "I gave it to him in the den."

Avra was laughing with a mix of tears and joy as she hurried up to the house and went into the den. Marlon was finishing the letter; he put it in a book as Avra entered.

She asked, "Did the mail arrive?" Without a word, Marlon nodded in the affirmative.

He had nothing else to say. And when Marlon has nothing to say, he means every word of it.

When she later told me the story, I asked, "Was Marlon smiling? Anything?" She shrugged, "You know Marlon; if he wants to keep something to himself, he keeps it to himself."

Hearing all this, I had to laugh a bit myself. Also, as I wrote about pages ago, Greg's letters were always works of art; not a word out of place, not an incorrect thought, not the slightest bit of "wrong" on the page. Whatever it was, I knew that the letter must've been amazing.

If it wasn't, Greg would not have sent it.

Not being able to help myself, I had to tell Tony. Not able to help himself, he told his mother. Tony and Veronique also got a warm chuckle over this, with Veronique telling Tony and me, "But we must never tell Greg that we know anything about this."

Of course, given all the circumstances, there were many ways that we could've talked about it with Greg - Thanked him, asked him about it - however the course of events might lead.

But with Marlon *also* saying nothing about it, well, it was clearly and only between Marlon and Greg.

Tony marveled, "Marlon knows you know us and he says nothing to Avra about Greg's letter?"

I said, "No. Just like Greg saying nothing to you."

Tony sighed a laugh as he shook his head.

"Wow. Men like these guys. Rare."

It was pure Greg: being a saint; not wanting to be caught being one.

It was pure Marlon: needing someone; not wanting to be caught needing.

INDEX

20th Century Fox, 13, 19, 40-42, 45, 52, 58, 60-63, 88, 144, 156, 185, 209, 244, 289
60 Minutes, 165

A

ABC television network, 14, 19-20, 31, 34, 45, 52, 108, 256-258, 266, 293, 307
Academy Award ("Oscar") 18, 26-27, 53, 66, 77-78, 80, 116, 119-121, 131, 159, 208, 212, 216-217, 245, 295, 297-298, 341, 346, 346-347
Academy of Motion Picture Arts and Sciences (The) 77-78, 120-121
ACT (American Conservatory Theater) 331, 333
Adler, Stella, 198, 312, 332
Adventures in the Screen Trade, 55
African Queen (The) 120
Ahmanson Theater, 133
Ali, Muhammad, 283
All About Eve, 57
All in the Family, vi, 6-7, 11, 47, 134, 174-175, 180, 182, 293
Allen, Woody, 9-10, 86, 137
Altman, Robert, 299
American Beauty, 331
American Family, 300
American Film Institute, 314, 341, 343
American in Paris (An) 347
Amblin Entertainment, 92
Amos 'n' Andy, 182
Amsterdam, Morey, 33
Andy Griffith Show (The) 356, 367
Anspach, Susan, 43-44
Apocalypse Now, 125, 213, 228, 245-246, 323, 333, 349, 389-391
Appaloosa (The) 48
Apprentice (The) 372
Archie Bunker's Place, 175
Arquette, David, 229
Arquette, Rosanna, 237
Assonitis, Ovidio, 104
Attic: The Hiding of Anne Frank (The) 288
Autism, 15-16, 286-287, 338-339, 351, 356, 362, 367
Avid Editing System, 16, 167, 283, 323
Ayres, Bernice ("Bunny", mother of Gregory Peck) 82

B

Bacall, Lauren, 81-82, 149, 384-385
Bad (song) 137, 140
Bad Boy Drive, 336, 366
Bailey, Richard, 375
Baldwin, Peter, 12
Ball, Lucille, 376
Balsam, Martin, 105
Barbeau, Francois, 229
Barrett, Rona, 180
Bashir, Martin, 141-142
Basic Instinct, 132
Beatles (The) 309
Beatty, Warren, 39, 327-338, 366, 369
Bedtime Story, 298, 282
Beebe, Steve, 368
Begley, Ed (Jr.) vii, 12, 14, 130-131, 329, 353-354, 357
Begley, Hayden, 354
Begley (Carson) Rachelle, vii, 12, 14, 353-355, 357
Behold a Pale Horse, 223
Behind the Mask, 257, 259-261, 269, 271, 273, 277
Bellocchio, Marco, 222
Bening, Annette, 328-335, 336-338
Benny, Jack, 81
Bergman, Ingmar, 15, 86-88, 90, 94-95, 131, 148, 382-386
Bergman, Ingrid, 54, 86
Bertolucci, Bernardo, 222, 251

Betsy (The) 101
Big Country (The) 384
Billie (Boston terrier) 121-122
Black Narcissus, 94
Black Sheep (screenplay) 40-42, 58-59, 61-63, 65, 168, 170, 209
Blazing Saddles, 133
Blockbuster Video, 367
Blue and the Gray (The) 257
Bochco, Steven, 12
Bodhi Tree, (The) 169
Bogart, Humphrey, 53-54, 78, 81, 120, 347, 374
Bonanza, 153
Bonnie and Clyde, 144
Bono, Sonny, 70
Bork, Robert, 115, 342
Boxleitner, Bruce, vi, 280
Boys From Brazil (The) 83, 101, 120, 245, 349
Brainerd, Minnesota, 5, 7, 27, 30, 35-38, 42, 57, 87, 134, 229, 386
Brainerd International Raceway, 35-36
Brando (The) (resort) 311, 375
Brando, Cheyenne, 20, 34-35, 96-97, 121, 133, 138, 153, 183, 361, 379, 392
Brando, Christian, 20, 34-35, 95, 121, 138, 146, 251, 379, 390, 392
Brando, Marlon,
  childhood, 82, 99, 198
  civil rights, 115-116, 310-311, 342-343, 394
  final days, 339-340, 362-367, 368-373
  Free Money, vii, 9, 15, 78, 168, 195-196, 208-222, 224-236, 239, 247-249, 251, 254, 257-258, 261, 270, 279-285, 303, 312, 333-334, 361-362, 373, 383-388, 390-391
  friendship with Michael Jackson, 63, 130, 134-143, 163, 183, 313, 332, 362
  Lying For a Living, 10, 85, 279, 308, 310, 313-316, 318, 322-323, 326-328, 337, 339, 362, 364, 368-369, 375, 381
  screenwriting method, 57, 89, 102-103, 277
  thoughts on Gregory Peck, 2, 18, 23, 25, 98
Brando, Marlon Sr. *(father of Marlon Brando)* 82
Brando, Miko, 95, 135, 137-138, 142, 313
Brando, Rebecca, 34, 49, 95-96, 138, 350, 352
Brando's Smile, 252
Brandstein, Eve, 175-176
Brave (The) 208, 251, 254
Breakfast at Tiffany's, 67
Brill Building (The) 134
Broderick, Matthew, 253
Brooks, James L. 46
Brown, Christy, 78
Brown, Nicole, 140, 351
Brown, Tina, 318-319
Bruce, Lenny, 281
Brutsman, Bud, 367-372
Brutsman, Jay, vi, 1, 4-7, 21, 38-39, 70, 75, 151, 153-154, 180
Brutsman, Joseph,
  acting, 5-6, 12-14, 17, 20, 31-32, 37, 44-45, 47-50, 98, 173, 175, 240-241, 288, 307-308
  Black Sheep, 40-42, 58-59, 61-63, 65, 168, 170, 209
  Brainerd, 5, 7, 27, 30, 35-38, 42, 57, 87, 134, 229, 386
  CalArts, 10
  cartoonist, vi, 5-8, 11, 17, 38, 83, 174, 176, 362
  Diary of a Sex Addict, 13-14, 236-237, 257, 263, 312, 353-354
  editor, 283
  education, 1-13, 27-31
  meeting Avra Douglas, 31-35
  meeting Gregory Peck, 35-44
  meeting Marlon Brando, 95-100
  meeting Tony Peck, 27-31
  Paul Bunyan, 167-172

reality TV, 16, 167, 354, 356, 362, 371-372
screenwriting, iii, viii, ix, 4, 13, 35, 41, 55-58, 74, 90, 148, 170-172, 186, 188, 222-223, 236, 248, 253, 270, 278, 307, 386
Tie You Up, 31, 40, 209, 217
Brutsman, Laura, (Busch) 4-7, 11, 27-28, 31, 37, 84, 154, 173, 176, 209, 241, 285-287
Brutsman, Marilyn, vi, 4, 5, 7, 21, 38, 39, 70, 98, 209, 285-287, 357
Brutsman, Molly, iii, vi, vii, 15-16, 73, 141-142, 285, 287, 317, 328, 331, 334, 338-339, 350-355, 362-366, 368-369, 373
Brutsman, Pam (Maasch) 4, 154, 209, 285-287
Bubble Factory (The) 172, 292
Buffalo Bill, 32, 48
Bugs Bunny, 38
Bugsy, 328
Bujold, Genevieve, 215
Bull Boy, 89, 263
Bullwinkle, 8
Burn, 251, 360
Burns, Allan, 8, 12, 33
Burns, George, 81
Burrows, James, 255
Bush, Barbara, 115, 118
Bush, George H.W., 115, 118
Buttons, Red, 157

C

CAA (Creative Artists Agency) 250, 257-261, 267-271, 273-277, 319, 362
Caesar, Sid, 277, 358
Cagney, James, 53, 120, 199
Caine Mutiny (The) 347
CalArts (California Institute of the Arts) 10
Cammell, Donald, 89
Canal+ 132
Candy, 251, 282, 360
Cannon, Dyan, 24, 41, 43

Cannon Group (The) 104
Cape Fear (1962) 77, 91-93, 94
Cape Fear (1991) 76-77, 91-93, 94, 105, 232
Capote, Truman, 67, 318
Cappa Films, 92
Captain Ahab, 83, 231, 257, 359
Captain Horatio Hornblower, 346-347
Carney's (diner) 157
Carrey, Jim, 8, 33
Carson, Johnny, 66, 157
Carter, Jack, 157
Carter, Jimmy, 118, 158
Carter, Rosalynn, 118
Casablanca, 120
Cash, Johnny, 39
Catch-22, 299
Cates, Gilbert, 12
Cathedral of Our Lady of the Angels, 351, 355, 359
Cavani, Liliana, 222-224
CBS television network, vi, 32, 45, 220, 250, 257, 259-273, 275-277, 279-280, 290, 293, 316, 362
Chaplin, Charlie, 66, 75, 90, 237-238, 308, 321
Charet, Bruce, 60
Charlie (Boston terrier) 122
Chase (The) 227
Chasen's, 157
Cheers, 51
Chekhov, Anton, 30
Cher, 63, 70, 177
Chirac, Jacques, 189, 191, 193
Chorus Line (A) 7
Christopher Columbus: The Discovery, 283
Chung, Connie, 361
Church, Thomas Hayden, 210, 225, 229-231, 284
Cimino, Michael, 340
Cleopatra, 156
Clermont, Nicolas, 211, 215, 217-222, 230, 234-235 280, 283-284
Clift, Montgomery, 22, 120, 199
Clinton, Bill, 118

Clinton, Hillary, 118
CNN, 114, 164-166
Coleman, Dabney, 14, 31-33, 43-44, 46-49, 53, 98, 100, 355
Columbia Pictures, 40, 143, 333
Comedy Central, 284
Cosby Show (The) 46, 50
Conversation with Gregory Peck (A) vii, 85, 232, 241, 308, 381-382
Connery, Sean, 253
Coolidge, Martha, 148, 382
Coppola, Francis, 144, 237, 245-246, 252, 270
Cotton Club (The) 145, 292
Countess from Hong Kong (A) 51, 66
Crockett, Davy, 171
Crossing Guard (The) 214, 219
Cruise, Tom, 89, 102-104, 219, 239
Cryer, Jon, 252
Culkin, Macaulay, 136
Cupid (screenplay) 172
Curtis, Tony, 70

D

Danis, Diane, 355
David and Bathsheba, 346-347
Davis, Marvin, 63
Davis, Miles, 281, 339
Days and Nights of Molly Dodd (The) 33, 34, 96
Days of Glory, 198
Dean, James, 22, 316, 376
Depp, Johnny, 130, 208, 251-254
De Niro, Robert, 89, 91-92, 102-105, 239, 249, 361
Devil's Own (The) 236, 239-242
Diagnosis: Murder, 51, 293
Diary of a Sex Addict, 13-14, 236-237, 257, 263, 312, 353-354
DiCaprio, Leonardo, 121, 313
Dick Powell's Zane Grey Theater, 116
Dick Tracy, 333
Dick Van Dyke Show (The) 30, 356-359
Dickinson, Angie, 24, 41, 43

Dickinson, Janice, 109
Diff'rent Strokes, 182
Diller, Barry, 45
Disney (brand/company) 1, 5, 7, 9, 10, 139, 143-144, 153, 168, 357
Disney, Walt, 5, 9, 153
Disneyland, 139
Divine Rapture, 171, 188-189, 233, 251, 259
Do You Remember Love? 259, 260
Doctor DeMott, 15, 86, 88, 90, 93-94, 98, 105, 113, 130-133, 145, 148-151, 195, 208, 210, 212-213, 221, 234-236, 301, 303, 382-386
Dodsworth, 148
Don Juan DeMarco, 246, 252-255, 257-258, 361
Donner, Richard, 243-245
Douglas, Alan, 281-283, 333, 339
Douglas, Avra
    Boston terriers, 121-122, 128
    caring for Cheyenne Brando, 20, 34-35, 96-97, 121, 133, 138, 153, 183, 361, 379, 392
    family, 288-305, 315-322
    in France, 35, 379
    meeting Gregory Peck, 161-163
    Molly Brutsman, iii, vi, vii, 15-16, 73, 141-142, 285, 287, 317, 328, 331, 334, 338-339, 350-355, 362-366, 368-369, 373
    pastry chef, 34
    Saint Jimmy, 263-277
    screenwriting, 267-277
    working for Marlon Brando, 19, 34, 95-99, 105-110, 121, 287, 312, 361, 379, 392-396
    working for Jay Tarses, 31-35, 49
Douglas, Jerry, 264, 281, 315-316
Douglas, Jod (Kaftan) 316-322
Douglas, Kirk, 54, 56
Dove (The) 144, 146, 149
Drollet, Dag, 20, 34-35, 96, 122, 392
Dry White Season (A) 206, 283
Duck Factory (The) 8, 33

Dutch, 165
Duvall, Robert, 228
Dylan, Bob, 282

E
E.T. The Extraterrestrial, 175
Earth in the Balance, 169
Eastwood, Clint, 163, 228, 283, 389
Easy Rider, 143, 167
Ed Wood, 252
Edward Scissorhands, 252
Empire Strikes Back (The) 300
Englund, George, 251, 322-326, 368
Entertainment Tonight, 1, 319
Epstein, Jeffrey, 142
Erman, John, 12
Ethel Barrymore Theatre (The) 241
Evans, Robert, vii, 144-148, 183, 292
Exorcist (The) 278

F
Fairbanks, Douglas, 90
Family Business, 253
Famous Teddy Z (The) 250, 252
Fan Tan, 89, 263
Fargo, 36, 228-229, 281
Farley, Chris, 39, 63
Fassbinder, Rainer Werner, 87
Fatburgers, 157, 338
Field, Sally, 159
Fields, W.C., 67, 374
Filmline International, 211, 221, 223, 284
First Artists, 90
Five Easy Pieces, 167
Flatley, Beth, 267
Fleetwood Mac, 118
Flip Wilson Show (The) 182
Flynn, David, 110
Flynn, Errol, 346-347
Fonda, Jane, 48, 77, 314-315
Foose, Chip, 368-372
Ford, Gerald, 117
Ford, Harrison, 239
Formula (The) 207, 245-246

Fox Network, 44-47, 277
Fox News, 45
Foxx, Redd, 181
France-Soir, 71
Franklin, Benjamin, 171
Frank's Place, 31
Frasier, 51
Fred Flintsone, 38
Free Money, vii, 9, 15, 78, 168, 195-196, 208-222, 224-236, 239, 247-249, 251, 254, 257-258, 261, 270, 279-285, 303, 312, 333-334, 361-362, 373, 383-388, 390-391
Freshman (The) 96, 206-207, 236, 282-283
Freud, Sigmund, 137
Fry's Electronics, 160
Fugitive Kind (The) 260, 322

G
Gable, Clark, 53-54, 70, 156, 282
Gaines, Boyd, 176-177, 180
Gallin, Sandy, 63
Garbo, Greta, 75
Garland, Judy, 314
Garson, Greer, 54
General Electric, 116
Gentleman's Agreement, 119, 155, 348, 361
Get Shorty, 211
Gilligan's Island, 29
Globus, Yoram, 104
Gloria, 175
Godfather (The) 27, 60, 101, 144, 146-148, 201, 207, 213, 238, 240, 244, 251, 281, 298, 322-323, 340, 341, 345, 349, 372, 375, 387
Godfather II (The) 147-148
Goldberg, Whoopi, 270, 313
Goldman, Ron, 140, 351
Goldman, William, 55, 307
Goldwater, Barry, 117
Gone with the Wind, 290, 340
Good Doctor (The) 30
Good Morning America, 108
Good Times, 182

Goodall, Jane, 335
Goodfellas, 76-78
Gore, Al, 118, 169
Gore, Tipper, 118
Graduate (The) 297
Grant, Cary, 22, 138-139, 316, 377
Gregory, Dick, 328
Grey Gardens, 364
Griffith, Andy, 51, 293, 356, 367
Griffith, D.W., 90
Grodin, Charles, 264
Guevara, Che, 376
Gunfighter (The) 206, 346
Guys and Dolls, 66, 240, 322

H

Hackett, Buddy, 157-158
Hackman, Gene, 254
Haley, Alex, 349
Hamburger Hamlet, 269
Hanks, Tom, 120
Hanna Barbera, 5, 38
Hanley, William, 288-291
Hansen, Courtney, vii, 368
Harrison, George, 309
HBO (Home Box Office) 265-266
Head (The Monkees) 143, 167
Hearts of Darkness, 246
Heaven Can Wait, 333
Heaven's Gate, 103, 340
Hecht, Ben, 55
Hefner, Hugh, 141
Hellcats of the Navy, 116
Hello Dolly, 144
Hepburn, Audrey, 82
Hepburn, Katharine, 54, 120, 135, 241
Hemingway, Ernest, 78
Hemingway, Mariel, 137
Hendrix, Jimi, 281-282
Herzog, Werner, 87
Heston, Charlton, 54, 115, 162, 184
Hill Street Blues, 292-293
Hirschfeld, Marc, 175
Hitchcock, Alfred, 55, 139, 237-238
Higgins, Michael, 188-191

History Channel (The) 368
Hoffman, Dustin, 77, 85, 90, 253
Hollywood Reporter (The) 93
Hollywood Schoolhouse (The) 254
How the West Was Won, 44, 240
Howe, Tina, 149
Hudson, Rock, 155
Huston, John, 139, 359
Huston, Walter, 148

I

I Spy, 182
In Living Color, 46, 277
In the Heat of the Night, 293
Inchon, 101
Indian Runner (The) 214, 219
Ingels, Marty, 298
Inland Empire, 132
Interiors, 82
Isham, Mark, 280
Ishtar, 333-334, 337
Island of Dr. Moreau (The) 173-174, 179, 229, 233, 361

J

Jackson 5 (The) 140
Jackson, Kate, 14, 280
Jackson, Michael, 63, 130, 134-143, 163, 183, 313, 332, 362
Jacobs, Chris, vii, 368
Jagger, Bianca, 109
Jannings, Emil, 67
Jean Hersholt Humanitarian Award, 120
Jeffersons (The) 175, 181-182
Jenner, Bruce, 351
Jericho, 89, 150-151, 263
Jewison, Norman, 105
Johnson, Lady Bird (Claudia) 115, 118
Johnson, Lyndon, 115, 342
Jones, James Earl, 349
Jones, Jennifer, 163
Jones, Shirley, 44, 298
Juilliard School of Theatre (The) vi, 5, 7-12, 19, 21, 27-29, 31-32, 37, 40, 41, 45, 48, 54, 69, 72, 77, 80, 83-84, 87, 98,

101, 127, 134, 162, 173-179, 222, 241, 288, 301, 312, 330-335, 375
Julia, 182
Julius Caesar, 57
Jungle Book (The) 168

K

Kallianiotes, Helena, 133, 335
Kantor, Jay, 250, 252
Kardashian family, 350-351
Kassar, Mario, 132
Kastner, Elliot, 59-60, 145, 270
Kaye, Tony, 310-314, 316, 324-325
Kazan, Elia, 200, 345, 347-348
Kelada, Asaad, 12
Kelly, Grace, 193
Kennedy, John, 116-117, 347
Kennedy, Robert, 116-117
Kershner, Irvin, 300-301, 303
Keys of the Kingdom (The) 53
Kilmer, Val, 28, 173-183
King, Larry, 85, 114, 163-167, 361
King, Martin Luther, 115
Kinski, Nastassja, 237
Kohner, Paul (Agency) 148
Kopple, Barbara, 381
Kubrick, Stanley, 384

L

L.A. Law, 100
La Traviata, 223
LaMourea, Andre, 5-6
Lancaster, Burt, 22, 54
Landau, Martin, 300
Langlois, Yves, 280
Larry King Live, 85, 114, 163-167, 361
Last Tango in Paris, 99, 213, 223, 238, 251, 323, 349
Laurel (Stanley) and Hardy (Oliver) 1, 75, 86
Lawrence of Arabia, 119, 156, 347
Lawrence, T. E., 156
Lazar, Irving ("Swifty") 40-42, 63, 77-80, 170
Lazar, Mary, 42, 77, 79

Le Dome, 157
Lean, David, 156, 297
Leaving Neverland, 142
Lear, Norman, 7, 9, 11, 46, 134, 174-182
Lee, Harper, 155
Lemmon, Jack, 24, 68-69, 136
Lennon, John, 309
Letterman, David, 292-293
Lewis, Daniel Day, 78
Lewis, Emmanuel, 136
Lewis, Jerry, 76, 222
Lewis, Sinclair, 148
Lifetime Network, 34
Lincoln, Abraham, 161, 257
Lincoln Center, 7, 8, 19, 27, 134, 176, 296
Lindsey, Robert, 164-165, 327
Lionsgate Entertainment, 284
Listen To Me Marlon, 381
Littlefeather, Sacheen, 298
Littwin, Susan, 45
Living with Ed, vii, 12, 14, 354
Living with Michael Jackson, 142
London, Jason, 131
London, Jeremy, 131
Loren, Sophia, 51
Los Angeles Midnight Mission (The) 357
Los Angeles Times (The) 34, 130
Love and Death, 87
Love Story, 143
Lovitz, Jon, 313
Lucas, George, 9
Lucy Ricardo, 37, 376
Lying For a Living, 10, 85, 279, 308, 310, 313-316, 318, 322-323, 326-328, 337, 339, 362, 364, 368-369, 375, 381
Lynch, David, 132, 256

M

Maasch, Mark, 286
*M*A*S*H*, 30, 144, 299
MacArthur, 120, 245
MacArthur, Douglas, 117
Macchio, Ralph, 104
MacLaine, Shirley, 24, 41, 43

MAD Magazine, 10
Madison Square Garden, 134
Magic Lantern (The) 386
Malden, Karl, 300
Malick, Terrence, 335
Manhattan, 137
Marooned, 1-3, 240
Marquand, Christian, 251
Marquez, Gabriel Garcia, 212-214, 216-217, 386
Married... with Children, 46-47, 50-52
Marshak, Alice, 379
Martel, Arlene ("Tasha") 288-305, 315-316
Martin, Steve, 70
Mary Tyler Moore Show (The) 8
Matlock, 51, 293
Matteo's (restaurant) 157-158
Matthau, Carol, 67, 128
Matthau, Walter, 24, 67-68, 136, 238, 295
Mature, Victor, 346-347
Mayer, Louis B. 54
Mazie, Mark, 271-273, 275-277
MCA Inc. (Music Corporation of America) 116
McCarthy, Joseph, 348
McCartney, Paul, 309
McCormack, Eric, 255
McMahon, Ed, 109
McNeill, Robert Duncan, 100
McQueen, Steve, 90, 299
Me Too (movement) 84, 324
ME TV, 304
Medavoy, Mike, 145, 217, 219-220, 292, 327-335, 374
Meet the Fockers, 374
Meisner, Sanford, 44, 198
Melville, Herman, 360
Men (The) 113, 198
Mengele, Josef, 83, 349
Mickey Mouse, 38
Michaels, Bret, 388
Midnight Cowboy, 144, 297
Milestone, Lewis, 156

Miller, Larry, 357
Miller, Penelope Ann, 236
Miss Piggy, 249
Missouri Breaks (The) 59
Mitchum, Robert, 105
Mizruchi, Susan, 252
Moby Dick (1956) 83, 359
Moby Dick (1998) 257
Modern Family, 51
Monroe, Marilyn, 321, 330, 375
Moonves, Les, 260-279, 362
Moore, Geoffrey, 133
Moore, Roger, 24, 72, 133, 136
Moriceau, Norma, 229
Morris, Edmund, 164-165
Morrison, Patt, 130
Morse, David, 131
Mrs. Dally Has a Lover, 288-289
Mulholland Dr. 132
Mullally, Megan, 255
Mulligan, Robert, 155
Muni, Paul, 83
Murdoch, Rupert, 44-45, 63
Mutiny on the Bounty (1962) 91, 103, 122, 128, 154-156, 251
My Left Foot, 78-80
My Three Sons, 6

N
NBC television network, 8, 32-34, 46, 100, 108, 255, 266, 292-293
Nealon, Kevin, 166
Neighborhood Playhouse, 44, 198
Neverland Ranch, 136, 138-139, 141-142
New Beverly Cinema (The) 187
New York Times (The) 359-361
New Yorker Magazine (The) 127, 318-319
Newman, Paul, 36-37, 42, 90, 106-107, 116
Newman, Randy, 357
Newman's Own, 106, 311
Newton, Wayne, 39
Nichols, Mike, 299
Nicholson, Jack, 65, 97, 120, 130, 133, 146, 210, 214, 328, 335, 366, 380, 395
Night of the Following Day, 113

Night Porter (The) 222
Nine to Five, 48
Nixon, Pat, 118
Nixon, Richard, 25, 78, 115-117, 159-160, 205
Nolte, Nick, 105, 313
Norma Desmond, 74
North Queensland, 173
Norton, Edward, 311

O

Obama, Barack, 118
O'Connor, Carroll, vi, 46, 181, 293
October Three, 140
Odd Couple (The) 30
Off the Wall (song/album) 137
Old Gringo, 120, 233
Oliver Peoples Eyewear, 375
Olivier, Laurence, 9, 22, 101
Olmos, Edward James, 300, 308, 313
Omen (The) 27, 91, 144, 201, 207, 243-245
O'Neill, Ed, 46-52, 53, 96, 100
On Golden Pond, 48
On the Waterfront, 119, 155, 200, 242, 322, 345-348, 387
One Day at a Time, 176, 180
One-Eyed Jacks, 227, 305, 322, 384
One Hundred Years of Solitude, 212, 386
Osmond, Donny, 135
Other People's Money, 105, 121, 233, 236, 310
O'Toole, Peter, 119, 156, 347
Overhaulin', vii, 368-372
Oz, Frank, 249

P

Pacino, Al, 65, 254
Painting Churches, 149, 384-387
Pakula, Alan, 155
Palmer, Adam (brother of Avra Douglas) 315-316
Paramount Studios, 143-147, 213, 233, 292, 294, 333, 375
Parton, Dolly, 63

Pasolini, Pier Paolo, 222
Passani, Veronique (see *Veronique Peck*)
Passion's Way, 290
Patton, 245
Paul Bunyan (screenplay) 167-172
Pearson, Noel, 148
Pearthree, Pippa, 32
Peck, Anthony (Tony)
   with Cheryl Tiegs, 31, 41, 71, 73, 107-112, 114, 130-131, 133, 151, 161, 183, 284
   Black Sheep, 40-42, 58-59, 61-63, 65, 168, 170, 209
   Diary of a Sex Addict, 13-14, 236-237, 257, 263, 312, 353-354
   education, 27-31
   meeting Marlon Brando, 183-186, 189, 191-196
   Paul Bunyan, 167-172
   with Paula Rice, 112
   screenwriting, 13, 35, 41, 55-58, 74, 90, 148, 170-172, 186, 188, 222-223, 236, 248, 253, 270, 278, 307, 386
Peck, Cecilia, 31, 71, 78-79, 121, 149, 161, 173, 177, 209, 222, 352, 381-382, 384
Peck, Gregory
   Carolwood gatherings, 24, 31, 39-41, 44, 59, 63, 65, 67-70, 72, 130, 133, 157, 163, 193, 194-195, 238, 295, 350, 351-352, 355
   childhood, 198
   civil rights, 115-116, 310-311, 342-343, 394
   comeback in 70's, 27, 90-91, 144, 201, 207-208, 243-245
   Doctor DeMott, 15, 86, 88, 90, 93-94, 98, 105, 113, 130-133, 145, 148-151, 195, 208, 210, 212-213, 221, 234-236, 301, 303, 382-386
   early career, 27, 53, 198-199
   final days, 303, 338-339, 343-344
   friendship with Frank Sinatra, 24-25, 39, 66, 68-70, 72, 109, 135-

136, 139, 157, 183, 193, 222, 283, 353
friendship with Michael Jackson, 133-143
meeting Veronique Passani, 70-74
letter writing, 81-82, 393-396
politics, 112-118, 205, 342, 343
thoughts on Marlon Brando, 2, 18, 24-25, 130
thoughts on Ronald Reagan, 112-118, 205
Peck, Gregory Pearl *(father of Gregory Peck)* 82
Peck, Greta (Kukkonen) 205, 386
Peck, Jonathan, 361, 386, 391
Peck, Veronique (Passani) 31, 40-42, 67, 69, 71-74, 77, 79-80, 93, 115, 129-130, 133, 135-136, 138-139, 161, 168-170, 183, 189, 193-195, 209, 231, 234, 256, 295, 350, 352, 354-355, 378, 380, 393-394, 396
Peck, Zackary, 114
Peeping Tom, 94
Penn, Arthur, 148-149, 382
Penn, Chris, 210
Penn, Sean, 15, 65, 95, 130-131, 148-149, 185, 210, 211- 221, 229, 233, 235, 284, 313, 328, 374, 382, 385-386
People Magazine, 45, 180
Phantom of the Opera (The) 133
Phillips, Mackenzie, 180
Phoenix Pictures, 217, 292
Pickford, Mary, 90, 364
Pirates, 29
Pitt, Brad, 219, 239-240
Platinum Toenail, 89, 100-105, 239, 263
Plummer, Christopher, 215
Poitier, Sidney, 24, 90
Poland Spring, 111
Polanski, Roman, 29, 237
Pontecorvo, Gillo, 251
Pork Chop Hill, 130
Portrait (The) 149, 384-385, 387
Powell, Michael, 94

Presley, Elvis, 70, 222, 321, 388
Puzo, Mario, 148

Q

Quando Quando Quando, 222
Quest for Fire, 280
Quiet Man (The) 387
Quinn, Anthony, 116, 139, 300

R

Rafelson, Bob, 143
Rainier III, Prince of Monaco, 193
Reagan, Nancy, 74, 116, 164
Reagan, Ronald, 25, 112, 114-118, 164-165, 205, 353
Reality TV, 16, 167, 354, 356, 362, 371-372
Redford, Robert, 280
Red River, 387
Red Shoes (The) 94
Reds, 333
Reed, Carol, 156
Reef (The) 290
Reiner, Carl, 356, 358-359
Renis, Tony, 222
Reynolds, Debbie, 44
Reynolds, Gene, 12
Rice, Paula, 112
Rickles, Don, 157
Rides, 368-369, 372
Rio Bravo, 387
Robbins, Jerome, 297
Robson, Wade, 142
Rockefeller Center 134
Rockwell, George Lincoln, 349
Rogers, Ginger, 298
Rogers, Will, 171
Rolling Stone Magazine, 322
Roman Holiday, 155, 224, 361, 387
Ronald Reagan Presidential Library, 114-118, 353
Rookie (The) 389
Rooney, Mickey, 76, 85
Roosevelt, Theodore, 164, 171
Roots, 182, 256, 258, 293

Roots: The Next Generations, 256, 258, 349
Rosemary's Baby, 143
Rosenman, Howard, 63-65, 332
Ruddy, Albert, 60, 145
Rudin, Scott, 329
Ryan, Eileen, 131

S
Safechuck, James, 142
Sahl, Mort, 328
Saint Jimmy, 263-277
Salicornia, 166
Sam Goody, 367
Sand Pebbles (The) 299
Sanford and Son, 180-182
Sanford, Isabel, 181
Saroyan, William, 67
Saturday Night Live (SNL) 166, 277, 293, 313
Sbarge, Raphael, 288
Scarecrow & Mrs. King, vi, 13-14, 32, 45, 280
Scarlet and the Black (The) 257
Scarlett, 290
Scary Movie 2, 277-279, 361
Schindler's List, 92
Schwarzenegger, Arnold, 117
Score (The) 249, 259, 311, 361
Scorsese, Martin, 15, 76, 91-95, 113, 131, 148, 195, 212, 232, 235, 237, 295, 301, 382, 385
Scott, George C., 245
Scott, Tony, 223
Screen Actors Guild (SAG) 116-117
Sea Wolves (The) 207-208
Seagal, Steven, 104
Searchers (The) 387
Sears & Roebuck, 109
Secret Storm (The) 5
Seymour, Jane, 110
Shakespeare, William, 99, 176, 346
Shampoo, 39-40
Shatner, William, 304

Sheen, Charlie, vii, 15, 210, 220, 225, 229, 232, 235, 373, 388-389, 391
Sheen, Martin, 125, 229, 232, 235, 246, 388-391
Sheinberg, Jon, 172
Sheinberg, Sidney, 172, 292
Sheridan, Jim, 148
Shootist (The) 386-387
Silver Spoons, 177
Silverman, Fred, 292-293
Simon, Neil, 30
Simoneau, Yves, 225-226, 230, 280, 284
Simpson, O.J., 35, 140, 142, 351
Simpsons (The) 46
Sinatra, Barbara, 68-69
Sinatra family, 353
Sinatra, Frank, 24-25, 39, 66, 68-70, 72, 109, 135-136, 139, 157, 183, 193, 222, 283, 353
Skuzz, 89, 263
"Slap" Maxwell Story (The) 13-14, 31-33, 43-44, 45-51, 96, 98, 100, 307, 355
Smith, Gary, 314-315
Smith, Kelly, 11
Soapdish, 159
Something About Amelia, 288
Sony Pictures, 13, 185, 217, 237, 257, 312, 353
Sorvino, Mira, 229, 247
Sound of Music (The) 294, 299-300
Spielberg, Steven, 92-93, 172, 292
Spacey, Kevin, 28, 83-85, 173, 331
Spade, David, 63
Spago, 78, 147
Spock (Mr.) 294
Straight Story, (The) 132
Stanislavski, Konstantin, 198
Stanton, Harry Dean, 24, 130, 313
States of Separation, 222-224
Star Magazine, 44-45
Star Search, 109
Star Trek, 294
Star Wars, 168, 249, 301

Starr, Ringo, 309
Steiger, Rod, 242
Stern, Howard, 134
Stewart, James, 22, 377
Stewart, Patrick, 257
Stewart, Rod, 70
Stoddard, Brandon, 34
Strasberg, Lee, 332
Streetcar Named Desire (A) 53, 120, 155, 207, 281, 322, 333, 347, 372, 387
Strindberg, August, 87
Streisand, Barbra, 70, 90, 314
Struthers, Sally, 175
Sullivan, Ed, 157
Sunset Boulevard, 74-75, 290
Superman, 91, 240, 244-245, 323
Sutherland, Donald, 215, 221, 229-230, 270, 388
Swank Motion Pictures Rental, 1-3, 86
Swingers (diner) 262

T

Tahiti Rain, 107-108, 110-112
Talk Magazine, 318-320
Tarses, Jay, 12, 31-34, 96
Tartikoff, Brandon, 8
Taylor, Elizabeth, 135, 137, 156
Teacher's Pet (Klassenziel Mord) 267-268
Teahouse of the August Moon (The) 83
Ten Commandments (The) 162
Terminator 2: Judgement Day, 132
Thriller, 134, 140
Tie You Up, 31, 40, 209, 217
Tiegs, Cheryl, 31, 41, 71, 73, 107-112, 114, 130-131, 133, 151, 161, 183, 284
Tim and His Friends, 89, 263, 270
TLC (The Learning Channel) 368, 371
TNT Network, 149
To Kill a Mockingbird, 1, 22, 88, 90-91, 93, 118, 119-120, 154-156, 297, 340, 342, 345-347, 349, 361, 375-376, 387
Today Show (The) 108

Torn Apart, 162
Total Recall, 132
Town & Country, 333
Toy Story, 357
Tracy, Spencer, 53, 120
Tracy Ullman Show (The) 46
Travolta, John, 166, 216
Treasure of the Sierra Madre (The) 269
Trial of the Catonsville Nine (The) 149
Tribeca Productions, 92
Trivial Pursuit, 297
True Grit, 387
Truffaut, Francois, 87
Trump, Donald, 117, 141, 169, 372
Tsubaki, Yachio, 186-190, 374
Turner, Ted, 149
Turner, Tina, 353
TV Guide, 45, 180
TV Land, 356-358
Twain, Mark, 171
Twin Peaks, 256
Two and a Half Men, 220

U

UC Berkeley (University of California Berkeley) 198
UCLA (University of California Los Angeles) 29
Ugly American (The) 91, 251
Underwood, Blair, 100
United Artists, 90, 144, 213
Universal Studios, 13, 40, 91-94, 116, 143, 155, 172, 174-176, 180, 185, 251, 289, 292

V

Vajna, Andrew, 132
Valenti, Jack, 342
Van Dyke, Dick, 30, 51, 293, 356-359
Vanity Fair, 319
Verdi, Giuseppe, 223
Victory Tour, 135
Vinokour, Bruce, 271-273, 275-276
Vito Corleone, 144, 193, 207, 298, 349, 395
Viva Zapata! 83, 200
Voight, Jon, 313

von Sydow, Max, 278

W
WABC, 134
Ward, Jay, 8
Warm Springs Productions, 17
Warner Brothers Studios, 5, 144, 280-281, 283, 333
Wasserman, Lew, 116, 342
Wayans, Keenen Ivory, 46, 277
Wayne, John, 184, 346-347, 376, 386-387
WCBS, 134
Weintraub, Jerry, 148
Welch, Raquel, 300-301
Welles, Orson, 297
West Side Story, 294, 299-300
Wharton, Edith, 290
What's Eating Gilbert Grape, 252
Whisper into My Good Ear, 288-305, 315
Wild One (The) 97, 200, 206, 331, 375
Wild Strawberries, 15, 88, 90, 94, 148, 382
Wilder, Billy, 24, 74, 295
Will & Grace, 255-256
William Morris Agency, 172, 215, 271, 285
Williams, Robin, 313, 332
Williams, Tennessee, 99, 346
Williamson, Marianne, 304
Willis, Bruce, 174
Wilson, Demond, 180
Wilson, Hugh, 31
Winfrey, Oprah, 138
Winters, Shelley, 75
Wise, Millicent, 294-296, 300
Wise, Robert, 293-300, 302
Witherspoon, Reese, 131
WNBC, 134
Woodward, Joanne, 259-260
Wright, Robin, 131
Writers Guild of America (WGA) 41, 88, 100-101, 269-270
Wyler, William, 384
Wyman, Jane, 116

X
Xerox, 108, 110, 178

Y
Yearling (The) 116
Yoda, 249
Young and the Restless (The) 264, 281, 315
YouTube, 81, 83, 243

Z
Ziegfeld Theater (The) 246
Zinnermann, Fred, 198
Zip A Tone graphics, 108

CPSIA information can be obtained
at www.ICGtesting.com
Printed in the USA
LVHW050531020222
709878LV00015B/425